U M L AND C + +

A PRACTICAL GUIDE TO
OBJECT-ORIENTED DEVELOPMENT

RICHARD C. LEE

Lucent Technologies
(Bell Laboratories)

WILLIAM M. TEPFENHART

AT&T

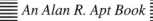

An Alan R. Apt Book

Prentice Hall, Upper Saddle River, New Jersey 07458

Library of Congress Cataloging-in-Publication Data
Lee, Richard C.
UML and C++: a practical guide to object-oriented development /
Richard C. Lee, William M. Tepfenhart.
p. cm.
"An Alan R. Apt book"
Includes bibliographical references and index.
ISBN 0-13-619719-1
1. Object-oriented programming (Computer Science).   2. Computer
software—Development.   3. C++ (Computer program language)
I. Tepfenhart, William M.   II. Title.
QA76.64.L45   1997
005.1'2—dc21   97-7688
                                                       CIP

Publisher: Alan Apt
Editor-in-Chief: Marcia Horton
Assitant Vice President of Production and
    Manufacturing: David W. Riccardi
Production Manager: Bayani Mendoza de Leon
Production Editor: Mona Pompili
Editor: Laura Steele

Manufacturing Buyer: Donna Sullivan
Creative Director: Paula Maylahn
Art Director: Heather Scott
Cover Designer: Tamara Newman Cavallo
Copy Editor: Nick Murray
Editorial Assistant: Toni Chavez

© 1997 by AT&T and Lucent Technologies
Published by Prentice-Hall, Inc.
Simon & Schuster / A Viacom Company
Upper Saddle River, New Jersey 07458

The author and publisher of this book have used their best efforts in preparing this book. These efforts include the development, research, and testing of the theories and programs to determine their effectiveness. The author and publisher shall not be liable in any event for incidental or consequential damages in connection with, or arrising out of, the furnishing, performance, or use of these programs

Printed in the United States of America

10 9 8 7 6 5 4

ISBN 0-13-619719-1

PRENTICE-HALL INTERNATIONAL (UK) LIMITED, *London*
PRENTICE-HALL OF AUSTRALIA PTY. LIMITED, *Sydney*
PRENTICE-HALL CANADA, INC., *Toronto*
PRENTICE-HALL HISPANOAMERICANA, S.A., *Mexico*
PRENTICE-HALL OF INDIA PRIVATE LIMITED, *New Delhi*
PRENTICE-HALLOF JAPAN, INC., *Tokyo*
SIMON & SCHUSTER ASIA PTE. LTD., *Singapore*
EDITORA PRENTICE-HALL DO BRASIL, LTDA., *Rio de Janeiro*

PREFACE

Axioms in Philosophy are not axioms until they are proved upon our pulses: we read fine things but never feel them to the full until we have gone the same steps as the author.

John Keats (1795-1821), Letter to J.H. Reynolds, May 3, 1818

UML and C++: A Practical Guide to Object-Oriented Development is for busy professional software analysts and developers who work on large systems, especially those who need to integrate their new systems with legacy systems. If you don't have time to take a class yet you need to learn and get up-to-speed on object-oriented (OO) technology using Unified Modeling Language (UML) and C++, this book is a self-teaching guide for you. It will help you understand the differences between OO analysis, OO design, and OO programming. Our goals are to

- teach you to build an OO application using C++ and make the right trade-off decisions to meet your business needs;
- clarify the basic concepts associated with OO technology;
- supply the necessary coverage for students and practitioners entering the field to get them up to speed;
- expose some of the myths surrounding OO technology while focusing on its practicality as a software engineering tool;
- give you a "recipe" or step-by-step guide to do all the steps of OO technology;

- advocate the view that OO, rule-based concepts, fuzzy logic, multimedia, and data modeling integrated into a single model can address the current and future business challenges for information technology organizations;

- provide a practical approach to analysis, design, and programming in the OO technology;

- show how to document using UML;

- show how to implement OO technology using C++ (though not an OO language) is an extremely powerful multiparadigm language); and

- balance theory with application practices in the existing literature.

You do not have to know computer science theory or advanced mathematics to understand the important OO concepts and issues in depth. Even the programming chapters do not require a background in C++; they illustrate how working code in C++ is produced.

Object-Oriented Technology

We are software developers of large systems. We believe that OO technology is the most important software evolution (revolution) of the 1990s. It is changing the way we build software and the way applications intercommunicate over worldwide networks and across multivendor computers. Moreover, the OO model is changing the way we design business processes and the way we think about an enterprise. Most enterprises need redesigning today to meet future business challenges.

Business process redesign is one of the most important functions of an information technology organization. A model that captures the business processes, procedures, policies, and rules facilitates redesign. Tools that translate the model automatically into an operational system speed the implementation of the redesign. When the market or business condition changes, these systems should be regenerated to reflect the changes by updating the model and using these tools. Information science (engineering) has taken us further and faster than any other approach in previous decades. However, it needs constant updating through even better, more refined methods to meet our business needs and challenges through OO modeling and OO programming. More and more people believe that OO technology will put a dent into the software crisis, meaning that the mechanisms of OO will become for software what the bolts, and beams are for the construction design and what the chip is for computer hardware design. This belief stems from the following:

- The proficiency of a higher-level OO model should provide the software designer with real-world, programmable components, thereby reducing software development costs.

- Its capability to share and reuse code with OO techniques that will reduce time to develop an application.

- Its capability to localize and minimize the effects of modifications through programming abstraction mechanisms, allowing for faster enhancement development and providing more reliable and more robust software.

- Its capability to manage complexity allows developers to address more difficult applications.

The collection of OO concepts is a tool set for modeling reality. The OO tool set gives developers the best means of managing the complexity. Certain OO concepts help developers produce flexible and maintainable software.

Why Unified Modeling Language?

As practitioners of OO technology, we know that all the methods, if practiced properly, result in the same or similar model. Different modeling language notations can be impediments to progress. We are interested in results that help us produce more maintainable software at less cost and in a more timely manner. Unified Modeling Language gives us all the drawing icons necessary to capture most of the concepts or *mechanisms* that we find valuable in solving real business problems. Also, it provides all the necessary diagrams that are vital for documenting our models. Finally, it is a living language that gives us the ability to extend the notation for mechanism not yet defined by the distinguished group of Grady Booch, James Rumbaugh, and Ivor Jacobson at Rational Software Corporation.

Why C++?

It is a misconception that C++ is exclusively an OO programming language. It is a multiparadigm language that supports a number of programming paradigms, including procedural, abstract data types, and OO. We show you how to map your OO model into the C++ constructs using the OO paradigm in C++. Also, we show you how to use other non-OO concepts of the language in the context of OO design to help you meet your business needs.

C++ is our language of choice for two practical reasons. First and foremost, most developers have to address real constraints: interfacing to legacy systems and technical limitations on databases, storage, and performance. C++ gives developers multiple paradigms that developers can tune as needed. Second, vendors supplying tools and compilers have put their money on C++.

Our Approach To Object-Oriented Technology

We are not OO purists nor are we theorists. We are developers willing to use any good idea that will help us achieve two very critical business goals: lower development cost and reduce time-to-market for enhancements. We believe that three technical objectives_reliability, maintainability, and flexibility_are critical to meeting these business goals.

Our approach to using OO technology is to manage the complexity of developing software so it is reliable, maintainable, and flexible. Managing complexity is the key to achieving these objectives and thus our business goals. To manage complexity in complex problem domains, we find that the developers are required to know how objects, classes, relationships, and rules fit into the object paradigm. When we model most complex problem domains, we find objects, classes, and many relationships among objects. In addition, we need to capture the rules (policies) within that domain. Thus, we have to use very rich static modeling techniques to capture the data (object) relationships

Many OO experts consider relationships as "bad" because they violate the encapsulation principle. From our perspective, it helps us manage the complexity of the problem domain and helps us achieve our business goals. We gladly use it and we look for more mechanisms and language support in this area. In chapter 9 on declarative semantics we write that rules and policies should be captured as an integral part of our model and not in special subsystem extensions.

Using mechanisms to help us model complex problem domains is consistent with our choice of UML as our modeling language and C++ as our programming language. Both UML and C++ allow us to define any needed mechanism that helps us build more manageable software.

We discuss behaviors (dynamic and static) and polymorphism for capturing the procedural aspects of the model. The use of finite state machine or some other state model helps us manage procedural complexity while addressing timing, synchronization, and interrupts. These areas are generally ignored or overlooked by most OO books. We do not address these issues in depth, but we lay the foundation so the reader can make use of the semantics added to UML.

We believe the key to success in building large OO systems requires that developers/programmers know more than what is taught in most OO books. Building large systems requires using mechanisms promoted by some OO experts but not accepted by all. Professional developers need to at least understand how these aspects of the problem domain can be handled before they can be a productive team member. This book will *not* make you an expert. You still need experts/consultants to develop the system. By applying the 80/20 rule, this book provides the 80 percent that can make you productive and understand how the experts solve the difficult 20 percent.

In this book we do not cover the latest trends or fads in OO technology, including object design patterns, the standard template library, and distributed-object computing. Although they are interesting, we are not convinced that they contribute significantly to our goal of providing a practical framework for enabling developers new to OO programming to get up to speed as soon as possible.

Finally, we do not agree with most experts that OO technology is a mature technology. We believe it is in its infancy; what impresses us is how much we can accomplish with such an infant technology. Object-oriented technology has the enormous potential to help us manage complexity that did not exist with the earlier technologies (procedural, functional, rule-based, etc.).

Organization of the Book

We take the reader through our rationale in applying OO techniques and methods. These are not a set absolute laws. Our goal is to make you think about good OO concepts and design principles when developing software and programming in C++. In the case study, we take a project through all the steps of OO analysis, design, and coding. Using specific OO techniques and applying fundamental OO concepts. The design is implemented in C++ with performance enhancements techniques of C++.

We have written and designed this book to be a self-teaching guide that should be read in sequential order. Although we have adopted a method that Richard has used for years teaching OO concepts and basic skills, we do not advocate this as a method for building OO systems. Each chapter discusses a major step of our approach to OO technology. Most chapters, conclude with a step-by-step guide or recipe. We hope the reader will uses these steps as a guide only; always rely on common sense rather than following prescribed steps blindly.

> **Chapter 1** provides the reasons why companies are interested in OO and why software professionals should understand OO.
>
> **Chapter 2** addresses the business of software and the need to manage complexity.
>
> **Chapter 3** describes how to find the basic terminology and key concepts in OO technology.
>
> **Chapter 4** describes how to find potential objects, the first step employing OO technology.
>
> **Chapter 5** describes how to differentiate between "real" and "false" objects by identifying attributes (data) and services associated with the object.
>
> **Chapter 6** demonstrates how to capture objects behavior.
>
> **Chapter 7** describes how to identify and describe dynamic behavior.
>
> **Chapter 8** describes the relationships (generalization/specialization, link, object aggregation, etc.) that are available for organizing all the objects in the system.
>
> **Chapter 9** describes how to incorporate declarative facts into the OO model about object knowledge and a rule-based mechanism for their implementation.
>
> **Chapter 10** describes how to make objects into classes to take advantage of C++.
>
> **Chapter 11** addresses some design issues with OO system development.[1]

---

[1]   Design is very complex and is a separate topic from OO technology.

Chapter 12 provides the C++ basics necessary to perform OO programming with C++. (Readers familiar with C++ can skip this chapter).

Chapter 13 teaches you how to implement a class, which is a template for creating objects.

Chapter 14 teaches you how to implement the behavior specifications developed in chapter 6.

Chapter 15 addresses how to create and destroy objects using the class mechanism of C++

Chapter 16 addresses how to implement generalization/specialization (one of the key OO concepts) by using the class derivation mechanism of C++.

Chapter 17 addresses how to implement other relationships not supported by C++.

Chapter 18 introduces a case study example demonstrating how to use the method discussed in chapters 4-17.

Chapter 19 presents one team's approach to performing the object analysis of the case study.

Chapter 20 presents a second team's approach to performing the object analysis of the case study.

Chapter 21 demonstrates how the object model in chapter 20 is translated into an object design and implemented in C++.

Acknowledgments

We owe so much to so many people. The impetus of this book came from the hundreds of students who have taken Richard Lee's class, his friends, and his many colleagues. He appreciates their persistence and their encouragement, ignoring the perils to his personal life.

Since we are developers (not researchers, academics, nor writers), we have leveraged off the work of OO researchers (who originated all the ideas) and OO writers (who presented these ideas to us in earlier writings). We simply apply these ideas to building real applications in a useful way. To all the originators and writers of the ideas, concepts, mechanisms, and techniques before us, we acknowledge and thank;. without them, this book would not have been possible.

Theories and ideas are wonderful; however, to practitioners, experience is the best teacher. We could not have produced this book without our experiences in applying OO technology and the methods to real projects. We thank our many bosses, present and past, who had the courage to let us do leading-edge (and many times bleeding-edge) software development. Without their support, we would not have been able to test what we have written.

Richard Lee thanks the multitude of people who have worked for him and were the pioneers in applying the ideas in this book to real projects. They shared both the excitement and the misery of being "first" to apply OO technology to large projects. (Or was it their folly to follow his lead and take challenges that no one else in the company wanted?) To all of you, Richard owes his thanks.

William Tepfenhart thanks his co-workers, past and present, each of whom has contributed to his understanding computer science better. He thanks Bill Case, Freid Elliot, and Dayton Eden, who allowed him to transition from *writing* FORTRAN models of physical systems to artificial intelligence models for *reasoning* about physical systems. He thanks his colleagues who broadened his modeling repertoire to include objects, relations, and rules.

We thank Barry Peiffer, David Simen, John Eddy, and Dan Dvorak for sharing their time and feedback. Steve Ruder did an excellent job as technical editor.

A lot of credit goes to our managers Dick Machol, Raj Warty, Moses Ling, and Raj Dube for their support. They allowed us the use of computer tools and resources during off-hours, or we wouldn't have been able to complete the book. However, do not construe this as being a book approved by AT&T or Bell Laboratories. This is our private view of OO technology based largely on Richard's 30 years in the software development business and his experiences with OO technology. William Tepfenhart provided many excellent "recipes" and organized the material so developers can quickly become contributing members on a development team.

Finally, we acknowledge and appreciate the valuable input from our reviewers: Rex Jaeschke, chair of the ANCI C committee and independent consultant and author, and Robert Taylor, Taylor Computing. As the authors, we are perfectly happy to take the blame for all errors, omissions, inaccuracies, falsehoods, fuzzy thinking, and any good qualities of this book. We welcome all constructive comments. We happily will ignore destructive ones.

Richard C. Lee
William M. Tepfenhart

CONTENTS

CHAPTER 1

The Information Management Dilemma

Since software construction is inherently a system effort—an exercise in complex interrelationships—communication effort is great, and it quickly dominates the decrease in individual task time brought about by partitioning. Adding more men then lengthens, not shortens, the schedule.

F. Brooks Jr., *The Mythical Man-Month,* © Addison-Wesley Publishing Company, Inc.
Reprinted by permission of Addison Wesley Longman, Inc.

Currently, there is a great deal of excitement and interest in object-oriented techniques in business and in the information technology (IT) industry. In the midst of all the ballyhoo, most practitioners in software engineering need to understand what the ballyhoo is all about.

The Problem

CORPORATIONS ARE BECOMING INFORMATION-BASED organizations that depend on a continuous flow of data for virtually every aspect of their operations. However, the volume of information is increasing faster than the capacity to process it. Thus, they are drowning in their own data.

The problem arises from the following conditions:

- Software project costs are going up, and hardware costs are going down.
- Software development time is getting longer, and maintenance costs are getting higher, while at the same time hardware development time is getting shorter and less costly.
- Software errors are becoming more frequent as hardware errors become almost nonexistent.
- Software is developed using a rigidly structured process that is inflexible.

This is confirmed by studies, as shown in Table 1-1 and Table 1-2.

TABLE 1-1 Software Project Costs by Development Phase

Work Step	%
Requirements	3
Design	8
Programming	7
Testing	15
Maintenance	67

Source: Bloor Research

TABLE 1-2 Costs of Correcting Software Errors

Software Development Phase	% of Dev. Funds	Errors Introduced (%)	Errors Found (%)	Relative Cost to Correct
Requirements Analysis	5	55	18	1.0
Design	25	30	10	1.0–1.5
Code and Unit Test	10			
Integration Test	50	10	50	1.0–5.0
Validation and Documentation	10			
Operational Maintenance		5	22	10–100

Source: Hughes Department of Defense Composite Software Error History

It is clear that our present software methods result in systems that are very expensive to maintain. Corporations are spending most of their money in testing and maintaining their systems. Unfortunately, the present methods are not effective in requirements analysis and design stages, where the cost of correction is very low. Furthermore, Table 1-2 shows that 85 percent of our errors are made during the requirements analysis and design stages. Improving these two steps is the most cost-effective way to improve the quality of software.

Modern Corporations Are Headed Toward Disaster

If we combine these software problems with the increasing rate of change in business conditions today, we have a recipe for disaster. A corporation's accounts receivable may be in good shape today, but decisions based on the output of incorrect software can threaten the ability of a business to be financially strong tomorrow.

Today, much of corporate software is obsolete long before delivery, and it is incapable of evolving to meet future business needs. Furthermore, some studies have shown that only 25 percent of all software projects result in working systems. Thus, historically there is strong evidence that computer systems have not satisfied their customers. If software professionals are to address this problem, they must first know their customers' needs.

What Does the Customer Want?

THE CUSTOMER WANTS A SOLUTION (system) that:

- Meets functional requirements
- Adapts to the rapidly changing business environment
- Fits the run-time (time/space) constraints

The customer wants software that is:

- Maintainable
- Developed within budgeted resources (time/space/material/people)
- Designed with appropriate longevity in mind

Since our classical development methods (structured methods, data modeling, ad-hoc, etc.) have not met our customers' needs, object-oriented consultants have told corporation managers that the use of object-oriented technology will meet these needs better than the classical methods. Now that we understand why businesses are excited about object-oriented technology, let us see why leading-edge software engineers are excited about it.

Why Object-Oriented Technology Is Important to Developers

IN THE 1960S, SOFTWARE DEVELOPERS were building small and relatively simple applications/systems. They used some very simple languages (assembly language, FORTRAN, and COBOL) that were designed specifically for their use. Developers used no method other than their own "creativity." Programming was considered a creative activity, and developers were hired based on their independent spirit. Unfortunately, this led to "spaghetti code" and the famous GOTOs in code that are a horror to maintain.

In the 1970s, Al Constantine and Ed Yourdon came up with a method of developing software that used the function as its building block. This method, known to most developers as structured analysis and design, helped developers organize the software by functions. At the time, this seemed very natural, because organizations were organized functionally. Since most computer systems and applications were written for a specific functional organization, the applications became extensions of that organization.

This seemed like a better way to build software, especially if you did modular programming in addition to structured analysis and design. Modular programming eliminated the unmanageable GOTOs. Structured analysis and design helped developers manage only the functions. However, it did very little to help developers manage data.

Despite being developed for "business applications," structured analysis and design was better suited for "scientific applications." In most scientific applications, functions are very stable; most of them are determined by laws of nature that rarely change. In business applications, however, the functions are human-defined and are subject to change at any time.

Although structured analysis and design was successfully applied to many scientific applications, it led to large maintenance organizations in business applications. For many of these applications, software professionals had to continuously change the building blocks (i.e., change the functions). Changes at such a fundamental level required basically rebuilding the application/system; thus, software professionals recognized the need for other methods of developing software.

In the 1980s, Peter Chen (who developed the entity-relationship diagram) and Ed Codd (designer of the relational database) provided developers with the foundation for a new way of developing software that was based on a collection of data items, called an entity, as its building block. This discovery seemed appropriate as the foundation of a new methodology for software development for business applications because software professionals and researchers at that time believed that data was the most stable part of the "business application."

As a result of the widely held belief that entities were stable, and because relational databases had an excellent mathematical basis, most companies in the 1980s began using data-modeling methods to develop software. However, data-modeling methods had the converse weakness of structured methods. Structured methods did help developers manage the data, but data-modeling methods did not help developers manage the functions. The theory was that all the functions could be defined by using language constructs that were consistent with first-order predicate calculus. Unfortunately, most of the problems that needed to be solved could not be done using first-order predicate calculus.

Now there is a need for a software development method that addresses the weaknesses of earlier methods. Earlier methods used only one view of the system as a building block and did not readily accommodate other views. For example, structured analysis and design focused on the function as the building block of a system. Data organization is very weakly supported in the data flow diagrams. Similarly, in the data analysis method (entity-relationship diagram), the building block was an entity, but the functions needed to satisfy the system requirements were virtually ignored in this method. Neither method deals well with capturing dynamic behavior. Declarative semantics (rules) and exception-handling mechanisms were totally ignored.

The object-oriented method is the only method we know that provides software developers with a paradigm that supports all views of a system equally well, and it does so in an orthogonal manner. As a result, developers can manage the complexity of the situation.

In object-oriented programming, the application (system) is a dynamic network of collaborating objects. With the addition of rules to the paradigm in an orthogonal manner, declarative semantics can be integrated with the procedural semantics into one system.

From a pragmatic point of view, the object-oriented method allows software developers to manage the complexity of the problem domain and its supporting technology. When developers can manage more aspects of the problem domain, they can produce more flexible and more maintainable software.

CHAPTER 2

Managing Complexity: Analysis and Design

What cannot be cured must be endured.

■ Francis Rabelais

In the early 1960s, developers used no method other than their own creativity. Performance and using less core (memory) were the major constraints. Writing spaghetti code and using the infamous GOTOs were accepted ways to increase performance and use less core. Most programs were neither large nor complex by today's standards. However, even then developers had difficulty remembering all the information they needed to know to develop, debug, and maintain their software.

For example, when one of the authors first started in this field in the early 1960s, he wrote some mission-critical software for his employer. This code is still in use today. About ten years ago, his former employer called him and asked him to help them make modifications to this code. The employer's programmers had studied the code, but could not figure out how the software worked. As his former employer succinctly put it, "We know that the program works, as we have been using it for 20 years, but when we study the code we cannot figure out how you made it work." His former employer sent the author the code to study. After a couple of weeks, he concluded that he could not help his former employer design the modification, even he did not know how he got it to work 20 years ago. Thus, his former employer had no choice but to leave the code untouched and make the modifications at a different level with code that was comprehensible.

In the late 1960s and early 1970s, higher-level languages (COBOL, FORTRAN, ALGOL) were introduced to help solve some of these problems. These languages certainly helped automate the management of local variables and did implicit matching of arguments to parameters.

In conjunction with these new languages, developers used a more structured method to design and develop software. Remember structured analysis and design? Remember modular programming? These techniques raised the expectations of what a computer could do in our user community. As developers attempted to satisfy their user community by trying to solve more complex problems using the computer, the tasks became so large and complex that even the best programmers could not comprehend them. So programming changed from a creative individual activity to a structured team activity.

When this happened, we observed that a program we expected one programmer to write in three years could not be written by *three* programmers working for *one* year. This phenomenon led to Fred Brooks' memorable phrase: "The bearing of a child takes nine months, no matter how many women are assigned." Of course, software complexity was the main reason behind the nonlinear behavior of the development effort.

In imperative programming, the interconnections between software components are very complicated, and a large amount of information has to be communicated among the various team members to get it correct.[1] The key question is what brings about this complexity? Sheer size alone cannot bring about complexity, for size itself is not a hindrance to the concept of partitioning the software into many pieces. In fact, the method of structured analysis and design assumed that large programs differ from small programs only because of size. If size was the issue, structured analysis and design would have solved the difficulty.

Unfortunately, the aspect of software development using the imperative programming model that makes it among the most complex tasks for humans is its high degree of *coupling*. Coupling refers to the dependence of one portion of

---

[1] See quote at beginning of chapter 1.

code on either another section of code and/or some data storage. A high degree of coupling is an inherent aspect of imperative programming.

In designing imperative programs, we partition our program into subroutines (essential tasks). However, if these subroutines are useful to other parts of the program, there must be some communication of information either into or out of these subroutines. Remember that data is not managed. Thus, a complete understanding of what is going on usually requires knowledge of the subroutine and all the routines that use it. This is poor *cohesion*. Cohesion refers to how well a set of code and its associated data fit together. This is especially true when you consider the data that may be needed. In most imperative-programming languages, variable names (means of accessing data) can be shared only if they are in a common pool.

In brief, much of the complexity of imperative programming came from the high degree of coupling and poor cohesion in the way we built the software.[2] It is now apparent to us that using classical methods in software development will almost always result in systems being built with poor cohesion and high coupling; this makes the system inflexible and unmaintainable. In our opinion, a better method is needed to develop software that gives developers a chance to meet their customers' needs. To be able to accomplish this, developers cannot use the same building blocks (functions, entities, or rules) that are used in classical methods. They need to use a new abstract mechanism as the building block for software. This new abstract mechanism is a *class*. The class will serve as our blueprint for manufacturing *objects,* which will be the building blocks for systems.

Abstraction Mechanism

TO UNDERSTAND HOW THE OBJECT-ORIENTED paradigm uses the abstraction mechanism to manage complexity, we will first review the various ways that software engineers/programmers have used abstraction prior to the object-oriented paradigm. From a historical perspective, object-oriented use of the abstraction mechanism may be seen as a natural progression of abstracting for functions, to modules, to abstract data types, and then to objects.

Functions

With the advent of imperative programming languages, functions and procedures became the early abstract mechanisms widely used to write programs. Functions allowed tasks that were used in many places, even in different applications, to be collected in one place and reused. Procedures allowed programmers to organize

---

2   Data modeling is still imperative programming, since most of the functions/transactions are still written using a procedural language. Moreover, rule-based systems (i.e., artificial intelligence systems) also involved coupling and cohesion issues.

repetitive tasks in one place. Both of these abstractions prevented code from being duplicated in several places.

Functions and procedures also gave programmers the ability to implement information hiding. One programmer writes a function or a set of functions that will be used by many other programmers. Other programmers do not need to know the exact details of the implementation; they only need to know the interface. Unfortunately, abstract functions are not an effective mechanism for information hiding. They only partially solve the problem of multiple programmers making use of the same names.

To illustrate this, we will look at how we write a set of functions to implement a simple stack. First, we establish our visible interfaces: init (initialize the stack), push (place something on the stack), and pop (take an item off the top of the stack). After defining the interface, we need to select some implementation technique such as an array with top-of-stack pointer, a linked list, and so on. We elect to implement the stack by using an array and proceed to code the functions. It is easy to see that the data contained in the stack itself cannot be made local to any of the functions, since all the functions need to use it; therefore, the variable must be shared.

In imperative programming languages, such as COBOL, or C prior to the introduction of the static modifier, the only choices for keeping data are local variables and global variables. As a result, the stack data must be maintained in global variables if we want the data to be shared by all the functions. Unfortunately, there is no way to limit the accessibility or visibility of global variable names.

Let's assume that we have named the array for our stack *stackarray*. All other programmers working on the project that use our functions must therefore know about stackarray, because they must not create a variable that has the same name. This is true even though the data is used only by the stack functions written by us and should not be used outside these functions. Similarly, the names init, pop, and push are now reserved and cannot be used by other programmers on the project for other purposes, even if that portion of code has nothing to do with the stack.

In advanced imperative programming languages such as ALGOL and Pascal, the block-scoping mechanism offered a slightly better control over name visibility than just local and global names. However, this mechanism did not solve the information-hiding problem presented above. To solve this problem, a different abstract mechanism had to be developed.

Modules

A module is an abstract mechanism that is useful for creating and managing name spaces. In its basic form, a module gives the programmer the ability to divide the name space into two parts, public and private. The public part is accessible to everyone, while the private part is accessible only within the module. Variables (data), functions, procedures, and types can all be defined in either part of the module. This abstract mechanism was popularized by David Parnas, and he gave us the following guidelines for using modules:

1. The designer of the module must provide the intended users with all the information needed to use the module correctly, and nothing more.
2. The designer of the module must provide the implementor with all the information necessary to complete (code) the module, and nothing more.

These guidelines are similar to the way the military handles secret documents via the "need to know." If you do not need to know some information, you do not have access to it. This explicit and intentional concealment of information is information hiding, which is the second principle of the object-oriented paradigm.[3]

The module, as an abstract mechanism, solves our information-hiding problem. We can now hide the details of the stack. Note that a module enforces the first two principles of the object-oriented paradigm, namely, encapsulation and information hiding. When a mechanism does this, it isolates one part of the system, namely the module, from all other parts of the system. This improves the maintainability of the software produced because the isolation allows code to be modified or extended and bugs to be fixed without the risk of introducing unnecessary or unintended side effects.

However, a module has a major shortcoming. Let's look at the stack problem again. What if a user wants to use two or more stacks? We cannot handle this with a module. As a mechanism, the module does not allow us to perform *instantiation*, which is the ability to make multiple copies of the data areas. This idea of instantiation is the sixth principle of the object-oriented paradigm.

For a better example of why instantiation is an important and desired capability, consider the following situation. We need to develop a new type of number called Complex. We define the arithmetic operations (addition, subtraction, multiplication, etc.) for complex numbers and functions to convert a conventional number (integer, float, double, etc.) to a complex number. If we were to use a module to capture our new type of number, we would have a small problem—we can manipulate only one complex number at a time. A complex number system with such a restriction would not be very useful.

Abstract Data Types

An abstract data type is a programmer-defined data type that can be manipulated in a manner similar to predefined data types. Like a predefined data type, an abstract data type corresponds to a set (perhaps an almost infinite set) of legal data values and a number of functions that can be performed on these values. Programmers can create instances of this abstract data type by assigning legal values to the variables. Furthermore, we can use the functions to manipulate the values assigned to the variables. In brief, an abstract data type mechanism allows us to do the following:

---

[3] The eight principles of the object-oriented paradigm are introduced in Chapter 3.

1. Extend a programming language by adding programmer-defined type(s)

2. Make available to other code a set of programmer-defined functions that are used to manipulate the instance data of the specific programmer-defined type

3. Protect (hide) the instance data associated with the type and limit access to the data, allowing access by only the programmer-defined functions

4. Make (unlimited) instances of the programmer-defined type

Modules, as defined above, can address only items 2 and 3 directly. With appropriate programming skills, some of the other capabilities may be addressed. However, packages found in languages such as Ada and CLU are a much better example of an implementation of the abstract data type mechanism.

Thus, we can solve our instantiation problem for the stack and for complex numbers by using an abstract data type.

Classes/Objects

MANY PEOPLE CONSIDER SMALLTALK "the object-oriented language." They would define a class as being a different name for an abstract data type and an object as an instance of an abstract data type. Technically, one can argue that they are correct; however, in our opinion, this definition leaves out the most important part of object-oriented programming. Today object-oriented programming has expanded on the idea of abstract data types and added to them some important innovations that help us better manage complexity. It is these additional innovations that give object-oriented technology all its power.

Message Passing

Object-oriented programming added several new ideas to the concept of abstract data types. First is the idea of *message passing*. In object-oriented programming, an action is initiated by a service request (message) sent to a specific object, not as in imperative programming by a function call using specific data. On the surface, this may appear to be just a change of emphasis. The imperative programming style places a primary importance on the functions, while the object-oriented style places primary importance on the object (value). For example, do you call the push function with a stack and a data value, or do you ask a stack to push a value onto itself?

If this is all there is to message passing, it would not be a very powerful mechanism. However, message passing gives us the ability to overload names and reuse software; this is not possible using the imperative programming functional call style. Implicit in message passing is the idea that the interpretation of a message can vary with objects in different classes. That is, the behavior (response that a message will elicit) depends on the class of the object that receives the message. Thus, our push function can mean one thing to our stack object and a very different thing to another object—a mechanical arm object, for example.

In object-oriented programming, names of functions are unique only within a class. We can use simple, direct, and meaningful names for our functions across classes, leading to more readable and more understandable code. This also provides for better cohesion at the implementation level than does a conventional imperative programming language.

Generalization/Specialization and Polymorphism

In addition to message passing, object-oriented programming added two more mechanisms to abstract data types: generalization/specialization[4] and polymorphism. Generalization/specialization allows classes to share the same code. This reduces the code size and provides for more maintainable software. In addition, it helps us by giving us good cohesion and a lower degree of coupling in our implementation. Polymorphism allows the shared code to be tailored to fit the specific circumstances of particular classes. These mechanisms work together to support the independence (low degree of coupling) of individual components (objects) that support an incremental development process (good cohesion).

As useful as generalization/specialization and polymorphism are in helping us organize (or structure) our classes and objects,[5] these mechanisms only help us manage relationships that are heritable. In reality, we certainly have heritable relationships with our children, parents, grandparents, and so on. However, we also have other types of relationships that need to be managed. For instance, married people have spouses that cannot be modeled by using generalization/specialization and/or polymorphism (even though many married people may wish they could polymorph their other half). Moreover, in most organizations people work in teams to get a job done, and there is a hierarchical structure of people who make up the organization. Again, these structures cannot be modeled by using the few mechanisms that we have discussed. We need more mechanisms to enable the object-oriented paradigm to accurately model our perception of reality.

Additional Relationships

IN THE PREVIOUS SECTION, WE introduced one type of relationship, namely, generalization/specialization. However, this type of relationship is not adequate for us to model our perception of reality. For example, we cannot capture the marriage relationship nor the supervisor-subordinate relationship by using generalization/specialization. We need additional mechanisms to help us model these concepts.

---

[4] Generalization/specialization is implemented by using inheritance in many object-oriented languages, including C++. If it helps, you may consider the two terms synonymous. However, in the design chapter (Chapter 11), we will discuss inheritance as a different concept.

[5] Thus, they also help us to manage complexity.

Associations

Let us look at an instance of marriage more closely. Suppose that Joe is married to Jane. From Joe's perspective, the marriage relationship captures the fact that Jane is his wife and provides a set of "wifely" services to Joe. Similarly, from Jane's perspective, the marriage relationship captures the fact that Joe is her husband and provides a set of "husbandly" services to Jane. Thus, it is very common to have role names (husband, wife) associated with a relationship (marriage). In some sense, the role names help us define what services are expected to be accessible via that relationship. For example, if Jane is also Joe's supervisor at work, a second relationship (supervisor-subordinate) must be established to capture the "subordinate" services of Joe. This second relationship is necessary to maintain the semantic consistency of the relationship. Joe can stop being Jane's subordinate at work and stay married to Jane. This kind of relationship, where one object knows about another object for specific services, is called a *link*.

If we define marriage as existing only between two persons of different gender, then we need to categorize people into two categories (classes): Male and Female. Note that Joe, an object, is an instance of Male and that Jane, another object, is an instance of Female. Now, since all marriage links are between one object of the class Male and another object of the class Female, we can capture all the marriage links by using a higher-level concept called an *association*. An association describes a group of links with common structure and common semantics. All links in an association must connect objects from the same class to objects from a second class. Note that from an object-oriented perspective, the common semantics means that the services provided by each object in the same class are the same. Also, remember that providing the same service does not mean that the behavior is identical. For instance, if we define "mow the lawn" as one of the services of husband, then every male object must have a "mow the lawn" service. However, the method that each male object uses to mow the lawn can be very different (polymorphism). Specifically, Joe can actually mow the lawn himself, while Jack may pay one of his kids to mow the lawn, and Jim may use a professional lawn mowing company.

With the marriage relationship, one can argue that not only is the behavior (how the service is provided) different, but also the services provided by each partner are different for each marriage. This is certainly more likely to be true today than when people had fixed concepts associated with the roles of husband and wife. If this is correct, we would not be able to abstract each of the marriage links into a group; we would require a unique template for each group of links with different services. That is, each marriage would be a different association.

Associations are bidirectional; thus, it is common to give a name to an association in each direction. In our marriage example, from Female's direction it is husband, and from the Male's direction it is wife. By the way, it is common practice to name a relationship with the same name as the class with which it is associated, but we do not recommend this practice, as it captures no semantic meaning (poor cohesion). It is effective only if there is only one association between the classes; if there is more than one association, a better convention should be used. For example, consider the relationship between a person and a company. It is very common for a person to be both an employee and a stockholder of a company, especially now with an increase of employee-owned companies. To model these two different relationships accurately, we would create two associations between the class Person and the class Company. One association would represent the employer/employee relationship and the second would represent the ownership relationship.

In theory, associations may be binary (between two classes), ternary (among three classes), or higher. In practice, however, the vast majority of associations are binary or ternary; we have only rarely used the higher forms. Higher-order associations are very difficult to draw, implement, and think about; they should be avoided if possible.

The notion of association is not a new concept; it has been widely used for years in database modeling. However, very few programming languages explicitly support the association mechanism. Nevertheless, we believe that we should model an association as a separate abstraction that contains information that depends on two or more classes rather than a single class.

Some would argue that capturing an association as a separate abstraction violates the encapsulation principle of a class. However, there is information that we need to model that naturally transcends a single class. In the marriage relationship, for example, the marriage date and the location where the ceremony is held are examples of information that naturally transcends either class of Female and Male.

Not capturing an association accurately causes programs to contain hidden assumptions and dependencies that make them hard to maintain. For instance, in our employer/employee example, a person's salary is not really information about a Person. Consider the case where you need to model a person who has two or three jobs with different employers.

Conceptually, and especially during analysis, we recommend that a link should be treated as an object. Since an object has attributes (i.e., may store information) and provides services, a link has the potential to store data and provide services. In our marriage relationship, for example, the attributes could be date of marriage and the church where the ceremony was held. Although associations (and aggregations) are not directly supported by present-day programming languages, our goal should be to demonstrate their usefulness and to encourage the development of programming languages that will support these mechanisms that help us manage complexity.

Aggregation

From the above examples, we can see that an association is a very weak relationship. People regularly change employers. In fact, management talks about people needing to change careers and employers many times. Furthermore, marriage in the United States is certainly not permanent.[6] Thus, an association is like a "Hollywood marriage"—it can be changed very rapidly.

---

[6] In most situations, we would model marriage as an association. In some societies, the marriage is permanent with no divorce.

But there are other relationships, like a car with its parts or a purchase order with its line items, that do not allow changes as easily. Furthermore, these specialized forms of an association have special properties. We would like to have another relationship mechanism to capture these more specialized forms of an association because the special properties need to be enforced. The new mechanism is called *aggregation*. [7] In this mechanism, an object that represents the whole is associated with a set of objects representing its components. A good example of a relationship that is probably best modeled by an aggregation is a bill-of-material and all of its associated line items.

Aggregation contains the following properties:

Transitivity. Transitivity is the property such that if object A is a part of object B and object B is a part of object C, then object A is a part of object C. In our example, consider the possibility that a line item may have sub–line items. By transitivity, the sub–line items are also part of the bill-of-material.

Antisymmetricity. Antisymmetricity is the property such that if object A is a part of object B, then object B cannot be a part of object A. Again using our example, a line item may not be part of a sub–line item.

Finally, some of the attributes and/or methods of the assembly usually propagate to its components as well. In our example, the bill-of-material usually has an order number that is also used by all the line-items and sub–line items.

There are at least two difficulties in dealing with aggregations. First, the components must all be of the same semantic domain.[8] For example, a computer terminal is composed of a CRT, keyboard, cables, and so on. However, a terminal is also made of glass, silicon, steel, and plastic. The "made_of" decomposition of the terminal is not the same as the "composed_of" decomposition; it would be incorrect to mix components in these two decompositions. The second difficulty has to do with "optional components." For example, a car normally has door handles. If all the door handles are removed, is the car still a car? Now we need to be careful; it appears that a car still exists. However, it may be true that door handles are optional, but what about tires? The logic can then be extended to include every part of a car. But if every part is optional, then a car may exist with no parts. We will see that we can allow only a certain amount of flexibility when we define the aggregation using conditional components.

---

[7] This is also called the whole-parts, assembly-parts, or the part-of relationship. In terms of a modeling mechanism, we can define an aggregation as relating an assembly class to a set of component classes. Aggregation reduces complexity by letting us treat many objects as one object and giving us a better mechanism than a link to model specific domain entities (e.g., purchase order, cars, assemblies).

[8] In a later chapter, we will see how we can identify this situation by identifying the different kinds of aggregations.

Behavior

RELATIONSHIP MECHANISMS GIVE US A way to organize classes/objects in both peer-to-peer (association) and hierarchial (generalization/specialization and aggregation) structures. This structure portion of the model is called the static model by many object-oriented experts. We prefer to use James Martin and James Odell's term and call it the *structure analysis*.

However, a structure analysis of an application/system is not adequate; we also need to do a *behavior analysis*. Behavior analysis is the process we use to look at how each object (class) provides its services (i.e., the methods).

With the class/object mechanism, we create the conceptual building blocks of our model. The class mechanism, like a blueprint, defines the data structure and provides an index for the system functions. Services (functions and procedures) are tied to a specific class, and an object (as well as its associated data) can only be manipulated by the functions associated with the class of which the object is an instance. Without classes and objects, we can neither define any data nor use any methods (code).

When we specify "how a service is provided," we are defining "how a class of objects will perform that service." From an analysis perspective, there are two types of behavior: static and dynamic

Static Behavior

In static behavior, the operation (code) within the method is not affected by any external or internal events (actions). A good example of static behavior is the "square root" service for Number. If one requests the "square root" service from the number 4, which is an instance of Number, the result will always be 2. No external or internal action can cause the method of Number to change the result of computing the square root. If there were only static methods in reality, we would have a very nice model by just managing the structure portion of the model. In fact, writing the method (code) would be easy, as we would use the same techniques we used in imperative programming.

Dynamic Behavior

If all behaviors in the world were static, it would not be interesting. Fortunately, we live in a dynamic world. For example, look at how a loan agent will respond to your asking, "What is the prime loan interest rate?" The answer to this question can change almost hourly. Similarly, how does the airline reservation clerk answer your question, "What is the lowest fare from New York to San Francisco for January 15?" This answer may change as you are trying to make a decision on the telephone. These are two examples of dynamic behavior. The reasons for these changes in behavior may be captured by letting an object exist in many different states. Then an object's response can be based on its state. This kind of behavior is not handled very well by using the imperative programming technique. Such methods are better captured by using another mechanism called a finite-state machine.

To better understand the concept of states, let us look at the reservation process in an airline reservation system. When a request comes in, a reservation is created and moves to the requested state. While in the requested state, if there are seats, it can confirm the reservation; however, if there are no seats, it puts the reservation on the wait list. When a confirmed reservation is canceled, the reservation is moved to the canceled state. If the person shows up and flies at the given time, the reservation is moved to the used state, and when the plane lands, the reservation is moved to the archived state. A similar scenario holds for a reservation on the wait list. Thus, the Reservation object could have the following states: Requested, Wait-listed, Confirmed, Canceled, Used, and Archived. A change of state may occur when a service of the object is requested. When a method associated with a service changes the state of the object, the state is recorded in the data portion of the object. Usually, there is a finite set of sequences of state changes that is allowed with an object. The complete set of sequences is called the lifecycle of the object. Because all possible sequences of state changes are usually programmed using a finite-state machine mechanism, we need a way to capture this information in graphic form. One such mechanism is the fence diagram. Figure 2-1 is a fence diagram that shows the lifecycle of the Reservation object.

This fence diagram shows the state and the transitions (movement from one state to another state) that are possible. However, it does not show what will cause the object to change its behavior or state, nor does it show what action (operations performed) is taken when the change of state is recognized. A better model for capturing these additional two aspects of dynamic behavior is a state transition diagram, which shows (1) state, (2) transition, (3) condition, and (4) action. The full description of the major components of a state transition diagram follow:

State: Mode of behavior of the object.

Transition: Represents the movement from one state to another state. The transition logically is modeled as taking no time (i.e., the object moves from

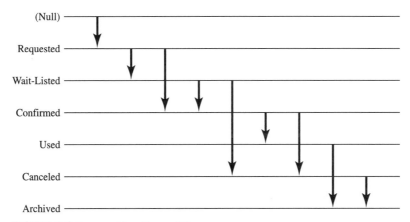

FIGURE 2-1 Reservation Fence Diagram

one state to another state instantly). A transition has two parts: transition condition and transition action.

Condition: When the transition condition is satisfied, the object moves from one state to another state. A condition can be the receipt of an external/ internal signal, a variable's reaching an absolute or relative value, or the receipt of a time signal.

Action: Operation (algorithm) executed by the object when it moves from one state to another state. Actions may include sending a signal to another object and triggering a transformation.

Figure 2-2 shows a template for a state transition diagram. Figure 2-3 shows a state transition diagram for the Reservation object.

UML has added some additional semantics to the dynamic model that address (1) interrupt handling (history state), (2) ongoing operations within a state that take time to complete (activities), (3) timing constraints (timing mark), (4) processes in threads (tasks), and (5) synchronization.

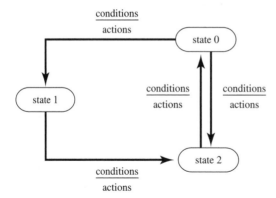

FIGURE 2-2 State Transition Diagram

Rules

WITH THE ADDITION OF RELATIONSHIPS (inheritance, aggregation, and association), object-oriented technology added some powerful mechanisms for specifying the data semantics of any application domain. Classical techniques for specifying static behavior and finite-state machines for specifying dynamic behaviors are powerful mechanisms for capturing the procedural semantic. However, one of the weaknesses of current object-oriented methods is the lack of mechanisms to support declarative semantics. In most object-oriented methods, declarative semantics (i.e., rules) are left to the inventiveness of the analyst/developer. If we assume that the purpose of the new method is to help us manage complexity by giving us mechanisms that model the full semantics of the problem domain, then we need to add mechanisms that handle rules (or declarative semantics) to our repertory.

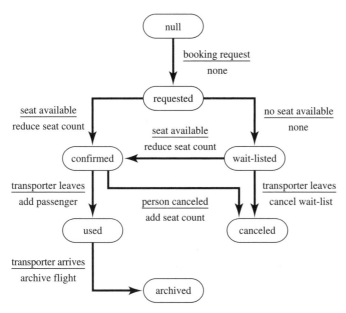

FIGURE 2-3 State Transition Diagram for the Reservation Object

For the novice, declarative semantics addresses the issues of global control description and business rules. Since most declarative semantics are explicitly specified in rules, we will focus on the issue of rules. The types of rules we are interested in capturing are (1) control rules, (2) business rules, (3) exception handling rules, (4) contention rules, and (5) triggers.

In a later chapter, we will look at a new language, R++, that extends C++ to give us some of the capabilities required to handle some of the rules types listed above. In a sense, R++ extends C++ to give us the additional mechanisms necessary to support full functional semantics (i.e., support for both procedural and declarative semantics).

Complex Systems

WE NOW HAVE PREVIEWED THE major mechanisms available via the object-oriented paradigm to manage complexity. There are other mechanisms that are more properly included in an advanced object-oriented book, of which several are currently available in the market for reference.

Before we can determine if a particular paradigm helps manage complexity better than other paradigms, we must first understand the characteristics (attributes) of complex applications or systems. Studies have identified five key attributes of complex application/systems:

- Complex systems take the form of a hierarchy. A complex system is composed of interrelated subsystems that have their own subsystems, and so on, until some lowest level of elementary components is reached.

■   The choice of which components in a system are primitive is relatively arbitrary and is largely up to the discretion of the observer of the system.

■   Intracomponent linkages are generally stronger than intercomponent linkages.

■   Hierarchical systems are usually composed of only a few different kinds of subsystems in various combinations and arrangements.

■   A complex system that works is invariably found to have evolved from a simple system that worked.

A good example of a complex system is a human being. Let us compare the mechanisms available in the object-oriented paradigm to the mechanisms that a biologist uses to analyze a human being. In biology, the building block (primitive component) is the cell, which is made from a membrane, cytoplasm, and the nuclei. Similarly, in the object-oriented paradigm, the primitive component is an object that has two subcomponents, data and function. Cells are joined together to form organs; similarly, objects are joined together via relationships to form subsystems. Organs are organized in some hierarchial manner to form biological systems; subsystems are joined via various relationships to form systems/applications.

In a human being, the "cell" and the "organ" behave in both a static (same every time) and a dynamic (not necessarily the same) manner. Object-oriented technology includes techniques to capture the dynamic behavior of both an object and a subsystem, Furthermore, a human may actually change its behavior completely by actually providing different services. Similarly in object-oriented technology there are techniques/mechanisms to transform an object of one type to another type. Moreover, additional techniques/mechanisms are still being developed to support other concepts necessary to model our perception of reality.

CHAPTER 3

Object-Oriented Programming

We hear desperate cries for a silver bullet—something to make software costs drop as rapidly as computer hardware costs do. But as we look to the horizon of a decade hence, we see no silver bullet. There is no single development in either technology or in management technique that promises even one order of magnitude improvement in productivity, in reliability, and in simplicity.

■ F. Brooks, The Silver Bullet, *Essence and Accidents of Software Engineering*

Maintainable, flexible, and reliable software is difficult to produce. Software systems are complex and, as suggested by Brooks, complexity is a part of the essence of the system. No process of abstraction can eliminate complexity in its entirety. However, we believe that we can create mechanisms that help us manage these complexities. Furthermore, we believe that some difficulties are not "accidents"; they arise as a consequence of the way software is constructed. It is our belief that changing the way we construct software will ameliorate these so-called "accidental" difficulties.

What Is Object-Oriented Programming?

Not a Silver Bullet

Programming a computer is, and will always be, one of the most difficult tasks ever undertaken by humans. Even with the advent of many tools, a proficient programmer must have intelligence, logic, the ability to find and use abstractions, experience, and creativity. Object-oriented programming is not the silver bullet or holy grail for which the managers of software development organizations are looking. However, object-oriented programming is more than simply a collection of new features added to an existing programming language; it is a new paradigm.

New Paradigm

Object-oriented programming is a new programming paradigm. A paradigm is "a set of theories, standards, and methods that together represent a way of organizing knowledge." This is the expanded definition of the word given in Thomas Kuhn's book *The Structure of Scientific Revolution.* Developers have been using other paradigms, such as imperative programming (C, Pascal, Cobol, Ada), logic programming (Prolog, C5), and functional programming (FP, ML).

For a compiler, the programming language we use directly influences the way we view (model) reality. In the 1970s when we were using programming languages such as C, Pascal, and PL/1, we used an imperative programming paradigm for modeling reality—the structured method. In the 1980s, when we were using SQL and 4GL with relational databases, we used a data-modeling paradigm for modeling reality—the entity-relationship diagram. Today as we program using C++, Smalltalk, and Objective C, we use the object-oriented paradigm to model reality.

For a compiler, the difference between an imperative language such as C and an object-oriented language such as C++ is only the addition of a few new keywords and data types. However, making effective use of these new facilities requires developers to shift their perception to an entirely different approach for modeling and problem solving. Object-oriented programming is a new way of thinking about what it means to compute, how we organize our information inside a computer system, and how we describe our view (model) of reality.

Basic Object-Oriented Programming Concepts

THE MOST FUNDAMENTAL CONCEPT/MECHANISM of object-oriented programming is an *object.* Since this is a book for developers, we will define an object as a software package consisting of the attributes (data) and the methods (code) that act on the data. The data is not directly accessible to the users of the object. Access to the data is granted only via the methods, or code, provided by object (i.e., function calls to its methods), as shown in Figure 3-1. This defines the first principle of the object-oriented paradigm—encapsulation.

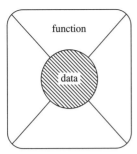

FIGURE 3-1 Object Has Data Encapsulated by Functions

Encapsulation.   The object contains both the data and the methods (code) that will manipulate or change that data.

The services of an object define how other objects gain access to its methods. Each object advertises the public services it is willing to provide to all objects. It also provides other services (protected and private) that are restricted only to specific other objects. We will discuss this in depth later. The idea of providing services defines the second principle of the object-oriented paradigm—information hiding.

Information Hiding.   The object that contains the attributes (data) defines what services (functions) are available to the other objects. In fact, other objects have neither access to nor knowledge of the data (attributes) or how (method/code) a service is provided.

Let us define an agent as an object that provides services and a client as an object that uses one or more of these services.[1] Before a client may use an agent's services, an interface must be defined. This interface definition is called the prototype of the service. The prototype is made from two parts: (1) the name of the service (called the selector by some experts), and (2) the arguments for the service (called the signature by some experts). Every object must define its prototype for each service it plans to provide. The set of defined prototypes is the protocol of the object (or, alternatively, it is the object's interface). The protocol defines how a client may invoke (or request) the services of this object.

A good example of an object and its interface is the icon system that we all use in a windowing system. A very common action in this system is to select an icon and then use a pull-down menu to get all of the services that we can choose for that icon. Thus, in an object-oriented system, the icon is really an object and the menu defines the object interface (or protocol).

---

[1]   An agent may also be called a server. *Agent* may be a better term during analysis, so that the term *server* may then be reserved to mean the actual object that does the work.

One object can use the public service of another object by using the message-passing mechanism (paradigm) to send a message that conforms to the prototype of the service. If object 1 (the client) wants to use a service of object 2 (the agent), the client sends a message to the agent requesting the specific service of the agent. Note that the message must be directed to a specific object and contain the name of the requested service. Furthermore, the message may contain additional information (arguments) needed by the agent to perform the requested service.

For example, in the programmer's parlance, object 1 makes a function call to the service (function) that belongs to object 2 and passes all the appropriate parameter values needed by the function call. Since we stated that message passing is implemented by a function call in C++, it is fair to ask in what sense a message-passing mechanism is different from a function-call mechanism. Certainly, in both cases there is an implicit request for action, and there is a set of well-defined operations that will be performed to fulfill the request. However, there are three important distinctions.

First, in a message-passing mechanism, each message is sent to a designated receiver (agent), as illustrated in Figure 3-2. In the imperative programming paradigm, a function-call mechanism has no designated receiver (agent). This distinction supports encapsulation.

Second, the interpretation of the message (method or set of operations/code used to fulfill the service request) depends on the receiver and can vary with different receivers. This distinction is necessary to support information hiding and polymorphism, which we will explain later. This leads to the third principle of the object-oriented paradigm—message passing.

Message Passing.   An object may communicate with another object only via the message-passing mechanism.

Each message must be sent to a designated receiver, and the interpretation of the message depends on the receiver.

Third, in the object-oriented paradigm, the specific receiver of any given message is not usually known until run time, so the determination of which method to invoke cannot be made until then. Thus, there is late binding between the message (service request/function call) and the method (code fragment) that will be used to fulfill the request for action. This can be contrasted to the early binding (compile or link time) of the function call to the code fragment in the imperative programming paradigm.

The support for late binding defines the fourth principle of the object-oriented paradigm—late binding.

Late Binding.   Support for the ability to determine the specific receiver and its corresponding method (code) to be executed for a message at run time.

From a client's perspective, it is the agent that provides the service. It is possible that the agent actually delegates the work to a third object. This leads to the fifth principle of the object-oriented paradigm—delegation.

Delegation.   Work is passed, via message passing, from one object (client) to another object (agent) because from the client's perspective the agent has the

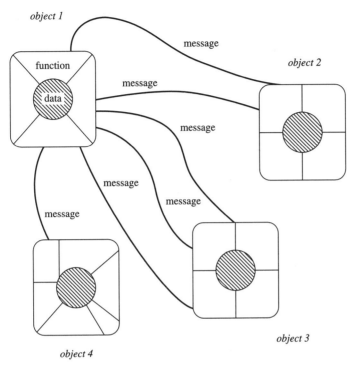

FIGURE 3-2 Message Passing Among Objects

services that the client needs. Work is continuously passed until it reaches the object that has both the data and the method (code) to perform the work.

Delegation is sometimes referred to as the perfect bureaucratic principle. Consider, for example, a corporation or a governmental organization. The chairperson of the board sends a service request (message) to the chief operating officer to build a new plant in Texas. From the perspective of the chairperson of the board, it is the chief operating officer's responsibility to provide the service. However, we all know that the chief operating officer has neither the skills nor the knowledge (information) to actually build a plant in Texas. So the chief operating officer has a method that delegates the work to the head of projects. The head of projects has a method that delegates the work to the chief engineer who has the staff to build a plant in Texas. In fact, the chief engineer's method delegates specific tasks to the appropriate heads of various disciplines to build the plant. It is the specific engineers who have the knowledge and the skills to design the plant to be built.

Here we see the fifth principle of the object-oriented paradigm applied. The work is delegated to the object that has the information (data) and the skills (method) to perform the task. The bureaucratic part comes from the fact that both the chief operating officer and the head of projects advertise the service "build a new plant," even though neither one has the information or the skills to perform the task. However, because they have access to resources (objects) that can perform the task, they can then take the responsibility for performing the task.

What got delegated is the authority to get the work done; responsibility cannot be delegated. From the chairperson of the board's perspective, it is the responsibility of the chief operating officer to fulfill the request to build a new plant in Texas. Similarly, from the chief operating officer's perspective, it is the responsibility of the head of projects to fulfill the request to build a new plant in Texas. When the head of projects accepts this request, he/she has accepted the responsibility from the chief operating officer to perform the work. However, neither the chief operating officer nor the chairperson knows how the work will be done. This is applying the principle of information hiding.

Now let us look at some other object-oriented concepts. Categorizing helps us organize the complex world in which we live. We can make certain assumptions about an object that is in a particular category. If an object is an instance of the category (class), it will fit the general pattern for that category. This leads us to the sixth principle of the object-oriented paradigm—class/instance/object.

Class/Instance/Object.   All objects are instances of a class. Instances can be created (instantiated) or destroyed (deleted) at run time.

How the object provides a service is determined by the class of which the object is an instance. Thus, all objects of the same class use the same method (code) in response to a specific service request (function call). Earlier we discussed the prototype of a service and the protocol as it relates to an object. Now with the concept of a class, we see that the prototypes and the protocol are really defined for a class and that they apply to every object that is an instance of that class.

Not only do we organize our objects into categories (classes), but we also arrange our categories into a hierarchy from the general to the specific. This leads us to the seventh principle of the object-oriented paradigm—generalization (without polymorphism).

Generalization without Polymorphism.   Classes can be organized by using a hierarchial inheritance structure. In the structure, the subclass will inherit the attributes, the relationships (defined below), and the methods from the superclass that is higher in the tree. An abstract superclass is a class that is used to create only subclasses. Thus, there are no direct instances of such a class.

However, there are always exceptions to the rule; in order to handle exceptions to the rule within our hierarchial structure, we define the seventh principle of the object-oriented paradigm—generalization with polymorphism, a modification of the sixth principle.

Generalization with Polymorphism.   Classes can be organized by using a hierarchial inheritance structure. In the structure, the subclass will inherit the attributes, relationships, and methods from the superclass that is higher in the tree. However, a subclass may create its own method to replace a method of any of its superclasses in providing a service that is available at the superclass level when an instance of that subclass is the agent.

For the subclass, its method will *override* the superclass method for providing the same service.

Though generalization is a powerful concept, some relationships between objects cannot be captured using this concept. This leads us to the eighth principle of the object-oriented paradigm—relationships.

Relationships. Collaborations[2] between objects to provide a service to a client are usually captured by an association relationship, which is technically called a *link*.

Later in this book, we will discuss the aggregation relationship; a link is sufficient here, as an aggregation is really a link with special properties.

Object-Oriented Programming Languages

BEFORE WE CAN DISCUSS C++, we should look briefly at the programming paradigms and the variety of languages used in object-oriented technology. This will give us a better perspective on the choice of C++ for this book. The programming paradigms and languages are described below.

Object-Based Programming

Object-based programming is a programming style that uses encapsulation and objects. The methods and attributes are hidden within the object, and each object is uniquely identified. There is no support for the class mechanism, inheritance, relationships, dynamic behavior, and rules. Ada is an example of an object-based language.

Class-Based Programming

Class-based programming includes all the mechanisms of object-based languages as well as the mechanisms for classes and instances. CLU is an example of a class-based programming language.

Object-Oriented Programming

Object-oriented programming includes all the mechanisms for class-based programming as well as mechanisms to support inheritance and self-recursion. Smalltalk is an example of an object-oriented programming language.

---

2   The definition of the different kind of relationships (i.e., association, aggregation, link, generalization, specialization) is explained in depth in later chapters.

Advanced Object-Oriented (OO) Programming

Advanced OO programming includes all the mechanisms for object-oriented programming and also includes capabilities to support multiple inheritance, association, aggregation, and dynamic behavior. C++ is an example of an advanced OO programming language.

Leading-Edge Object-Oriented Programming

Leading-edge OO programming includes all the mechanisms of an advanced OO programming style as well as mechanisms for supporting implementation of rules. R++ is an example of a leading-edge programming language.

Why C++?

THE C LANGUAGE WAS DEVELOPED by Dennis Ritchie in the early 1970s as a system implementation language and was used to build UNIX. The design philosophy of the C language is as follows:

- Make it portable.
- Keep the language small and simple.
- Make it fast.
- Trust the programmer.
- Do not prevent the programmer from doing what needs to be done.

With the use of the UNIX systems and because it was a terse and small language, C became widely used as a general-purpose programming language.

C++ was created by Bjarne Stroustrup in the early 1980s. Bjarne had four main goals in the design of the language:

1. Make C++ compatible with C.
2. Extend C with a class construct similar to the class construct of Simula 67.
3. Support strong typing.
4. Retain the design philosophy of the C language.

To achieve the above goals, C++ retained much of the C language, including a rich set of operators, nearly orthogonal design, terseness, and extensibility.

For us, the selection of C++ as our development language was largely determined by the above goals. First, we wanted a programming language that would preserve the design philosophy of C, as we do not believe that developing software will ever be so easy that all you need is an "object-oriented language." Second, we wanted a language that would facilitate interfacing our new systems to legacy systems.

The technical capabilities of C++ helped make our decision easy:

1. C++ is a highly portable language, since there is now an ANSI standard for C++. Also, there are compilers for the language on nearly every computer and operating system.

2. A C++ program can be fast because it does not incur the run-time expense of type checking and garbage collection as do most "pure object-oriented" languages.

3. C++ does not require a graphic environment and is relatively inexpensive.

4. C++ is a marriage of low-level (assembly language) and high-level (object-oriented constructs). The developer may write code at the appropriate level to accurately model the particular solution and still maintain machine-level implementation details.

5. C++ is a multiparadigm language that gives the developer a range of choices in designing and coding a solution. We will use these choices to demonstrate techniques that work, rather than insisting on paradigmatic dogma.

In brief, one may view C++ as a professional developer's object-oriented language alternative to "pure object-oriented" languages such as Smalltalk, Objective C, Eiffel, and so on. The language trusts the programmer and does not prevent the programmer from extending the language to support useful abstract mechanisms or from using non-object-oriented techniques when appropriate. Furthermore, it is an extension of a programming language that has been used to write a large number of applications on a wide range of machines.

These capabilities are important from a practical point of view because we know of very few commercial systems that live up to the "pure concepts of object-orientation" as defined by the object-oriented pundits. For most of the systems we built, we needed to go beyond the "pure concepts" to produce systems to meet the limitations of time, resources, and budgets, and/or to interface with legacy systems written in imperative programming languages such as C. There is no better language, other than a multiparadigm language, to give leading-edge developers a way to use their creativity and experience in a controlled context to solve real problems, meet business constraints, and still exact the benefits of the promised new technology.

When we discuss rules, we will look at R++, a leading-edge programming language from AT&T.

Ways of Organizing Reality

IN PRIOR YEARS, SOFTWARE DEVELOPERS used various paradigms (ways of viewing or modeling reality) to organize and manage software. However, each of the earlier paradigms supported modeling a specific view of a system. The four essential views of a system are as follows:

■ **Data/entity view**
Entity-relationship diagram

■ **Functional view**
Functional decomposition
(structured techniques)

■ **Behavioral view**
State transition diagrams
(state charts)

■ **Control view**
Rule-based systems

Major software methodologies have been developed using one of these views as a fundamental building block.

For example, structured analysis and design is based on using the functional view as the essential building block of its paradigm of reality. In this model, the computer is a data manipulator. It has some set of instructions that will cause it to go into memory and pull values (data) out of various slots (memory addresses), transform them in some manner, and then store the results back in another slot. Although it is a fairly accurate reflection of the way a computer works, this model does not reflect the way most people go about solving problems. This has been called the pigeon-hole model of computation.

The relational database (data analysis) methodology is based on the data/entity view of reality. In this model, the computer is a data manager that organizes data into collections (called entities) that are the building blocks of the system. The computer then manipulates the data within the entities to get the information it needs to process. However, this methodology was silent on how the computer was to take advantage of the entity in processing the data. Thus, most practitioners who used this methodology for data analysis still used the pigeon-hole model of computation for processing the data.

The finite state machine (statemate) methodology is based on the behavioral view of reality. In this model, the computer is a state manager. It organizes the processing based on the state of the system. The state is the building block of this system, and the data that gets manipulated is state-dependent. This methodology does not address data management. Moreover, in designing the functions and actions of this methodology, practitioners continued to use the pigeon-hole model of computation.

The rule-based system (part of artificial intelligence systems) is based on a control view of reality. In this model, the computer is an inference engine that executes a set of rules (if-then statements). In theory, the sequence in which the rules were executed was not material. However, in practice, most of us were not able to find rules that were truly decoupled. Since there was no structure to organize the rules, there was also very poor cohesion. Furthermore, rule-based systems did not help us manage the data and did not support procedural concepts.

Nearly all these methodologies are still based on the pigeon-hole model of computation, and all are very weak in modeling alternate views of the system. In brief, a rich enough methodology to manage the information about a complex problem domain did not exist.

Software engineers and software researchers have been trying for at least thirty years to improve the techniques for building software applications/systems. Attempts to address this issue have come from innovations in programming languages and from various structured approaches to application development. That is, we used structured methods, 4GLs, CASE tools, prototyping techniques, and code generators to address this issue.

The extent to which these efforts have succeeded is questioned in recent reports (Butler Cox, 1990). These reports show that structured methods impaired both the productivity of the developers and the quality of the end product. Furthermore, in very complex applications 4GLs may actually degrade productivity and, due to the restrictiveness of high-level languages, cause the switch to 3GL coding.

It was time for software professionals to understand why they were having these difficulties when

- software became the predominant cost of delivering and maintaining a system, and
- not even the most skilled programmers could produce resilient and correct code.

To gain understanding, computer scientists began to research software development.

It has taken software researchers all this time to understand how difficult it is to build "good" software. In their research, they have found software difficult to build for the following reasons:

- The complexity of the problem domain
- The difficulty of managing the development process
- The flexibility possible through software
- The problem of characterizing the behavior of a continuous system

In this book, we address mainly the first reason. The last reason is discussed in our case study. We also discuss the proper use of the flexibility of object-oriented techniques in the case study and the flexibility of C++ in the coding sections. Managing the development process is outside the scope of this book.

The Simulation Model of Computation

THE PROBLEM-SOLVING VIEW OF object-oriented programming is very different from the pigeon-hole model used in imperative programming. In the object-oriented paradigm, we never used any of the conventional terms, such as *assignments, variables,* or *memory addresses.* Instead, we use terms such as *objects, messages,* and *services.* We have a universe of well-behaved objects that courteously ask each other to perform services. We have a community of helpers that assist us in solving problems.

The idea of creating a universe of helpers is very similar to a style of computer simulation called "discrete event-driven simulation." In this style, the user creates models of various elements of the simulation and describes how they interact with each other. Then some discrete event sets the elements in motion.

This is almost identical to the way we do object-oriented modeling/programming. We define various objects in the universe that will help us solve the problem as well as how they interact with each other, and then we set them in motion. As a result, we consider object-oriented programming as using a simulation model of computation instead of a pigeon-hole model of computation.

This simulation model also provides the designer/programmer with a better metaphor for problem solving. When we think in terms of services and methods (how to provide the service), we can bring a wealth of experience, understanding, ideas, and intuition from everyday life. In contrast, most of us have very little insight into how to structure a program that views problem solving in terms of pigeon-holes or slots containing values.

The Object-Oriented Way of Organizing Reality

To ILLUSTRATE HOW THE OBJECT-ORIENTED paradigm helps us manage complexity, let us apply this modeling technique to a real-world situation. First we will describe the situation, and then we will discuss how we would use the object-oriented paradigm to capture the situation.

In this example, we have a family with a father (John), a mother (Jane), two sons (Peter and Paul), and two daughters (Elizabeth and Mary). John is an actor and Jane is a dentist. All the children are students, and the family dog is Lassie. Their family physician is Alice. This family owns a house in the suburbs. Although mowing the family lawn is normally a chore for the father, it can also be a paid chore for any one of the children. Working within the neighborhood is Jack, a professional lawn mower.

One morning, Jane notices that the lawn needs mowing, so she mentions to John that it is time to mow the lawn. John agrees and says that he will mow the lawn this evening. Later that evening, John comes home exhausted from a long day at the studio and decides to pay one of his children to mow the lawn. He looks for one of his children; he sees Mary first. He asks Mary to mow the lawn for five dollars. Mary agrees; however, Mary knows that Jack, a professional lawn mower, is willing to mow the lawn for four dollars. So Mary calls Jack to mow the lawn for four dollars, and Jack agrees to mow the lawn. Jane comes home later that evening and she sees the lawn mowed. Thinking that John mowed the lawn, Jane compliments John on the excellent condition of the lawn.

Now let us do an object-oriented analysis of this situation. There are the following tangible objects in our model: John, Jane, Peter, Paul, Elizabeth, Mary, Lassie, the family lawn, Jack and Alice. Jack, the professional lawn mower, advertises a lawn-mowing service. John, as the father of the house, also provides a lawn-mowing service that is limited to the family lawn. Each of the children also provides a lawn-mowing service, for a specific price.

The prototype of the lawn-mowing service is not the same for each of the objects. For example, the prototype for Jack's lawn-mowing service may have the name (selector) "mow the lawn" and the following arguments (signature): address of the lawn, whom to bill, billing address. The four children's prototype for "mow the lawn" service may look similar to Jack's, as the children are willing to mow any lawn for cash. The children's prototype may have the name "mow the lawn," and these arguments: address of the lawn, money (in form of cash). Finally, John will only mow the family lawn as his chore. John's prototype may have the name "mow the lawn" and no arguments. John had a default value for the lawn to mowed, namely the family's lawn, when Jane asked him to mow the lawn. He also knew that he would not get paid for mowing the family lawn.

Jane, the client, solves the problem of getting the lawn mowed by finding an appropriate agent, John, to whom she passes a message containing her request for service. In order for John to process the message, Jane's message must follow the protocol/prototype that John has defined for the service. Since Jane sent a message that John can interpret (i.e., the message is consistent with a prototype within the protocol that John has advertised), John must have a method (some algorithm or set of operations) to perform the requested service ("mow the lawn").

In this case, John behaves in a dynamic manner. If he is not tired at the end of the day, he mows the lawn himself; if he is tired, however, he asks one of his children to mow the lawn. Alternatively, if John always mows the lawn himself, as Jane apparently assumed, then his behavior would be considered static. In either scenario (whether John used a dynamic or static method for his behavior), when John accepted the message, he accepted the responsibility to satisfy Jane's request. Similarly, when Mary accepted the request from John to "mow the lawn" for five dollars, Mary accepted the responsibility to satisfy John's request.

Jane did not know, and probably did not want to know, the particular method that John used to provide the service "mow the lawn." She was very content that the lawn was mowed when she got home. If she had investigated, however, Jane would have found that Jack mowed the lawn for four dollars. Similarly, John did not know the particular method that Mary used to mow the lawn. This is the client's view of the principle of information hiding.

In the object-oriented paradigm, the agent's service is defined to the client in terms of responsibilities. Jane's request for action (i.e., service from John) must indicate only the desired outcome (mow the lawn). John is free to pursue any technique that achieves the desired results and is not hampered by interference from Jane. It is John's responsibility to define how he will provide the requested service by defining the method of providing the service.

John's method was an algorithm based on whether or not he was tired at the end of the day. As we know, on this particular day, he delegated the work to his daughter, Mary. Furthermore, Mary subsequently delegated the work to Jack.

From this example, we see another principle, all too human, in message passing. The first thought of every client and agent is to find someone else to perform the work. This is the application of the principle of delegation. Of course, objects cannot always respond to a message by asking another object to perform an action. If this were allowed, there would be an infinite circle of requests, like a bureaucracy of paper pushers, each passing papers to some other member of the organization. At some point, at least a few objects need to perform some work other than passing the request to some other object. These ideas are used in our example. From Jane's perspective, her husband John has provided the service "mow the lawn," which is the reason she compliments John for the excellent condition of the lawn. From John's perspective, it was Mary who mowed the lawn. John, then, may also thank Mary for the excellent job that she did. But in fact, if the behaviors or methods (how we provide the services) were not hidden (information hiding) from Jane, she would have known that Jack mowed the lawn.

To better understand the message-passing mechanism, let us look at a different scenario. John could have sent his message "mow the lawn" to one of his sons. Let us assume that he sent it to Peter instead of Mary. Peter's behavior or method is different from Mary's. Specifically, he needs all five dollars to pay for the gasoline to get to tomorrow's ball game. So, Peter mows the lawn himself. John and Jane had a choice of which person to ask for the service (or send the message to). However, the client must send the message to a designated receiver, and the designated receiver must provide the service. If Jane had asked Alice, the family physician, to mow the lawn, she would have been in error, since Alice does not provide that service. If Alice understands the message, she would probably send back an error message, "Physicians do not mow lawns." More likely, this would result in an invalid message for the recipient.

Now let us look at some other object-oriented concepts. Although Mary may never have dealt with Jack, she has some ideas about what behavior to expect from Jack when she requests his service; she knows that Jack is a professional lawn mower and she has information about lawn-mowing professionals. Since Jack is an instance of the category (class) **LawnMower,** he will fit the general pattern for lawn mowers. We can use the name **LawnMower** to represent the category of all lawn mowers. This is an application of the class/instance/object principle.

Mary has additional information about Jack that goes beyond his being an instance of the class **LawnMower.** She also has generic information about Jack, because Jack is also in the class **HouseCareProfessional.** She knows that Jack will come to the house to do the mowing, just as the other house care professionals such as the rug cleaner and the gardener. This is different from instances of the class **HealthCareProfessional,** who usually do not make house calls. Furthermore, Mary knows Jack is also in the class **SmallBusinessOwner,** and as such he will ask for money as part of the service and will give a receipt, as would any other small business owner. Mary has organized her knowledge of Jack in terms of a hierarchy of classes. The generalization tree with Mary's organization is shown in Figure 3-3.

Jack is an instance of the class **LawnMower,** but the **LawnMower** is a specialized form (subclass) of the class **HouseCareProfessional.** Furthermore, **HouseCareProfessional** is a subclass of the generalized form (superclass) of **SmallBusinessOwner,** and she can continue up the hierarchy to **OrganicMatter**

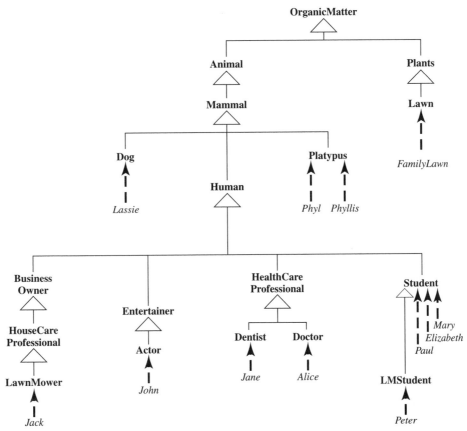

FIGURE 3-3 Generalization/Specialization—Hierarchy for the Lawn-Mowing Example

via **Human** and **Mammal.** Thus, Mary has a lot of generic information about Jack that is not directly attributed to his being in the class **LawnMower;** Mary assumes that the knowledge of a more general class applies to a specialization of that class. Mary's classification of Jack is the application of the generalization without poly-morphism principle.

Generalization (inheritance) works just as every parent would wish. The children (subclasses) inherit all the attributes (knowledge) and all the methods (behavior) of the parent (superclass). In addition, children can have additional attributes (smarter than the parent) and have additional methods (can do more than parent). This is what we call the "good child" form of specialization. Unfor-tunately, not all children are "good children." We need a way of modeling the "bad child." Let us look at this next.

We know that most mammals reproduce by giving birth; certainly humans do and so does the dog Lassie. However, Phyllis, the female platypus, reproduces by laying eggs instead of giving birth. Thus, the subclass **Platypus** provides the service of reproduction in a different manner than do the rest of the mammals.

If we want to capture this fact and still use our generalization hierarchy, we must have a way of handling the exceptions to the general rule. We do this by providing a way for the subclass to provide a different method for a service that is defined in the superclass (parent class). In our example, the superclass **Mammal** has defined a service called "reproduce." The method for the service "reproduce" is to give birth to live offspring. **Platypus** is a subclass of **Mammal.** In the "good child" form of specialization, Phyllis would reproduce by giving birth to live offspring. However, Phyllis is a "bad child"; she reproduces by laying eggs. In this form of specialization, called generalization with polymorphism, Phyllis provides her own method (i.e., laying eggs) for the service "reproduce." Thus, Phyllis uses a different method of providing the service "reproduce" than Lassie. Phyllis is an example of the need to modify the generalization without polymorphism principle.

In our example, we need to use generalization with polymorphism. Mary and all the other students will respond to the "mow the lawn" message by delegating any request that pays over five dollars to Jack as he will mow the lawn for four dollars. However, Peter is an exception; he will always respond to the "mow the lawn" request by doing it himself. Thus, we must use generalization with polymorphism to capture Peter's behavior (see above figure).

Let us look more closely at the method that Mary uses to "mow the lawn." In order to call Jack to mow the lawn, Mary has to have access to Jack. Normally, Jack sends flyers around the neighborhood advertising his service. Mary sees the flyer and puts Jack's name and telephone number into her address book. Although this action may seem innocuous, Mary has established a relationship with Jack. At the instant Mary recorded his name, she decided to consider using his service when the occasion arises. A connection was established between Mary and Jack. The reason Jack sends out the flyers is to establish such relationships and add to his customer base. Every person who reads the flyer and saves Jack's name, telephone number, and kind of service has established a relationship with Jack. We can name that relationship from two perspectives: (1) from Jack's perspective, all the people who keep the flyer information are customers, and (2) from these people's (and Mary's) perspective, Jack is a professional lawn mower.

This kind of relationship, where one object knows about another object for specific services, is called a *link*. Let us presume that the neighborhood is called FunTown and that we have a category (class) of people called **FunTowner.** Since Jack is an instance of **LawnMower** and every one of his customers is an instance of **FunTowner,** we can capture this link by a higher-level concept called *association*. An association describes a group of links with a common structure and common semantics. All links in an association must connect objects from one class to objects from a second class. Thus, if we have a second person Joan who also is an instance of **LawnMower** and every one of her customers is an instance of **FunTowner,** we have a second link that belongs to the same association.

Associations are bidirectional. It is common to give a name to an association in each direction. In our example, from **LawnMower**'s direction, it is **Customer,** and from the **FunTowner**'s direction, it is **LawnMower.**[3] Without the association, there would be no way for Mary to access the services of Jack.

Table 3-1 summarizes the key object-oriented concepts using the "mowing the lawn" example. We have used some notations from UML in Figure 3-3. Generalization/specialization (inheritance) is shown as a solid line from subclass to

TABLE 3-1 OO Concepts with Examples

OO Concept	Explanation/Example
Client	Requestor of the service (i.e., sender of the message—Jane)
Agent (server)	Agent to whom the message is sent (i.e., John)
Object	Jane, John, Mary, Lassie
Message sending	Mary's request to John to "mow the lawn"
Signature	Additional information (arguments) needed to carry out the request (i.e., amount to be paid)
Responsibility	John's responsibility to satisfy Jane's request
Attributes	Name, age, etc.
Services	John and Jack both provide the service "mow the lawn."
Method	This is the operation(s) of providing the service, which is hidden from the client.
Collaboration	Object that helps another object in performing the method (i.e., Jack helps Mary in providing the "mow the lawn" service).
Class	Mammal, BusinessOwner
Instance	Same as an object.
Inheritance	LawnMower is a specialized form of a HouseCareProfessional. HouseCareProfessional is a Human, which is a specialized form of Mammal.
Polymorphism	Phyllis laying eggs.
Subclass	Subclass will inherit attributes and methods from its superclass(es) (i.e., Human will inherit all the attributes and methods of Mammal).
Superclass	Dentist is a subclass of the superclass HealthCareProfessional.
Abstract superclass	Class used to create only subclasses (i.e., Mammal).

---

[3] In actuality, a link is implemented via pointers from one object to another object(s). A *pointer* is an explicit reference to an object; thus an association is implemented in a class as a class pointer attribute to the other class. For example, in the data portion of class **FunTowner** there may be a data member *lawn mower* that points to a **LawnMower** object. Conversely, the data portion of class **LawnMower** may contain a data member *customer* that points to a set of **FunTowner** objects that are the customers.

superclass with a triangular arrowhead on the superclass end. Instantiation of a class is shown with a dashed arrow from the object to the class. Both of these notations are from UML. A class is shown by using bold font, and an object is shown using underline font. In UML, a class is drawn as a solid-outline rectangular box with three compartments, with class name in the top compartment, a list of attributes in the middle compartment, and a list of operations in the bottom compartment; an object is drawn as a solid-outline rectangular box with three compartments, with object name underlined in the top compartment, a list of attributes, and so on. We will see these symbols later in the text for classes and objects.

■ ■ SUMMARY

The principles of the object-oriented paradigm are as follows:

1. **Encapsulation**
   An object contains both the data and the methods (code) that will manipulate or change the data.

2. **Information Hiding**
   The services of an object define how other objects have access to its methods and, therefore, its data. Each object advertises public services that it can provide to other objects.

3. **Message Passing**
   An object (client) may communicate with another object (agent) only via the message-passing mechanism. A client requests a service of an agent by sending a message that matches a predefined protocol that the agent defines for that service.

4. **Late Binding**
   The specific receiver of any given message will not be known until run time, so the determination of which method to invoke cannot be made until then. Remember inheritance with polymorphism.

5. **Delegation**
   Work is passed, via the message-passing mechanism, from one object (client) to another object (agent) because from the client's perspective the agent has the services that the client needs. Work is continuously passed until it reaches the object that has both the data and the method (code) to perform the work. Delegation is sometimes called the perfect bureaucratic principle.

6. **Class and Objects**
   All objects are instances of a class. How an object provides a service is determined by the class of which the object is an instance. Thus, all objects of the same class use the same method (code) in response to a specific service request.

7. **Inheritance and Polymorphism**
   Classes can be organized by using a hierarchial inheritance structure. In the structure, the subclass will inherit the attributes and the methods from the superclass(es) higher in the tree. However, a subclass may create its own method to replace the method of any of its superclasses in providing a service

that is available at the superclass level. When the subclass is the agent for that specific service, the method of the subclass will override the method of the superclass(es) for providing the same service.

8.   **Relationships**

Association and aggregation are used to capture the collaboration between objects that is necessary to provide a service to a client.

CHAPTER 4

Finding the Objects

I have a cat named Trash. . . . if I were trying to sell him (at least to a computer scientist), I would not stress that he is gentle to humans and is self-sufficient, living mostly on field mice. Rather, I would argue that he is object-oriented.

■ Roger King, *My Cat Is Object-Oriented*

This chapter describes the first step in our method for building an OO model. We begin at a logical starting point—finding the objects. We cover many different techniques for identifying objects in this chapter. The goal here isn't to master all of them, but to provide a solid background by which developers can direct their efforts. We recommend one technique, recognizing that it isn't the newest, most comprehensive, or trendy approach. Instead, we concentrate on presenting a technique that is easy for someone new to the objected-oriented paradigm to apply.

Object-Oriented Analysis: Model of Reality

WHEN WE ANALYZE SYSTEMS, WE create models of the application domain of interest to our business. The model can be very specific and highly specialized (i.e., a vendor ledger system), or it can cover a whole enterprise. In either case, the model represents an aspect of reality and is built in a manner that helps us to manage complexity and understand the business reality. The model is always much simpler than reality, just as any toy model is simpler than the real thing. In our case, however, if the model is rich enough, we can manipulate it to help us invent or redesign our businesses.

With traditional analysis methods, we model the world using functions or behaviors as our building blocks. We have seen some of the weaknesses of such a modeling paradigm. With object-oriented analysis, we model reality with objects as our building blocks, hoping to eliminate the shortcomings of a modeling paradigm based on functions. In the object-oriented paradigm, we describe our world using object types (classes) and describe the services of these object types. Then we model the behavior of the world as a sequence of messages that are sent between various objects. By using this form of analysis, we can more easily design and program the software in an object-oriented manner and achieve the benefits of doing so.

Building the OO Model

IN TRADITIONAL TEXTBOOKS, BUILDING THE OO model is considered the requirements phase of the project. What makes this phase very confusing to developers is that two very distinct but related activities are taking place simultaneously: problem analysis (domain analysis) and business solution description (product description).

There are at least two reasons to keep these activities nonsequential and not mutually exclusive. First, a large number of product developments require little or no problem analysis. Usually, problem analysis is applied only to new, difficult, or yet unsolved problems. Companies usually do not waste time or resources on a problem that is already well understood. Second, when doing problem analysis, most teams use it only for that portion of the business problem that is not well understood. When some part of the problem or problem domain is well understood, the teams start to work on the business solution description to solve that part of the problem. This back-and-forth process gives the team an effective way of monitoring its own progress.

The goal of problem analysis is a relatively complete understanding of the problem and the constraints on the possible business solutions. The goals of business solution description are a correct, complete, unambiguous, verifiable, consistent, modifiable, traceable, organized, and concise description of the business solution that is understandable to the user. This does not mean that the goals of a business solution description are always met, but one should come close.

In problem analysis, the developers/analysts/system engineers acquire knowledge of the problem (and the problem domain) at hand and identify all the possible constraints on the problem's solution. Much of the time is spent interviewing users and business/domain experts and brainstorming ideas. During this period, there is considerable expansion of information and knowledge about the problem to be solved. The issues that need to be addressed during this activity are (1) finding a way of trading off constraints, and (2) finding ways to organize the information and knowledge acquired.

In a business solution description, the developers/analysts/system engineers make some of the difficult decisions on constraint trade-offs and describe the external behavior of the product to be built. In this activity, (1) ideals are organized, (2) conflicting views are resolved, and (3) inconsistencies and ambiguities are eliminated.

The end result of problem analysis and business solution description should be a model that does the following:

- Organizes the data into objects and classes, and gives the data a structure via relationships of inheritance, aggregation, and association
- Specifies local functional behaviors and defines their external interfaces (service prototypes)
- Captures control or global behavior (event trace diagrams)
- Captures constraints (limits and rules)

In our version of object-oriented analysis, we do not differentiate between problem analysis and business solution description; we build a model of reality that should capture both. This is consistent with the idea that a good and effective method should have seamless steps and preferably no transformation from one step to another. The first step in this method is finding the objects.

Identification of Objects

IDENTIFYING OBJECTS (AND CLASSES)[1] IS the most important and difficult step in any object-oriented method. Identifying them is important because the requirements specification, design, and code will use them as the building blocks; mistakes in properly identifying them will affect the extensibility and maintainability of the software. Identifying them is difficult (at least for most beginners) because it requires in-depth knowledge and skill in the object-oriented paradigm and the ability to apply it to the applications. It typically takes three months to one year of practice for the necessary skills to mature, and it may take longer

---

[1] Technically a class is also an object. In the next few chapters, we will treat a class as an object. For the experienced reader, we are really interested in finding classes and not instances of a class in this chapter.

depending on the person's attitude (toward object orientation), aptitude, and amount of on-the-job training/experience.

In theory, identifying objects and classes should not be difficult. We deal with objects and classes every day of our lives. For example, a child's toy (a toy fire truck or a doll) is merely a model of a real-world entity (a truck or a person). The toy fire truck has attributes that are either constant (i.e., height, width, color) or variable (i.e., battery level and relative state of newness or disrepair), as well as services (i.e., move forward, move backward, turn on siren). It also has exception conditions such as battery drained, broken wheel, and so on.

Making mental models and using abstractions are standard human approaches for dealing with the complexity of everyday life. Therefore, if software professionals understand their application domain, identifying objects and classes requires merely capturing the relevant models/abstractions of the application domain needed to solve the problem. Then why is identification still so difficult?

The biggest problem is that developers have learned and practiced a much less natural and less powerful approach to software development—the functional approach (structured analysis and functional decomposition). As mentioned earlier, due to the limitations of computers and programming languages, developers needed to use a paradigm that mimicked a computer. This resulted in a functional approach to modeling reality that focused on the procedural step-by-step operations.

Human inertia makes it difficult for experienced developers to break this habit, especially since functional approaches are unnatural (until the skill is developed) and developers have spent years honing that skill. Furthermore, thinking in terms of objects in everyday life may appear to be easy and natural, but thinking about software development analogies in terms of objects will take some time. When developers first apply an object-oriented method, they are often unsure of what constitutes a software object or class. Even when they know the definition, they are not always sure that something meets the definition of an object or a class.

This difficulty has provoked a philosophical debate and much confusion. There are two fundamentally different views of how objects and classes came to be: empiricist and phenomenalist. The empiricist view says that they are out there just waiting to be perceived. According to Betrand Meyers, "the objects are just there for the picking." Therefore, developers must be blinded to them because they are too accustomed to functional decomposition and are still trying to use functions as their building blocks.

The phenomenalist view says that objects come from both the world and our consciousness through a dialectical process. Other phenomenalists suggest that real-world objects are a reflection of social relations and human thinking processes.

We are members of the phenomenalist school. Not only do we believe that objects comes from our consciousness, but we must also now "objectify" the world to get maximum benefit from this new technology. It is this "objectifying" that makes object identification difficult even for experienced object-oriented analysts.

Over the past ten years, object-oriented practitioners and researchers have developed many techniques (often indirect) to resolve this issue. These techniques were based on the assumption that there is a mapping (ideally, one-to-one) between things that neophytes can identify as well as objects and/or classes that neophytes have difficulty recognizing. This allows object-oriented neophytes to do useful work while acquiring the skills and experiences to make the full paradigm shift to the object-oriented approach.

Different methodologists have their own favorite approaches, and many of these techniques are tightly coupled to a few approaches. Most books and articles discuss only a small number of these identification techniques, and some approaches are rarely taught. Some of the techniques are well suited for object-oriented design,[2] but less useful during object-oriented domain analysis (i.e., requirements analysis). Some techniques are safe in the sense that they identify a minimal number of false objects and are easy to use, but will identify only the obvious objects and classes.

Because there is not necessarily an easy one-to-one mapping among objects and classes and "other things," all these techniques have shortcomings, namely, that using these techniques may produce false-positive identification and that none of these techniques provide a complete list of objects.[3] We believe that there neither is nor will be a technique that will help us find all the objects and only all the objects. This is consistent with our phenomenalist view; we believe that we will mature our perception of reality via a dialectical process because the real world of objects is a reflection of social relations and our thinking processes. As with most things, it is the responsibility of you and your management to manage this risk.

The following techniques give us a list of potential objects, albeit an incomplete list. They may be divided into two categories, current and traditional. Current techniques are the most effective and state-of-the art, although they require significant training and experience to be used effectively. Traditional techniques are usually highly indirect and are easy to use and misuse, especially for beginners. Miscellaneous techniques are limited in scope, but useful given the right situation.

Current Techniques

CURRENT TECHNIQUES RELY ON EXPERIENCE and knowledge of the domain to be captured in the object model. They cover the range from using the things to be modeled to extending existing models of the domain.

---

[2]   In our definition of design, we mean modeling the technology domain.

[3]   For example, all the abstractions of concepts or ideas that need to be modeled as objects.

Using the Things to Be Modeled

Using the things to be modeled is the preferred method of experienced object-oriented software engineers. It recognizes that the application domain entities need to be identified before identifying the corresponding objects and classes. This technique is advocated by such noted authors as Coad and Yourdon, Shlaer and Mellor, and so on.

The technique is highly effective because it is natural, direct, and reliable. Unfortunately, it tends to help only in finding the terminators[4] and other tangible objects that are the easiest entities to identify. Abstract classes are not readily identified using this technique. Furthermore, this technique requires the user to make the paradigm shift to the object-oriented mindset. Although this paradigm shift should be the ultimate goal, on-the-job training to accomplish it may be very expensive.

Following are the steps of this technique:

1. Identify individual or group things, such as persons, roles, organizations, locations, logs, reports, forms, and so on, in the application domain that is to be modeled.
2. Identify the corresponding objects and classes.

Using the Definitions of Objects and Classes

Using definitions assumes that the most effective approach is a direct approach and that the software engineer has experience in identifying objects and classes. The technique is very simple; the developer uses object abstraction, knowledge of the application domain, and the definition of class to intuitively identify objects and classes. This is the same way experienced developers would recognize functional and process abstractions.

This is a direct and effective approach that provides the best partitioning of the requirements into classes. When used properly, this technique produces the fewest false-positive identifications. This technique has no limitations, but it requires a significant paradigm shift for the developer.

Making this paradigm shift requires significant training, practice, intuition, and experience, which usually takes at least six months of on-the-job training. Moreover, there are no tricks or tools to help in this technique; the tools are designed only to document the results.

Using Object Decomposition

Object decomposition assumes that many objects and classes are aggregates of component objects and classes. Furthermore, it assumes that decomposition is a

---

[4] Terminators are classes that have no subclasses, and abstract classes are those that have subclasses. When one talks about an object, one is usually referring to an instance of a terminating class.

good way to identify the component objects and classes and that you have some of these aggregate objects or classes identified.

The steps of this technique follow:

1. Find the aggregate objects or classes.
2. Use object decomposition to identify their component objects or classes.

This technique is a natural way to deal with aggregates; unfortunately, not all objects and/or classes are aggregates or components of an aggregate. Furthermore, real-world aggregates normally physically contain their components; because of this property, novices often nest the implementation components within this aggregate when an association relationship may be a better model of the implementation components. This can lead to both subtle modeling issues and technical issues such as recompilation, reuse, and maintenance.

Using Generalization

Generalization assumes that objects are identified prior to the identification of their classes, that every object is an instance of some class, and that the commonalities among objects can be used to generalize classes.

The steps of this technique follow:

1. Identify all objects.
2. Look for two or more objects that share the same attributes and services.
3. Generalize these common aspects to form a class.
4. To continue finding classes, see "Using Subclasses."

The primary benefit of this approach is that it promotes reuse and supports the development of one or more classification hierarchies.

Using Subclasses

When using subclasses, we skip finding objects and directly start identifying classes. It assumes that separate classes often contain common resources (i.e., attributes, services, methods, etc.) and that they can be changed into subclasses that inherit the common resources from a common superclass.

Here are the steps of this technique:

1. Identify classes that share common resources (i.e., attributes, methods, service name, aggregation relationship, association relationship, etc.).
2. Factor out the common resources to form a superclass (parent), and then use inheritance for all classes that share these resources to form simpler subclasses.

The key benefit of this technique is reuse, but it has some serious drawbacks. When misused, it leads to unmaintainable and opaque classes that reuse randomly unrelated resources that do not logically belong to subclasses of the same superclass. It also may produce inappropriate or excessive inheritance coupling.

Using Object-Oriented Domain Analysis

If an object-oriented domain analysis (OODA) of an application in the same problem domain has been done previously, it can be used to identify objects and classes. Given the OODA, the steps of this technique are as follows:

1. Analyze the results of the given OODA (in the same domain).
2. Reuse (with or without modification) objects or classes from the OODA.

This technique supports reuse and tends to maximize cohesion in classes and minimize message and inheritance coupling. If one assumes that the previous OODA is solid, this technique also naturally gives a "reality check" on the current project, because the objects and classes should be the similar to the ones in the previous OODA. Thus, considerable time and effort could be saved if the original OODA is relevant and complete. Unfortunately, this technique has limitations.

Today, finding adequate and relevant OODA is not easy. Most systems have either incomplete OODA or no OODA model at all. For reuse to be effective, the problem domain must be well documented and understood by the developers. Tailoring for performance and other business constraints in a specific project may lower reuse. Finally, although it is easier to reuse than to reinvent, the not-invented-here (NIH) syndrome of many developers must be successfully overcome.

Reusing an Application Framework

In some cases at least one OODA has been done to create an application framework of reusable classes. An application framework is a reusable, domain-specific template of classes and/or subassemblies and all its associated classes that implement some common capabilities. Because it is domain-specific, it usually applies specifically to other applications that are in the same domain.

The steps of this technique follow:

1. Identify one or more relevant application frameworks in the same application domain.
2. Reuse both objects (instances of classes) and classes from previously developed frameworks. Note that some of the classes may need to be modified to be reused in your specific application.

This technique may be considered an enhancement of the OODA technique described above; thus, it has all the advantages and limitations of that technique.

Moreover, it has additional limitations. Your current developers must be able to identify one or more relevant application frameworks that have been previously developed and stored in a repository. Most likely, not all the needed classes will be in the application framework(s) examined.

Reusing Class Hierarchies

We can reuse class hierarchies if a reuse repository with relevant reusable class hierarchies has been developed. To use this technique, we follow these steps:

1. Look for classes in the reuse repository that can be reused, either with or without modification.
2. After identifying the classes, attempt to reuse the associated class hierarchy.
3. After modifying the classes, attempt to create new abstract classes by grouping common attributes and methods.
4. If the classes are parameterized, supply the generic formal parameters.

This technique has the same advantages as using OODA. In addition, it maximizes the use of inheritance and is a natural fit for Smalltalk (an OO language). As with all techniques, it has additional limitations beyond those for OODA. The existing classification hierarchies may not be relevant to the current application. Existing classes may need to be parameterized, or new subclasses may need to be derived.

Reusing Individual Objects and Classes

If a reuse repository with relevant reusable objects and classes has been developed, we can reuse specific objects and classes.
The steps of this technique follow:

1. Look for relevant objects and classes in the reuse repository that can be applied to the application.
2. If necessary, modify the objects and/or classes.
3. Supply generic formal parameters to parameterize classes as necessary.

This technique has some very serious shortcomings that we will discuss later.

Using Subassemblies

Using subassemblies is possible if developers are incrementally developing subassemblies using a recursive development process. This technique is similar to functional decomposition; instead of a function, take an object and decompose it into other objects (subassemblies). Continue the decomposition until there are only terminal objects (i.e., those that do not need to send messages to other objects at a lower level) at the leaves of the decomposition.

The steps of this technique follow:

1. Identify all the objects (classes) at the current level that must remain temporarily incomplete because they depend on one or more as yet unidentified objects or classes.
2. Develop a skeleton specification/design for the methods of the temporarily incomplete object using either (1) narrative English, (2) an object-oriented specification language such as OOSDL, or (3) a program design language (PDL).
3. Create the appropriate child subassemblies (objects) at the next lower level to handle the messages for the incomplete objects at the higher level.
4. Do step 1 at the current level that has the new subassemblies.

This technique has several advantages. It supports incremental identification of objects/classes. It also identifies all the subassemblies in an application domain. It is very similar to functional decomposition, so there is less culture shock for developers trained in the structured methodology. However, there are limitations to this technique; it identifies only assembled objects. Thus, one must have some other technique to identify fundamental components of the subassemblies.

Using Personal Experience

The use of personal experience will eventually become more popular and may be the most viable of all the techniques described here as developers gain more experience in using the object-oriented methodology. It assumes that the developers have previously designed one or more relevant classes in the application domain. To build the new models, the developers reuse some of the objects and classes that have been developed on the previous projects.

The steps of this technique follow:

1. Find objects and classes that correspond to ones found in previous models that are in the same application domain.
2. Modify the classes as necessary to support the present project.

By building on experience, this technique provides a reasonable "reality check" on the current project. Thus, the quality of the classes and objects may be substantially improved, as they are based on classes and objects that are already built and tested. It is also very natural to want to leverage off the application experience of the developer.

However, there are drawbacks. This technique assumes relevant previous experience, which is not always present. When previous experience is based on functional decomposition projects, the developers have a tendency to identify suboptimal classes. In such a situation, past experience may be of limited value and possibly even misleading. Moreover, this technique is very informal, and different developers may identify substantially different objects and classes given the same starting information; thus, it is a highly subjective technique. Also, it may not minimize the message and inheritance coupling.

Traditional Techniques

TRADITIONAL TECHNIQUES FOCUS MORE ON discovering a domain model rather than using existing domain models. We feel that it is a good practice for an individual learning object-modeling techniques to understand and apply these techniques before using current techniques.

Using Nouns

Pioneered by Russell J. Abbott and popularized by Grady Booch, the technique of using nouns was widely used between 1983 and 1986 and was included in many object-oriented development methods.

The steps of this technique follow:

1. Obtain (i.e., from a requirement document) or use narrative English to develop an informal description of the problem to be solved in words of the application domain (i.e., use the terms of the domain experts).
2. Use the nouns, pronouns, and noun phrases to identify objects and classes (find the "real-world" objects and classes). Singular proper nouns (Jim, he, she, employee number 5, my workstation, my home) and nouns of direct reference (the sixth player, the one-millionth purchase) are used to identify objects. Plural nouns (people, customers, vendors, users, employees) and common nouns (everyone, a player, a customer, an employee, a workstation) are used to identify classes.
3. Verbs (pay, collect, read, request) and predicate phrases (are all paid, have simultaneously changed) are used to identify the services.

This technique has many advantages. Narrative languages (English, Chinese, French, German, Japanese, etc.) are well understood by everyone on a project and can be an effective communication medium for both technical and nontechnical project staff. Moreover, there usually is one-to-one mapping from nouns to objects or classes.

Using nouns requires no learning curve; the technique is straightforward and well defined, and does not require a complete paradigm shift for the beginner. Moreover, this technique does not require a prior OODA; you can apply it to an existing requirement specification written for structural analysis and/or any other methodology.

This technique has some shortcomings, however. For one thing, it is an indirect approach to finding objects and classes. Nouns are not always classes or objects in the problem domain. Many sentences in a functional specification are in the wrong form for easy identification of the objects and classes. For example, "roll back the transaction" or "the software will compute the average salary." In many cases, the nouns, especially subjects of sentences, refer to (1) an entire assembly or a computer software configuration (i.e., CICS), (2) a subassembly or a software component, (3) an attribute, or (4) a service. Later, we will discuss these shortcomings and how we can address them.

Using Traditional Data Flow Diagrams

The use of data flow diagrams arose among the many software developers and managers who had invested heavily in expensive CASE tools that supported data flow diagrams (DFDs). In their need to make a transition from functional decomposition requirements analysis methods (i.e., structured analysis) to object-oriented design, they wanted a "Holy Grail" that would protect their investment and make the transition easier. This technique was first published by Ed Seidewitz and Mike Stark of NASA's Goddard Space Flight Center.

This technique uses the following diagrams:

- Terminators on context diagrams (CDs)
- Data stores on DFDs
- Complex data flows on DFDs

Before you use this technique, a structural analysis must be completed, and all the CDs and DFDs must be written.

To use this technique, do the following:

1. Map each terminator on the CDs to an object to encapsulate the interface.
2. Identify one class to encapsulate the interface of each set of similar or identical "terminator" objects.
3. Map each data store on the DFDs to an object.
4. Map data stores that contain more than one data field to an aggregate object.
5. Map all or part of the data transformation associated with the data store to the service of the object, and thus of the class.
6. Map complex data flows (i.e., records with numerous fields) to an object.
7. Identify subtransformations associated with the parts of the data flow and then map these subtransformations to services of the object.

The major benefit of this technique is that it requires no paradigm shift by the analysts and developers. If the original DFDs are well constructed, false-positive identification of objects and classes is rare. Finally, there are a lot of projects that already have the CDs and DFDs.

Unfortunately, the shortcoming is also directly related to not making the paradigm shift. Nearly all the DFDs were originally written for functional decomposition, and they have a tendency to create a top-heavy architecture of classes.

With functional decomposition, there is a tendency to assume that the stem is an assembly of subassemblies at the appropriate level. Moreover, one tends to assign services at the corresponding level where the subassembly was found. This may cause objects to be identified in the wrong subassembly. Although false-positive identification of objects and classes is rare, not all the objects or classes are identified. The rareness of false-positive identification is totally dependent on the quality of the original DFDs. This is still an indirect method of finding objects and classes; it is based on data abstraction and not on object abstraction.

In many instances, an object or class contains more than one data store. Thus, their attributes may be mapped to objects and classes while their associated objects and classes remain unidentified.

Since the DFDs represent functional decomposition, pieces of an object may be scattered across several DFDs assigned to different persons. As a result, different variants of the same object may be redundantly and independently identified. Finally, transforms are not restricted to a single service of a single object. Therefore, transforms are often compound operations that need to be assigned to multiple objects. If the objects are not properly identified, this leads to fragmented objects and classes.

Using Class-Responsibility-Collaboration (CRC) Cards

The use of CRC cards was developed by Rebecca Wirfs-Brock and others. These developers observed that identifying objects and classes is a human activity that can be stimulated by the use of small pieces of paper (i.e., CRC cards or Post-it Notes) to represent the objects/classes. It was found that by handling the CRC cards, developers with experience, creativity, and intuition can often identify new objects/classes by noticing holes in the current set of cards. Thus, the cards served both as a vehicle to document the previously identified objects and classes and to stimulate the developers to find iteratively and incrementally new objects and classes not currently documented.

For the classical version of this technique, do the following:

1. On a CRC card, document the name of the class and list both the responsibilities (i.e., which services it provides) and collaborators (i.e., objects/classes it needs to fulfill its responsibilities).

2. Identify missing objects and/or classes that should be added to the existing set of CRC cards. Specifically, look for responsibilities that cannot be allocated to existing classes and collaborators that have not yet been assigned to a class.

For the modern version of this technique, do the following:

1. On a Post-it Note, document the name and list the responsibilities of the class.

2. Position all the classes on a whiteboard and draw association arcs between the classes to represent the collaborators.

3. Identify missing objects and/or classes that should be added to the existing set of classes. Look for attributes and services that cannot be allocated to the current classes.

This technique is inexpensive and easy to use. Little effort is invested in making the classes, and they can be easily discarded. Also, the method stimulates communication and is not intimidating to beginners.

Unfortunately, this technique is better suited for thinking about and designing objects and classes than for identifying them. You must already have objects and classes in order to use this technique to identify additional objects and classes. Finally, the developers must have significant experience, creativity, and intuition for this technique to be consistently successful.

Recommended Approaches

WHICH APPROACH TO USE DEPENDS on the situation and the experience of your team. No single approach or technique will be suitable for all, especially when you take into consideration time to market and cost. In spite of this caveat, we present here the most common preferences. If you have tested relevant application frameworks as well as their associated repository, the "reusing application frameworks" technique is the best approach. If the frameworks do not exist, there should be a separate effort using OODA.

However, for the novice, this book presents a different approach that uses many of the above-mentioned techniques (proven to be more usable by those unfamiliar with this new object-oriented paradigm).

We will start by doing the following:

1. Because most analysts/developers are still given a requirements document in narrative English (native language) that uses the terms of the domain expert, it is not unreasonable to use the "using nouns" technique of Abbott/Booch with the caveat that this technique is used to find potential objects and will not find all the objects.

2. Identify all "potential objects" in the problem domain by interactive dialog with the domain expert. Remember that both we and the domain expert are dealing with objects every day. Furthermore, domain experts make mental models and use abstraction to deal with the complexity of their respective businesses. We want to capture the objects that are in the mental models of the domain experts. If we can do this, we can deliver software to the marketplace faster and enhance that software package faster because it is consistent with the mental

model of the domain experts. The goal of this step is to identify all the objects that the domain experts would identify.

3.   Use the "using the things to be modeled" technique to elicit more potential objects. In an attempt to find objects, some object-oriented pundits have suggested this technique as a way to trigger our recognition of "potential objects." The categories as given by some leading experts are shown in Tables 4-1, 4-2, and 4-3.

TABLE 4-1 Categories According to Coad and Yourdon

Categories	Explanation
Structure	"Kind-of" and "part-of" relationships
Other systems	External systems
Devices	
Events remembered	A historical event that must be recorded
Roles played	The different role(s) that users play
Locations	
Organization units	Groups to which the user belongs

TABLE 4-2 Categories According to Shlaer and Mellor

Categories	Explanation
Tangibles	Cars, telemetry data, sensors
Roles	Mother, teacher, programmer
Incidents	Landing, interrupt, collision
Interactions	Loan, meeting, marriage
Specification	Product specification, standards

TABLE 4-3 Categories According to Ross

Categories	Explanation
People	Humans who carry out some function
Places	Areas set aside for people or things
Things	Physical objects
Organizations	Collections of people, resources, facilities, and capabilities having a defined mission
Concepts	Principles or ideas not tangible, per se
Events	Things that happen (usually at a given date and time); steps in an ordered sequence

4. As a guide to help eliminate some potential false problem domain objects, apply the following definition test. An object can be considered as

- ■ Any real-world entity
- ■ Important to the discussion of the requirements
- ■ Crisply defined boundary

A real-world entity attempts to keep the analysis in the problem domain and helps to eliminate implementation objects (design objects) such as stacks, keyboards, and programming languages. The phrase "important to the discussion of the requirements" helps to exclude some of the objects that are not relevant to the present problem. For example, the space shuttle is a real-world entity, but it is hard to believe that it is important to our "mow the lawn" problem domain. The phrase "crisply defined boundary" comes from Booch and helps to exclude verb phrases such as "going to the store" from being considered as objects.

Example

Let us return to our lawn-mowing example and apply our approach. In step 1, we apply the "using nouns" technique. Below is the statement of the lawn-mowing example with nouns in italics.

We have a *family* with a *father*, *John*, a *mother*, *Jane*, two *sons*, *Peter* and *Paul*, and two *daughters*, *Elizabeth* and *Mary*. John is an *actor*, and Jane is a *dentist*. All the *children* are *students*, and the *family dog* is *Lassie*. Their *family physician* is *Alice*. This family owns a *house* in the *suburbs* of *New York City* and though mowing the *family lawn* is normally a *chore* for the father, it can also be a *paid chore* for any one of the children. Working within the *neighborhood* is *Jack*, a *professional lawn mower*.

If we now apply our domain knowledge, step 2, we may add lawn mower as a generalization of professional lawn mower, lawn as a generalization of family lawn, and dog as a generalization of family dog. In addition, we may add studio as a place where John works and office as a place where Jane and Alice practice their professions. In step 3, we may add the "is_married" relationship and "mowing the lawn" to the list. Table 4-4 illustrates a typical result of applying the combined technique. This may have left us with some "false positives"—for example, "mowing the lawn" might be better modeled as a service than as an object.

TABLE 4-4 Initial List of Potential Objects for Lawn-Mowing Example

Potential Objects/Classes	
John	Jane
Peter	Paul

**TABLE 4-4 Initial List of Potential Objects
for Lawn-Mowing Example (Continued)**

Potential Objects/Classes	
Elizabeth	Mary
Lassie	family lawn
Jack	Alice
Family	Children
Lawn mower	Physician
Professional lawn mower	Family physician
Dentist	Actor
Mother	Father
Daughter	Son
New York City	Dog
Students	Family dog
House	Suburb
Chore	Paid chore
Office	Studio
Neighborhood	Lawn
"Mowing the lawn"	Is_married

■ ■ ■ SUMMARY

These are the standard four steps that we recommend:

1. Given a requirements document in narrative English (native language) that uses the terms of the domain expert, use the "using nouns" technique of Abbott/Booch with the caveat that this technique is used to find potential objects, and it will not find all the objects.

2. Identify all "potential objects" in the problem domain by interactive dialog with the domain expert. We want to capture the objects that are in the mental model of the domain experts.

3. Use the "using the things to be modeled" technique to elicit more potential objects.

4. As a guide to help eliminate some potential false problem domain objects, apply the following definition test. An object can be considered as (1) any real-world entity, (2) that is important to the discussion of the requirements, and (3) has a crisply defined boundary.

When you get more experience, we suggest the following steps for finding a list of potential objects/classes:

1. Underline all the nouns in the requirements document.

2. Filter the list of nouns to identify things outside the scope of the system. These are usually "external objects" to which the system interfaces. These external objects will be useful for the context diagram. Technically, they are not objects in the final model of the application/system, so they are not objects that we want to refine. We can therefore eliminate them from our list of potential objects as part of the application/system.

3. Usually several different nouns, or noun phrases, are used to describe the same thing (concept or idea). We must select a single term and eliminate the alternative. For example, the "workplace" and the "office" are probably the same concept in nearly all problem domains. If a different term is used to describe the same physical thing in a different semantic domain (i.e., to capture a different concept), you need to capture both concepts. For example, you might use *mother* and *dentist* as problem domain terms that apply to Jane in our lawn-mowing example. However, each term captures a different concept, so these terms represent two different potential objects. Specifically, *mother* captures a concept that has to deal with the parenting semantic domain, while *dentist* captures a concept in a work/healthcare semantic domain.

4. Sometimes the same noun is used to capture two different concepts, and a new term(s) must be created to ensure that each concept, or "thing," is captured. For example, consider the term *floor*. There are two concepts that we can capture using this word: (1) we can refer to a floor as part of a room and, (2) we can refer to a floor (or a level) in a building. These are two separate concepts (or ideas), and they may not be represented by the same object. Remember that an object is a way of capturing a concept or idea.

5. Use the category lists given by our experts in Tables 4-1 through 4-3 to see if there are other concepts or ideas that we should add to the list.

6. As a guide to help eliminate some potential false problem domain objects, apply the following definition test: an object can be considered as (1) any real-world entity, (2) that is important to the discussion of the requirements, and (3) has a crisply defined boundary.

CHAPTER **5**

Identifying Responsibilities

Present themselves as objects recognized, in flashes, and with glory not their own.

■ William Wordsworth

In the first step of our method, we created a list of "potential objects." Now we need to determine if these potential objects are "real objects" that we want to put into our model. Thus, the second step in our method is to determine if these objects have any responsibility in our application/system.

Before we can do this, however, we have to know what an object is and what we mean by responsibility.

What Is an Object?

IN CHAPTER 3 WE DEFINED an object from a developer's perspective as it relates to the production of software. In chapter 4 we provided a different definition for use in finding objects in the problem domain. Now we want to use a more technical definition, from the problem domain perspective, to help us eliminate "false objects" from the list of potential objects. Here is a domain analysis view or definition of an object:

Object: An object is an abstraction of something in the problem domain, reflecting the capabilities of a system to keep information about it, interact with it, or both.

Humans have always formed concepts in order to understand the world. Each concept captures a particular idea or understanding that we have of the world in which we live. As we acquire and organize more concepts, we use them to help us make sense of and reason about things in our world.

An object is one of those things to which we apply our concepts: for example, invoice, employee, paycheck, train, train engine, boxcar, passenger car, dining car, computer, computer keyboard, joystick, screen, icon on a screen, mouse pad, organization, department, office, and the process of writing this line. Note in the examples that a train is composed of a train engine, boxcar, passenger car, and dining car. Thus, an object may be composed of other objects. These objects, in turn, may be composed of other objects, and so on. For example, the passenger car is composed of doors, seats, windows, and so on. Another example is a machine that is composed of subassemblies that are made from other subassemblies. Moreover, the object may be a real thing (e.g., train, car, computer) or an abstract thing (e.g., mammal, marriage, time).

In object-oriented analysis and design, we are interested in an object for its services. Remember that the way an object-oriented system works is that one object requests the service of another object via the message-passing paradigm. Thus, from an external (or system) perspective, an object is defined by its public services, that is, an object is defined by the services that it advertises. So, technically, the protocol defines the class/object. However, we know as software developers that the protocol (collection of prototypes) alone is not adequate. During analysis, we expect to identify the business data and the associated business methods necessary to support the defined business services. For analysis, then, an object is an encapsulation of business attribute values (data) and their associated business methods (how services are provided). To preserve the encapsulation and information-hiding principles, an object also defines an external view of its public methods for access by other objects. This external view is its public business services. These public services are defined via prototypes and constitute the only means by which another object may access its methods and thus its data. According to Wirfs-Brock, responsibility is the set of public services that an object provides and the associated data necessary to provide the services.

For most people, however, it is more natural to be able to relate attributes (i.e., data) to an object than to define its services, so we will look at identifying both attributes and services for an object together as one step.

What Is an Attribute?

THINGS IN THE REAL WORLD have characteristics. For example, a person can be described in terms of height, weight, hair color, eye color, and so on. Each characteristic that is common to all instances of the object/class is abstracted as a separate attribute. For example, Joe is 6' tall, weighs 175 pounds, and has red hair and brown eyes, while James is 5'10" tall, weighs 160 pounds, and has black hair and green eyes. For a person, potential attributes are height, weight, hair color, and eye color. Note that the characteristics that are abstracted into attributes are highly problem-dependent. Consider the "person" object. Most of us can come up with a large number of characteristics for a "person" conceptually. When we limit our abstraction of a person to a specific problem domain or to a specific problem, we reduce the number of applicable characteristics.

Thus, for the purposes of analysis, an attribute is an abstraction of a single characteristic that is applicable to the business domain and is common to all the entities that were themselves abstracted as objects. From a technical perspective, an attribute is some variable (data item or state information) for which each object (instance) has its own value. Each attribute must be provided with a name that is unique within the object/class. Because each attribute may take on values, the range of legal values allowed for an attribute should also be captured.

According to some object-oriented authors, there are a four types of attributes: descriptive, naming, state information, and referential. State-information attributes are used to keep a history of the entity; this is usually needed to capture the states of the finite state machines used to implement the dynamic aspect of behavior. Referential attributes are facts that tie one object to another and are used to capture relationships. However, capturing states and relationships using attributes is an implementation issue. In this book, states and relationships are represented pictorially, and not as part of the attribute list of an object or class. In this chapter, we address only descriptive attributes and naming attributes.

Descriptive Attributes

Descriptive attributes are facts that are intrinsic to each entity. If the value of a descriptive attribute changes, it means only that some aspect of an entity (instance) has changed. From a problem domain perspective, it is still the same entity. For example, if Joe gains 1 pound, from nearly all problem domain perspectives, Joe is still a person. More importantly, Joe is still the same person as he was before he gained 1 pound.

Naming Attributes

Naming attributes are used to name or label an entity. Typically, they are somewhat arbitrary. These attributes are frequently used as identifiers or as part of an identifier. If the value of a naming attribute changes, it only means that a new name has been given to the same entity. In fact, naming attributes do not have to be unique. For example, if Joe changes his name to James, that is all that is changed; his weight, height, and so on are still the same.[1]

What Is a Service?

A SERVICE MAY BE DEFINED as work done for others. In a sense, the services of an object are the advertised or public work that an object is willing to perform when requested by another object via the message-passing paradigm. These services are defined by prototypes. The prototype is made from two parts: (1) the name of the service (called the selector by some experts), and (2) the arguments for the service (called the signature by some experts). Thus, every object must define its prototype for each service it plans to provide.

The defined collection of prototypes is the protocol of the class/object, which is the object's interface (i.e., all its advertised services). The selector (i.e., the name of the service) should be externally focused. For example, a service of a local restaurant may be "changing bills for coins."[2] The "changing bills for coins" is defining a service from the user's perspective, while naming the service "changing coins for bills" is an internal perspective of the service. Naming services is difficult because we want names that reflect an external perspective and are consistent with the semantic domain in which the object resides.

What Is a Method?

TECHNICALLY, A METHOD IS A detailed set of operations that an object performs when another object requests a service.[3] However, a behavior by definition is a set of actions that an object is responsible for exhibiting—so alternatively, a method specifies a behavior of an object. A method is similar to a function in functional decomposition. However, there are some very important differences. Remember that these methods can only be accessed via the message-passing paradigm, and each method may only use its own data and data passed to it via its argument

---

[1]   During analysis in the early days, many developers also required a unique naming attribute that was used as a key to map objects into a relational database. Better support for object-oriented technology exists today, so this requirement is no longer needed.

[2]   The reason that the restaurant provides the service may be that it gets a lot of loose change from tips and the bank does not accept coins for deposit.

[3]   Conversely, a service of an object defines how another object may gain access to a specific behavior (method/function).

list.[4] Perhaps most important, these services should be specified to a level of depth that is consistent with the semantic domain in which the object resides.

Identifying Attributes

The key issue here is what data do we believe the object is responsible for knowing and owning. The following questions must be asked about each potential object:

- How is this object described in general?
- What parts of the general description are applicable to this problem domain?
- What is the minimal description needed for this application?

If you take the Eastern, or Taoist, approach to object-oriented analysis, you will design your system by asking only the first two questions. You will not be concerned with the specific application that you are implementing. We have found that this approach tends to produce a more flexible and robust model from a business perspective. You will then be able to respond to changes in the marketplace more quickly. This flexibility is usually achieved at the expense of performance and space utilization.

If you ask all three questions and look only at the present application (Western approach), you will tend to produce a fine-tuned, high-performance system with good space utilization that makes more effective use of the hardware. However, it will be at the expense of having fewer reusable classes/objects and having less flexibility to respond to the marketplace.

Attributes are rarely fully described in a requirements document. Fortunately, they seldom affect the basic structure of the model. You must draw upon your knowledge of the application domain and the real world to find them.

Because most guidelines for identifying attributes do not help differentiate false attributes from real attributes, Rumbaugh et al. (1991) offer the following suggestions to help eliminate false attributes:

1. **Objects.** If the independent existence, rather than just the value, of the attribute is important, then the attribute is an object and there must be a link to it. For example, consider a Person object. Is the address or city in which the person lives an attribute or another object? If, in your application, you do not manipulate the address without knowing to which person the address belongs, then it is an attribute. However, if you manipulate the address as an entity by itself, then the address should be an object with a link between it and the person.

---

[4] In a later chapter we will see that it also has access to other data via services of other objects with which it has relationships.

2. **Qualifiers.** If the value of an attribute depends on a particular context, then consider restating it as a qualifier. For example, an employee number is not really an attribute of a Person object. Consider a person with two jobs. It really qualifies as a link "employs" between the Company object and the Person object.[5]

3. **Names.** A name is an attribute when it does not depend on the context. For example, a person's name is an attribute of Person. Note that an attribute, as in a person's name, does not have to be unique. However, names are usually qualifiers and not attributes. As such, they usually either define a role in an association or define a subclass or superclass abstraction. For example, parent and teacher are not attributes of Person. Both are probably roles for associations. Another example is gender. There are two ways to capture this: Consider gender as an attribute of Person or make two subclasses.[6]

4. **Identifiers.** Make sure not to list the unique identifier that object-oriented languages need as a way to unambiguously refer to an object. This is implicitly assumed to be part of the model. However, do list the application domain identifiers. For example, an account code is an attribute of Account, while a transaction identification is probably not an attribute.

5. **Link attributes.** If the proposed attribute depends on the presence of a link, then it is an attribute of the link and not of the objects in the link. Make the link an associative object, and make the proposed attribute one of its attributes. For example, let us assume that Jim is married to Mary. The date of their marriage is an attribute of the is_married association and not an attribute of Jim or Mary.

6. **Fine details.** Omit minor attributes that do not affect the methods.

7. **Discordant attributes.** An attribute that seems completely unrelated to all other attributes may indicate that the object may need to be split into two objects. A class should be coherent and simple (i.e., must represent a concept that operates in a single semantic domain).

To aid you in finding attributes, we suggest you begin by using the adjectives and possessive phrases in the requirements document. For example, *red* car, the *40-year-old* man, the *color* of the truck, the *position* of the cursor. Then, after identifying a few attributes, you should ask the above questions to identify more attributes.

---

[5] If it is not important to the application that a person has a second employer, then making that fact an attribute of the Person object may be satisfactory.

[6] Technically, making two subclasses is the most accurate model. However, if we never have services or relationships that are gender-specific, then it is appropriate to make gender an attribute during implementation.

Specifying Attributes

COAD AND YOURDON STATED IT very well when they said, "Make each attribute capture an atomic concept," which means that an attribute will contain a single value or a tightly related grouping of values that the application treats as a whole. Examples of attributes include individual data items (such as age, salary, and weight) and composite data items (such as legal name, address, and birth date).

Issues of normalization, performance, object identification, and keeping recalculable information should be left to design and implementation. However, the form of the data (character, integer, string, color, etc.) should be specified. Its range, constraints, and invariants should also be captured. We recommend capturing constraints and invariants using declarative semantics. See later chapters for discussion on rules.

Because identifying attributes is difficult, Shlaer and Mellor (1988) have suggested properties to which an attribute must adhere. We have added an additional property, identified in the following list as Property Zero.

Property Zero: An attribute must capture a characteristic that is consistent with the semantic domain in which this object (as a concept or idea) resides. For instance, consider the object Programmer. A programmer may have years of experience in writing computer programs. However, age is probably not an attribute of Programmer; it is probably an attribute of Person, which is a different object from Programmer. Now if we make the dangerous assumption that all programmers are also people, then we can create a Human Programmer object by having it inherit the programmer's attributes (e.g., years of writing computer programs) from the Programmer object and the human attributes (e.g., age) from the Person object. Thus, Human Programmer is a composite of two objects.

Property One: An instance (entity) has exactly one value (within its range) for each attribute at any given time. For example, we can choose eye color as an attribute of the Person object with the range of black, brown, blue, and green. If we discover that a person, Carey, who should be an instance of Person, has one green eye and one brown eye, then we cannot assign both green and brown as the eye color of Carey.[7]

Property Two: An attribute must not contain an internal structure. For example, if we made name an attribute of Person, then we must not be interested in manipulating the given name and the family name independently in the problem domain.

Property Three: An attribute must be a characteristic of the entire entity, not a characteristic of its composite parts. For example, if we specify a Computer object that is composed of a terminal, keyboard, mouse, and CPU, the screen size is an attribute of terminal and not computer.

---

[7]   This can be easily solved by making eye color an attribute of an object Eye and having Person own (have a referential attribute to) two eyes; however, this requires that the model be changed.

Property Four: When an object is an abstraction of a concept that interacts with other objects (especially tangible objects), the attributes of the object must be associated with the concept and not the other objects. For example, let us assume we want to transfer oil from a holding tank to a separator tank, and we define an Oil Transfer object to capture the concept of the body of liquid that moves. Then, if we assign the attribute gallon to the object Oil Transfer, it must represent the number of gallons that are transferred. It may not be used to represent the number of gallons in the holding tank nor in the separator tank.

Property Five: When an object has a relationship with another object, especially an object of the same kind (class), the attributes must capture the characteristics of the object, and not the relationship or the other object(s) in the relationship. For example, if we add salary as an attribute and a spousal relationship to Person, we cannot use the spouse's pay as the value for the salary attribute of a nonworking spouse, and the date of their marriage is not an attribute of either spouse.

Identifying Services

ACCORDING TO COAD AND YOURDON, services provided by objects can be categorized as either algorithmically simple or algorithmically complex. Within each of these categories, services can be broken down into various types. Each category and its types are given in Table 5-1 and Table 5-2. Coad and Yourdon believe that 80–90% of services will be algorithmically simple. We believe that the number is closer to 60%.

TABLE 5-1 Algorithmically Simple Services

Create	Creates and initializes a new object
Connect	Connects an object with another object
Access	Gets or sets attribute values
Disconnect	Disconnects an object from another object
Delete	Deletes an object

TABLE 5-2 Algorithmically Complex Services

Calculate	Calculations that the object is responsible for performing on its values
Monitor	Monitoring what the object is responsible for in order to detect or respond to external system or device or internal object
Query	Computes a functional value without modifying the object.

Algorithmically simple services are not usually placed in an object-oriented model. Every class/object is assumed to have these services. This makes the model simpler and aids in reading large and complex models. In this step, we are only interested in identifying those algorithmically complex business services that must be provided by the object.

To aid us in finding services, we should use the verbs in our requirements document. Typically, an English sentence is in the form "subject—action verb—object." In this case, the action verb is usually defining a method that must be provided by the object of the sentence.[8] For example, "A person hit the ball." The tendency of a novice is to define a "hit" service for the Person object. In OD, the sentence is used to define a "receiving a hit" service for the Ball object. For the Person object to hit the Ball object, the Ball must have a prototype service within its protocol to receive the "hit" message request from Person.

After using the verbs to identify services (application-specific case), we should consider generalizing the service name for the domain. Remember that the name should be given from an external perspective (user of the service). We want to use as generic a word as possible to give us an opportunity to find abstract classes, which are the most difficult objects/classes to discover.

Specifying Services

SPECIFYING THE SERVICE IS DONE by defining the prototype for the service. Recall from chapter 3 that the prototype is made from the name of the service and the signature of the service. The name chosen should reflect either an external item or a user's view of the service. The signature is a list of arguments that need to be passed to the object so that it can perform the named service. This is the additional data that an object does not have and expects to be given by the calling object.

Normally, it is good practice to specify only the arguments that are necessary for the specific object to perform (execute) the method associated with the service. However, because we are trying to capture concepts and not technical definitions, the argument list may be adjusted to take advantage of polymorphism later. So during this step, the name of the service should be considered very carefully, and we can be a little more lax about the arguments.

Recommended Approach

OUR APPROACH FOR IDENTIFYING RESPONSIBILITIES follows:

1. Identify attributes

   a. Look at all the adjectives and possessive phrases in the requirements document.

---

8   In the object-oriented paradigm, interaction between objects occurs via message passing.

    b. Ask the following questions:

        1. How is this object described in general?

        2. What parts of the general description are applicable to this problem domain?

    c. If you want to follow the Western school, ask this question also:

        1. What is the minimal description needed for this application?

    d. Use Rumbaugh et al.'s suggestions to eliminate false attributes.

2. Specify attributes

    a. Make each attribute an "atomic concept."

    b. Eliminate attributes that are calculable or derivable from the basic attributes.

    c. Eliminate attributes that address normalization, performance, or object identification during this step.

    d. Test to verify that each attribute adheres to all the properties suggested by Shlaer and Mellor and that as a group the attributes are in the same semantic domain (good cohesion).

3. Identify services

    a. Look at the verbs in a requirements document. Remember the verb usually defines the services of the object of the sentence.

    b. Look at the user scenarios, which usually indirectly identify many services.

    c. Look at each feature, which usually requires services from many objects.

4. Specify services

    a. Give a name to the service that is externally (relative to itself) focused.

    b. Define the signature of the service by identifying its argument list.

Example

Let us return to our lawn-mowing example. In this example, we have very few adjectives that would help us define attributes for the potential objects we identified in step 1a. However, we are dealing with objects that we all know, as well as with a problem domain that we can all readily understand. So we can start with step 1b, question number 1. Let us start with the eight Person objects: John, Jane, Peter, Paul, Elizabeth, Mary, Jack, and Alice. Examples of descriptive attributes that Person objects probably have are birth date, height, weight, hair color, eye color, and gender; naming attributes are GivenName and SocialSecurityNumber (see Table 5-3).

TABLE 5-3 Attributes and Values for a Selection of Objects in the Lawn-Mowing Example

Attribute Name	John	Jane	Peter	Paul
Birth date	9/12/40	2/24/42	8/30/69	3/5/71
Height	5'8"	5'10"	6'2"	6'6"
Weight	110 lb	160 lb	210 lb	195 lb
Hair color	gray	white	black	blond
Eye color	blue	grey	green	black
Gender	male	female	male	male
Name	John Doe	Jane Doe	Peter Doe	Paul Doe
SSN	123-45-6789	234-56-7899	345-67-1234	456-78-0123

Before moving to question 2, we have to decide on the problem domain. We could decide that we want to define our problem domain to cover everything, but then our attribute list would have to be extended to cover the area of a person's health, employment, taxes, investments, social relationships, and so on. This would make the object very large, and neither maintainable nor usable to any application, unless it has unlimited CPU and space resources. (There goes management's idea of one class/object definition for all usage.) However, it is not as bad as all that. Normally, every business is bound by the kind of domain for which they are in business.

Let us now limit our domain to home owner property care. We are interested in capturing applications like mowing the lawn, fertilizing the lawn, seeding the lawn, trimming the bushes, cleaning the pool, carpet cleaning, house painting, roof repair, gutter cleaning, chimney-sweeping, and so on.

If we think very carefully about the problem domain, we will probably realize that none of the attributes we have identified are applicable to our problem domain of "home owner property care." However, from the requirements description, we can see that the schedule of a person's time is useful and that some state information (is Dad tired or not?) may be needed.

Furthermore, since family physicians are not within the domain of HomeOwnerPropertyCare, we can drop Alice and FamilyPhysician from our list of potential objects. With similar logic, we can probably drop Studio, Dentist, Actor, Student, and Suburb from the list. It is also probably safe to drop Father, Mother, Son and Daughter from the list,[9] especially in these modern days of equal chores for all. We have kept Lassie and Dog on the list, because a dog may be an alternative to chemical fertilizer. The house is needed for other applications, such as house painting. We are not sure about Chore and PaidChore. We suspect that we will need LawnMower, ProfessionalLawnMower, and FamilyLawn for our application.

[9] This is actually incorrect. We will see in a later chapter that we need to use the father-child relationship. However, since "parenting" is a different semantic domain than "home owner property care," we have a tendency to eliminate these objects during this step.

After applying question 2, we have the following revised attribute list:

For John, Jane, Peter, Paul, Elizabeth, and Mary, there is one attribute: schedule.

For Jack and ProfessionalLawnMower, the attributes are Address, TelephoneNumber, and Schedule.

For Lassie and Dog, there is one attribute: schedule.

For House, the attributes are Address, TelephoneNumber, DateOfLastPainting, DateOfLastRoofRepair, and so on.

For the FamilyLawn, the attributes are: heightOfGrass, lastSeeded, lastFertilized, and so on.

For Chore and PaidChore, no attributes were found.

Now, we are ready for question 3; our application is "mowing the lawn." If we restrict ourselves only to our application, we would eliminate the following potential objects from consideration: Lassie, Dog, Chore, Paid Chore, and House.

After applying question 3, our revised attribute list is as follows:

For John, Jane, Peter, Paul, Elizabeth and Mary, there is one attribute: schedule.

For Jack and ProfessionalLawnMower, the attributes are address, telephoneNumber, schedule.

For FamilyLawn, there is one attribute: heightOfGrass.

In applying question 3, we have eliminated objects (and if we had a lot of attributes, probably some attributes) that are applicable to the general problem domain, but not to our specific application.

In Taoist philosophy, the focus is on the path rather than on the destination or, in our terminology, the process rather than the goal. When we translate this into object-oriented modeling, the Taoist philosophy tells us to focus on capturing the objects in the problem domain rather than on the objects that will help us solve the immediate problem. It is the belief of the Taoist that focusing on the goal will cause you to ignore valuable information, while focusing on the process will let the path show you the way. In terms of object-oriented technology, focusing on the specific problem or application will cause you to ignore important concepts and, as a result, will make your classes (objects) less reusable.

If you are trying to produce flexible and reusable software, you should apply an Eastern or Taoist philosophy to problem solving and object-oriented modeling. In Eastern philosophy, we would not have asked question 3. We would expect that the proper modeling of the problem domain would automatically also contain our business solution to our application. This kind of philosophy is based on experimentation, in contrast to our classical Western thinking, which is based on planning.

Step 2 for attributes is left to the reader.

Now let us perform steps 3 and 4 for services. Since we have contrived a very simple example, the only service is "mow the lawn." If we look at people in general, the number of services that they provide is endless; but we do not want to capture all these services. If we were to consider services in the domain of "home owner property care," we would add services such as house painting, lawn fertilizing, lawn seeding, house cleaning, gutter cleaning, sweeping the sidewalk, trimming the bushes, and raking the leaves. However, when we get back to our specific application, we are back to one service: "mow the lawn."

Thus, we have the following objects with a "mow the lawn" service: John, Peter, Paul, Elizabeth, Mary, Jack, and ProfessionalLawnMower.

Note that the family lawn already has a changeHeight or setHeight height of grass service because it is algorithmically simple.

As useful as the Eastern philosophy is in helping us perform better object specification, we still do not want to include in our final model either objects or services that are not needed for our specific application. So when all is said and done, we still need to apply the following test to ensure that we have only the necessary (but at this time, probably not sufficient) objects.

Tests:

1. The object must provide some service for some other object in the application/system or an external interface service to some external object.

2. In general, the object must have multiple attributes. In some cases, an object may only provide services and have no attribute.[10]

Sometimes it is useful to keep an object (an abstraction) that may help us in organizing our structural model, which captures the relationships between objects. The only services of such objects may be its constructor and destructor.

■ ■ SUMMARY

Our approach for identifying responsibilities follows:

1. Identify attributes
2. Specify attributes
3. Identify services
4. Specify services

---

[10] Such objects should be rare, and they would not usually be discovered during this step.

CHAPTER **6**

Specifying Static Behavior

$$\nabla^2\Psi = -\frac{2\mu}{\hbar^2}(E - V)\Psi$$

■ Time Independent Schroedinger Equation

In the second step of our method, we created a list of "real objects." In the process of finding them, we identified attributes and services of these objects. However, during that step, we took an external view of the service. More specifically, we did not concern ourselves with how the object would provide (perform) the service. In the third step of our method, we need to capture how each object provides the services identified in step 2 and how these services are controlled (sequenced and synchronized) to respond to the customer's request. In the process of specifying these services and how they are controlled, we may also identify additional services that other objects must provide.

What Is Behavior?

IN THE PREVIOUS CHAPTER, WE defined a service as "work done for others."[1] Behavior can be defined as the set of actions that an object is responsible for exhibiting when it provides a specific service. Another object may access a specific behavior of an object only via the appropriate service. This behavior is usually captured as a method (function) in the object.

A behavior is defined when the following are specified: (1) all the inputs (arguments to the service), (2) all the outputs, and (3) how (from a domain perspective) the object will provide the service. Behavior can be either static or dynamic. This chapter presents techniques for capturing static behavior. Techniques for capturing dynamic behavior are addressed in chapter 7.

In static behavior, the set of actions is captured by the operations (code) within the method. By definition, the operations within the method will not be affected by any external or internal events[2] (actions). A good example of static behavior is the "square root" service for Number. If one requests the "square root" service from the number 4, which is an instance of Number, the result will always be 2. There is no external or internal action that would cause the method of Number to change the algorithm for computing the square root and thus providing a different result.

The most natural way to document behavior[3] is to use any natural language. Unfortunately, all natural language is rich in ambiguities and inconsistencies. When it is spoken, some clarification is provided by intonation, hand movements, and body language. In many situations, however, especially in specification, even spoken words do not alleviate the ambiguities or inconsistencies. The problem is that natural language is a set of atomic elements (words) that lack well-defined semantics (consistent and unambiguous definition in the problem domain). The resulting collection of words that form sentences or paragraphs becomes ambiguous or inconsistent; thus, the behavior descriptions written in natural language becomes inconsistent and ambiguous.

One solution is to build a shell around the natural language with well-defined semantics. This technique is used in every field of endeavor. For example, in accounting, words such as *ledger, debit,* and *credit* have very precise and well-defined semantics. Similarly, in the computer world, words such as *input, output, bit,* and *byte* have well-defined semantics.

When we construct a shell around the English language to provide a richer set of semantically clear constructs, this is really modeling. The purpose of a model is to provide a richer, higher-level, and more semantically precise set of constructs (usually words) than those of the underlying natural language. The model is designed to reduce ambiguities and inconsistencies, manage complexity, facilitate checks for completeness, and improve understandability. Associated

---

[1]   Technically, an object can provide services to itself. This is quite common for complex objects.

[2]   If they were true, we would model this with dynamic behavior.

[3]   For example, how the object will provide the service.

with each of the models are techniques for capturing the behavior (function/ method) of the model. Thus, the following techniques for documenting behavior are based on a relatively formal underlying model.

Techniques for Specifying Static Behavior

THERE ARE AT LEAST TWO ways of specifying static behavior:[4] (1) giving the before and the after conditions on its execution and (2) decomposing the service into a series of activities and tasks that can be mapped to basic operations of the class or service calls to other objects.

From a formal language perspective, the first way is preferred. In fact, UML uses this technique for operation specification, of which static behavior is a special case. However, we have found that analysts had a great deal of difficulty in recognizing the necessary preconditions and postconditions. Furthermore, this technique does not help us to understand the business nor to find additional services that are not identified in our process. Thus, we prefer to perform a business service analysis, which is the second way of specifying static behavior.

A service is comprised of a series of activities and tasks that perform the work of that service. Thus, a service is a set of activities and tasks that is organized and proceduralized to accomplish a specific subgoal. The tasks and activities are interdependent, and there is a well-defined flow of control between them. The definition of the behavior is the identification of the activities and tasks that are to be performed in support of the named service.

The easiest way to specify static behavior is to perform a service (task) analysis, in which you identify the set of activities and tasks necessary to perform a given service. In this process, the activities and tasks are reduced to operations of the following types: basic operations of the class and service calls to other objects.

In capturing activities and tasks, the following questions should be answered:

■ How are they performed?
■ Why are they performed?
■ What are their interrelationships?

For use in control specification and design, the following additional information should be gathered:

■ Is it part of a transaction (if you are using the transaction paradigm)?
■ Timing
■ Frequency
■ Volume
■ Variants

---

[4] This is called operation specification in UML.

- Business rules on verification and validation
- Processing algorithms
- Saved and/or stored data
- Reports
- Control points and check points, if any
- Error detection, correction, and recovery

The steps are very simple. Begin with the service trigger,[5] document all the manual and mental steps that must be performed, document every decision point, document each test and calculation or change made in an attribute, and document all possible results from a decision point. Finally, consider exceptions and special cases.

The following three points of caution are appropriate:

1. Be careful with modeling manual processes. The ideas behind the object-oriented paradigm is that the object that has the data does the work. Therefore many manual processes should not be done by a conceptual human object in the system; these are done by the object itself. For example, a purchase order can fill itself. This may seem a little unnatural to a novice, but the purchase order has all the data needed to process itself. Similarly, a check in most banking applications will basically process itself.

2. In many situations, only the activities are in the same semantic domain as the object—the tasks are in a different semantic domain. In such a situation, the task needs services supplied by other objects, which are usually related to the present object either through inheritance, association, or aggregation. Capturing each service in the correct object is critical to having low coupling and good cohesion in the model. Remember that low coupling and good cohesion of objects lead to reusable and flexible software.

3. Operations allowed as part of service specification in the object-oriented approach are bounded. Operations can only change data that the object owns (i.e., its attributes), and have access only to the object's data and data passed to it via the argument list. Furthermore, an object can only access the services of other objects that it knows about. In the next chapter,[6] we will discuss how an object knows about another object.

---

[5] The service call from some other object, usually an external object.

[6] These constraints are consistent with the encapsulation and information-hiding principles of the object-oriented paradigm. Fundamental to building good systems is the fact that the services of each object must be in the same semantic domain.

Techniques for Specifying Control

FINDING THE SERVICES AND DESCRIBING each one as a sequence of actions that produce the intended result is one of the issues that is not well addressed in most object-oriented books or courses. We will attempt to give the reader some guidance in this area.

We believe that just as we have borrowed techniques for documenting behavior from other methodologies, we need to borrow a technique from an existing method (McMenamin and Palmer) to help us specify the behavior of objects and capture the necessary additional services that will meet all the requirements. This method was adopted and modified by Jacobson for capturing requirements in object-oriented analysis in his Objectory method.

The steps described by McMenamin and Palmer are very simple:

1. List all the external and internal events to which the application/system needs to respond. The users and the interface system(s) are external to the system. A good way to get a list of external events is to perform a task analysis for the users and the external systems. In the terminology of the Objectory method, this would be called identifying the actors.

2. For each event, usually a message, determine how and in what sequence the necessary messages will be passed among objects to satisfy the request. This particular series of interactions among objects is called a scenario. A scenario shows a single execution of the application/system in time. When the scenario requires specific sequencing and synchronization beyond what is provided as part of the services of objects in the scenario, a task object should be created to capture the scenario controls. A scenario is equivalent to a transaction in many applications. Thus, a task is commonly used to capture the control aspects of a transaction.

3. Capture the above sequences by drawing an event trace diagram[7] for each scenario and its variations. These scenarios, or sequences of messages, are useful for understanding the application/system and for integrated testing. This step is different from both McMenamin and Palmer and Jacobson's Objectory method. In structured methods, usually a state machine for the whole system is designed to capture the scenarios; similarly, in the Objectory method, a state model is used to represent the system. This makes sense for both of the above methods because they are used in the early part of these methods before decomposition. We are using this technique after detail analysis (domain analysis) of the application/system in order to verify the validity of the domain analysis in addressing the specific application. This is a critical

---

[7] In UML, this is called a sequence diagram.

difference; we believe that using the scenarios to validate our domain model is a better way to develop reusable classes than to start the model process from the application, as originally suggested by McMenamin and Palmer.

4. Capture the details of how each service is provided. By thinking through each scenario, the analyst/developer can specify precisely what must be done in each of the object services. Then the details of the actions that need to be taken within a service are captured. Again, this is different from the classical method, which would have taken a system view. We are now taking a decomposed view of the system.

5. Consider modeling the scenarios as use cases to reduce the number of scenario diagrams. Jacobson has developed a sophisticated structure for scenarios, using object-oriented technology to organize the scenarios. This structure is extremely useful for managing the complexity of the scenarios. This sophisticated structure will be supported by UML.

Techniques for Documenting Control

Process Flow Diagrams

Process flow diagrams use processes (functions) as building blocks. The response is captured as a series of processes that operate on a set of data. This technique for documenting event response is well suited to functional decomposition. In many applications, this would be the level-1 diagram of a functional decomposition.[8] From a technical perspective, one can argue that the activities and tasks are captured as "processes" (i.e., bubbles on the diagram) in lower-level diagrams. If we were performing functional decomposition, this would be correct. However, in object-oriented analysis, it is not always correct to map every activity or task to a service of an object. Often we will map a task to an object.[9]

Although there are many different notations used, a generic notation is described. Data flow (i.e., information) is represented by a labeled arrow. Processes are represented by labeled bubbles. The keywords *and* and *or* are used to link data flows.

Object Interaction Diagram (Collaboration Diagram[10])

An object interaction diagram shows the sequence of messages that implement a service or transaction. It shows the objects and links that exist just before the service begins and also the objects and links created (and possibly destroyed) during

---

[8] The context diagram is level 0.

[9] Mapping a task to an object is one technical solution. A more correct approach would be to reengineer the process so that it could be mapped to the service of a single object.

[10] The term used in UML is *collaboration diagram*, but earlier OO writings have used other terms.

the performance of the service. A message from one object to another is indicated by a label consisting of a sequence number, the name of the service requested, and the arguments list with an arrow showing the message-flow direction. In UML, there are additional options to handle synchronization with other threads of control, nested procedural calling sequences, concurrent threads, iteration, and possible conditional expressions.

Event Trace Diagram (Sequence Diagram[11])

This technique uses objects as its building blocks. In this analysis technique, you trace the response of an event as a series of messages between objects. Each message is a request for services from another object. In using this technique, one must already have some idea about the objects that are in the system. This is one reason why we identify objects as the first step of our object-oriented method.

A generic notation for use in event trace diagrams is described. A straight vertical line is used to represent an object. Its name is shown at the top of the line. An event (external service request) is used to label the diagram. A service call to another object is represented by a direct horizontal arrow with the prototype of the service call as its label. Time proceeds vertically, so event timing sequences can be seen easily. To indicate events that require time to deliver, the event line can be slanted downward so that the sending and receiving message are distinct. Timing marks can be added to the diagram to show timing constraints. In UML, a special form of the sequence diagram is also specified to show the period of time that an object has a thread of control.

The Use-Case Model[12]

A scenario is an instance of a use case. Each scenario provides a prototypical thread through its associated use case. Thus, a use case typically characterizes multiple scenarios. A use-case diagram shows the set of external actors (interfaces) and the application/system use cases in which the actors participate. In the diagram, the system is represented by a large rectangle, and the use cases are drawn as ellipses within the icon for the system. The actors are drawn as object icons (hexagons) outside the system icon. Solid lines are drawn from the actors to the use cases in which they participate. If desirable, each participation relationship can be labeled with the event(s) and/or message(s) that are exchanged between the actor and the use case. Also, if desirable, a dashed arrow from one use case to another may be used to show that the first use case includes the behavior of the second use case.

---

[11] The term used by UML is *sequence diagram*, but earlier OO writings have used event trace diagram.

[12] The use-case model is part of UML.

Techniques for Documenting Static Behavior

Preconditions and Postconditions

In UML specifications, the recommended way of specifying preconditions and postconditions is via textual specification. The textual specification would have the following sections: service name, inputs, output(s), elements of the object modified, preconditions, and postconditions. We recommend adding invariant conditions to the list, if you choose to use this technique.

Flowcharting

A flowchart is the oldest technique for specifying a method/function. Many object-oriented methods use this technique and have highly specialized notations for documenting the behavior.

A generic flowcharting technique is described. A rectangle is used to capture the calculation or operations, and the diamond is used to capture the decision. Flow of control is shown via arrows. Words are placed on arrows from a diamond (decision point), as each arrow from the diamond represents one of the possible results.

Data Flow Diagrams

Data flow diagrams (DFDs) are an integral part of a number of methods (e.g., Rumbaugh et al.). Each specific method uses a slightly different notation. A generic notation is described. Data flow (i.e., information) is represented by a labeled arrow. Operations (actions or transformations) are represented by labeled bubbles. Information sources or sinks are represented by labeled boxes. Attributes (stored information) are represented by double horizontal lines. The keywords *and* and *or* are used to link data flows.

Structured English

Structured English is also used in some methods. It is widely used by system engineers who have no formal training in computers. The generic guidelines for using structured English are as follows:

1. Use command verbs to describe operations, transformations, or actions.
2. Use attribute names for data to be manipulated.
3. Use prepositions and conjunctions to show logical relationships.
4. Commonly understood (semantically precise) mathematical, physical, business, and technical terms may be used.
5. Mathematical equations as well as illustrations such as tables, diagrams, and graphs may also be used for clarification.

6. Words other than the above should be used sparingly and only to help document the behavior.

7. Sentence or paragraph structures must be simple, with single-entry, single-exit constructs. The constructs should consist only of the following:

- Sequence: actions that occur in a specified time sequence
- Concurrence: more than one action taking place simultaneously
- Decision: a branch in the flow of actions based on the results of a test
- Repetition: the same action(s) repeated until some specified limit or result is reached

Examples are given in Figure 6-1. Words that appear in all capitals are attributes (i.e., data), and lines that are indented represent subordination.

```
1. Sequence example
   Find INTEREST DUE as
       RATE x INSTALLATION PERIOD x PRINCIPAL.
   Next, subtract INTEREST DUE from ACCOUNT BALANCE.
   Next, issue REMAINING BALANCE as ACCOUNT BALANCE.
2. Concurrency Example
   Calculate NAVAID DISTANCE as great circle distance from
       AIRCRAFT POSITION to NAVAID POSITION.
   Calculate ALT DIFFERENCE as
       AIRCRAFT ALTITUDE - NAVAID ALTITUDE.
3. Decision example
   If AMOUNT REQUESTED is greater than LIMIT,
   then:
       return "NOT APPROVED"
   else:
       subtract AMOUNT REQUESTED from LIMIT.
       Next, return "APPROVED"
   endif:
4. Repetition example
   For each member of selected Accounts:
       ask each account to change its INTERESTRATE to NEWINTERESTRATE.
   endfor:
```

FIGURE 6-1 Examples of Structured English

Recommended Approach

ALTHOUGH THE USE OF PROCESS flow diagrams may be more familiar to most of us, we do not recommend it. When they are used, analysts and developers have a tendency to directly map activities onto services of objects and to use the task analysis as the specification of the services. This is very bad practice because many of our activities violate the encapsulation and information-hiding principles of object-oriented technology. When these principles are violated, a system with high coupling and poor cohesion is created. A highly coupled system of objects with poor cohesion means that software is less maintainable and less flexible. We believe that the improper use of process flow diagrams will cause the development of poor-quality software.

We recommend using the existing method of McMenamin and Palmer to specify the behavior of objects. The steps are very simple:

1. List all the external and internal events to which the application/system needs to respond.

2. For each event, usually a message, determine how and in what sequence the necessary messages will be passed among objects to satisfy the request.

3. Capture the above sequences by drawing a sequence diagram for each scenario and its variations. These scenarios, or sequences of messages, are useful for understanding the application/system and for integrated testing. (See step 4 when there are a large number of scenarios.)

4. (Added by the authors) If useful, create a use-case model for the scenarios. This is almost necessary for large systems, as the number of actual scenarios or sequence diagrams would be overwhelming.

5. Capture the details of how each service is provided. By thinking through each scenario or use case, the analyst/developer can specify precisely what must be done in each of the object services. Then the details of the actions that need to be taken within a service are captured using structured English.[13] It should be noted that UML supports specification of the service (method) as an option of the language.

Example

Based on earlier analysis, we have the following objects with a mowTheLawn service: John, Peter, Paul, Elizabeth, Mary, Jack, and ProfessionalLawnMower.

---

[13] Although there are advantages and disadvantages to all techniques of documenting the behavior, we recommend using structured English for the following reasons: (1) In many organizations the analysis is performed by non–computer scientists/programmers, and for them, structured English is easier to understand than other techniques. (2) DFDs and flowcharting should be used with a computer-aided software engineering (CASE) tool. Unfortunately, most CASE tools today do not provide satisfactory end-to-end support. (3) Furthermore, current CASE tools for object-oriented methods are neither easy to use nor conducive to the way we really do analysis and design. (4) Many of us still assume that when we use DFDs or flowcharts, we can revert back to functional decomposition. When we do this, we negate the benefits of object-oriented technology. Again, most CASE tools have not enforced the additional semantic constraints on DFDs and flowcharts that are really implied by using these same techniques for documenting object (class) behavior.

Remember that we are assuming that the family lawn already has a change or set HeightOfGrass service because it is algorithmically simple. The definition of service for mowTheLawn for each object is shown in Figure 6-2 using structured English.

For this model to work, we will need an external object (such as an object based on the Unix mechanism of a cron job) that will periodically (i.e., every 15 minutes) ask each object, including John, to start the service/task that is on its schedule. This is a very common external event; many services are called on the basis of a predetermined schedule. Let us presume that John's "mow the lawn" service has scheduled the actual mowing (mowFamilyLawn service) to occur at 7 P.M. when John comes home. Thus, when John comes home, he will immediately perform the mowFamilyLawn service. Figure 6-2 defines the mowFamilyLawn service.

OBJECT NAME	**John**
SERVICE: "mowFamilyLawn (no arguments)"	
If MYCONDITION is equal to "tired",	
then:	
for each child in selected Children	
ask each child to "mow the lawn" for 5 dollars.	
if answer is "yes",	
then:	
remove "mowFamilylawn" from SCHEDULE.	
return;	
else:	
endif:	
endfor:	
perform mowing the lawn.	
else:	
perform mowing the lawn.	
endif:	

FIGURE 6-2 Service Provisions of John for Mowing the Lawn

We have not refined the actual mowing of the lawn. We have also assumed that John has a way of contacting all his children. We will show how contacting his children can be accomplished in a later chapter.

Now, let us look at the mowTheLawn service for the children. All of the children, with the exception of Peter, will delegate any lawn-mowing request that pays over five dollars to Jack, who will mow any lawn for four dollars. Peter always mows the lawn, regardless of the pay. His service is defined in Figure 6-3. The service for the other children is defined in Figure 6-4.

The children have a mowTheLawn service instead of a mowFamilyLawn service, as the children will mow any lawn. Because of this flexibility, we needed to associate a lawn address with that service. We did not do this for John, because he will only mow the family lawn. Also, it is assumed that the children have access to Jack's telephone number via the telephone book. In a later chapter, we discuss the various vehicles by which one object has access to another object's services. The definition of the "mow the lawn" service for Jack and for the ProfessionalLawnMower is left to the reader.

If we think about the performance of a service, which is a sequence of actions, we quickly realize that most of our behaviors have to do with elapsed time. For example, we wake up after having slept for x number of hours, go to sleep at y o'clock, and eat at a certain time. Thus, the only external event in this

OBJECT NAME	**Peter**
SERVICE: mowTheLawn (ADDRESS_OF_LAWN, DOLLAR_AMOUNT)"	
get SCHEDULE for evening (7P.M. – 9P.M.)	
Next, if SCHEDULE has open slot,	
then:	
place mowLawn in slot.	
associate ADDRESS_OF_LAWN with mowLawn.	
return "Yes, I will mow the lawn this evening."	
else:	
return "No, I cannot mow the lawn."	
endif	

FIGURE 6-3 CRC Card for Peter in the Lawn-Mowing Example

OBJECT NAMES	Paul, Elizabeth, Mary

SERVICE: mowTheLawn (ADDRESS_OF_LAWN, DOLLAR_AMOUNT)
if DOLLAR_AMOUNT is less than 5 dollars,
then:
get SCHEDULE for evening (7P.M. – 9P.M.)
Next, if SCHEDULE has open slot,
then:
place mowLawn in slot.
associate ADDRESS_OF_LAWN with mowLawn.
return "Yes, I will mow lawn this evening."
else:
return "No, I cannot mow the lawn."
endif
else:
get Jack's TELEPHONE NUMBER from Telephone Book.
ask Jack to mow the lawn (ADDRESS_OF_LAWN, self, ADDRESS)
if Jack's response is "yes,"
then:
return "Yes, I will mow lawn this evening."
else
return "No, I cannot mow the lawn."
endif:
endif;

FIGURE 6-4 CRC Card for Paul, Elizabeth, and Mary in the Lawn-Mowing Example

application is time elapsed. A reasonable model of this "real-world" situation is to assume that it only needs to be modeled at 15-minute intervals, so that people can schedule their lives at 15-minute intervals and at no finer granularity. Thus, the high-level sequence diagram may look like the one illustrated in Figure 6-5.

The Scheduler is a new object; its sole purpose is to ask an object that uses scheduling to perform a required task based on what the time is now. Each object

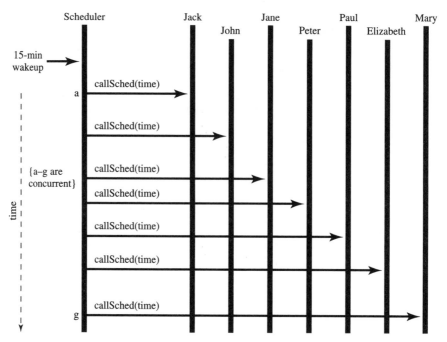

FIGURE 6-5 Scheduler's Sequence Diagram from Lawn Mower Example

operates as if it can perform some service (function) every 15 minutes. If one of the objects were scheduled to "mowLawn" at 7 P.M., the Scheduler will send a message to that object to execute its callSched with the argument of 7 P.M. In each object, the callSched method is the same; it checks its schedule to see what service (function) needs to be performed. In this case, it would be the mowLawn service.

■ ■ SUMMARY

Below are the detailed steps of our approach to specifying static behavior and to capturing the controls for an application/system:

1. List all the external and internal events to which the application/system needs to respond.
2. From each event, usually a message, determine how and in what sequence the necessary messages will be passed among objects to satisfy the request.
3. Define and draw a sequence diagram (event trace diagram) for each scenario and its variations.
4. If the number of scenarios is large, consider creating a use-case model to reduce the number of diagrams.
5. Capture the details of each service associated with the sequence diagram by using one of the documentation techniques given in this chapter.

CHAPTER

7

Dynamic Behavior

Action is transitory, —a step, a blow; The motion of a muscle, this way or that.

■ William Wordsworth, *The Borderers*

This chapter presents techniques for capturing dynamic behavior. For applications that are not control-based, most objects (i.e., classes) will not undergo significant state changes, so that only a few (if any) will require state diagrams. However, in many control-based applications, the state diagrams may be the dominant aspect of the model.

Technically, state diagrams are the formal specifications of the behavior of a class, and thus of an object. Static behavior is really a special case of a modeless state diagram. A modeless state diagram occurs when an object (class) always responds the same way to external and internal events (stimuli). Note that scenarios are not state diagrams; they are examples of execution of the system. They involve usually several objects playing various roles. Thus, they are instances of behavior, and as such they can only illustrate behavior; they cannot define it. Technically, when all state diagrams have been created, all scenarios can be derived from this entire set of state diagrams. In fact, many of us use scenarios to check for the sanity of the model. Similarly, since a scenario is an instance of a use case, a use case is a "slice" of the system behavior across state diagrams from multiple classes.

Introduction

OBJECT-ORIENTED ANALYSIS IS OFTEN described in terms of structure, behavior, and rules. The structural analysis captures the static vision of how the objects are related to each other; it essentially captures the data semantics of the application. A visual, spatial metaphor is used to document these relationships. In all the earlier chapters, we have focused on capturing the structural aspects of the application. In contrast, behavior analysis captures the time-dependent aspects of the application. For example, it is used to specify how to hire employees, dismiss employees, add diagrams to a document, or delete words from a document. Thus, whether the behavior is static or dynamic, the method description captures the procedural semantics of the application. Rules, which are discussed in a later chapter, capture the declarative semantics of the application.

If the application has no time-dependent behavior, then capturing the structural aspects of the system and performing static behavioral analysis is sufficient to build the application. This is the situation with our case study so far. However, the world we live in is not static; it changes over time. Dynamic modeling mechanisms allow us to capture the behavior of objects, and thus the behavior of the application, over time.

Temporal relationships are difficult to capture. The typical application is best understood by first examining its static structure (data semantics), that is, the structure of its objects and their relationships (inheritance, association, aggregation) to each other in a moment of time. After capturing this aspect of the application, we want to examine the changes in the objects and their relationships over time. Those aspects (procedural semantics) of an application that concern these changes over time are captured in the *dynamic* model. Thus, this chapter presents mechanisms that help us capture flow of control, interactions, and sequencing of operations in an object-oriented application. The major concepts of dynamic modeling are *events*, which are the stimuli, and *states*, which are configurations of objects at some point in time. Thus, an application can be described in terms of object behaviors, that is, an orderly sequence of state changes of objects over time, and the behavior of an object is captured as a chain (or probably a network) of cause (stimuli) and effect (state change) over time.

For example, the chain of cause and effect for an Order object in an order processing system may be as follows: at placing the order: requisition state; at filling a line item of the order; partially filled state; at shipping of line item: partially shipped state; when all the line items have been filled and shipped: shipped state. When the order is shipped, an Invoice object is created, the Order object's data is archived, and the object is deleted from the system. Figure 7-1 shows a chain diagram depicting this. Note that the state is drawn using a rounded box, and the initial state is shown by a solid arrow from a filled circle to that state. The end state, if applicable, is shown as a filled circle enclosed in an unfilled circle. We have labeled them in the diagram as start and end. The labels are not part of UML.

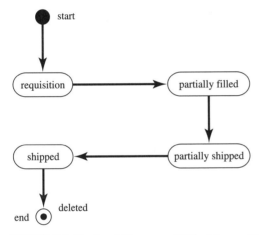

FIGURE 7-1 Chain of Cause and Effect for an Order Object

Techniques for Identifying Dynamic Behavior

AN OBJECT IN THE REAL world normally has a lifetime. Often it is created or comes into existence, progresses through certain stages, and then dies or vanishes. For example, a human being is conceived and born, passes through stages (baby, child, preschooler, grammar school, teenager, young adult, mature adult, senior citizen), and eventually dies. Some individuals do not visit all the stages, and others appear to have reverted to an earlier stage. However, all humans follow this basic pattern of dynamic behavior throughout their lifetimes.

From our general observations of behavior patterns for different things in the real world, we conclude as follows:

- Most things go through various stages during their lifetimes.
- The order in which a thing progresses through its stages forms a pattern that helps in classifying the kind of thing it is.

■   In a pattern, not all progressions between stages are allowed. Some progressions are forbidden by laws of physics, some by statute, and so on.

■   There are incidents/events in the real world that cause a thing to progress (or indicate that it has progressed) between stages.

For technical reasons, we also add the following assumptions:

■   A thing is in exactly one and only one stage of its behavior pattern at any given time.

■   Things progress from one stage to another stage instantaneously.

Note that the granularity of time depends on the degree of abstraction and can vary at different levels of the application. Basically, however, the progression (transition) must be atomic, that is, noninterruptible, at the given level of abstraction. Thus, the incident or event that causes the progression must be treated as atomic, for an incident occurs at a point in time, while a stage (state) is a configuration of objects that exists between incidents.

Let us now test these observations and assumptions on a second example. Figure 7-2 shows the behavior pattern for an airplane. In this example, the airplane goes through numerous stages, which are shown by oval rectangles. They include parked at gate, taxiing to runway, and so on. The pattern is simple and is shown in the figure by using arrows. This pattern of progressing through stages applies to all instances of airplane. Not all progressions between stages are allowed; for example, an airplane cannot progress directly from being parked at the gate to being in flight. There are incidents/events that signal the progression between states, which are shown as labels on the arrows. For example, when the airplane is in the "taking-off" stage, "wheels leave ground" signals the progression from the "taking-off" stage to the "in flight" stage. The wheels leave the

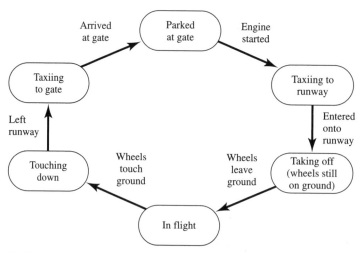

FIGURE 7-2 Behavior Pattern for an Airplane

ground instantaneously, and at any given instant of time, we can assume that the airplane is in one of the above stages.

It is very important to note that the stages are defined by our perception (model) of reality, and that some of the incidents/events are really indicators of the progression (change of state) from one stage to another. We will see later that the progressions (changes of state) are used as a way to cause an action (execution of code) to occur during the "instantaneous" progression from one stage to another stage. Thus, stages are defined because the object may need to take some action when the incident/event occurs. For instance, in the airplane example, when the wheels leave the ground, they need to be lifted back into the airplane. Also, when the airplane touches down, the brakes are applied, and usually the engines are reversed.

Common Lifecycle Forms

The pattern that characterizes a Class is called its *lifecycle form*. While any pattern/form is possible, two forms appear to dominate the modeling of computer applications at this time. Shlaer and Mellor (1988) have given names to these forms:

- Circular lifecycle
  The circular lifecycle generally applies when the object/class has an operational cycle for its behavior. Examples include the airplane, a microwave oven, a robotic drill.

- Born-and-die lifecycle
  When an instance gets created and deleted (or rests in a final state) during the life of the system being analyzed, the class is well characterized by the born-and-die lifecycle. Examples include a human in the history of mankind, an account in a banking system, a logging record, a bar of candy in the course of a few days.

Models for Capturing the Lifecycle

According to all object-oriented experts, it is best to express a lifecycle with a state model. Four forms of the state model are widely used in analysis: (1) Mealy, (2) Moore, (3) Harel, and (4) modified Harel (UML). The differences between these four models will be apparent below. All four forms use the following components:

- A set of *states*
  Each state represents a stage in the lifecycle of a typical object. A stage is technically a period of time during which an object is waiting for an event to occur.

- A set of *events*
  Each event represents an incident/event or indication that a progression is to happen. Technically, it is an occurrence at a point in time. The granularity of time depends on the degree of abstraction. Though the granularity of time may vary at different levels of the same application,

an event must be atomic (i.e., noninterruptible) at the given level of abstraction. An event is a one-way asynchronous transmission[1] of information from one object to another. It may have parameters with names and types as part of the message sent.

- *Transition*

  A transition is a response to an event received by an object that is in a certain state. Based on the type of state model used, it may invoke an action. (Action is defined below.) At a specific moment of time, an object is in a particular state, called the current state. When an event is received by an object, only the transitions leading from the current state are eligible to be triggered by the occurrence of that event. Associated with a transition may be a guard condition (UML) or transition rule (state machine).

- *Transition rules (guard conditions).*

  A transition rule is a Boolean expression in terms of event parameters and the state variables and functions of the object to which the state diagram belongs. When an event triggers the transition, the value of the transition rule is evaluated. If the value evaluates to true, the transition occurs; otherwise, the transition does not occur.

- *Actions*

  An action is an operation or set of operations that must be accomplished[2]

  1. when the transition is occurring (Mealy),
  2. when an object enters into the state (Moore),[3]
  3. when the transition is occurring (Harel)
  4. when the transition is occurring,
     when an object enters in the state,
     and when an object departs from the state (modified Harel).

  An action is atomic and instantaneous; that is, it is noninterruptible at the abstraction level of the associated state.

Note that the modified Harel model allows for three possible actions to occur during a transition:[4] an action associated with exiting from the current state,

---

[1] Two-way information flow (e.g., call-and-return) can always be modeled as two one-way information flows.

[2] There are other models, such as Petri nets. Furthermore, there are models that support actions at transition, at entry into the state, and at exit from the state. Thus, any combinations of the three are possible. However, in practice, we usually only need one.

[3] In this model the transition rule is the precondition rule for that state.

[4] The two additional actions for entry and exit are not theoretically necessary; the same effect could be obtained by attaching the action to all transactions entering or exiting the state. In practice, we would prefer not to do this.

a second action associated with the transition itself, and a third action associated with entry into a new state (which may be the same as the current state).

In UML, three additional constructs are added: *history state, activity,* and *timing mark.* A *history state* is used to capture the concept that a state must "remember" its substate when it is exited and be able to resume the same substate on subsequent reentry into the state. An *activity* is an operation or set of operations within a state that takes time to complete. Thus, it is not instantaneous and can be interrupted. Some activities continue until they are terminated by an external event (usually a state change) and others terminate on their own accord. A *timing mark* construct is used to capture real-time constraints on transitions. The most common use of a timing mark is to capture the maximum limits on the elapsed time between events.

These state models are usually represented graphically by *state transition diagrams.* We will use the Mealy model in the case study.

Identifying and Specifying Events

AS THE PRECEDING DISCUSSION OF the lifecycle model suggests, one of the key components that we need to identify is the event. In this section, we learn techniques to identify and specify events.

Use Case and Scenario

A *use case* is a generic description of an entire transaction involving several objects. It has been used in structured methods to identify external events for an application/system. Typically, it is used to analyze the interactions between the application/system and one or more external objects. A use case is typically written as a text description of the external actors (objects) and the sequences of events involving the various objects that constitute one of the many transactions supported by the application/system.

A *scenario* is an instance of a use case. It shows a particular series of interactions among objects in a single execution of the system. This single execution of the system typically constitutes a transaction (from the external object's perspective) between the external object and the application/system.

Scenarios can be shown in two different ways:

1. *Event trace diagram*[5]
    This shows the interaction among a set of objects in temporal order, which is very useful in understanding timing issues. An alternate form is a text dialog, which is widely used by nontechnical requirement writers.

---

[5] In UML, this is called a sequence diagram.

2. *Object interaction diagram*[6]

    This shows the interactions among a set of objects as nodes in a graph, which is helpful in understanding software structure, since all the interactions that affect an object are localized around it.

Event Trace Diagram

Of the two ways to show scenarios, we present only the event trace diagram in this book. An *event trace diagram* is drawn as follows. Objects (not classes) in a scenario are drawn as vertical lines. An event (incident) is drawn as a labeled horizontal arrow from the sending object's line to the receiving object's line. Time proceeds vertically, so event-timing sequences can be easily determined. An object can send simultaneous events to other objects; however, simultaneous reception of events is not meaningful and should be avoided.

There is a variant form of the event trace diagram that captures procedure-calling sequences in situations where there is a single point of control at any given time. In this scheme, a double line is used to show the period of time an object has a thread of control. Thus, a single line indicates that the object is blocked (not in control) and is waiting for an event to give it control. This may be useful for situations where we have a single processor with a single thread of control; however, it is less useful in a fully concurrent system situation.

Example

For better understanding, let us borrow an example from Shlaer and Mellor. Suppose we want to model a scaled-down microwave oven, the OneMinute Microwaver. The product requirements are as follows:

1. There is a single control button available.
2. If the oven door is closed and a user pushes the button, the oven will cook (i.e., energize the tube) for 1 minute.
3. Pushing the button at any time when the oven is cooking adds an additional minute of cooking time. For example, if the user has 31 seconds more cooking time to go and pushes the button twice, the cooking time will be 2 minutes and 31 seconds.
4. Pushing the button with the door open has no effect.
5. There is a light inside the oven.
6. Any time the oven is cooking, the light must be turned on (so that the user can look inside and see if the food is boiling over.)
7. Any time the door is open, the light must be on (so that the user can see the food or have enough light to clean the oven).
8. User can stop the cooking by opening the door.

---

[6] In UML, this is called a collaboration diagram.

9. If user closes the door, the light goes out.
This is the normal configuration when someone has just placed food inside the oven but has not yet pushed the control button.

10. If the oven times out (cooks until the desired preset time), it turns off both the power tube and the light. It also then emits a warning beep to tell the user that the food is ready.

From the textual requirements, we identify the following pertinent incidents:

- Opening the door
- Closing the door
- Pushing the control button
- Completion of the prescribed cooking interval

These incidents are events that may cause the oven to perform some operations and also change its state. The incidents are abstracted or captured as events. With those external events, we can create the following set of event trace diagrams for the microwave oven using use cases and scenarios. Scenario 1 is the normal case and is shown in Figure 7-3. Note that all scenarios are developed from an external (user's) perspective. In scenario 2, no additional time was added.

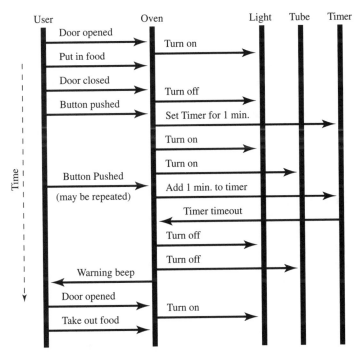

FIGURE 7-3 Event Trace Diagram for Microwave Oven in Scenario 1

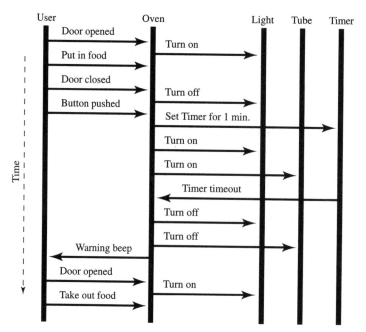

FIGURE 7-4 Event Trace Diagram for Microwave Oven in Scenario 2

This is shown in Figure 7-4. In scenario 3, shown in Figure 7-5, the user opens the door while food is cooking.

These scenarios cover all the various sequences that are pertinent to the building of the state model. Technically, the user opens the door, and the door notifies the oven that the door is open; similarly for closing the door. The user also pushes the button, and the button notifies the oven that the button has been pushed. However, neither the button nor the door takes any action on its own in these incidents. We modeled it as if the user who opens the door is sending a signal to the oven directly; this simplifies the model with no loss of information for our purposes; see Figure 7-6.

Specifying Dynamic Behavior

USE CASES AND SCENARIOS ARE not sufficient documentation for development. We will now look at ways of documenting the events and documenting the dynamic behavior in a form more suited for programming.

Event List

AN *EVENT* IS THE ABSTRACTION of an incident or signal in the real world that tells some object in the system that it is (or may be) moving to a new state. In the abstraction process, four aspects of an event should be specified:

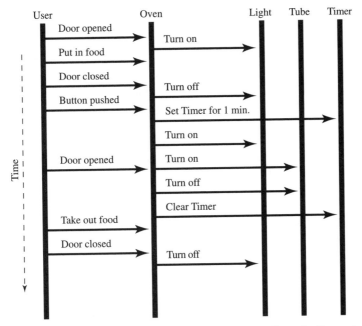

FIGURE 7-5 Event Trace Diagram for Microwave Oven in Scenario 3

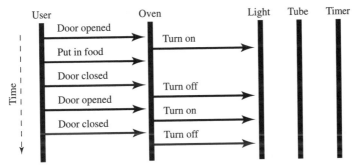

FIGURE 7-6 Event Trace Diagram for Microwave Oven in Scenario 4

1. Meaning
    The meaning of an event is usually captured in a short phrase that tells what is going on in the real world. For example, "wheels leave ground" in the airplane example and "door open" in the microwave example.

2. Destination
    The object[7] that receives the event. By convention, the event is sent only to one receiver.

---

[7] The state model is part of an object. Since patterns are by class, we define the state model for the entire class.

3. Label

A unique label must be provided for each event to distinguish different events from each other. This is very important when there are distinct events with similar meanings. Though the label is arbitrary, the suggested format for labeling is to use letter-number combinations. A convenient convention is to use destination-based labeling, in which all the events that are received by the same class begin with the class's key letter(s).[8]

4. Event data

An event should be thought of as a service request. Thus, it can and usually does carry data that is given to the object as parameters of the service request.

An *event list* is simply a list of all the events from the scenarios involved in the definition of the state models for the objects within the application/system. The event list for the microwave is given in Table 7-1.

TABLE 7-1 Event List

Label	Meaning	Source	Destination	Data
V1	Door open	User	Oven	None
V2	Door closed	User	Oven	None
V3	Button pushed	User	Oven	None
V4	Timer timeout	Timer	Oven	None
L1	Turn on light.	Oven	Light	None
L2	Turn off light.	Oven	Light	None
P1	Turn on tube (energize tube).	Oven	Tube	None
P2	Turn off tube (deenergize tube).	Oven	Tube	None
T1	Set timer for 1 minute.	Oven	Timer	None
T2	Add 1 minute to timer.	Oven	Timer	None
T3	Clear timer.	Oven	Timer	None

Without the event trace diagram, most of us would consider "putting in the food" and "taking out the food" as important incidents. However, the event trace diagram shows that they do not cause any action to occur and thus are not material to the modeling process. This may seem strange to the novice, because the primary purpose of the microwave is to heat food. In reality, the microwave will work with no food in it; we can turn it on with nothing in it. So our model does

---

[8] A class's key letters are given in a label tag used to provide a convenient marker for the class. For the classes in the microwave oven example, we might use Usr, MO, LGT, TB, and TMR.

capture accurately how a microwave is actually designed and built. Also the warning beep is an incident, but the processing of that event is handled by the external object (user). Thus, it is not an event that the system will process and thus not on our event list.

State Transition Table

In dynamic behavior modeling, a *state* is given a number and a name that are unique within the state model. The number is used in the state transition table to depict the next state; it does not prescribe the order in which an object would occupy the states. An *action* is a set of operations that must be performed when the transition occurs. The following operations are allowed:

- Read and write operations involving its own attributes.
- Generate an event to be sent to any other object, including itself.
- Generate an event to something outside the scope of analysis (e.g., an operator, a hardware device, or an object in another system/subsystem).
- Create, delete, set, reset, read a timer.
- Access the services of another object, including objects in its own class.

Since the operations allowed are very liberal in their action, it is the responsibility of the analyst/developer to ensure the consistency of the state model as a whole. Thus, analysts should ensure the following:

- Leave the object consistent.
  If an attribute is updated, any attribute that computationally depends on it must be updated.
- Ensure consistency of relationship.
  If the action creates or deletes an object, it must ensure that any relationships involving those objects are made consistent with the rules stated in the model.
- Leave subtypes and supertypes consistent.
  If action transforms an object from one type to another type, it must ensure that all the proper objects and relationships are managed.

In a *state transition table*, each row represents one of the possible states (stages) of the state model,[9] and each column represents an event that has this state model as its destination. The cells of the table are filled in with the specification of what happens when an instance of a class (e.g., your specific microwave oven) in a given state (row in the table) receives a particular event (the column).

---

9   The state model belongs to an object.

The process of creating the state transition table for each class is as follows:[10]

1. Place all the events that have the same destination in the columns of the table.

2. Start with one row if you have not identified any stages, or use your stages as possible states.

3. Take each scenario and start filling in the cells in the table, showing the next state above the line and the action below the line.

4. When you run into a conflict (e.g., a cell has to respond to an event differently for two different scenarios), add a new state to the model, because this means that there was a change in state (stage) that has not been captured in the original analysis.[11]

5. Repeat steps 3 and 4 until all the scenarios are captured in a consistent manner in the table.

6. Now check the empty cells and decide if these are "event ignored" or "can't happen" situations.[12]

7. Finally, reduce any identical rows to one row if you are using the Mealy model.

The state transition tables for the microwave oven are shown in Tables 7-2, 7-3, and 7-4.

Observe in Table 7-2 that states 1 and 6 are identical state transitions; states 3 and 4 are also identical. However, in each case, the precondition for entering each state is different. For instance, you can only get into the "cooking interrupted" state from prior states when the power tube is on and the timer is turned on, while a person can be opening and closing the microwave door to cause the state model to move from state 1 to state 2 and back to state 1, which would not require that the timer be cleared and the tube deenergized. When we get to diagramming the state models, we will see the impact of these preconditions on the different state models.

We can assume that these objects have methods that really turn the physical devices on and off.

---

[10] Since patterns hold for an entire class, we define the state model for the class. Each object gets its own state model, as with attributes.

[11] This is usually seen as the need to perform different actions when the event is received in the different scenarios.

[12] Steps 6 and 7 are very important to ensure the completeness of the analysis.

TABLE 7-2 Microwave Oven

States	V1: Door Open	V2: Door Closed	V3: Button Pushed	V4: Timer Timeout
1. Idle with door open	Can't happen [1]	2 Turn off light.	Event ignored	Can't happen [2]
2. Idle with door closed	1 Turn on light.	Can't happen [3]	3 Set timer to 1 minute; turn on light; turn on tube.	Can't happen [2]
3. Initial cooking period	6 Turn off tube; Clear timer.	Can't happen [3]	4 Add 1 minute to timer.	5 Turn off tube; turn off light; sound warning beep.
4. Extended cooking period	6 Turn off tube; Clear timer.	Can't happen [3]	4 Add 1 minute to timer.	5 Turn off tube; turn off light; sound warning beep.
5. Cooking complete	1 Turn on light.	Can't happen [3]	Event ignored [4]	Can't happen [2]
6. Cooking interrupted	Can't happen [1]	2 Turn off light.	Event ignored	Can't happen [2]

Note 1: Door is already open.
Note 3: Door is already closed.
Note 2: Timer is not running.
Note 4: One could argue that this entry should be identical with that in state 2.

TABLE 7-3 Light

States	L1: Turn On	L2: Turn Off
1. On	Event ignored [5]	2 None
2. Off	1 None	Event ignored [5]

Note 5: When light is on, ignore "on" request; similarly for "off."

TABLE 7-4 Power Tube

States	P1: Turn On	P2: Turn Off
1. On	Event ignored [6]	2 None
2. Off	1 None	Event ignored [6]

Note 6: When tube is energized, ignore "on" request; similarly for "off."

TABLE 7-5 Timer

State	T1: Set Timer	T2: Add Time	T3: Clear Timer	T4: Clock Tick	T5: Fire
1. Idle	2 Set time remaining to 1 minute; set up ticking mechanism.	Can't happen [7]	Can't happen [7]	Can't happen [8]	Can't happen [10]
2. Set	Can't happen [7]	5 Add 1 minute to time remaining.	1 Clear time remaining; unset tick mechanism.	3 Subtract 1 time tick from remaining time.	Can't happen [10]
3. Counting down	Can't happen [9]	5 Add 1 minute to time remaining.	1 Clear time remaining; unset tick mechanism.	3 Subtract 1 time tick from remaining time; check if time remaining is <= 0; if so, generate internal T5 signal to cause transition to firing state.	4 Generate T3 signal to effect transition from firing to idle.
4. Firing	Can't happen [9]	Event ignored [11]	1 Clear time remaining; unset tick mechanism.	Event ignored [11]	Can't happen [10]
5. Adding	Can't happen [11]	5 Add 1 minute to time remaining.	1 Clear time remaining; unset tick mechanism.	3 Subtract 1 time tick from remaining time.	Can't happen [10]

Note 7: Timer is not active.
Note 8: Tick mechanism is not active.
Note 9: Timer is already set.
Note 10: T5 is an internal signal that is generated only when it is in state 3.
Note 11: Too late.

Documenting Dynamic Behavior

WE WILL LOOK AT A graphic form, the state diagram, for documenting the state model in a class.[13]

State Diagrams

A *state diagram* is a graphic form for displaying the lifecycle of objects in a class. It describes in pictorial form all the possible ways in which the objects respond to events sent by other objects.[14]

Historically, state diagrams were used with structured methods to show how a system behaves when it receives external events from objects outside of the system. One weakness of this technique was that we lumped the system into one large object, which made the number of states very large. Today, we normally identify controllers, objects that are part of the system, to receive these signals and maintain the system and control (or sequence the actions of other objects within the system). However, the more powerful use of state diagrams is to capture the lifecycle of an object that undergoes a sequence of operations that takes the object into fundamentally different states.

A state diagram is a directed chart of states (nodes) connected by transitions (directed arcs). The directed arcs are labeled with the transition event and any necessary guard rules associated with the transition. The guard rule must be evaluated to be true before the transition occurs. Normally, the allowable variables used in the guard rules are limited to the arguments of the event, state variables, and the services of the class. In our microwave example, there are no guard rules. Figures 7-7 and 7-8 show the state diagrams (Mealy and Moore, respectively) for the state transition diagram of the microwave oven. In the Mealy model, states from the transition table were collapsed because the actions are associated with the transition. V1, V2, V3, V4 refer to the labels used in Figure 7-7.

In the Moore model, the action is associated with the state. We cannot eliminate identical rows from the model.[15] In our model, the action is associated with the entry into the state. There are models that allow us to associate action with exit from a state also. Some authors have suggested a model that allows actions with transition, entry into a state, and exit from a state. However, in practice, we normally associate the action with the transition. The Harel model also associates the action with the transition, but it also allows substates and other powerful capabilities. State machines are not the only model that can be used to capture dynamic behavior; other models, such as Petri nets, exist to handle more sophisticated dynamic behavior. The state machine is usually sufficient for most practitioners.

---

[13] Though each object has its own state model, we define the template for the state model in the class. Remember that all objects in the same class have copies of the same state model.

[14] Events may be external or internal.

[15] This is unlike the Mealy model, in which we eliminated identical rows.

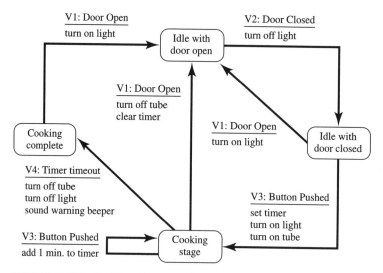

FIGURE 7-7 Mealy State Diagram for Microwave Oven

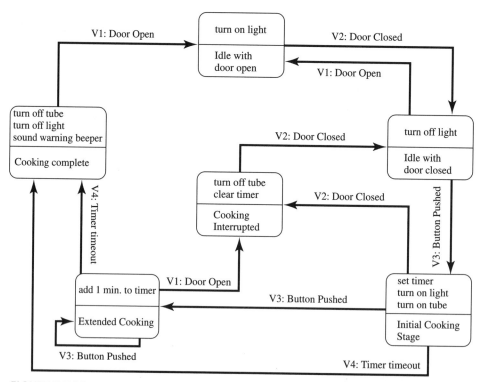

FIGURE 7-8 Moore State Diagram for Microwave Oven

Recommended Approach

WE RECOMMEND THE FOLLOWING STEPS for performing behavioral analysis:

1. Prepare scenarios of all the typical interaction sequences.
2. Prepare scenarios of all the accepted business exception cases.
3. If appropriate, prepare scenarios of all the failure and rare cases. Failures include error conditions, equipment failures, and undesirable and unusual behaviors.[16] In object-oriented methods, the failure conditions that are to be processed by the application/system should be formalized into the analysis model along with normal behaviors.[17]
4. Develop an event trace diagram for all cases that will help identify events.
5. Use the event trace diagram to generate an event list. Note that in the example, we assumed that the transition depended only on the reception of one event. In some situations a transition may depend upon the arrival of two or more events from different sources. There are two ways to handle this situation. First, you can create an intermediate state to hold the reception of one of the event and use it as a holding state for reception of the other event(s). The other choice is to add an attribute or object to hold the data. This would require the programmer to initialize and clean up the attribute or object at the appropriate time.
6. Use the event list and your knowledge of classes to create state transition tables.
7. Use the state transition table to create your state diagrams.
8. Check the state diagrams by testing the scenarios against the diagrams.

---

[16] Many of us who work with real-time process control know this as failure analysis and understand that proper analysis is highly problem-dependent. The purpose of failure analysis is to take into account the effects of certain kinds of malfunctions and errors and to evaluate strategies for dealing with them. In process control, the goal is to maintain control, or recover control, or have a graceful and safe shutdown of an industrial or external process. Frequently the failure analysis leads to additional requirements, installation of new sensors, addition of electrical/mechanical safeguards, writing an emergency procedure instruction book, and so on.

[17] A word of caution to the meticulous thinker: It is very easy to get carried away and investigate a myriad of possible failures. Economic and time constraints, balanced with safety, should be applied to limit the failure analysis to real and reasonable scenarios. Far-fetched scenarios should not be designed into the system. However, if there is a safety or economic damage concern, it is strongly recommended that a manual procedure be written to handle these situations. Abnormal behaviors are usually extremely complex, which can cause the model to grow larger and more complex. This will make the system more difficult to maintain and to modify.

■ ■ SUMMARY

Historically, capturing the changes to objects and their relationships over time has been very difficult to manage. In this chapter, we presented a concept and its associated mechanisms to capture this aspect of the application/system. This concept is called dynamic behavior. We learned the following about dynamic behavior:

- ■ How to identify it by recognizing common lifecycle forms: circular and born-and-die
- ■ How to identify and to specify events that are the key stimuli in causing objects to change state
- ■ How to use the events to help us identify and specify the dynamic behaviors, using state transition tables
- ■ How to document this specification in the graphic form of a state diagram
- ■ A couple of types of finite state machines that may be used to implement the dynamic behavior captured in the state transition table.

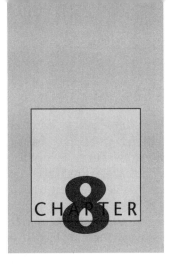

CHAPTER 8

Identifying
Relationships

A poor relation is the most irrelevant thing in nature.

Charles Lamb

In the third step of our method, we captured how each object provides services. In the process of specifying how it was done, we also demonstrated that some objects need access to services (functions) of other objects to perform the operations necessary to supply the original service. However, in the object-oriented paradigm (unlike the procedural paradigm), an object cannot just call a service (function). The message-passing paradigm requires that a service request be directed to an object. In the fourth step, we address how an object accesses the services of another object.

Accessing Another Object's Services

ONE OF THE FUNDAMENTAL DIFFERENCES between the object-oriented paradigm and the procedural paradigm is that in the object-oriented paradigm every service request (function call) must be sent to a specific object, while in the procedural paradigm a function can be called directly. For example, in order for object A to send a message[1] to object B, object A must have a "handle"[2] to object B. Thus, in object-oriented technology, the analysts/developers should understand the various vehicles available to give an object access to the handle of another object.

There are three basic ways for one object to access another object's services:[3]

1. The calling object, which has a handle, passes the handle of the other object as one of the arguments of the function (message) signature.
2. The called object has a relationship (aggregation or link[4]) to the other object. A relationship gives handle(s) to other objects in the relationship.
3. The needed service belongs to an "ancestor" class.[5]

Relationships

IN A WORLD OF PERFECT reuse and portability, each object and/or class would be independent of every other object and/or class. Then during step 3, we would be able to specify all the operations of every method with operations that only use data belonging to the object and/or that is passed to the object from the calling object. In this perfect world, all services would be provided using only data associated with the object itself and the calling object. This would make reuse and portability a very easy issue.[6]

Unfortunately, *No object is an island, independent of all others.* Objects typically depend on other objects for services and possibly for error handling, constant

---

[1] In C++, call a function.

[2] In C++, a reference or pointer.

[3] There is a fourth way, the access of static class functions, which may be considered a managed global function.

[4] A link is a relationship between objects, and an association is a relationship between classes.

[5] The standard object-oriented term for ancestor class is *superclass*. In brief, the service is inherited from the ancestor.

[6] There are object-oriented experts who argue that the use of relationships (association and aggregation) violates the encapsulation and information-hiding principles. This is a correct statement. Unfortunately, all relationships, including generalization (a.k.a. inheritance), violate the encapsulation and information-hiding principles; there are very few experts who would argue against inheritance and polymorphism. We take a more practical approach to object-oriented technology. If a mechanism helps us manage complexity, then we are willing to use it. In practice, one or more groups of collaborating objects are needed to implement a large number of the services. Experience has shown that all the mechanisms/constructs (and then some) that we will be discussing are needed to implement any application/system of any significant capability.

data, and exception handling. Some objects are components of other objects, and some objects are used to join other objects. Moreover, objects are, by definition, instances of classes, and classes may inherit attributes and services from other classes. In most applications, the model needs to capture these interdependencies of the various objects.

These interdependencies are called relationships. A relationship is not merely a link that ties one object to another so that it can access the other object's services. A relationship also carries a semantic meaning. Object-oriented technology gives both analysts and developers a rich set of mechanisms or constructs to capture these semantic relationships.

In this chapter, we discuss three very important relationships: generalization, links, and aggregation.[7] These are certainly not new concepts; we work with them every day. For example, we all learned generalization when we studied taxonomies in biology class. An excellent example of a link is marriage, and an example of aggregation (whole-parts) is a car. Moreover, links in the form of associations have been widely used for years in the database modeling community.[8]

Generalization

GENERALIZATION, AS WE WILL USE it, has its roots in the knowledge-representation paradigm used in artificial intelligence. Ross Quillian's psychological model of associative memory is one example. In that representation, Quillian introduced the node-link model for representing a semantic knowledge network. The nodes represented classes, and the links represented relationships between objects in the respective classes at the nodes. In a semantic network, both the node and the link had labels. One of the most powerful labels represented the generalization relationship. That link was called the *is_a*. The concept of the is_a relationship is quite simple. If object A has an is_a relationship with object B, then all the attributes and services of object B are also attributes and services of object A. For example, suppose we have two objects: Person and Employee. Reasonable attributes for Person could be name, age, weight, and height. But an Employee is_a Person. By the definition of the is_a relationship, the attributes of Person are also the attributes of Employee. Note that normally the Employee has additional attributes such as salary, position, organization number, and employee identification number. In this example, the Person object is referred to as the *ancestor* (or parent) node, and the

---

[7]   Unfortunately, few programming languages explicitly support all these mechanisms.

[8]   Some object-oriented authors believe that every piece of information should be attached to a single class; thus, a link violates the encapsulation principle and should not be allowed. However, most of us who have developed large and complex applications/systems believe that some information transcends a single class, and that the failure to treat a link on an equal footing with objects will lead to a model (program) that contains hidden assumptions and dependencies. Thus, during analysis one should model a link to indicate that the information it contains is not subordinate to a single object (class), but dependent on two or more objects (classes).

Employee object is the descendent (or child) node. The ancestor is a generalization of the descendent; conversely, the descendent is a specialization of the ancestor.

Generalization relationships have some important properties that differentiate them from other relationships.[9] These properties are the following:

1. Structural properties

   a. Attributes
      The descendent will have all the attributes of the ancestor. For instance, Employee will have the age attribute because it is a descendent class of Person.

   b. Nongeneralization relationships
      The descendent will have all the nongeneralization relationships of the ancestor. For example, if we add a marriage link between two Persons,[10] Employee will also have a marriage link because it is a descendent of Person.

2. Interface properties

   All services provided by the ancestor must also be provided by the descendent.[11] For instance, if the Person object had an addWeight service, then Employee will also have an addWeight service because Employee is a descendent of Person.

3. Behavior properties

   a. Generalization without polymorphism (good child)
      In generalization without polymorphism, all methods supplied by the ancestor for its services are also used by the descendent to provide the corresponding services.

   b. Generalization with polymorphism (bad child)
      In generalization with polymorphism, some methods supplied by the ancestor for its services are also used by the descendent to

---

[9] In theory, all three aspects (attribute, service, and behavior) can be redefined in the subclass, We have limited the redefinition for a very practical purpose and consistent with the implementation of inheritance in C++. Other languages may give you more flexibility in redefinition and this may seem more powerful. However, there can be too much flexibility. In most languages, the additional flexibility will result in software that is less safe as we cannot guarantee that the software is well tested.

[10] A *link* is relationship between two objects. We will learn later that Person is really a class and, therefore, the relationship is really an association.

[11] Even if the service of a descendent effectively removes the behavior, it must still provide the interface for that service.

provide the corresponding services. For the remaining services of the ancestor, the descendent supplies its own customized methods that replace the ancestor's corresponding methods.[12]

4. Mathematical properties

  a. Antisymmetry
     If object A is_a descendent of object B, then object B may not have an is_a relationship with object A (object B is not a descendent of object A). For example, Employee is_a Person, but not all persons are employees.

  b. Transitivity
     If object A is_a object B and object B is_a object C, then object A is_a object C.[13] For example, if we add the fact that a SalesPerson is_a Employee to our example, then SalesPerson is also a Person. Furthermore, it also has the age attribute because of properties 1a and 4b.

Generalization/specialization is a critical mechanism in the object-oriented paradigm because finding the correct ancestor(s) to assign the services and attributes to is crucial to designing a good model. Unfortunately, it is very difficult for novices to realize that most of the objects with which they work are composites of other objects.

To overcome this difficulty, novices should consider every object as a complex object that may be viewed as many different subobjects. Each subobject represents that complex object in a single semantic domain. For example, we are (1) employees in the work domain, (2) taxpayers in the governmental domain, (3) parents and/or children in the family domain, and (4) members in the social club domain.[14] The services we provide and the relationships we have are different for each domain. For example, consider the services *hire, promote, retire,* and *fire.* All these services are intimately tied to the fact that each of us is also an employee. When a person is unemployed, these services do not apply. As a taxpayer, a tax audit relationship with a tax auditor may exist. This is a relationship that is very intimately tied to each of us as taxpayers. It would be improper to use this relationship in the other domains. For instance, taxpayers do not want their auditors known by their employers or social clubs.

---

[12] This is perhaps a good time to remind the reader that the "bad" child is often an excellent model in object-oriented analysis and design.

[13] Transitivity enables us to show generalization hierarchies diagrammatically as directed acyclic graphs. The use of single inheritance makes it possible to organize the objects in a hierarchy. Because many people use only single inheritance, generalization is often diagrammatically shown as an ancestral tree.

[14] Although some of these names may also be role names in some applications, we will assume that we want to capture these concepts as objects.

The proper use of generalization helps us represent composite objects in a manner that manages complexity and thus makes software more maintainable and flexible to change. Although a descendent can be thought of as having all the attributes, nongeneralization relationships, and services of all its ancestors, it is better to consider the descendent as having access to all these things via the appropriate subobject of which it is a specialization. This forces us to keep the attributes, relationships, and services in the appropriate semantic domain, which reduces coupling and provides higher cohesion. Lower coupling and higher cohesion lead to more maintainable and more flexible software.

Identifying and Specifying Generalization/Specialization

WE RECOMMEND USING THE ORIGINAL list of potential objects minus the objects external to the application domain as our list of objects that may potentially be used in an is_a relationship. With this list, we apply the following test to each possible pairing of the objects. We ask, "Is object A an object B?" "Is object B an object A?" The allowable answers are *always*, *sometimes*, and *never*. If the answer to both questions is *never*, the two objects are not in an is_a relationship with each other. If both answers are *always*, object A and object B are synonymous.[15] If the answer to "Is object A an object B?" is *always*, and the answer to "Is object B an object A?" is *sometimes*, then object A has an is_a relationship with object B.[16]

For example, let us look at the following list of objects: Officer, Manager, Supervisor, Advisor, Engineer, Contractor, and Representative. We will apply our test to these objects in a typical corporate environment. The answers are shown in Table 8-1.

TABLE 8-1 An is_a Analysis Table.

Is A a B?	O	M	S	Ad	E	C	R
Officer	X	a	n	n	n	n	a
Manager	s	X	s	n	n	n	a
Supervisor	n	a	X	n	n	n	a
Advisor	n	n	n	X	n	n	a
Engineer	n	n	n	n	X	s	n
Contractor	n	n	n	n	a	X	n
Representative	s	s	s	s	n	n	X

A is the row, B is the column, O = Officer, M = Manager, S = Supervisor, Ad = Advisor, E = Engineer, C = Contractor, and R = Representative. In the cells, a = always, s = sometimes, and n = never.

---

[15] They are either instances of the same class, or they are different names for the same class.

[16] The only remaining combination will mean that object B has an is_a relationship with object A.

To use this table effectively, we look at the columns with at least one *a* and then start with the columns containing the smallest numbers of *a*'s. In this example, it would be the Engineer column. From the table, a Contractor is_a Engineer. The next column with the least *a*'s is Manager. From the table, Supervisor is_a Manager and Officer is_a Manager. Finally, we are ready for the Representative column. If we use the results of the table directly, we have four is_a relationships:

- Officer is_a Representative
- Manager is_a Representative
- Supervisor is_a Representative
- Advisor is_a Representative

However, from earlier is_a relationships, we know that both a supervisor and an officer are also managers. So probably the proper semantics are that Manager is_a Representative and Advisor is_a Representative. Supervisor and Officer inherit this relationship from Manager.

As an exercise, consider adding the following three objects to the table: (1) Jim, who is an Officer; (2) Jack, who is a Supervisor, and (3) Joe, who is an Engineer. When doing this exercise, you should note that the three objects (Jim, Jack, Joe) all satisfy the is_a test.[17]

Object Aggregation

TO VIEW AN OBJECT AS composed of subobjects, each of which operates in a single semantic domain[18] is not the same as viewing an object as consisting of components of objects. To support this second view, another mechanism, *aggregation*, is provided in the object-oriented paradigm. *Aggregation* (or *whole-parts*) is not a new concept to us. Analysts and developers are constantly dealing with aggregate entities consisting of component entities.[19] For example, a purchase order is composed of line items, a weekly timesheet is composed of numerous daily time records, and a system is composed of subsystems made from hardware, software, and so on.

Aggregation, like generalization, has some important properties:[20]

---

[17] We will learn in a later chapter that generalization/specialization is really applied to classes. Jim, Jack, and Joe are instances. Although a case can be made for an instance being a specialization of a class object, the object-oriented paradigm uses a different mechanism to capture this special case: instantiation.

[18] For example, the generalization/specialization view of an object.

[19] Note: The aggregate is the whole, and the components are the parts.

[20] These properties must be satisfied by all instances of an aggregation. Furthermore, when these aggregations are implemented, these properties should be managed. Unfortunately, this is rarely done, because most programming languages do not provide the language mechanisms to support aggregation.

1. **Structural properties**

   The parts must have some structural or functional relationship to the whole of which they are constituents.

2. **Mathematical properties**

   a. Antisymmetry

      If object A is a part of object B, then object B cannot be a part of object A. For example, a purchase order is composed of line items. By antisymmetry, a purchase order is not part of a line item. Note that the line item may be composed of sub–line items. Even in this case, a line item may not be part of a sub–line item.

   b. Transitivity

      If object A is a part of object B and object B is a part of object C, then object A is a part of object C. For example, a purchase order is composed of line items, which may be composed of sub–line items. By transitivity, a sub–line item is also part of the purchase order.

Attributes, relationships, services, and methods are not inherited in aggregation, in contrast to generalization. Because the properties of an aggregation are very weak, aggregation may be either static or dynamic, and a component of an aggregate may also be conditional. A *static aggregation* has fixed (invariant) components and cannot be changed. A *dynamic aggregation* has components that may vary over time. A *conditional component* either is or is not a component of an aggregate, depending on whether a specific condition holds.[21]

Aggregations are very useful. They reduce complexity by treating many objects as one object. They provide a construct or mechanism that better models specific application domain entities (e.g., purchase order) than does a link. Aggregations also ensure the proper visibility (information and service hiding) of the interactions among the components. For example, the individual lights of a traffic signal must be turned on and off in a specific sequence. Thus, the creation of a traffic light object that aggregates the three traffic lights as components will allow modeling the control of the individual components via the aggregate. This is very powerful, as it hides all the complexity from the users of the traffic signal.

Classification of Aggregation

UNFORTUNATELY, BECAUSE THE OBJECT-ORIENTED paradigm has not defined the aggregation mechanism very well, most of us have difficulties applying this mechanism properly in practice. The latest literature on this topic argues that this is due

---

[21] Novices should be very careful with conditional components. They should rarely be used; normally, it is better to capture a variation by specialization (subclassing).

to the fact that aggregation, itself, is an "ancestor" concept. We believe that we need to use the "descendent" concepts (more specialization) to be able to use this mechanism effectively. These descendent concepts, or different kinds of aggregation, will capture additional properties that will help us better manage complexity.

From a theoretical perspective, linguists, logicians, and psychologists have studied the nature of relationships. One of the relationships that has been studied reasonably well is that between parts and the wholes that they make up. In a joint paper, Morton Winston, Roger Chaffin, and Douglas Herrmann discussed this whole-parts relationship. They described several kinds of aggregation (composition or meronymic relationships). In their study, the kind of relationship is determined by the combination of the following basic properties:

- Configuration: whether or not the parts bear a particular functional or structural relationship either to one another or to the whole that they constitute.
- Homeomorphic: whether or not the parts are the same kind of thing as the whole.
- Invariance: whether or not the parts can be separated from the whole.

The paper identified six types of aggregation; we have added a seventh:

1. Assembly-parts (component-integral composition)
2. Material-object composition
3. Portion-object composition
4. Place-area composition
5. Collection-members composition
6. Container-content (member-bunch composition)
7. Member-partnership composition

Assembly-Parts (Component-Integral Composition)

In the assembly-parts aggregation, the whole is comprised of components that maintain their identity even when they are part of the whole. To form an aggregation of this kind, the parts must have a specific functional or structural relationship to one another as well as the whole that they constitute. For example, frames are part of a roll of film, bristles are part of a brush, wheels are part of a car, analytical geometry is part of mathematics. In addition, an integral object (whole) is divided into component parts that are objects in their own right. Furthermore, the components may not be haphazardly arranged, but must bear a particular relationship, either structurally or functionally, with one another and with the whole. Thus, the whole exhibits a patterned structure or organization. Examples include traffic signals, cars, airplanes, toys, machines, and computers.

These items are assembled from parts since, in an assembly-parts aggregation, the assembly does not exist without parts. The whole may be tangible (car, toothbrush, airplane, printer), abstract (mathematics, physics, physiology, accounting, jokes), organizational (NATO, United States, Exxon), or temporal (musical performance, film showing).

However, when a component ceases to support the overall pattern of the object, a different relationship is established. For example, if a memory card is taken out of a computer, the memory card is no longer considered part of the computer. However, the memory card is still considered a computer part or a piece of a computer. Unlike a component, a part or a piece does not participate in the overall pattern of the whole and provides no functional support for the whole. In a component-integral object, a component of the whole can be removed without materially affecting the concept of the whole.

When looking for component-integral object composition in a requirements document, look for the key phrases "is part of" and "is assembled from." Examples of this are as follows:

- A keyboard is part of a computer.
- Nuclear physics is part of physics.
- Windows are parts of a house.
- A piano recital is part of the performance.
- Chairs are parts of the office.
- A telephone is assembled from its parts.
- An orchestra is assembled from its various instrument sections.

As these examples show, it is not difficult to identify assembly-part relationships from a requirements document.

Material-Object Composition

In the material-object aggregation, the parts (materials) lose their identity when they are used to make the whole. In fact, the relationship among parts is no longer known once they become part of the whole. Thus, a material-object composition relationship defines an invariant configuration of parts within the whole, since no part may be removed from the whole. For example, "Bread is made from the following ingredients: flour, sugar, yeast," and "A car is made from materials such as iron, plastic, and glass."

Note that while material-object composition defines what the whole is made of, a component-integral object defines the parts of the whole. For example, to describe a component-integral object relationship we would say, "A car has the following clearly identifiable parts: wheels, engine, doors, and so on." Thus, components can be physically separated from the whole because the relationship is extrinsic. Note that a material-object relationship is not extrinsic; you cannot separate the flour from the bread once the bread is made.

When looking for material-object composition in a requirements document, look for key phrases such as "is partly" and "is made of." Some examples follow:

■ Cappuccino is partly milk.

■ A chair is partly iron.

■ A table is made of wood.

■ A high-rise building is partly steel.

■ Candy is made partly from sugar.

■ Bread is made from flour.

Note that "partly" is not necessary for a material-object relationship. For instance, a mirror may be made of all glass (not "partly" of glass). Furthermore, whether you choose to use the material-object or component-integral object to represent a relationship may be domain-dependent. For example, in most situations one would model the ceramics of a sparkplug as material-object composition. However, if in your problem domain you can separate the ceramic from the spark plug, you will need to use the component-integral object composition to capture the relationship.

Portion-Object Composition

In the portion-object aggregation, the relationship defines a homeomorphic (same kind of thing as the whole) configuration of parts in the whole. Usually, portions of the objects can be identified using standard measures such as inches, millimeters, liters, gallons, hours, or minutes. In this manner, the portion-object composition supports the arithmetic operations of subtraction, addition, multiplication, and division.

When looking for portion-object composition in a requirements document, look for such key phrases as "portion of," "slice," "helping of," "segment of," "lump of," "drop of," "spoonful of." Examples of this are as follows:

■ A slice of bread is a portion of a loaf of bread.

■ A spoonful of cereal is a portion of a bowl of cereal.

■ A second is part of a day.

■ A meter is part of kilometer.

■ A cup of coffee is usually part of a pot of coffee.

When the word "piece" is used, however, care must be taken to ensure that the pieces are similar in nature. For example, a piece of candy is candy, and a piece of rotten apple is apple, but a piece from an exploded car is not a car.

Note that each slice of bread, is considered bread and each cup of coffee is considered coffee. Moreover, both second and day are units of measurement on which you can perform a mix-and-match for the basic arithmetic operations. This observation also holds true for the meter and kilometer units of measurements. However, you may not mix and match seconds with kilometers, because they are different semantic concepts. This similarity between a portion and the whole permits the analyst/designer to allow a portion to selectively inherit properties from the whole. For example, the ingredients in a loaf of bread are the same as in a slice of bread. The component-integral object composition also allows certain properties of the whole to apply to its parts. For example, the velocity of a ball can also be used to imply the velocity of each of its parts.

Place-Area Composition

In the place-area aggregation, the relationship defines a homeomorphic (same kind of thing as the whole) and invariant configuration of parts and the whole. This relationship is commonly used to identify links between places and particular locations within them. Like the portion-object composition, all the places (pieces, slices) must be similar in nature, but they differ in that the places cannot be separated from the area of which they are parts.

When looking for place-area composition in a requirements document, look at the preliminary portion-object composition and ask if this relationship is invariant. If it is, then it is a place-area composition instead of a portion-object composition. Also look at the container-content relationships (see below) and ask, "Are all the contents homeomorphic and also nonremovable." If the answer is yes, again it is a place-area composition instead of a container-content relationship. Some examples follow:

- New York City is part of New York State.
- Los Angeles is part of the United States.
- A peak is part of a mountain.
- A floor is part of a room.
- Yosemite is part of California.

Spend a little extra time to convince yourself that a room as part of a hotel is an example of a place-area composition.

Collection-Members Composition

Collection-members composition is a specialized version of place-area composition. In addition to being a monomeric and invariant configuration of parts within a whole, there is an implied order to its members. One example is an airline reservation with its various flight segments. Here, the order of each flight segment in the itinerary is a very important part of the reservation. Other examples include monthly timesheet—daily timesheets, monthly planner—daily plans; people—organization chart; name—telephone book; name—roledex; file—file cabinet.

When looking for collection-members composition in a requirements document, look at the preliminary place-area composition and ask if this relationship has an implied order. If it does, then it is a collection-members composition instead of a place-area composition.

Container-Content (Member-Bunch Composition)

The member-bunch composition defines a collection of parts as a whole. The parts (contents) bear neither a functional nor a structural relationship to each other or to the whole. Furthermore, the contents are neither homeomorphic nor invariant. The only requirement is that there be a spatial, temporal, or social connection for determining when a member is part of the collection. The container exists and has properties and behaviors of its own. That is, it exists even if there are no contents.

Examples include purchase order—line items; bag—contents of bag; box—contents of box; union—members; company—employees, and so on. In the first example, it is very common for one to place a "blanket" purchase order with no line items. The specific items/works (line items) are added later and there is no implied order in the line items. Furthermore, note that the organization-chart relationship for employee has an implied order and invariant property, while the company—employees relationship is not invariant, nor does it capture any implied order.

This type of aggregation should not be confused with inheritance (classification). For example, "Jason is a human" and "airplane is a transport vehicle" are classifications. Jason possesses all the attributes and provides all the services of a human. Similarly, airplane has all the attributes and provides all the services of a transport vehicle.

The container-content relationship is different. It is usually based on spatial or social connections. For example, to say that a shrub is part of a garden implies that it is within the geographical confines of the garden and probably close to other plants within the garden. Similarly, an employee's being a member of a club implies a social connection. However, for a shrub to be classified as a garden, every shrub would have to be a garden. Similarly, every employee would have to be a club. This relationship has a tendency to be a catch-all for aggregation-type relationships.

Member-Partnership Composition

The member-partnership composition defines an invariant form of the container-content relationship. It defines an invariant collection of parts as a whole.

Examples of this type of relationship include the following:

- Ginger Rogers and Fred Astaire as a dance couple
- Laurel and Hardy as a comedy team
- Jacoby and Myers as attorneys at law
- Lee and Tepfenhart as authors of this book

Members in this relationship may not be removed without destroying the relationship (partnership). For instance, if Laurel leaves Hardy, the comedy team of Laurel and Hardy no longer exists. Hardy can now form a new comedy team with a new partner, but it will be a different partnership.

When looking for member-partnership relationships, review the preliminary list of container-content relationships for invariance. If the relationship is invariant, then make it a member-partnership relationship.

Objects and Aggregation Relationships

Now that we understand aggregations better, we should make two observations about them:

1. An object can be viewed as more than one aggregation. For example, a loaf of bread may be viewed as an aggregate of slices (portion-object composition) and it may be viewed as being made from flour, sugar, yeast, and so on (material-object composition). Both views can be supported simultaneously in the object-oriented paradigm.

2. Transitivity holds only for aggregations of the same kind. For example, the microwave oven is part of a kitchen (component-integral composition) and the kitchen is part of a house (place-area composition). However, the microwave oven is not part of the house. Furthermore, a computer can be an aggregation of a terminal, hardware box, keyboard, and mouse. The hardware box usually comprises of a CPU, memory, hard disk drive, and floppy disk drive. By transitivity, a CPU is part of the computer. However, a terminal is made of glass, silicon, steel, and plastic. This decomposition of the terminal is not the same as the above decomposition of the hardware box.[22] Most of us would not apply the transitivity or antisymmetric properties to the material composition of the terminal in conjunction with the component-integral composition of the computer. At best we would say that the material composition of the computer is a union of the material composition of the parts.

Links Between Objects

GENERALIZATION AND AGGREGATION HELP US capture relationships between objects when we want to view an object as a set of other objects. There are relationships between objects that are not generalizations or aggregations. For example, the marriage relationship between a person and his/her spouse. Certainly, this relationship is not viewed as a generalization. If it were, a person would have to inherit all the in-law relationships of his/her spouse. It is also not an aggregation, in spite of the religious ceremony, as divorces are legal. Thus, we

---

[22] Both of the earlier aggregations are component-integral compositions.

need another mechanism to capture all these other relationships between objects. In the object-oriented paradigm, this "catch-all" relationship is called a *link*.

From a technical perspective, a *link* is a relationship (physical or conceptual) between objects that lets one object know about another object so that one object may request the services of another. However, a link should also have a semantic meaning that is consistent with the semantic domain within which the object resides.

In object-oriented modeling, all links are considered bidirectional.[23] Thus, once a link is established between two objects, each object may request the services of the other. A *role name* uniquely identifies one end of a relationship and provides a vehicle for viewing a relationship as a traversal from one object to a set of associated objects.[24]

The role name allows an object at one end of the relationship to traverse the relationship without explicitly using the relationship name. Role names are necessary for a link (association) between two objects of the same class. For example, in a *supervise* relationship between employees in the class **Employee**, the role names Supervisor and Subordinate would help distinguish between two employees participating in the supervise relationship. Role names are also useful to distinguish multiple links between two objects. For example, consider a manual car wash. The role names from car to employee could be *washer, dryer, waxer, polisher*, and *buffer*. For a specific instance (object) of a **Car** (class), Joe (an instance of **Employee**) is the washer and the buffer, since he both washes and buffs the car.

Furthermore, a link can be binary (between two objects), ternary (between three objects), or higher. In practice, it is rare to find links with a semantic meaning that tie together objects of three different object types (classes).[25]

An *association* describes the set of links between two (or more) objects of a single class or of different classes with the same semantic meaning. Thus, a link may be viewed as an instance of an association. Examples of associations between the same class for class **Person** are married To and works For. Today, with the two-income family, two persons may be married to each other and one of them may also be the supervisor of the other in the workplace. We cannot use one link to capture this situation because the two relationships have different semantic meanings. The couple can get a divorce, but still maintain the same work relationship. An example of an association between two classes is the employment relationship as applied to the classes **Company** and **Person**. That is, "Joe is Employed By Exxon" is an instance of a link in this association. Since every link (and thus, the corresponding association) is bidirectional, "Exxon employs Joe" is the link in the reverse direction.

---

[23] All links are considered bidirectional during modeling. However, in implementation it is not uncommon practice to drop one direction of a link.

[24] *Set* means one or more objects. From an object's perspective, traversing a relationship is an operation that yields the related (associated) objects. Thus, in implementation the role name is a derived attribute whose value is a set of related objects.

[25] An example of a ternary link would be the relation between concert, concert ticket, and attendee.

Because an association is an abstraction of a concept, it may also have attributes and services. It may have the same properties and capabilities as a class.[26] Because we normally do not think of a link as an object, novices should be very careful not to assign attributes of the relationship to one of the classes in the relationship. For example, consider a person's salary. It is normally modeled as an attribute in the class **Person.** However, it is actually an attribute of the employment relationship between the classes **Person** and **Company.** If you still have doubts, consider the case where a person has two jobs with two different employers.

The last example raises a pragmatic point: When does one make salary an attribute of **Person**, and when does one make it an attribute of the association. Theoretically, the correct answer is that salary is an attribute of the association. From a modeling perspective, we recommend that you use what is appropriate for your business situation. To decide which is appropriate requires good engineering judgment. We recommend that you consider the problem domain, future direction of product, and next release features as factors during the analysis phase.[27]

Identifying and Specifying Links and Aggregations

THE BEST SOURCE FOR INITIALLY identifying some of the links (associations) and aggregations is the requirements document. Reread the requirements document and look for situations where one object may be part of another object. These are potential aggregations. Use the suggestions of key phrases and tests described above.

Also, look for links in the requirements document. Links, like services, are often seen as verbs in a requirements document. Phrases that usually imply a link include "which it gets from," "keeps track of," "changes with," and "depends upon." Furthermore, the detailed description of a service is also a source of identifying links. Most objects that need to collaborate (i.e., use services) with other objects and to access these other objects usually require a link.

Other sources to help find links are the event trace diagrams and the behavior specification documents. Each service request from another object must be supported by some access vehicle. If the "handle" is not passed as an argument, then a relationship must be established between the two objects. Care should be given to naming the relationship, usually a link, in a manner that captures its semantic meaning.

When you are studying the behavior specification document, only put in links that have semantic meaning. If you cannot find a good name for the link, consider whether this handle should have been part of the signature (should have been passed to this object from the calling object).

---

[26] However, in many situations, neither the attributes nor the services of the relationship need to be captured in the model.

[27] In design, we need to consider modifiability, reusability, simplicity, and performance.

Remember the following rules to determine whether you have found a link or an object aggregation:

1. An aggregation may not connect an object of one class to another object of the same class. This would violate the antisymmetric property of aggregation. However, a link may connect two objects of the same class. For example, supervise is a relation between two employees (instances) of the class Employee. The most common example given is marriage between two persons. However, this example is flawed since our society does not legally recognize the union of two persons of any gender as a marriage. Marriage in most societies today is a relationship between an instance of class **Female** and an instance of class **Male**. This example, therefore, captures the constraints on the relationship as defined by present societal standards and shows the importance of capturing the link/association upon the correct object or abstraction. Thus, we see how difficult it is to model properly and capture all the implied constraints.

2. Multiple connections between objects are legal. Each connection should be used to capture a distinct semantic meaning. For example, consider sending a car through a manual car wash. Employees are needed to wash, dry, wax, polish, and, finally, buff the car. Every task may be performed by one employee, or each task may be performed be a different employee. If we model these as links to the employees who performed the various tasks, we would have multiple links for an instance (object) of **Employee** (class). For example, Joe could have both washed and buffed the car.

3. Self-associations are possible and common. In this case, role names are essential to capture the relationship accurately.

4. Multiple association does not imply that the same two objects are related twice.

Managing Relationships

ONE OF MOST DIFFICULT TASKS in building an object-oriented model is to determine whether a potential relationship is better captured as an argument in the signature of the service (function), or as a link, aggregation, or generalization/specialization.

The following are some guidelines for this task:

■ If the relationship is permanent (static), then it must be captured as a relationship. Now, what does permanent mean? If you consider a scenario as a unit of time, then permanent means that the relationship needs to be known across scenarios. Note that permanent is a relative term. Basically, if it has to be stored in memory for use by some other independent process, then it is permanent.

■ A relationship must capture some concept that applies to the problem domain or some subdomain that is needed for implementation. In other words, there must be a semantic meaning to the relationship. A service should only traverse (use) the relationship when its usage is consistent with that semantic meaning. For example, consider the link for two Person objects: married_to. Today, with two-income families, it is possible for one spouse to work for another spouse. It would be improper and poor modeling to use the married To relationship to access work-domain services of the other spouse. A second link (works_for) needs to be established to capture this different semantic relationship.

■ If you think you have an aggregation, make sure that all the parts are in the same domain and provide the same functional or structural configuration to the whole. Apply transitivity and antisymmetric tests to check for consistency. Note that transitivity is possible only with aggregations of the same kind. It is very common for novices to mix parts of different kinds of aggregations in one aggregation. This will cause the transitivity test to fail. When this happens, you probably need to look at the parts to see if the are different types of aggregates. For example, consider a building with the following parts: windows, floors, offices, elevators, ceilings, walls, stairs, meeting rooms, cafeteria, atrium, sundry shop. If you put all these parts into one aggregation, you have mixed parts from two different semantic aggregations. The offices, floors (meaning one level in a building), meeting rooms, cafeteria, atrium and sundry shop are defining a functional configuration of the building; while the windows, floors (meaning the physical floor), ceilings, and walls are defining a structural configuration of the building. These parts must be captured in two different aggregations because they have different semantics.

■ An aggregation may not connect two objects of the same kind to each other. This would violate the antisymmetric property of aggregation. For example, a person may not be an aggregate of other persons. However, a link may connect two objects of the same kind. For example, supervise is a relationship between two employees (instances) that is valid.

■ Aggregation is often confused with topological inclusion. Topological inclusion is a relationship between a container, area, or temporal duration and that which is contained by it. For example, (1) the customer is in the room, (2) the meeting is in the evening, and (3) Monument Valley is in Arizona and Utah. In each case, the subject is surrounded by the container; however, it is not part of the container in any meaningful semantic domain. For example, a customer is not part of a room, nor is a meeting part of an evening. Furthermore, no part of Monument Valley is Arizona or Utah, because it is part of the Navaho reservation. Topological inclusion is most commonly confused with place-area composition. Note that every part of Dallas is in Texas, while no part of Monument Valley is in Arizona.

- Sometimes, novices confuse attributes with aggregation. Attributes describe the object as a whole (a black box approach); aggregation describes the parts that make the whole (white box approach). Thus, a house may have attributes such as width, length, and height, but it is made from wood, glass, bricks, and so on.

- Attachment of one object to another object does not guarantee aggregation. Certainly toes are attached to the feet, and they are part of the feet; however, earrings are attached to the ear, but they are not part of the ear. Note that toes provide functional support to the feet, while earrings do not supply any functional or structural support.

- Ownership may also be confused with aggregation. Certainly a car has wheels, and wheels are part of a car. However, the fact that James has a car does not imply that the car is part of James. Thus, ownership is captured by a link.

- Multiple links between objects are legal. Each link should be used to capture a distinct semantic meaning. (See the car wash example for Joe.)

Documenting Relationships

NEARLY EVERY MAJOR OBJECT-ORIENTED methodologist has his/her own way of documenting classes, objects, relationships, and behaviors. It is our opinion that nearly all the techniques are similar and that their differences are not as substantial as we are led to believe. We have chosen to use UML's notation to document the relationships. The notation templates are shown Figure 8-1.

In a generalization diagram, we see that a class is represented by a rectangular icon, and the generalization/specialization is drawn as a solid line from the specialized class to the generalized class with a large triangular arrowhead on the generalized class end. Normally, the specialization classes of the same parent are different alternatives in the same semantic domain and provide for a partitioning of the parent class; however, some applications require that we use specialization in several dimensions simultaneously; in these cases, UML allows a discriminator label to be attached to a generalization arc. Arcs with the same label represent specialization in the same dimension. Different dimensions represent orthogonal abstract ways of describing an object of the parent class. Though UML notation doesn't preclude the concepts of multiple classification and dynamic classification, it does not explicitly support these concepts.

Aggregation is a special form of association that deals with the composition of the aggregator class. In an aggregation diagram, a class is represented by a rectangular icon, and the aggregation is drawn as solid lines from the aggregates (parts) to the aggregator (whole) with a diamond arrowhead on the aggregator's end. The multiplicity of the aggregator may be one, many, and optionally one. Multiplicity is captured by using a text expression. The expression is a comma-separated list of integer ranges. A range is indicated by an integer (the lower value), two dots, and an integer (the upper value); a single integer and the symbol '*' are also legal ranges. The symbol '*' indicates any number, including none.

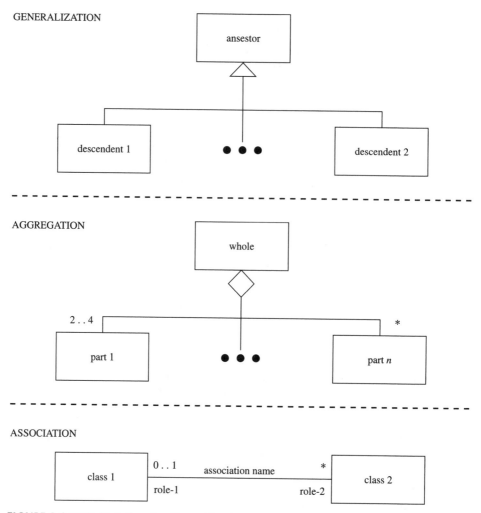

GENERALIZATION

AGGREGATION

ASSOCIATION

FIGURE 8-1 UML Notation for Generalization, Aggregation, and Association

In an association diagram, classes are represented by rectangular icons, and a binary association is represented by a straight solid line between two rectangular icons.[28] An association may have a name with an optional small "direction arrow" (solid triangle with no tail) showing how to read the association. The

---

[28] Ternary relationships are drawn using an additional diamond icon to tie the lines together. This diamond icon is also used for all other higher-order relationships. An association that needs to be a class is captured as a class, and its association with the relation is shown with a dashed line from the class icon for the association to the association (solid line) between the two classes participating in the association.

name is placed on or adjacent to the association line.[29] The association name may be omitted if role names are used. At each end of an association is a *role*. Each role may have a name that describes how its class is viewed by the other class(es); this is called the *role name*. The role names opposite a class must be unique. The role name is placed next to the end of the line and adjacent to the class icon. The role also determines the multiplicity of its class, that is, the number of instances of the class that can be associated with one instance of the other class. Multiplicity is captured by using a text expression. The expression is a comma-separated list of integer ranges. A range is indicated by an integer (the lower value), two dots, and an integer (the upper value); a single integer and the symbol '*' are also legal ranges. The symbol '*' indicates any number including none. If the multiplicity is more than one, the keyword {ordered} may be placed on the role, indicating that the instances in the association have an explicit order.

Recommended Approach

OUR STEPS FOR FINDING RELATIONSHIPS are as follows:

1. Get a list of potential objects that may be involved in generalization.
2. Create a table of these objects for the is_a test.
3. Fill in the cells of the table, using only *always*, *sometimes*, and *never*.
4. Use the table to find all the generalizations. Remember to eliminate the instantiations.
5. Draw a hierarchial diagram of the generalizations between classes, using UML notation.
6. Reread the requirements document and look for aggregations and links (associations). Use the key phrases given earlier as clues to finding these relationships.
7. Look for role names, which appear as nouns in most requirements documents. Although many object-oriented authors have stated that role names are optional, we strongly recommend using them. It is often easier and less confusing to assign role names instead of, or in addition to, relationship names.
8. Reread the specifications for all the services and identify the relationships needed to support those services. By rereading each service, the analyst/developer will be able to refine what must be done in each of the object services.
9. If the sequence diagrams, use-case model, and behavior specifications are documented, read these documents to find additional links.

---

[29] In theory, an association may have different names in each direction. We do not recommend trying to name associations in both directions.

10. Determine whether each potential relationship is better captured as an argument in the signature of the service (function), or as a link, aggregation, or generalization/specialization.

11. Document the results using UML notation.

Example

LET US RETURN TO OUR lawn-mowing example. Based on the previous analysis, we have the following objects: John, Jane, Peter, Paul, Elizabeth (Lisa), Mary, Jack, and ProfessionalLawnMower. We will discuss generalization in the next chapter. So now after reviewing the requirements document and the behavior specifications, we realize that capturing the family and its relationships is useful to this application. Figure 8-2 and Figure 8-3 illustrate object aggregations and links that we consider useful in our example. The objects are represented by underlining the name in compliance with the UML specification. The design of the UML association diagram and aggregation diagram is described in the next chapter.

In this example, Jane has access to John's services via the is-married link. John has access to all the children's services via the father/child links. Mary has access to Jack via the lawn-mowing link. Mary's sibling link, mother/child link and father/child link are permanent; they always apply over time. These are called *static* (and invariant) *relationships*.

However, Mary's lawn-mowing link with Jack is less permanent. Mary may choose to change to another professional lawn mower at any time. However, her relationship with a professional lawn mower may be permanent in that there is some professional lawn mower that she uses. In such a case, we consider the link static and variant. In the next chapter, we use the links to define associations, and we use the object aggregation to define class aggregation.

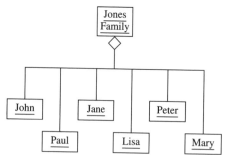

FIGURE 8-2 Aggregation Diagram for the Lawn-Mowing Example

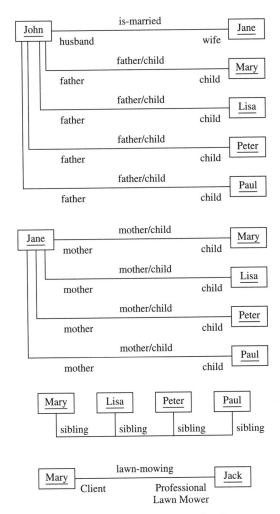

**FIGURE 8-3 Association Diagram for the
Lawn-Mowing Example**

■ ■ SUMMARY

Our steps for finding relationships are as follows:

1. Get a list of potential objects that may be involved in generalization.
2. Create a table of these objects for the is_a test.
3. Fill in the cells of the tables, using only *always*, *sometimes*, and *never*.

4. Use the table to find all the generalizations. Remember to eliminate the instantiations.

5. Draw a hierarchial diagram of these generalizations between classes, using UML notation.

6. Reread the requirements document and look for aggregations and links (associations). Use the key phrases given earlier as clues to finding these relationships.

7. Look also for role names. They appear as nouns in most requirements documents. Although many object-oriented authors have stated that role names are optional, we strongly recommend using them. It is often easier and less confusing to assign role names instead of, or in addition to, relationship names.

8. Reread the specifications for all the services and identify the relationships needed to support those services. By rereading each service, the analyst/developer will be able to refine what must be done in each of the object services.

9. If the event trace diagrams and the behavior specifications are documented, read these documents to find additional links.

10. Determine whether each potential relationship is better captured as an argument in the signature of the service (function), or as a link, an aggregation, or a generalization/specialization.

11. Document the results via some graphic notation.

Rules

What we have presented so far is a collection of mechanisms integrated into a consistent paradigm that helps us to manage the complexity of the procedural aspects of functional modeling.[1] However, there are aspects of an application/system that are nonprocedural (declarative) and are better modeled using other mechanisms. In this chapter, we discuss how the object-oriented paradigm can be extended to include the capability to manage declarative aspects of an application.

---

[1] Functional modeling has two aspects: procedural and declarative.

Introduction

THE CONCEPTS OF ABSTRACTION, ENCAPSULATION, inheritance, relationship, and polymorphism in object-oriented methods support the design and implementation of sophisticated procedural applications. Most object-oriented methods are presently based on the assumption that all aspects of the application/system will be modeled within the procedural paradigm.

However, some applications may have requirements given in a declarative manner.[2] When this occurs, the handling of the declarative semantics[3] (rules and facts) is left to the analyst/developer. One of the most difficult tasks for developers is transforming declarative statements into the procedural paradigm. It is very natural for developers to incorporate these declarative statements across the methods of various classes. However, when a declarative statement affects several methods, especially across multiple classes, it must be written in several places. This is not a good practice because (1) there is a transformation of declarative semantics into procedural semantics, and (2) it creates hidden coupling between methods. The first reason makes the model less readily understandable and violates the goal of modeling reality the way the domain experts see it. The second reason makes maintaining and changing the model very difficult.

Applications tend to grow; as they grow, developers encounter more situations in which declarative statements have been distributed across methods. Soon, the model becomes unmaintainable. For example, maintaining an invariant involving two objects may require that similar but not identical tests be inserted a variety of places within the code. This leads to errors of omission and logic by analysts, designers, and programmers as the application is extended. Because the invariant is not in one place, it is never explicitly stated. Unstated assumptions make modifications of code difficult and error-prone. We need both a method and a mechanism to handle declarative statements.

The needed implementation mechanism is a *data-driven mechanism*. This mechanism simplifies the task of maintaining model integrity in two important ways. First, it enables invariants and constraints to be stated explicitly in a single place, rather than having them scattered in multiple places. This makes the model (and thus code) easier to understand and modify. Second, because it is data-driven, invariants and constraints are reevaluated *automatically* whenever relevant changes are made to an object's attribute. This relieves the analyst/programmer of the burden of explicitly incorporating data-integrity rules into the procedural logic. The application's procedural logic is no longer cluttered with code for maintaining model integrity.

---

[2] We can distinguish between declarative and procedural languages or statements. Most of us have worked with procedural programming languages. They give us the constructs so that we can write a set of instructions that must be executed sequentially. The sequence may vary depending on conditions tested, and a group of instructions may be executed repetitively. However, declarative languages declare a set of facts and rules. They do not specify the sequence of steps for doing the processing.

[3] Declarative semantics are written with rules and facts.

The data-driven mechanism is important because many of our declarative requirements are given to us in a data-driven manner. This gives us a way to capture reality as domain experts see it—without the need to transform a declarative requirement (or solution) into a purely procedural model. Declarative statements are usually written at a higher level of abstraction than procedural statements. Implementing declarative statements using this mechanism frees the analyst, designer, and programmer from having to manage flow of control for these statements.

Rules

RULES CAPTURING DECLARATIVE SEMANTICS ARE employed for a variety of purposes, such as enforcing invariants in a domain model, auditing complex data structures, monitoring the state of a state machine, or checking constraints while a user inputs data. There are all kind of rules: some are best captured directly in the classical object-oriented paradigm, while others are better captured via other mechanisms.

One kind of rule that is better captured via another mechanism is the *data-driven rule*. This is due to the property that it requires a mechanism to act as a "monitor" of the model while it observes changes to an object's attributes and reacts when a condition is satisfied. Many applications naturally require this capability. Examples are (1) applications that monitor a physical system, (2) applications that apply business policies or engineering guidelines, and (3) software development tools.

The data-driven mechanism is well suited to handling rules that monitor things. It supports the situation–action directive without complicating an application's procedural logic. It also satisfies two very important goals of the object-oriented paradigm: (1) the model should be built to reflect the way the domain experts see reality, and (2) whenever possible, the code for the application should be generated from a model that is easy for the domain experts and the end users to understand.

To satisfy the above two goals, declarative statements (including rules) need to be rigorous. They must be understandable to the end users, so that they can verify that the rules correctly represent business policies and desired application/system behavior. Thus, declarative statements, including rules, should be written in structured English.

Identifying Declarative Statements

DECLARATIVE STATEMENTS ARE DIFFERENT FROM procedural statements. Identifying declarative statements in a requirements document is relatively simple. While procedural statements are always part of a specified sequence (e.g., a procedure, an activity, or a task), a declarative statement stands alone. A declarative statement is independent of any sequence of other statements. It declares a *fact* or a *rule*.

A *fact* statement may be expressed in various ways. The following are all examples of facts:

■   A record

Book	Author(s)	Publisher
Object-Oriented Analysis	Coad/Yourdon	Yourdon Press
UML and C++: A Practical Guide to Object-Oriented Development	Lee/Tepfenhart	Prentice Hall

■   A set of values in a spreadsheet
■   A plain statement (e.g., All surgeons are medical doctors.)
■   A stand-alone equation:

MIN_MONTHLY_PAYMENT = (PRINCIPAL * INTEREST_RATE)/ 12

Rules usually capture information about how the business should operate. Rules encapsulate business knowledge. Common key phrases in declarative statements that indicate a rule are the following:

■   It must always hold that . . .
■   It must always be true that . . .
■   Under all conditions, when . . . then . . .
■   Under all conditions, if . . . then . . .
■   When . . . if . . . then . . .
■   . . . if only . . .
■   . . . is correct only if . . .

A rule may be used as a declarative requirement to

■   enforce *"things that should always be true"* (invariants),
■   detect *"things that should never be true"* (constraint violations),
■   maintain the integrity of your domain model,
■   monitor for and react to important events,
■   express domain knowledge (*business policies, engineering rules,* and *situation–action heuristics*),
■   specify an operation (function) that would have to be used in many methods, and
■   exploit the data-driven or event-driven nature of rules.

Specifying and Documenting Rules

WHEN A REQUIREMENT IS WRITTEN as a declarative statement, the best practice is to specify it as a rule.[4] A technique that captures rules explicitly and makes them easy to read[5] is structured English. The details of the constructs available in structured English must wait until after the classification of (business) rules.

James Martin has constructed the following classification scheme for rules. His scheme describes the following types of rules:

- *Integrity rules* state that something must always be true (e.g., a value for an attribute must be in the integer range from 1 to 5).

- *Derivation rules* state how a value (or set of values) is computed (e.g., Tax Withheld = Federal Income Tax + State Income Tax).

- *Behavior rules* describe the dynamic aspects of behavior, such as what conditions must be true for an action to performed (e.g., when the door is open, the light in the oven is turned on).

To facilitate mapping these rules into the object-oriented paradigm, we can further refine James Martin's rule categories. Our categories are as follows:

1. *Data integrity* rules state that something must be true about an attribute(s) (e.g., a value for an attribute must be in the integral range from 1 to 5).

2. *Relationship integrity* rules state that something must be true about a relationship (e.g., a manager may not supervise more than ten employees).

3. *Derivation rules,* including facts, state how a value or set of values is computed (PRICE = 1.5 * COST).

4. *Service precondition* rules state that something must be true before a service will be performed (e.g., a cash advance will not be given unless it is past the fifth of the month).

5. *Service postcondition* rules state that something must be true after a service is performed (e.g., order Product is correctly completed only if the supplier is an approved vendor).

6. *Action trigger* rules define the causal relationship between events and actions (e.g., when an order is accepted, send the bill immediately).

---

4   Facts can be expressed as rules very easily. They will be derivation rules. Derivation rules are explained below.

5   Ideally, we want a technique that captures rules explicitly in a manner that is easy to read and will generate the correct code.

7. *Data trigger* rules define the causal relationship between an attribute's condition and an action (e.g., when the stock is below reorder level, then reorder).

8. *Control-condition* rules handle situations where multiple triggers are involved in the rule (e.g., if the product has been sent and the money received or if the purchase order has been canceled and the deposit returned, then the purchase order is closed).

Based on our classification scheme, the constructs in structured English shown in Figure 9-1 capture the rules. In these constructs, a condition is a Boolean expression, an event is a stimulus (signal), and an action is an invocation of a procedural statement.

Mapping Rules to the Proper Object-Oriented Concepts

IN THE 1980S ARTIFICIAL INTELLIGENCE systems became highly fashionable. The mechanism on which these systems were built was primarily an *inference engine*. An inference engine processes a collection of facts and rules to make deductions using logical inference. The rules an inference engine processes are called *production rules*. Most of us understand declarative semantics from this perspective.

1. For triggers and control conditions,

   IF condition THEN action

   or

   WHEN event IF condition THEN action

2. For integrity rules,

   IT MUST ALWAYS BE THAT statement of fact

   or

   IT MUST ALWAYS BE THAT IF condition THEN action

3. For service precondition,

   BEFORE service that is to be performed IT MUST BE THAT fact

4. For service postcondition,

   AFTER service that has been performed IT MUST BE THAT fact

5. For derivation rules, fact, usually an equation

   or

   WHEN condition or event THEN action

   or

   IF condition or event THEN action

FIGURE 9-1 Structured English Constructs

However, the rules discussed in this chapter are not production rules.[6] They are rules linked with the object-oriented model to provide a meaningful and useful model for implementation.

The mapping guidelines for taking a rule into an OO concept are as follows:

1. Service precondition
   A service precondition is mapped onto a service. As suggested by Meyers, the precondition is a requirement that should be guaranteed by the calling object.[7]

2. Service postcondition
   A service postcondition is also mapped onto a service. It is a rule that must be checked by the author of this service. The service must guarantee that the postcondition is satisfied.

3. Control condition
   A control condition is mapped onto a finite state machine. It is usually a condition needed for a change of state.

4. Action trigger
   An action trigger is mapped onto a finite state machine. It is usually an event in a state transition diagram.

5. Relationship integrity
   A relationship integrity is mapped onto a relationship. It normally affects the instantiation, deletion of, and addition to a relationship.

6. Data integrity or data trigger
   Data integrity and data triggers are mapped onto an attribute. Normally, they are checked every time the attribute changes value.

7. Derivation
   A derivation is difficult to map. It is usually used as part of a method. However, there are situations where it is implemented as a trigger. Care must be taken when you have a derivation rule.

---

[6] An inference engine may be used to implement a method in a class; however, we do not recommend this technique.

[7] Meyers says that "one of the main sources of complexity in programs is the constant need to check whether data passed to a processing element (method) satisfy the requirements for correct processing. Where should these checks be performed: in the method itself or in its client? Unless class designers formally agree on a precise distribution of responsibilities, the checks end up not being done at all, a very unsafe situation or, out of concern for safety, being done several times.

"Redundant checking may seem harmless, but it is not. It hampers efficiency, of course; but even more important is the conceptual pollution that it brings to software systems. Complexity is probably the single most important enemy of software quality. The distribution of redundant checks all over a software system destroys the conceptual simplicity of the system, increases the risk of error, and hampers such qualities as extensibility, understandability, and maintainability.

"The recommended approach is to systematically use preconditions, and then allow the service author to assume when writing the method that the corresponding precondition is satisfied. The aim is to permit a simple style of programming, favoring readability, maintainability, and other associated qualities."

Documenting the Rules Using UML

THE DOCUMENTING GUIDELINES FOR THE various rules are as follows:

1. Service precondition
    A service precondition is mapped onto a service. This needs to be cap-
    tured as part of the entrance criteria. If there is an *operation specification*
    for the service, use the precondition section of the operational specifi-
    cation to document this. If not, include this as a comment in the
    method description.
2. Service postcondition
    A service postcondition is also mapped onto a service. If an operation
    specification is written for the service, use the postconditions section to
    document this. The postconditions must also be included in the
    method description.
3. Control condition
    A control condition is mapped onto a finite state machine. It is usually
    a condition needed for a change of state. This is documented as a
    guard condition in UML.
4. Action trigger
    An action trigger is mapped onto a finite state machine. It is usually an
    event in a state transition diagram. This is documented as an event in
    UML.
5. Relationship integrity
    A relationship integrity is mapped onto a relationship. It normally
    affects the instantiation, deletion of, and addition to a relationship.
    This is documented as a constraint in UML.
6. Data integrity or data trigger
    Data integrity and data triggers are mapped onto an attribute. Nor-
    mally, they are checked every time the attribute changes value. This is
    best documented by creating a new stereotype, called "data trigger,"
    which is used to capture the actions associated with the rule(s). Then
    artificial associations are drawn between the classes that need data
    triggers and the data trigger class.
7. Derivation
    A derivation is documented as part of the method.

Implementing Rules

THE MAPPING GUIDELINES GIVEN ABOVE show that service precondition rules, service postcondition rules, control-condition rules, action triggers, and derivation
rules map very nicely into the classical object-oriented model. However, relationship integrity rules, data integrity rules, and data triggers are not well supported
in our model. To handle these rules, we need a data-driven mechanism. There are
two ways to supply a data-driven mechanism:

1. Use the triggers in the database system.
    Using triggers in the database system is the classical method of handling data integrity and data trigger rules. Every time the database recognizes a change in data value, it triggers a routine written by the user. The appropriate rules are implemented in that routine. This is reasonably straightforward for simple data-driven rules, but it is a little more tricky for complex rules (such as relationship constraints).

2. Use a language that extends C++ to include rules.
    At AT&T Bell Laboratories, researchers and developers have created a new language with constructs that directly support the data-driven mechanisms. This language is R++. R++ is an extension to C++ that bridges the gap between object-oriented procedural semantics and data-driven rules. C++ classes contain two kinds of members: data members and member functions. R++ extends the C++ class construct with a new kind of member, a rule.[8] This enables object-oriented applications to employ data-driven computation. As an extension to C++, R++ fits comfortably with C++ concepts and practices. R++ rules are relatively easy to learn, since the syntax is similar and the behavior is much like that of a "reactive" member function.

An R++ rule is syntactically defined as follows:

> rule *class-name* :: *rule-name* {*condition* => *action* }.

The condition-action pair behaves as an if-then statement:

> if *condition*   then *action*s.

The action is automatically executed when the condition evaluates to true. The system monitors the data members appearing in the rule's condition, and when a data member changes its data values, it creates a trigger event. The trigger event causes the rule to reevaluate the condition, taking into account new/ changed data. If the condition is satisfied, the rule "fires." (When a rule fires, the action is executed.)

Within the condition, part of the rule existential quantifiers (*all* and *exists*) and logical operators (*and* and *or*) are supported. Existential qualifiers and logical operators are used to form compound conditions. In addition, the language supports accessing related objects (thus their associated services) via a concept called *binding*. Service calls (function calls) are also supported in the condition.

Recommended Approach

WHEN DECLARATIVE STATEMENTS APPEAR IN the requirements document, the following steps are recommended:

---

[8]   What R++ calls rules are really only data-driven rules.

1. Separate the declarative statements from the procedural statements.
2. Restate the declarative statements in structured English as rules, taking care that the rules are rigorous and implementable.
3. Map the rules onto the appropriate OO mechanism.
4. If data-driven rules are used, employ a data-driven mechanism to model these rules. We recommend R++ over using database triggers.

■ ■ SUMMARY

Declarative statements, or rules, are another natural form in which domain experts and end users state their requirements. We, as analysts and developers, should accept declarative statements as a natural part of textual requirements. It follows that declarative statements should be captured within a model. To do this, we must translate the textual declarative requirements into structured English to assure that we have rigorous and implementable requirements. After stating all the declarative requirements in structured English, we should map each declarative statement into a rule category. The rule category allows each statement to be properly assigned to the appropriate object-oriented mechanism in the model.

Because not every rule category could be assigned to a classical object-oriented mechanism, we introduced the data-driven mechanism. This mechanism supports rules triggered by a change in the value of an attribute. As discussed, this is a very valuable extension to the object-oriented paradigm. Historically, triggers in a database system were used to implement this mechanism. However, documenting database trigger functions and getting people to read the documentation were not easily accomplished. An alternative approach was developed at AT&T Bell Laboratories. Researchers and developers chose to extend the C++ language to provide a data-driven mechanism as an integral part of the language. This solution is highly desirable, since we can see all the code in one place.

As with any tool, data-driven rules are good for some tasks and not as effective for others. We recommend them for the following:

- ■ Enforcing invariants
- ■ Maintaining data integrity
- ■ Maintaining relationship integrity
- ■ Detecting constraint violations
- ■ Stating business policies and engineering guidelines

A data-driven rule is like a demon that constantly monitors attributes and reacts when appropriate. The action portion of the code sits apart from the routine procedural code and is automatically triggered by relevant changes in the objects the rule monitors. This relieves the analyst/developer from designing and programming explicit control for the data-driven rule.

CHAPTER **10**

The Model

The sublime and the ridiculous are often so nearly related, that it is difficult to class them separately. One step above the sublime, makes the ridiculous; and one step above the ridiculous, makes the sublime again.

■ Tom Paine

At the end of our fourth step, we actually built an integrated model of the system. If we had executed each step perfectly, we would have our model. Unfortunately, the substeps and guidelines are not adequate to guarantee this result. In fact, the weakness in our method is its inability to help an analyst/ developer identify abstract classes.[1] In the fifth step, we will help you find these classes. This is the refinement phase of our method.

---

[1] This is the inherent weakness in all object-oriented methods. Now we know why people say objects are hard to find. Since abstract classes capture concepts from our minds, we do not anticipate a technique in the foreseeable future that will help us capture conception.

Concepts

ALTHOUGH MOST OF US WILL tell you that the strength of object-oriented technology is that it gives you the mechanism to model reality, in fact it is not an approach that models reality. Anyone who has studied philosophy knows that reality is the state of mind of each individual. So what is object-oriented technology really doing? It models people's understanding and processing of reality by capturing the concepts they have acquired. Thus, a vital part of learning this technology is acquiring an understanding of what a concept is and how it is used in object-oriented analysis.

Each concept is a particular idea or understanding that a person has of the world. We know that we have a concept when we can apply it successfully to surrounding things/objects. For example, a car and a telephone are widely held and understood concepts. We can certainly apply them to things/objects and determine if a thing/object is an instance of a car, a telephone, or neither.

The formation of concepts helps us organize the reality of our world. Psychologists believe that babies start life in a world of confusion and gradually acquire concepts to reduce the confusion. For example, at a very young age a baby learns to differentiate between the sounds of its mother and father.

Humans seem to possess an innate ability to perceive regularities and similarities among the many objects in the world. Every time we recognize these regularities and similarities, we create a concept to organize them. Eventually, we develop concepts (e.g., red and car) and learn to combine concepts to form new concepts (i.e., red car). As we grow older, we construct more elaborate conceptual constructs that lead to increased semantic meaning, precision, and subtleties.

Because we define them, the concepts we form and use are indeed varied. Concepts may be *concrete* (person, car, table, house), *intangible* (time, quality, company), or *relational* (marriage, partnership, supervision, ownership). They may indicate *roles* (mother, programmer, teacher, student), *events* (sale, interrupt, collision, takeoff), *displayables* (string, icon, video), *judgments* (high pay, good example, excellent job), and other things (signal, atom, gnome, tooth fairy).

These concepts serve as mental lenses with which we try to make sense of and reason about objects in our world. For example, the concept of person helps us reason about several billion objects on this earth. New concepts may (1) help us perceive the same objects in a different way, (2) help us reason about an existing object in a different manner, and (3) add new objects to our awareness. For example, the concept of employee helps us reason in a new way about people. The concept of atomic particle adds new objects to our awareness, and particle spin as it applies to an atomic particle helps us reason about an existing object in a different manner.

People can possess concepts about things that have existed, do exist, may exist, and probably will not exist. Two concepts, Santa Claus and Fairy Godmother, are objects for some people, yet they are not for others. Concepts like total world peace do not apply to anything today, but this may not be so in the future. It is highly unlikely that the concept of perpetual motion will apply to anything today or in the future. People also form concepts for which no objects exist. For example, many people have a concept of a perfect mate, yet no object has passed the concept's test.

Concepts and Object-Oriented Model

BY DEFINITION, A PRIVATELY HELD idea or understanding is called a conception. When that idea or understanding is shared by others, it becomes a concept. To communicate with others, we must share our individually held conceptions and arrive at mutually agreed upon concepts. For example, if your conception of a car is only a 1970 silver Lamborghini and your spouse's conception of a car is a family station wagon, you may want to come to a common understanding on the concept of a car before the family goes car shopping.

The process of object-oriented analysis is really the process of capturing a set of shared concepts among domain experts, users, managers, and developers. These concepts underlie every organizational process, define a shared organizational reality, and form the basis for an organizational language that is used for communication.

To help specify these concepts, the object-oriented paradigm has the following basic mechanisms: class, association, aggregation, generalization/specialization, polymorphism, and instantiation. In later chapters, we will add mechanisms to support concepts that deal with dynamic behavior and to deal with rules. Since this is a living technology, more mechanisms are being developed to provide better support for modeling concepts that are needed to help us better manage complexity. In this section of the book we review these basic mechanisms.

Class

A class describes a group of objects with identical attributes, common behavior, common relationships (link and aggregation), and common semantics. Examples of classes are person, employee, timesheet, company, and department. Each object in a class will have the same attributes and behavior patterns. Most objects get their individuality by having different values for their attributes and having different objects in their relationships. However, objects with identical attribute values and/or identical relational objects are allowed.

The important key to placing two objects in the same class is that they share a common semantic purpose in the application domain, beyond the fact that they have the same attributes, common relationships, and common behaviors. For example, consider a grain silo and a cow. If these were objects in a financial application, the only two attributes of importance might be age and cost, and both the silo and the cow might actually be in the same class of farm assets. However, if the application were a farming application, then it is unlikely that the silo and the cow would be in the same class. Thus, interpreting the semantics depends on the application and the judgment of the domain expert.

Association

An association describes a group of links with common structure and semantics. An association is a way to capture the links between objects in a meaningful way via their classes (object types). An association describes a set of potential links in the same way that a class describes a set of potential objects. In object-oriented modeling, all links, and thus all associations, are considered as bidirectional. Once a link is established between two objects, each object may request the services of the other. However, the proper usage of the association should require that the association (i.e., the links) be used only to access services consistent with the semantic meaning of the association. In theory, an association can be binary (between two classes), ternary (among three classes), or some higher order. In practice, most associations are binary.

Class Aggregation

A class aggregation describes a group of *object aggregations* with common structure and semantics. Thus, class aggregation is a way to capture the object aggregations between objects in a meaningful way via their classes (object types). Examples of aggregation are purchase order, with its associated line items, and a timesheet with its associated hourly accounting. Although many aggregations are implemented as unidirectional, in analysis these relationships should be considered as bidirectional.

An aggregation may be either static or dynamic, and a component of an aggregate may also be conditional. A *static aggregation* has fixed components that cannot be changed. A *dynamic aggregation* has components that may vary over time. A *conditional component* either is or is not a component of an aggregate, depending on whether a specific condition holds.

Aggregation has become such a useful mechanism for analysis that seven distinct kinds of aggregation have been identified:

- Assembly-parts (component-integral) composition
- Material-object composition
- Portion-object composition
- Place-area composition
- Collection-members composition
- Container-content (member-bunch) composition
- Member-partnership composition

These were described in chapter 8.

Generalization/Specialization

Generalization is an abstraction mechanism for sharing similarities among classes while preserving their differences.[2] Generalization is the relationship between a class and one or more refined versions of that class. The class being refined is

---

[2]   In most object-oriented languages, including C++, this is implemented using inheritance.

called the *superclass*[3] and each refined version is called a *subclass*.[4] For example, an aircraft has a manufacturer, identification number, weight, and cost. A helicopter, which also has propellers, and a jet fighter, which also has missiles, are refined versions of an aircraft. Generalization gives us the capability to define the features of an aircraft once and then just add the additional features for helicopter and jet fighter. In our example, the aircraft is the superclass, and the helicopter and jet fighter are the subclasses.

Attributes, relationships, and services with the same semantic meaning are attached to the superclass and inherited by the subclasses. Each subclass inherits all the attributes, services, and relationships of the superclass. For example, the jet fighter inherits the attributes, manufacturer, identification number, weight, and cost from the aircraft. *It inherited the attributes and not the values.* The jet fighter must determine its own values for these attributes. Generalization is commonly called the is_a relationship because each instance of a subclass is also an instance of the superclass.

Generalization is transitive across any number of levels of generalization. The term *ancestors* refers to the generalization of classes across multiple levels. An instance of a subclass is simultaneously an instance of all its ancestor classes. Furthermore, the subclass includes values for every attribute of every ancestor class and relational objects for each relationship in its ancestral classes. In addition, all the services and associated methods of all the ancestral classes may be applied to the subclass.

Each subclass not only inherits all of the above, but usually adds specific attributes, relationships (associations and maybe aggregations), and services with their associated methods as well. In our example, the jet fighter added missiles as an attribute and probably fireMissile as a service. This attribute and service are not shared by other aircraft.

Polymorphism

One of the goals of OO technology is to reuse code; generalization is one of the most effective ways to facilitate code reuse. However, some methods may need to be tailored to meet business needs. When such tailoring is required for a subclass, object-oriented technology has a mechanism, called *polymorphism*, that allows the subclass to have a method (behavior) that replaces its superclass's method for a specific service. Thus, when that service is requested from an instance of the subclass, the subclass method is invoked. However, when the service is requested from other instances (assuming no other subclass has also made a replacement method for this service), the superclass method is invoked.

For example, consider this simple example. We have class *Employee* that has a subclass *Executive*. From a modeling perspective, an executive is also an employee. One of the services that applies to all employees is payRaise. For all

---

[3]   Called a *base class* in C++.

[4]   Called a *derived class* in C++.

employees, the pay raise is the employee's salary multiplied by the annual inflation. This has been the corporate policy for the last ten years. With generalization,
this has worked very well. Each year at raise time, the payRaise service is invoked
for all employees, including the executives. Even though executives are employees, the directors of the corporation decided that executive pay raises should be
computed differently than for the rest of the employees. Executive pay raises are
five times the annual inflation rate plus a bonus of 15% of the gross revenue.

What mechanism does object-oriented technology have for handling this situation? In this situation, the subclass Executive can have a method that replaces
Employee's payRaise method every time this service is requested for an executive. Although these methods are different, they accomplish the same business
purpose (have the same semantics of payRaise). This phenomenon is known as
polymorphism. The method that gets invoked depends on the class of the object.
Thus, the employee and executive example can be captured by making the
payRaise service polymorphic.[5]

Instantiation

Instantiation is a mechanism in the object-oriented paradigm by which we can create instances of a class. These instances (objects) are the keepers of the data that
will make our application/system work. This mechanism is one of the vehicles
that we use to make our model dynamic.

Refining the Model

THE STEPS FOR REFINEMENT ARE as follows:

1. Group all objects with the same attributes, similar relationships, and
    common behavior. If there is a concept within the application domain
    that defines these objects, use that name for the class. If not, ask the
    domain expert what concept this may resemble. Use the class that the
    domain expert provides and regroup your objects.

2. Group the links and object aggregations into associations and class
    aggregations. Remember that all the members of the group must carry
    the same semantic meaning.

3. Determine whether the classes are specializations of a common super-
    class. Look for identical attributes, relationships, services, and
    behaviors across classes and, with them, try to form a class. Again, ask

---

[5]   Note that the name and signature of the service are preserved. This differs from C++ function over-
      loading, where the name of the function or the operator is reused, but the arguments are different.
      Thus, function overloading is not a vehicle for implementing polymorphism in C++. Polymor-
      phism is implemented in C++ by using virtual functions.

the domain expert if these properties capture a useful domain concept. Remember that these new objects must operate in a useful semantic domain.

4. Look for polymorphism. See if there are services of objects that are the same or similar, but differ in behavior (how the service is provided). If these objects operate in the same semantic domain, make the service polymorphic. Perform all the above steps again until no new super-class is found.

Subsystems

IN BUILDING LARGE APPLICATIONS/SYSTEMS, the analyst/developer has to deal with a number of interesting and different subject matters. For example, in a typical application, we have the following subject matters: the application, interface to external systems, user interface, alarm subsystem, and logging subsystem.[6] This is normally too much material for most of us to deal with as a whole. Consequently, we need a strategy for organizing these different matters into more manageable subsystems. The strategy or technique we will use is based on the work of Shlaer and Mellor. Their strategy relies on the concept of domain.

Domain

A domain is a separate real, hypothetical, or abstract world inhabited by a distinct set of objects that behave according to rules and policies that characterize that domain. For example, an Airline Management domain would be concerned with airplanes, air routes, airports, and gates, as well as with the operating policies and FAA regulations governing their use. However, the User Interface domain is concerned with windows, pulldown menus, dialog boxes, and icons together with a different set of operating policies.

Each domain forms a separate but cohesive whole. The principle of cohesion helps us keep closely related ideas together and unrelated ideas separate. Since a domain represents a set of closely related objects, rules, and policies, it can be treated as a unit (subsystem) for the purpose of analysis.

To better understand domain, we can look at this concept in terms of objects:

1. An object is defined in one domain.
2. The object in a domain requires the existence of other objects in the same domain.
3. The objects in one domain do not require the existence of objects in a different domain.

---

[6] In design, we add the screen subsystem, database subsystem, and so on. The operating system, programming languages, software packages, and development environment are all considered part of design.

For example, consider an airline management application. (1) The air route should be only in the Airline Management domain. (2) Air route by itself is not much use to us without airplanes and airports. (3) Air routes and airplanes can exist without windows or dialog boxes. Conversely, windows and icons can exist without air routes and airplanes.

Although an object in one domain does not require the existence of an object in another domain, it is very common for an object in one domain to have a counterpart instance in another domain. For example, an airplane in the Airline Management domain may have a counterpart airplane icon in the User Interface domain.

To help us recognize domains, Shlaer and Mellor provide a classification scheme:[7]

1. *Application domain.* This is the subject matter from the customer/user perspective. This is what we normally call business requirements analysis.

2. *Service domain.* This domain provides generic mechanisms and utility functions to support the application domain. These are the domains that are hard for us to identify.

3. *Architectural domain.* This domain provides the generic mechanisms and structures for managing data and control for the system as a whole.

4. *Implementation domain.* This domain includes the programming language, operating systems, networks, and common class libraries.

Bridge

According to Shlaer and Mellor, a bridge exists between two domains when one domain needs to use the mechanisms and/or capabilities provided by the other domain. The domain that requires the capabilities is known as the *client*, while the domain that provides them is called the *server*. For example, the Airline Management domain (client) may use the User Interface domain to display the air routes to the user. During analysis, the bridge defines a set of external services (from the client's perspective) and a set of requirements (from the server's perspective). For instance, in our airplane example the airplane icon must be able to derive its position from the position of the airplane object in the Airline Management domain.

Organizing Subsystems

ACCORDING TO RUMBAUGH ET AL., the decomposition of a system into subsystems may be done both horizontally and vertically. Although most of us have numer-

---

[7] In analysis, we are concerned only with application domains and service domains. In design, architectural domains and implementation domains are considered.

ous ways to decompose a system, any decomposition reduces to one or the other or a combination of these two kinds.

Horizontal Layers

A layer system is a set of semantic domains (virtual reality), each built in terms of the ones below it and providing the basis of implementation for the ones above it. Examples of this approach are the protocol layers of OSI and the TNM layers for telecommunication operating support systems. An interactive graphic system is another example. Here, windows are made from screens that are made from pixels driving some I/O device. The layers are the application domain, window domain, screen domain, pixel domain, and hardware domain.

The goal is to make each layer as independent as possible. Although there is usually some correspondence among objects in different layers, the communication between layers is basically one-way. A subsystem knows about the layers below it,[8] but has no knowledge of the layers above it. Thus, a client-server relationship exists between the layers.[9]

Usually only the top layer, which is the application domain, and the bottom layer, which is the hardware domain, are specified in the requirements document. One of the purposes of analysis is to find all the intermediate layers. It is good practice to have at least one layer (service domain) between the application layer and the hardware layer in order to facilitate porting to other hardware/software platforms.

Vertical Partitions

Vertical partitions divide a system into several weakly coupled subsystems,[10] each of which provides one kind of service. For example, consider a computerized work management system for maintenance personnel. There may be separate subsystems for routine work, troubleshooting, time reporting, and salary administration. There is only a very weak coupling among these subsystems. Routine work is only coupled to time reporting by the hours worked. Salary administration uses time reporting to determine how much to pay; however, it has neither coupling to routine work nor troubleshooting.

---

[8] In some paradigms, the communication may only be to the layer immediately below it. This restriction preserves the information-hiding and encapsulation principles between layers and makes software more maintainable, since a designer only needs to check the layer below it. However, in practice this is too restrictive. During design, performance considerations usually force us to allow the upper layer to access all the services in any lower layer.

[9] The upper layers are the clients for the lower layers.

[10] If the subsystems are independent of each other, then it is more effective to consider them as separate systems.

Combination

A system can be successively decomposed into subsystems by using both vertical partitions and horizontal layers in various combinations. Horizontal layers may be partitioned, and vertical partitions may be layered. Most large systems require this kind of mixture.

Identifying Subsystems

TO IDENTIFY SUBSYSTEMS, WE USE the fact that there should be coupling between objects in the same domain and low coupling across domains. If we draw a model that captures only the associations and class aggregations, we would find a clustering of classes. We will use each cluster as a potential subsystem. To help us determine if the cluster is a subsystem, Shlaer and Mellor have the following suggestions:

1. Give the domain a name and prepare a mission statement for it.
2. Find the bridges (services to other subsystems) for the domain.
3. See if these services are consistent with the mission statement.
4. Determine if you can replace this set of objects with a different set of objects with the same mission.

If all the above can be done, the cluster is a subsystem. If you find a number of intersubsystem relationships defined between the same two subsystems, a cluster may have been split improperly. Look again at your class definitions, and see if you can redefine the classes to make the clusters better behaved.

Recommended Approach

OUR RECOMMENDED APPROACH CONSISTS OF the following steps:

1. Group all the objects with the same attributes, similar relationships, and common behavior. If there is a concept within the application domain that defines these objects, use that name for the class. If not, ask the domain expert what concept this may resemble. Use the class that the domain expert provides and regroup your objects.
2. Group the links and object aggregations into associations and class aggregations. Remember that all the members of the group must carry the same semantic meaning.
3. Determine whether the classes are specializations of a common superclass. Look for identical attributes, relationships, services, and behaviors across classes and try to form a class. Again, ask the domain expert if these properties capture a useful domain concept. Remember that these new objects must operate in a useful semantic domain.

4. Look for polymorphism. See if there are services of objects that are the same or similar, but differ in behavior (how the service is provided). If these objects operate in the same semantic domain, make the service polymorphic. Perform all the above steps again until no new super-classes are found.

5. Draw a model that captures only the associations and class aggregations.

6. Identify the cluster of classes and assume they are potential subsystems.

7. Give this cluster a name and a mission statement.

8. Use the bridge and replacement tests to determine if it is a subsystem (separate domain).

9. Document the subsystem using the component diagram(s) in UML.

Example

Let us return to our lawn-mowing example. We will only apply refinement to our model, as this example is in only one semantic domain.[11] Based on the analysis, we have the following objects: John, Jane, Peter, Paul, Elizabeth, Mary, Jack, Family-Lawn, and ProfessionalLawnMower.

We will start by trying to group objects together. First, Paul, Elizabeth and Mary are objects that have the same attributes, common relationships, and common behavior. Jack and ProfessionalLawnMower also appear to be in the same class. In fact, ProfessionalLawnMower is a class, and Jack is an instance of that class.

Although we have identified ProfessionalLawnMower as an object, it is also a class. This is one of the difficulties in reading a requirements document. In one usage, a name of a class is used to refer to itself as an object, and in another usage, the name is used to refer to itself as a collection of instances of an object type. Now you understand the problem with step 1; when you list objects, you are also list-ing classes.[12] Our first cut at listing objects is shown in Figure 10-1.

Class	Instance(s)
Family	*Jones*
Professional Lawn Mower	Jack
ChildA	Mary, Elizabeth, Paul
ChildB	Peter
Father	John
Mother	Jane
Lawn	FamilyLawn

FIGURE 10-1 List of Initial Classes Instances for the Lawn-Mowing Example

---

[11] The subsystem identification steps are shown in the case study.

[12] This cannot be wrong, for every class is also an object. However, the reverse is not true (i.e., some objects are not classes).

If we review all the classes, we notice that class **childA** and class **childB** are almost identical. The difference is that the two classes have different methods for the mowTheLawn service. Since the semantic meaning and signature for the service are the same, this situation is best captured by polymorphism. Thus, we can create a superclass **Child** for subclasses **ChildA** and **ChildB**. This model is adequate if we presume that we deal only with one generation of a family and ignore the fact that a professional lawn mower can also be in a family. This more flexible and more accurate model is left as an exercise for the reader. The model shown in Figures 10-2, 10-3, and 10-4 is adequate for our limited application. The class descriptions are illustrated in Figures 10-5 through 10-9, which follow.

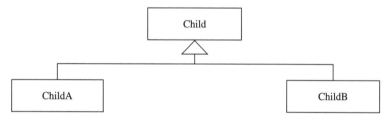

FIGURE 10-2 Class Generalization Diagram for Lawn-Mowing Example

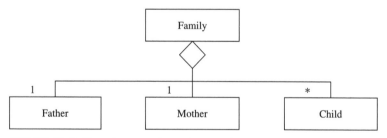

FIGURE 10-3 Class Aggregation Diagram for Lawn-Mowing Example

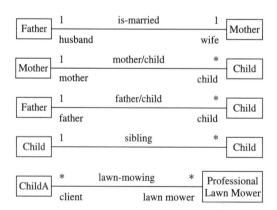

**FIGURE 10-4 Class Association Diagram for
Lawn-Mowing Example**

CLASS NAME	Family
ATTRIBUTES	
none	
SERVICES	
constructor will create the family (see later chapter)	

FIGURE 10-5 Example of a Class CRC Card for Family

CLASS NAME	Father
ATTRIBUTES	
schedule, mycondition	
SERVICES	
prototype: mowTheLawn (no arguments)	
{	
get SCHEDULE for evening (7P.M. – 9P.M.)	
Next, if SCHEDULE has open slot,	
then:	
place mowFamilyLawn in slot.	
return "Yes, I will mow the lawn this evening."	
else:	
return "No, I cannot mow the lawn."	
endif	
}	
prototype: mowFamilyLawn (no arguments)	
{	
If MYCONDITION is equal to "tired,"	
then: // get children via father/child association	
for each child in selected Children	
ask each child to "mow the lawn" for 5 dollars.	

if answer is "yes,"
then:
remove "mowFamilylawn" from SCHEDULE.
return;
else:
endif:
endfor:
perform mowing the lawn.
else:
perform mowing the lawn.
endif:
}

FIGURE 10-6 Example of a Class CRC Card for Father

CLASS NAME	**Child**
SUBCLASSES	**ChildA, ChildB**

ATTRIBUTES
schedule

SERVICES

prototype: mow_the_lawn (address_of_lawn, dollar_amount)
　　// there is no method specified, we will require that each
　　// subclass specify a method for providing this service.

FIGURE 10-7 Example of a Class CRC Card for Child

CLASS NAME	ChildB
SUPERCLASS	Child

ATTRIBUTES
no additional attributes; remember, it will inherit schedule from child

SERVICES
prototype: mow_the_lawn (address_of_lawn, dollar_amount)
{
get SCHEDULE for evening (7pm-9pm)
Next, if SCHEDULE has open slot,
then:
place mowLawn in slot.
associate ADDRESS_OF_LAWN with mowLawn.
return "Yes, I will mow the lawn this evening."
else:
return "No, I cannot mow the lawn."
endif:
}

FIGURE 10-8 Example of a Class CRC Card for Child B

SUPERCLASS	
CLASS NAME	

ATTRIBUTES
no additional attributes; remember, it will inherit schedule from child

SERVICES
prototype: mow_the_lawn (address_of_lawn, dollar_amount)
{
if DOLLAR_AMOUNT is less than $5,

then:
get SCHEDULE for evening (7pm-9pm)
Next, if SCHEDULE has open slot,
then:
place mowLawn in slot.
associate ADDRESS_OF_LAWN with mowLawn.
return "Yes, I will mow the lawn this evening."
else:
return "No, I cannot mow the lawn."
endif
else:
use lawn-mowing association to get
a professional lawn mower: plm
ask plm to "mow the lawn (ADDRESS_OF_LAWN, self, ADDRESS)".
if plm's response is "yes"
then:
return "Yes, I will mow the lawn this evening."
else
return "No, I cannot mow the lawn."
endif:
endif:
}

FIGURE 10-9 Example of a Class CRC Card for Child A

In this example, we have introduced a second form of polymorphism. In the earlier example, the superclass **Employee** had a method specified for the service payRaise; the subclass **Executive** then specified its own method for payRaise. However, we could have added another subclass, **Supervisors**, that did not specify its own method for payRaise. In that event, instances of **Supervisors** would use the method specified in the superclass **Employee**. Here, the superclass **Child** defines the prototype for the service mowTheLawn, but did not specify a method for performing the service. When this is done, every subclass must specify its own method for handling the service. There is no default specification in the superclass. Both subclasses **ChildA** and **ChildB** must have methods for the service mowTheLawn.

You should also recognize that the differences between **ChildA** and **ChildB** are that they have different methods for implementing the service mowTheLawn, and that only **ChildA** has an association with **ProfessionalLawnMower**. The rest of the class descriptions are left as an exercise for the reader.

■ ■ SUMMARY

The substeps of model refinement and subsystem identification are as follows:

1. Group all objects with the same attributes, similar relationships, and common behavior. If there is a concept within the application domain that defines these objects, use that name for the class. If not, ask the domain expert what concept this may resemble. Use the class that the domain expert provides and regroup your objects.

2. Group the links and object aggregations into associations and class aggregations. Remember that all the members of the group must carry the same semantic meaning.

3. Determine whether the classes are specializations of a common superclass. Look for identical attributes, relationships, services, and behaviors across classes. With these common attributes, relationships, services, and behaviors, try to form a class. Again, ask the domain expert if these properties capture a useful domain concept. Remember these new objects must operate in a useful semantic domain.

4. Look for polymorphism. See if there are services of objects that are the same or similar, but differ in behavior (how the service is provided). If these objects operate in the same semantic domain, make the service polymorphic. Perform all the above steps again until no new superclasses are found.

5. Now draw a model that only captures the associations and class aggregations.

6. Identify the cluster of classes and assume they are potential subsystems.

7. Give this cluster a name and a mission statement.

8. Use the bridge and replacement test to determine if it is a subsystem (separate domain).

Design

Many things difficult to design prove easy to performance.

■ Samuel Johnson

At the end of the fifth step, we completed the application model. Now we are ready to consider the technology necessary to implement the model. In this chapter, we add to the model all the technology-dependent objects (classes), so that the application can be implemented.

We do not discuss or describe object design patterns in this book, despite the large degree of interest this topic area has generated. We justify this by our observation that the use of design patterns by people without significant experience in object-oriented methods has led to considerable problems. Design patterns, although simple and easy to understand in themselves, can be very difficult for inexperienced people to apply correctly. We have observed that novices tend to warp their object models into the patterns that they understand best. Instead we have chosen to give a few general rules on how to map an object model into a good and usable design that can be easily implemented. We are leaving design patterns to an advanced book on design.

Introduction

AFTER YOU HAVE MODELED A business solution to your application/system, you must decide how to implement that solution using available technology. *System design* is the high-level strategy for implementing the business solution, and *detailed design* is the low-level strategy of the implementation of the application/ system.

In system design, the developer must do the following:

- Organize the system into subsystems.
- Identify concurrency inherent in the model.
- Allocate the subsystems to processors and tasks.
- Choose a vehicle and an approach for data storage.
- Determine a control strategy for accessing global resources.
- Choose an implement of control for the software.
- Consider start-up, shut-down, and failure strategies.

In detailed design, the developer must do the following:

- Add the objects/classes from the architectural and implementation domains.
- Design efficient algorithms for complex services.
- Optimize the design of the application/system.
- Maximize the use of inheritance.
- Redesign the associations for efficiency.
- Determine the best representation of classes.
- Package the classes and associations into reusable units.

Obviously, detailed design follows system design.

System Design

ALTHOUGH ALL THE ISSUES AND decisions a developer must make in system design are critical to the success of the project, we will only discuss dividing the system into a small number of components and the control strategy for the software.

Subsystems

Each major component of the system is called a *subsystem*.[1] Each subsystem should deal with a separate subject matter called a domain. Each domain can be independent of the rest of the system.[2] A good clue to a domain is that it has its own terminology with a different semantic meaning; it is a separate real, hypothetical, or abstract world that is inhabited by a distinct set of objects that behave according to the rules and policies of the domain. A subsystem is neither an object nor a function, but a package of classes, associations, operations, events, and constraints that are interrelated and that has a reasonably well-defined and, ideally, small number of interfaces with the rest of the system.

A subsystem is usually defined by the services it provides, just as an object or class is. The relationship between the rest of the system and the subsystem can be peer-to-peer or client/server.

In a peer-to-peer relationship, either side may have access to the other's services. Communication is not necessarily done by a request followed by an immediate response, so there can be communication cycles, which can lead to subtle design errors.

The client/server relationship, however, is much simpler; the client calls on the server, which performs some service and replies with the results. The client needs to know the interface of the supplier, but the supplier does not need to know the interface of the client. All the interactions are done through the supplier's interface.

There are all kinds of suggestions on how to decompose a system. The decomposed system can be organized in two ways: by horizontal layers or by vertical partitions.

A layered system is an ordered set of subsystems in which each subsystem is built in terms of the ones below it and provides the basis for building the subsystem above it. The objects in each layer can be independent, although there is some correspondence between the objects of various layers. However, knowledge is only one-way; a subsystem knows about the layers below, but it does not know about the subsystems above it. Thus, a client/server relationship exists between

---

[1] This is the same concept as discussed earlier. In analysis, we use subsystems to manage complexity in the application domain. Now, in design, we use subsystems to manage the complexity in the architectural and implementation domains.

[2] It is our opinion that effective reuse is not at the object/class level as proclaimed by most experts, but at the domain level. An example of successful domain reuse is seen with the many service domain application packages available.

layers. An example of a layered system is a windowing system for a computer user interface.

A vertically partitioned system divides a system into several independent or weakly coupled subsystems, each providing one kind of service. For example, an operating system includes a file subsystem, device controller, virtual management subsystem, and an event-interrupt handler. In a vertical partition system, a peer-to-peer relationship exists between subsystems.

A real system may be successfully decomposed into subsystems using both layers and partitions in various combinations; a layer can be partitioned, and a partition can be layered. Most large systems require a combination of layers and partitions.

Architectural Frameworks

In reality, since many of the decisions that should be made at the system design stage are given to the developers, much of the design process involves figuring out how to integrate these givens into a working system. One of the major improvements in software development is that software vendors have given developers subsystems that perform specific services very well for applications. Thus, developers should take advantage of written and tested subsystems when possible. Moreover, most developers have built certain architectural frameworks that are well suited for certain kinds of applications. If you have applications with similar characteristics, you should use these corresponding architectures as a starting point for your design.

The kinds of systems are as follows:

- **Batch**. A data transformation is done on an entire set of inputs.
- **Continuous**. As input changes in real-time, a data transformation is performed in real-time.
- **Interactive**. External interactions dominate the application.
- **Transaction**. The application is concerned with storing and updating data, often including concurrent access by many users and from many different locations.
- **Rule-based**. The application is dominated by concern about enforcing rules.
- **Simulation**. The application simulates evolving, real-world objects.
- **Real-time**. The application is dominated by strict timing constraints.

The steps for performing an object-oriented system design for the first four architectural frameworks are given below.

Batch Architectural Framework

1. Break the transformation into subtransformations, so that each sub-transformation performs one part of the transformation.

2. Define temporary objects for the data flows between subtransformations. Then each subtransformation only needs to know about the objects on each side of itself (i.e., its inputs and outputs).

3. Expand each subtransformation into other subtransformations until the operations are straightforward to implement.

4. Restructure the pipeline for optimization.

5. Use the new set of objects to form classes that loosely couple to the original object model.

Continuous Architectural Framework

1. Identify all the objects that need continuous updates.

2. Draw an event trace diagram for the continuous transformation.

3. Make the inputs and outputs of the services temporary objects that contain the values that change continuously.

4. Refine or define methods for each object/class that will process the incremental changes for the object.

5. Add any additional objects needed for optimization.

6. Use the new set of objects to form classes that loosely couple to the original object model.

Interactive Architectural Framework

1. Separate the objects that form the interface from the objects that define the semantics of the application; they are in two different domains.

2. Use predefined (library) objects to interface with external agents. For example, most windowing systems have libraries that give developers the windows, menus, and buttons for usage.

3. Use an event-driven (callback) approach to decomposition.

4. Separate physical events from logical events and assign them to the correct objects. Logical events are part of the application, and physical events are probably part of the interface domain. Be careful; a logical event often corresponds to multiple physical events or more than one physical event.

Transaction Architectural Framework

1. Map the object model into a database.

2. Determine the resources that cannot be shared.

3. Determine the unit of a transaction (the objects that must be accessed together during a transaction) using an event trace diagram.

4. Design the concurrency control for the transactions. Most database systems support this.

Software Control Within a Framework

There are two kinds of control flows within a software system: external and internal. External control is the flow of externally visible events among the objects in the system, while internal control is the flow of control within a method.

There are three ways to control external flows: procedure-driven sequential, event-driven sequential, and concurrent. Similarly, the three ways to control internal flows are procedure calls, quasi-concurrent intertask calls, and concurrent intertask calls. Both the internal and external control strategies chosen are highly dependent on the resources (language, operating system, etc.) available and the pattern of interactions in the application.

Since all the major object-oriented languages, such as Smalltalk, C++, and Objective C, are procedural languages, procedure-driven sequential is the most common way to control external flow. In this style, the control resides within the application code. The application code issues requests for external inputs and waits for them to arrive. When they arrive, control is resumed within the procedure that made the call. Although this style is easy for most developers to implement, the developer must convert the events in a sequential flow of operations (methods) between objects. This is done using an event trace diagram.[3] This style of control is useful when there is a regularity of external events. However, this style is not very good for handling asynchronous events, error conditions, flexible user interfaces, and process control systems.

In the event-driven sequential style, the control resides within a dispatcher or monitor provided by either the language, subsystem, or operating system. Application procedures are attached to events and are called by the dispatcher when the corresponding events occur (callback). The application makes procedure calls to the dispatcher for input/output, but does not wait for it in-line. Events are handled by the dispatcher, and all application procedures return control to the dispatcher instead of retaining control until input arrives.

Event-control style is more difficult to implement with standard programming languages (Smalltalk, C++, or Objective C). This style permits a more flexible pattern of control than the procedural style. Since it simulates cooperating processes within a single multithreaded task, a single errant method can block an entire application. However, event style produces more modular design and can better handle error conditions.

In the concurrent style, control resides in several independent objects, where each is a separate task. A task can wait for input, but other tasks continue to execute. There is a queuing mechanism for events, and the operating system resolves scheduling conflicts among tasks. JAVA is an object-oriented languages directly support tasking or concurrency.

---

3   Event trace diagrams are discussed in chapter 6 on static behavior.

Detailed Design

DURING ANALYSIS, WE DETERMINED THE objects/classes, their associations and their structure from an application perspective. During design, we have to add the implementation objects and optimize data structures and algorithms for coding.

There is a shift in emphasis from application domain concepts to computer concepts. Given the classes from the application, the designer must choose among different ways to implement them. Factors that may be important include execution time, memory usage, and disk I/O access. However, optimization of design should not be carried to excess, as there must be a practical trade-off between optimization and ease of implementation, maintainability, and extensibility of the final product.

Usually, the simplest and best approach is to take the classes found in analysis into design. Design then becomes the process of adding implementation objects, adding implementation details, and making implementation decisions. Occasionally, an analysis object/class does not appear in the design, but is distributed among other objects/classes for computational efficiency. Some redundant attributes or an object/class may be added for efficiency.

Thus, detailed design is primarily a process of refinement and adding implementation objects that are technology-dependent. These new objects and additional details should help better organize the application and augment the analysis model.

Class Design

During analysis, we focused on the logical structure of the information that is needed to build a business solution. During design, we need to look at the best way to implement the logical structure in order to optimize the application performance. Many of the effective implementation structures that we need are instances of container classes; examples are arrays, lists, queues, stacks, sets, bags, dictionaries, associations, and trees. Most object-oriented languages already have libraries that provide such classes.

Although we have defined business algorithms for building a business solution during analysis, we may need to optimize the algorithms for implementation. During optimization, we may add new classes to hold intermediate results and new low-level methods. These new classes are usually implementation classes not mentioned directly in the client's requirements document. They are usually service domain classes that support the building of the application classes. When new methods are added, some have obvious target objects as their owners. However, some methods may have several target objects as their owners. Assigning responsibility for the latter kind of service can be very frustrating.[4] This

---

[4] These "implementation" services can also be easily overlooked, because they are not inherently services of only one class.

is the fundamental problem when we invent implementation objects; they are somewhat arbitrary, and their boundaries are more a matter of convenience than of logical necessity.[5]

If we need to avoid recomputation to improve performance, we should define new objects/classes to hold these derived attributes (data). Remember that derived attributes must be updated when base values change. This can be done by using the following:

1. **Explicit code**. Since each derived attribute is defined in terms of one or more attributes of base objects, one way to update the derived attribute is to insert code in the updateAttribute method of the base object(s). This additional code would explicitly update the derived attribute that is dependent on the attribute of the base object. This is synchronizing by *explicit code*.

2. **Periodic recomputation**. When base values are changed in a bunch, it may be possible to recompute all the derived attributes periodically after all the base values are changed. This is called *periodic recomputation*.

3. **Triggers**. An active attribute has dependent attributes. Each dependent attribute must register itself with the active attribute. When the active attribute is being updated, a trigger will be fired that will inform all the objects containing the dependent attributes that the active attribute has a changed value. Then it is the responsibility of the derived object to update its derived attribute. This is called updating by *triggers*.

Sometimes the same service is defined across several classes and can be easily inherited from a common superclass. However, often the services in different classes are similar but not identical. By slightly modifying the prototype of the service, the services can be made to match, so that they can be handled by a single inherited service. When this is done, not only must the name and the signature of the service match, but they should all have the same semantic meaning. The following adjustments are commonly made to increase inheritance:

1. When some services have fewer arguments than other services, the missing arguments are added, but ignored in the method.

2. When a service has few arguments because it is a special case of a more general service, you can implement the special service by calling the general services with all the arguments.

3. When attributes in different classes have the same semantic meaning, choose one name for the attribute and move it to a common superclass.

---

[5] The problem becomes more difficult when we need to assign a service in an inheritance hierarchy. For implementation classes, the definitions of subclasses may be quite arbitrary and fluid. It is quite common to see services move up and down the hierarchy during the design step.

4. When services in different classes have the same semantic meaning, choose one name for the service and apply 1 or 2 to take advantage of polymorphism.

5. When a service is defined in several different classes, but not in other classes that semantically should be in one group, define the service in the superclass and declare it as a no-op method in the class that does not care about providing this service.

6. When common behavior has been recognized, a common superclass can be created to implement the shared behavior, leaving the specialized behavior in the subclasses. Usually, this new superclass is an abstract class.[6]

It is strongly recommended that you do not use inheritance purely as an implementation technique. This happens when developers find an existing class that has implemented a large number of the services needed by a newly defined class, even though semantically the two classes are different. The developer may then want to use inheritance to achieve partial implementation of the new class. This can lead to side effects because some of the inherited methods may provide unwanted behaviors. A better technique is to use delegation,[7] which allows the newly formed class to delegate only the appropriate services.[8]

Association Design

In implementing associations, the designer must consider the access pattern and the relative frequencies of the different kinds of access. If the number of hits from queries is low because only a fraction of the objects satisfy the criteria, an index should be used to improve the access to objects that are frequently retrieved. However, this is costly in terms of memory and slower updates. Sometimes adding a new association that is derived from the base association will provide direct access to the appropriate data.

If the association is only traversed in one direction, an association can be implemented as an attribute that contains an object reference. If the multiplicity is 1, it is simply a pointer to the other object. If the multiplicity is >1, then it is a pointer to a set of pointers to objects. If the "many" end is ordered, a list is used in place of a set. A qualified association can be implemented using a dictionary object.

---

[6] Sometimes it is worthwhile to abstract out a superclass even if there is only one subclass in your application that inherits from it. If it has useful semantics, it will probably be needed in future extensions of the application or in other applications.

[7] In delegation, you create an association between the class and the newly formed class. Then the newly formed class can delegate the service from itself to the corresponding service of the existing class.

[8] Languages such as C++ let a subclass selectively make service public. When used properly, inheritance can do the equivalent of delegation for such languages.

A two-way association can be implemented as follows:

1. Add an attribute to the class on one side of the association and perform a search when a reverse traversal is required.
2. Add an attribute to both sides of the association. Use the same multiplicity techniques as for an association that is traversed in one direction.
3. Create an associate class, independent of either class. An associate class is a set of pairs of related objects stored in a single-variable-size object. For efficiency, it is common to implement an associative object as two dictionary objects.

If the association has no services, but has attributes, attributes of an association can be implemented as follows:

1. If the association is one-to-one, the association attributes can be stored as attributes of either class.
2. If the association is many-to-one, the association attributes may be stored in the class on the many side.
3. If the association is many-to-many, it is best to create an associative class and assign the association attributes to the associative class.

Generalization and Inheritance

Most object-oriented languages incorporate generalization via class inheritance. Typically, a child class can inherit the attributes, services, behaviors, and relationships of the parent class(es).[9] In this way, the object-oriented paradigm gives analysts/developers a very powerful mechanism that not only helps to organize complex objects, but also facilitates code sharing and code reuse in implementation. The properties of class inheritance are as follows:[10]

1. Structural

    a. Attributes
        Objects (instances) of the descendent class, which is a child class of the parent class, will have values for all the attributes of the ancestor classes.

---

[9] Parent and ancestor classes are also called superclasses. Child classes are often referred to as subclasses. We feel that the use of ancestor, parent and child in discussing inheritance gives a little better insight into the inheritance relationships among classes. Conversely, we prefer the use of subclass and superclass when talking about mathematical relationships.

[10] This is not as simple a topic as we may lead you to believe. The assumptions made about these properties are quite varied among the object-oriented languages. We have given you the properties that are consistent with C++ and will implement generalization/specialization as defined in analysis.

b. Nongeneralization relationships
Objects (instances) of the descendent class, which is a child class of the parent class, will have all the nongeneralization relationships of the ancestor classes.

2. Interface

All the services that are provided by the ancestor class must also be provided by the descendent class, for an object that is an instance of the descendent class is simultaneously an instance of its ancestor class.

3. Behavioral

a. Inheritance without polymorphism (good child)
In inheritance without polymorphism, *all* the methods that are supplied by the ancestor class for its services are also used by the descendent class to provide the corresponding services. This is code reuse and code sharing.

b. Inheritance with polymorphism (bad child)
In inheritance with polymorphism, some of the methods that are supplied by the ancestor class for its services are also used by the descendent class to provide the corresponding services. For the remaining services of the ancestor class, the descendent class substitutes its own customized methods for use by instances of the descendent class.

4. Mathematical

a. Antisymmetry
If class A is a subclass of class B, then class B may not be a subclass of class A. If object A is a descendent of object B, then object B can not also be a descendent of object A.

b. Transitivity[11]
If class A is a subclass of class B and class B is a subclass of class C, then class A is a subclass of class B. An instance of class A is also an instance of class C and class B.

Delegation

The object-oriented model that we have built is based on the notion of class and not on the notion of an object. However, there are object-oriented computational models that are based on the object. These systems are usually called prototype systems. In a prototype system, there is no such mechanism as a class. Only

---

[11] Transitivity makes it possible to organize the objects (classes) in a hierarchial manner. Because of this property, generalization is diagrammatically shown as an ancestral tree.

objects exist, and an object may have a delegation relationship with any other object. When a service is requested from an object, it does the following:

1. If it has a method for the service, it will execute its own method.
2. If it has no method, it will delegate the execution of that service to an object that has a delegation relationship with it.
3. The delegation relationship is transitive. So if the delegated object does not have a method for the service, it will attempt to delegate the execution of the service to other objects with which it has a delegation relationship.

Note that relationship is between objects, and that the delegation relationship is more generic than the is_a relationship, since it can be used between any two objects.[12] Moreover, delegation can be established dynamically (at run time), while class inheritance is fixed at creation time.

For a prototype system, analysis is done by thinking about a particular object and then drawing similarities and/or differences for other objects based on the particular object(s). Any object may be a prototype object during the analysis. The idea is to start with an individual objects and then to specialize and generalize them as more complex cases are considered.[13] Lieberman has described this approach as compared to the object-oriented approach:

> Prototype systems allow creating concepts first, then generalizing them by saying what aspects of the concept are allowed to vary. Set-oriented (object-oriented) systems require creating the abstraction description of the set (class) before individual instances can be installed as members.

In a sense, this method of analysis is much closer to the way humans learn. We learn by either generalizing or specializing from instances. From this, one may be led to conclude that delegation is a better mechanism for implementing generalization/specialization. However, we will see in the next section that it is not quite that simple.

Orlando Treaty

Historically, there has been much debate over which mechanism (inheritance or delegation) is a more powerful concept for implementing generalization/specialization. Since 1987, we have seen that delegation can model inheritance, and conversely inheritance can model delegation. During OOPSLA 1987, which took place in Orlando, Florida, Lynn Stein, Henry Lieberman, and David Unger discussed their differences about delegation and inheritance and came up with a

---

[12] Furthermore, in some languages not only can the execution of services be delegated, but the attributes can also be inherited or shared.

[13] Our method is a modified prototype approach to building an object-oriented system.

statement that reflected a need for both mechanisms. That resolution became known as the Orlando Treaty. In essence, the treaty recognizes two modes of code sharing: anticipatory sharing and unanticipatory sharing. Class inheritance-based systems are best for anticipatory code sharing and delegation-based systems are more suited for unanticipated code sharing.

The treaty characterized three dimensions for code sharing:

1. **Static versus dynamic**. Is the sharing determined when the object is created (static), or can it be determined dynamically (at run time)?
2. **Implicit versus explicit**. Are there explicit operations to indicate the code sharing?
3. **Per object versus per group**. Is sharing defined for whole groups of objects, or could it supported by individual objects?

Traditional object-oriented languages (i.e., C++, Smalltalk, and Simula) use static, implicit, per-group strategies in the design of their languages. By contrast, delegation-based languages use dynamic, explicit, and per-object strategies in the design of their languages.

The Orlando Treaty further acknowledges that

> no definite answer as to what set of these choices is best can be reached. Rather, . . . different programming situations call for different combinations of these features: for exploratory, experimental programming environments, it may be desirable to allow the flexibility of dynamic, explicit, per object sharing; while for large relatively routine software production, restricting to the complementary set choices—strictly static, implicit, and group-oriented—may be more appropriate.

There is a trade-off here between the two strategies. Delegation requires less space, but execution time is slower because of run-time binding. In contrast, class inheritance offers faster execution but requires more space. If the class system is strongly typed,[14] there is an additional trade-off between safety versus flexibility. From the above discussion, one can conclude that delegation is great for building prototype systems; however, high-performance and production-quality systems will be better if they use a strongly typed class-based language, like C++.

Multiple Inheritance

We have intentionally given examples that use only single inheritance (each subclass has one and only one immediate superclass). However, there are real situations that are very effectively modeled by letting a subclass inherit from more than one immediate superclass. For instance, in our Person example, we

---

[14] C++ is a strongly typed language. This was one of the main features requested from development, so that more testable and more reliable software could be delivered.

assumed that all students were not employees. However, a better model may be that a person is both a student and an employee. With single inheritance, we would not be able to directly represent this multiple parent relationship. Other examples are German car manufacturer, BorderedTextWindow, and transformer toy. A German car manufacturer has properties that are due to its being a German company and also properties that are due to its being a car manufacturer. BorderedTextWindow has properties of a bordered window and properties of a text window. Finally, a transformer toy can act as a robot, car, plane, and boat. The mechanism that allows us to model these situations is called *multiple inheritance.*

With multiple inheritance, we can combine several existing (parent) classes to form a new subclass of all the parent classes. It can access all the methods and contain all the attributes and relationships of all the parent classes. For example, let us use the inheritance tree from our original example that includes the Platypus. In this inheritance tree, shown in Figure 11-1 the class **Platypus** inherits from both **Mammal** and **Endangered.** This is an example of multiple inheritance.

Here is a more comprehensive example. Let Carol, Frank, Mary, Susan, and Karen be employees of a company. Carol is in administration, and her manager is Frank. Susan is in engineering, and her manager is Mary. Karen works part-time and is also a student. Adam is also a student, but he does not work for the company. The inheritance tree for this example is shown in Figure 11-2.

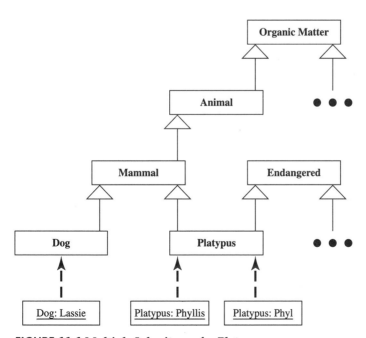

FIGURE 11-1 Multiple Inheritance for Platypus

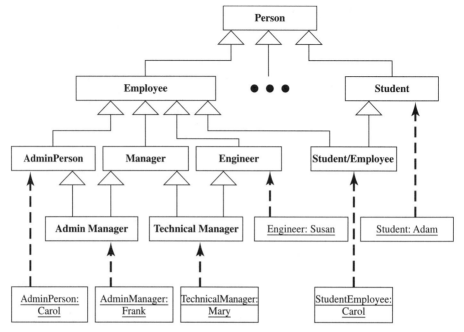

FIGURE 11-2 Multiple Inheritance for Student Employee Karen

■ ■ SUMMARY

In this chapter, we briefly discussed design. Despite our brevity on this topic, we have presented a few recommendations:

1. In system design, we believe that a subsystem must be a collection of objects (classes) in a single semantic domain.

2. In system design, we believe in using the client-server paradigm for establishing communication relationships between subsystems. We believe this will produce more robust and more maintainable software.

3. For software control, we believe that both procedural-driven and event-driven approaches are applicable, depending on the application/system to be built. In fact, we have used both simultaneously in one system.

4. We recommend using UML's deployment diagram to capture the physical topology upon which the software application/system will reside.

5. We recommend using the Utilities class of UML to capture underlying support functions of the operating system and non-OO libraries.

6. In detailed design of classes, it is best to take classes as found in analysis and keep them in the design. Then we should add implementation classes.[15]

---

[15] Adding implementation classes follows the same method as we described in the book, except now the domain is the appropriate technology.

7. In detailed design of association, we recommend implementing all associations with their attribute(s) as classes unless there are performance issues. A class implementation of association with attribute(s) accurately models the application/system, and thus will help make the software more maintainable and flexible for future features.

8. In detailed design, use delegation instead of inheritance if you expect to have the subclass and the superclass implemented on different processors.

9. In detailed design, multiple inheritance should be used only if all the parent classes will reside on the same processor. If the parent class(es) reside on different processors, use delegation to implement multiple inheritance.

10. Consult with an OO expert to find opportunities to use (1) templates, (2) patterns, (3) stereotypes, and composites capabilities of UML. Also have the expert review all your diagrams. Ensure that the expert reviews closely (1) multiple inheritance, (2) aggregation, (3) nonbinary associations, (4) category classes, (5) mapping of rules to constraints, and (6) exception handling. Adjust your diagrams to reflect the opportunities recommended by the expert.

11. We recommend using the component diagram of UML to capture your detailed physical design of components.

CHAPTER

12

C++ Fundamentals

The idea is that to be useful, a language feature must not only be elegant, it must also be affordable in the context of a real program.

■ Bjarne Stroustrup, *The C++ Programming Language,* © 1991 AT&T Bell Laboratories, Inc.
Reprinted by permission of Addison Wesley Longman, Inc.

After completion of the design steps, we have built a model that is now ready for implementation in C++. However, before we show how the model maps easily into C++, we need to cover the fundamentals for C++. Readers who know C++ may skip this chapter.

The purpose of this chapter and the next five chapters is not to teach the reader how to program in C++. The intent is to show how a design created by following the methods in this book translates into C++ code. This is consistent with our goal of providing a practical guide for the development of object-oriented applications using C++. We recommend that readers unfamiliar with C++ purchase a good book on the C++ language and one on programming in C++ for their development environment.

History

THE C PROGRAMMING LANGUAGE WAS developed by Kernighan and Ritchie at AT&T Bell Laboratories in 1978. Their goal was to develop a portable, small, simple, and fast programming language that did not prevent the programmer from doing what needed to be done. It basically put *full trust* in the programmer. In 1988 an ANSI Standard for the language was approved by the ANSI committee X3J11.

C++ development started in 1983 and was inspired by SIMULA67. Bjarne Stroustrup, also of AT&T Bell Laboratories, developed it as an evolution of C. Within six months of its first release from AT&T in 1985, there were commercial ports of C++ available on more than 24 platforms, ranging from PCs to mainframes. Today, there is an ANSI standards committee to formalize the language.

C++ is the most widely used programming language for object-oriented programming. Because most of its enhancements of the C language support creating classes with the same richness as the built-in data types, C++ supports the object-oriented concepts and mechanisms discussed in this book. In addition, C++ added stronger type checking than most languages to prevent many conversion errors and illegal initialization of data structures. These and other capabilities make it the ideal language for object-oriented development of large software systems. However, it neither requires nor enforces object-oriented paradigm usage in writing programs. C++ is first and foremost a multiparadigm language; it allows you to write code in the classical procedural paradigm of structured methods as well as the new object-oriented paradigm of object-oriented methods (i.e., Rumbaugh et al., Booch).

Programming Elements

A PROGRAM IS COMPOSED OF elements called *tokens*, which are a collection of characters (alphabetic, numeric, and special) that constitute the basic vocabulary recognized by the compiler. The compiler translates these tokens into instructions that the computer understands. Tokens are separated by white space and/or comment text inserted for readability and documentation.

In C, a comment is written as follows:

```
/* possibly many lines */
```

C++ added a rest-of-the line comment written as follows:

```
// this is a new C++ comment
```

This comment extends only until the end of the line, while the C comment may contain the C++ comments. For example;

```
/*    begin C comment

      x = x + y;          // this is the new C++ comment

      end of C comment     */
```

There are five kinds of tokens:

- Keywords
- Identifiers
- Literals
- Operators
- Punctuators

Each of these are discussed in the paragraphs that follow.

Keywords

Keywords are explicitly reserved words that have a predefined meaning in C++. They include words for data type declaration, statement formulation, and access control. Table 12-1 lists the keywords.[1] The underlined keywords are not part of the ANSI C standard. The bold keywords are necessary for supporting object-oriented programming. The italic keywords are interesting for implementation reasons.

Identifiers

An identifier is a sequence of alphanumeric characters, including the underscore character. The identifier must not start with a digit. Although legal, it is not advisable to use an underscore as the first character because the compilers and hidden library code use the underscore as the first character. Uppercase letters and lowercase letters are treated as distinct characters. In theory, an identifier can be arbitrarily long, but due to limitations in some compilers, 31 characters is a good limit.

---

[1]   For details on each keyword, consult an introductory to C++ programming book.

TABLE 12-1 C++ Keywords

and	and_eq	asm	auto	bitand
bitor	**bool**	break	case	catch
char	**class**	compl	const	const_cast
continue	default	**delete**	do	double
dynamic_cast	else	enum	extern	float
for	**friend**	goto	if	*inline*
int	long	namespace	**new**	not
not_eq	operator	or	or_eq	overload
private	*protected*	**public**	register	reinterpret_cast
return	short	signed	sizeof	static
static_cast	struct	switch	*template*	**this**
throw	try	typedef	**typeid**	union
unsigned	**virtual**	void	volatile	while

According to the ANSI C Standard Library naming convention, all uppercase letters should be used for constants, macros, and structures. Mixed uppercase and lowercase are used for functions and variable names.

Literals

Literals are constant values (e.g., 1 and 3.14159). All native C++ data types (see "Native Data Types") may have literals.

Operators

Operators are characters and/or character sequences with a special meaning. Most of the operators are used to perform arithmetic or logical operations. Table 12-2 lists the arithmetic and assignment operators. The equality, relational, and logical operators are given in Table 12-3.

Punctuators

Punctuators include parentheses, braces, commas, and colons. They are used to give structure to other tokens of the language.[2]

---

[2] Consult an introduction to C++ for more details.

TABLE 12-2 C++ Arithmetic Operators

Operator	Function
%	Modulus (remainder)
+	Addition
++	Increment
-	Subtraction
--	Decrement
*	Multiplication
/	Division

TABLE 12-3 C++ Relational and Logical Operators

Operator	Function
!	Logical NOT
<	Less than
<=	Less than or equal
>	Greater than
>=	Greater than or equal
==	Equal
!=	Inequality (not equal)
&&	Logical AND
| |	Logical OR
&	Bitwise AND
|	Bitwise inclusive OR
^	Bitwise exclusive OR
?	Conditional operator

Native Data Types

C++ provides a predefined set of data types and the operators to manipulate these data types. The following data types are predefined:

- Basic data types
- Constant values
- Symbolic variables
- Pointer types
- Constant types

- Reference types
- Enumeration types
- Array types
- Typedef names

Each of these is described in the paragraphs that follow.

Basic Data Types

The following basic data types[3] are predefined:

- integer (int, short, long)
  (e.g., 1, 111, 1050)
- floating-point decimal (float, double, long double)
  (e.g., 1.1, 123.3456)
- character (char)
  (e.g., 'a,''d,''2')
- character string (char*)
  (e.g., "the big black cat," "license plate X123")
- Boolean (bool)
  (e.g., true, false)

The integral types[4] are char, short, int, and long. They may be signed or unsigned. The single and double quotes are necessary in the character and string examples respectively.

Constant Values

Every literal constant has an associated basic data type and is nonaddressable. The different kinds follow:

1. Literal integer constant (decimal, octal, hex)
   (e.g., 1, 024, 0x1A, 0X1B2)
2. Signed/unsigned and long[5]
   (e.g., 1L, 8LU, 27lu)
3. Literal floating-point constant (scientific, decimal)
   (e.g., 1.23e–3, 2.14E3, 3.14159)
4. Single precision (F/f) and double precision (L/l)
   (e.g., 1.23e–3F, 3.14159L)

---

[3] The name is followed with the keywords in parenthesis. The keywords are used in the language to identify them.

[4] *Integral* means that all these types may be treated as integers.

[5] 27lu is legal, but a long unsigned number is not good practice.

5. Literal character constant
   (e.g.,'a','d','2',")
6. Nonprintable characters plus' and " use a backslash
   (e.g., \n, \', \", \?, \\, \7 (bell))
7. Literal string constant[6]
   (e.g., "", "a," "\a string?{}[]")

Symbolic Variables

In ANSI C (and thus in C++), a symbolic variable is identified by a user-supplied name. Each variable is composed of a specific data type and is addressable. Two values are associated with a symbolic variable:

- rvalue: its data value
- lvalue: its location value (memory location)

For example,

```
char c;
c = c - '0';
```

The first line is a definition as storage is allocated; we could have made it a declaration by using the keyword extern. The second line will subtract the rvalue of the constant '0' from the rvalue of the symbolic variable c. The lvalue of '0' is determined by the compiler and is not directly accessible by the programmer.

The following example also includes initializing the rvalue of the symbolic variables:

```
int y = 40;
char c ('d');
```

In the first line, the symbolic variable y is defined and its rvalue is initialized to 40. In the second line, the symbolic variable c is defined and is initialized to the character d.

Pointer Types

In ANSI C (and thus in C++), a pointer variable holds an address as its value in memory. This provides for indirect reference, and because C++ is a strongly typed language, each pointer has an associated data type. For example,

---

[6]   The compiler adds a null character at the end of the string.

```
int* ptr1;                    /* legal, but bad practice */
unsigned char *ptr2;
int *ptr3, num;               // preferred style
int xx, *ptr4;
```

In lines 1 and 2, we showed that the * may be placed next to the data type or next to the variable. In lines 3 and 4, we see that placing the * next to the variable is better practice. It makes code more readable.

A pointer may be initialized with an lvalue of the data element of the same type. For example,

```
int j;
int *ptr = &j;
```

In line 2, the pointer variable ptr will be initialized with the lvalue of j.

In C++, all string manipulations are done using character pointers (char *). Every string constant is of type char*, and the *n* variable of type char* may be initialized to a string. For example,

```
char *strptr = "This is it\n";
```

This line will make the rvalue of strptr equal to "This is it" with a new line control character and a null character following that literal string.

Constant Types

The const modifier to a symbolic variable transforms the variable into a symbolic constant. It is a read-only variable, so it must be initialized. For example,

```
const int bufSize = 1024;
```

Its address may not be assigned to a pointer, but a pointer to a const data is allowed. For example,[7]

```
const int *ptr_to_const;
```

A const pointer is also allowed. For example,

```
int *const const_ptr;
const int const *const_ptr_to_const;
```

---

[7] Assignment of either a const variable or a non-const variable to a constant pointer is allowed. However, in both cases, the data cannot be changed using the constant pointer.

In the latter line, both the pointer and what the pointer points to must be specified at the point of instantiation and may never be changed.

Reference Types

A reference type is defined by following the type specifier with the address operator (&). This variable, which we also call the reference type, must be initialized. It is an alias and cannot be made to alias another variable, so it is a const reference. All operations on the reference or the variable act on the variable (object) to which it refers. For example,

```
int &y;
```

In the example, int is the type specifier, & is the address operator, and y is the reference or the variable.

Here is a second example:

```
double y = 11.12345;
double &refY = y;
refY += 2.54321;              // y = 13.66666
```

It is commonly used in arguments and as the return type of a function.

Enumeration Types

An enumeration is declared with the enum keyword and a list of enumerators that are separated by commas and enclosed in braces. For example,

```
enum {yes, no, maybe};
```

It declares a set of symbolic integral constants, and there is no addressable storage associated with each enumerator. A value may be explicitly assigned to an enumerator, and a tag name may be assigned and used as a type specifier. For example,

```
enum Opinion2 {yes, no = 30, maybe};
Opinion2 reply = no;          // legal
Opinion2 reply = 1;           // illegal
```

Line 3 is not legal because reply is an instance of data type Opinion2 and can only be assigned a value from the set of symbolic integral constants. The only symbolic integral constants defined for Opionion2 are yes, no, and maybe.

Array Types

An array definition consists of a type specifier, an identifier, and a dimension. For example,

```
float float_array[100];
```

The dimension value is computed at compile time and must be a constant expression.

An array is a collection of data of a single data type. Access and assignment are by position in the array. For example,

```
float   yy = float_array[10];
```

Elements of the array are numbered beginning with 0. The language provides no compile or run-time range checking on indexes.

Typedef Names

A typedef definition begins with the typedef keyword followed by the data type and the identifier (typedef name). For example,

```
typedef int Length;
```

In this example, Length may be used anywhere int is allowed in the language. It provides mnemonic synonyms for existing predefined, derived, and user-defined data types. The identifier is not a new data type, but a synonym for the existing data type. Furthermore, the identifier may be used anywhere a type name may appear. Typedef is used to make programs more readable and to encapsulate machine-dependent aspects of the program.

What Is a Statement?

A statement is the smallest executable unit within a C++ program. There is a large variety of statement types, but they are all terminated by a semicolon. The simplest statement is the empty statement or *null statement*, which takes the following form:

```
;    // null statement is like a no-op
```

A null statement is useful when the syntax of the language requires a statement, but the logic of the application does not.

One of the most commonly seen statements is the *assignment statement*. For example,

```
x = y + 1;
```

The right-hand side of this statement is evaluated and converted to a value compatible with the left-hand side variable (y +1 is assigned to x). C++ provides assignment operators that combine an assignment and some other operator. For example,

```
x += y;      // this is same as x = x + y;
x *= y;      // this is same as x = x * y;
```

C++ provides autoincrement and autodecrement operators in both prefix and postfix form. For example,

```
++k;            // this is same as   k = k + 1;
l = --k;        // this is same as   k = k - 1; l = k;
m = k++;        // this is same as   m = k; k = k + 1;
```

Expressions

An expression is composed of one or more operations. Operations are captured in C++ by operators. For example, the addition operation is captured by the operator +. The arguments of the operation are referred to as operands. For example, the addition operation requires two operands.

Nearly all operations are unary (requiring only one operand) or binary (requiring two operands). Binary operators have a left and a right operand. Care must be taken because some operators represent both unary and binary operations. For example, the operator * is used to capture the dereference operation when it is used as a unary operator. However, as a binary operator, it is used to capture the multiplication operation.

An expression evaluation performs all the operations captured in the expression and yields a result. Usually, the result is an rvalue of a data type that is determined by the data types of the operand(s). The order of the operator evaluation is determined by the precedence and associativity of the operators. Though ordering is very natural, the reader should consult an introductory C++ book for the actual ordering.

Compound Statements

A compound statement is a series of statements surrounded by braces, { and }, and is used principally to group statements into an executable unit. For example, a C++ function is a compound statement. A compound statement is also used when the language syntax permits only a single statement to be specified and the application logic requires two or more statements to be executed.[8]

Statement Flow Control

The default flow of control is sequential in C++, so every C++ program begins with the statement main(). Each statement is executed in turn. When the final statement is executed, the program ends. However, sequential execution of state-

---

[8] Although it is possible to place a compound statement where you can place a statement, a compound statement is not terminated by a semicolon.

ments is probably inadequate except for the simplest programs. In the following sections, we look at some of the control statements available in C++.[9]

If statement

An if statement tests a particular condition. The form of an if statement is as follows:

```
if (expression) statement;
```

Whenever the expression evaluates to true (nonzero), a statement (or a compound statement) is executed. Otherwise, the statement is skipped. In either event, the following statement is executed after the if statement has completed.

Closely related to the if statement is the if-else statement. It has the following form:

```
if (expression) statement-1;
else            statement-2;
```

If the expression is nonzero, then statement-1 is executed and statement-2 is skipped. However, if the expression is zero, then statement-1 is skipped and statement-2 is executed. As with the if statement, after the if-else statement has completed, the following statement is executed.

Here is an example of using the if-else statement to get the minimum of two numbers:

```
if (y < x)
      min = y;
else
      min = x;
/* Below is the "following statement"   */
cout << "minimum is " << min;
```

If y < x evaluates to true, then the min is assigned the value of y; if y < x evaluates to false, then min is assigned the value of x. In either case, min is printed.

For statement

The for statement is an iterative statement typically used with a variable that is incremented or decremented. It is most commonly used to step through a fixed-length data structure, such as an array. The syntactic form of a for statement is

```
for (init-statement; expression-1; expression-2)
statement;
```

---

[9]   Please consult an introductory C++ book for details and for a complete set of control statements.

The init-statement can either be a declaration or an expression. It is usually used to initialize a variable; however, it may be null. Expression-1 serves as the loop control. Iterations are performed as long as expression-1 evaluates to true. In each iteration, the statement is executed. The statement may either be a single statement or a compound statement. If the first evaluation of expression-1 is false, the statement is never executed. Expression-2 is evaluated after each iteration of the loop. It is usually used to modify the variable initialized in the init-statement. If the first evaluation of expression-1 is false, expression-2 is never evaluated.

The following is a simple example of initializing:[10]

```
const int Max = 50;
float float_array[Max];
for (int i = 0; i <Max; i++)
{
float_array[i] = i;
}
```

In this example, each member of the array is initialized to its own index value as a floating-point number. For instance, float_array[0] = 0.0, and float_array[15] = 15.0.

What Is a Function?

Whether we are using structured methods or object-oriented methods, there is a stepwise refinement process that involves decomposing a process (a service in object-oriented technology) into smaller subprocesses. Function constructs are used to capture the processes and subprocesses. The "main" program in C++ is a sequence of function calls that may call other functions.

C++ provides the function mechanisms to perform some tasks, and the C++ libraries provide additional function mechanisms. One of the most important libraries for non-C programmers to understand is the string.h package of functions. The C community, and thus the C++ community, have agreed to treat the type char* as a form of string type. The understanding is that strings will be terminated by the character value of zero and that programmers will use the functions provided in string.h to manipulate the abstraction. The language partly supports this abstraction by defining string literals as being null-terminated; thus, a char* or char[ ] can be initialized with a literal string. For example, the C++ statement

```
char *aString = "Hello";
```

will result in aString[0] = 'H', aString[1] = 'e', aString[2] = 'l', aString[3] = 'l', aString[4] = 'o', aString[5] = '\0'.

---

[10] Notice that we begin initialization at index 0. All arrays in C++ begin with an index of 0.

The string.h package includes over 20 functions; the following are the most commonly used:

- strlen, which computes the string length
- strcpy, which copies a string
- strcmp, which checks if two strings are the same

A second example of additional function mechanisms supplied by libraries is the input/output mechanisms that experienced C++ programmers take for granted. In fact, input/output is not directly part of the language. The reader should be aware that there are several standard libraries for input/output in use with C++. There are the ANSI C standard library, stdio.h; the early C++ stream library, stream.h; and the newest C++ stream library, iostream.h. In this book, we will use iostream and teach you only the basics.[11]

The iostream.h library defines and declares three standard streams for the programmer. These are shown in Table 12-4. The iostream.h library overloads the two bit-shift operators for getting inputs and to send outputs as described in Table 12-5. In addition to all the library functions, user-defined services for a class of objects are also functions.

TABLE 12-4 Standard C++ Input and Output Objects

Stream	Description
cout	Standard out, normally the screen
cin	Standard in, normally the keyboard
cerr	Standard error, normally also the screen

TABLE 12-5 Iostream Operators

Operator	Description
<<	"Put to" output stream
>>	"Get from" input stream

Function Invocation

A C++ program is made up of one or more functions, one of which is main(). Every program execution begins with main(). When a C++ program is executing and encounters a function name, the function is called,[12] and control is passed to

---

[11] Please consult an introductory C++ programming book for details.

[12] In many textbooks, this is called invocation (i.e., the function is invoked).

that function. After the function does its work, control is passed back to the calling environment, which can then continue its processing. A simple example of a program is as follows:

```
#include <iostream.h>
#include <string.h>

main()
{
   char * s;
   cout << "\nHello, all" << endl;
   cout<< "\nPlease enter your name" << endl;
   cin >> s;
   if (strlen(s) > 20)
      cerr << "Error, name is" << strlen(s) -20;
      cerr << "characters toomany" << endl;
}
```

This program uses both the string and the iostream libraries. The first output statement puts a string "Hello, all" on the screen. The "\n" ensures a new line, and the endl is a special identifier that flushes the stream and adds a new line. The second output statement is similar to the first input statement, which expects a string of characters followed by the Enter (Return) key. The following statement uses the strlen function to get the length of the input string. If the input string is greater than 20 characters, it informs the user that the string is x characters too long.

Function Definition

The C++ code that describes what a function does is called the *function definition*. It takes the following form:

```
function header
 {
    statements
}
```

Everything before the left brace is part of the header of the function definition, and everything between the braces is the body of the function definition. The function header takes the following form:

```
return-type function-name (signature)
```

The return-type that precedes the function-name determines the data type of the value that the function returns. The return mechanism is explained below. The function-name is self-explanatory, and the signature is a list of parameters (arguments) that the function expects the caller of the function to provide.

Parameters are syntactically identifiers, and as such they can be used in the body of the function. Technically, these are formal parameters, since they are placeholders for actual values that are passed to the function when it is called. Upon function invocation, the values of the argument corresponding to the formal parameter are used in the body of the function when it is executed. Below is a function definition for the minimum function:

```
int min(const int x, const int y)
  {
   if (y < x)
        return (y);
   else
        return (x);
  }
```

The return statement has two purposes. First, when a return statement is executed, control is passed immediately back to the caller. Second, if an expression follows the keyword return, the value of the expression is returned to the caller. When an expression exists, it must be assignment-convertible to the return-type of the function definition header. Note that when there is no expression, the return-type of the function must be void. This is used when the caller does not expect a value to be returned.

Function Prototype

In C++, a function must declared before it is defined. This capability is used in object-oriented programming to preserve encapsulation. Such a declaration is called a function prototype and has the following form:

```
type name (argument-declaration list);
```

Here, type is the return type of the function, which may be either a user-defined data type or void. The name is the function name, and the argument-declaration list is a comma-separated list of data types. This list defines the data types of the values that the caller must provide to the function. It is also very common to have argument identifiers in the list; thus, the prototype can be identical to the function header.

Inlining

In C++, when the keyword inline prefaces a function declaration, the compiler will attempt to replace the function call with code. The compiler will parse the function and provide the semantic equivalent of a non-inline version of the function. The compiler will not allow complex functions to be inlined. This keyword basically replaces the Macro expansion.

Storage Class

Every variable and function in the C++ kernel language has two attributes: type and storage class. We have discussed native data types; now we need to discuss the storage classes. There are four storage classes: automatic, external, register, and static. Their corresponding keywords are: *auto, extern, register,* and *static.*

Auto

Variables declared within a function body are, by default, automatic, which is usually the most commonly used storage class. If a compound statement contains variable declarations, then the variables can only be acted upon within the scope of the enclosing compound statement. Declarations of variables within blocks are implicitly of storage class automatic. The keyword auto is used only to explicitly specify the automatic storage class.

When a block is entered, the system allocates memory (usually from the stack space) for the automatic variables. Within the block, these variables are defined and are considered local to the block. When the block is exited, the system releases the memory reserved for the automatic variables. The values for these variables are no longer available. If the block is reentered, the system will once again allocate memory for the automatic variables, but the previous values are lost.

Extern

When a variable is declared outside a function, storage is permanently assigned to it, and its storage class is extern. Such a variable is considered global to all the functions declared after it. Furthermore, upon block or function exits, the extern variable remains in existence. External variables never disappear; they exist throughout the life of the program. They are used to transmit values across functions. However, this can be dangerous, since the variable can be hidden if the identifier is redefined. The keyword extern is used to tell the compiler to look elsewhere for the definition of this variable. The variable may be in this file or some other file.

Since functions can also get information via the parameter-passing mechanism, most object-oriented experts would recommend infrequent use of external variables because they violate the encapsulation principle.

Register

The register storage class tells the compiler that the associated variables should be stored in high-speed memory registers if it is physically and semantically possible. Since resource[13] and semantic constraints may not make this possible, the variables will default to automatic when they cannot be made register.

---

[13] There are three or less than three registers available in most environments.

This storage class should be used only when the programmer is concerned with speed. Then choose a few variables that are most frequently accessed and declare them to be of the storage class register. However, be aware that contemporary optimizing compilers are frequently more astute than the programmer. Explicitly declaring something to have a register storage class may defeat the optimizer. Most of us consider this storage class to be of limited usefulness.

Static

Static declarations have two important uses. The first and more elementary use is to allow a local variable to retain its previous value when the block or function is reentered. This is in contrast to an automatic variable, which loses its value upon exit and must be reinitialized upon reentry. An example of this value-retention use of static is shown by adding code to the min function to maintain a count of the number of times it is called:

```
int min(const int x, const int y)
  {
    static int called_count = 0;
    called_count++;
    if (y < x)
        return (y);
    else
        return (x);
}
```

The second and more subtle use of static in external declarations is that it provides a privacy mechanism that is very important to maintaining the modularity of programs. The term *privacy* refers to the visibility or scope restrictions on the accessibility of variables and functions. Static external declarations are visible only within the file in which they are defined. Thus, unlike external variables that can be accessed by other files, a static declaration is available only throughout its own file.

In C++, external variables and static variables are initialized to zero if they are not explicitly initialized by the programmer. In contrast, automatic and register variables are not initialized by the system and can start with "garbage" values. For object-oriented programming, static should be used only as a privacy mechanism.

■ ■ SUMMARY

In this chapter, we learned about the following fundamentals of C++:

1. Tokens
2. Important keywords

3. Native data types

4. Statements

5. Two flow-of-control statements (if and for)

6. Functions

7. Invoking a function

8. Storage classes

CHAPTER

13

Implementing Class

To know what we think, to be masters of our own meaning, will make a solid foundation for great and weighty thought.

■ C. S. Peirce, *How to Make Our Ideas Clear*

The class mechanism in C++ allows developers to define their own data types in addition to the ones native to the language. At the initial implementation of the application/system, developers use this mechanism to implement the classes found in the model. In future releases of the application, developers will find the class mechanism useful when (1) they need to add functionality to an existing data type (either native or user-defined), and (2) they need to introduce a new abstraction that cannot map onto one of the defined data types or be derived from it.

191

Components of a Class

A C++ CLASS IS COMPOSED of four major parts:

1. **Collection of data members.** In object-oriented technology, this is the collection of attributes. There may be zero or more data members of any data type in this collection.

2. **Collection of member functions declaration.** This is the set of function prototypes that can be applied to the objects of that class. In object-oriented technology, this corresponds to the services. There may be zero or more function prototypes in the collection.

3. **Level of visibility.** Each member (data or function) may be specified as having one of the following levels of access (visibility): private, protected, or public. In object-oriented technology, all the data members should be private and all the services should be public.[1]

4. **Associated tag name.** This name serves as a type specifier for the user-defined class. Thus, the name may be used in the program where the native data type may appear.

The public member functions are referred to as the *class interface*. A class with private data members and public member functions is called an *abstract data type*.[2] A class in C++ supports the principle of information hiding and encapsulation. It also binds a collection of data members to a set of functions, and defines the characteristics of all instances created by that class. In brief, it provides the basic unit of reusability.

Class Definition

A CLASS DEFINITION IS COMPOSED of two parts: class header and class body. The class header is composed of the keyword class followed by the class tag name. The class body is enclosed by a pair of curly braces; the closing brace must be followed by either a semicolon or a declaration list. For example,

```
class Person
{
private:
            char name[40];
            char sex;
            int age;
};
```

---

[1] This is the implementation of the information-hiding and encapsulation principles.

[2] Now you know why some people call object-oriented analysis the discovery of abstract data types.

```
class Dog
{
 private:
                char name[40];
                int age;
} myDog, Lassie;
```

Note that in the Person example there is no declaration list. However, in the Dog example, two objects MyDog and Lassie are declared.

Class Body

WITHIN THE CLASS BODY, DATA members, member functions, and their associated levels of visibility are specified.

Visibility

Each member of the class has a level of visibility. There are three levels of visibility (public, private, protected) that a member may have. If a level of visibility is not explicitly stated for a member, the default visibility of private is used. The rules for using levels of visibility within the class body follow:

- All member declarations following a *public:* keyword are accessible by other classes (objects).
- All member declarations following a *private:* keyword are accessible only by the class itself.
- All member declarations following a *protected:* keyword are accessible only by the class and its subclasses.
- A subsequent use of *public:, protected:,* or *private:* will override earlier definitions only for the members that follow the keywords *public:, protected:,* or *private:*.

The preferred order for organizing the members of the class is public, protected, and private. When an object is instantiated, all members (data and functions) are accessible to its member functions. The level of visibility applies only to functions of another object, whether it is in the same class or in a different class. When a function has access to the private data of all objects of its class, it has *class scope.* Most member functions have access only to the private data of the object against which they are invoked; this is the *object scope.*

Data Members

The declaration of data members is the same as variable declarations in the language, with the exception that an explicit initializer is not allowed. For example, the following code will not work:

```
class Person
{
        /* Illegal Example    */
        int height = 0; int weight; char * name;
}
```

Initialization is done in the constructor for the class (see later chapter).

As with variable declarations, it is legal to combine the int declaration into one declaration. For example:

```
class Person
{
        int height, weight; char * name;
}
```

When possible, declare data members in increasing size of storage to optimize the alignment of storage on all machines. However, data members can also be of user-defined types. A class object can be declared as a data member only if the class definition has already been seen by the compiler before its use as a data member. However, when a declaration of a data member is a pointer or a reference to a class, a forward declaration of the class may be used. For example, the following is a definition of Woman using a forward declaration of Man:

```
class Man;      // forward declaration
class Woman
{
 private:
            char name[40];
        // pointer to Man object that is husband
            Man * husband;
};
```

A class is not considered defined until the closing brace of the class body is seen by the compiler; however, the class is considered to be declared after the opening brace. This allows a class to define pointers and references to itself as data members. Consider a link list of persons:

```
class LinkPerson
{
 private:
            Person me;
            LinkPerson *next;
            LinkPerson * prev;
};
```

Member Functions

Member functions of a class are declared inside the class body. A declaration consists of the function prototype. The function prototype is composed of a return type and a name, followed by a signature enclosed in parentheses. The signature consists of a comma-separated list of argument types. An argument type is any native type, derived type, or user-defined type. An argument name may follow each type specifier.

An example of declaring member functions follows:

```
class Person
{
 public:    // member functions
    char*     getName();
    char      getSex();
    int       getAge();
    void      setName(char *)
    void      setSex(char s);
    void      setAge(int a);
 private:   // data members
    char      name[40];
    char      sex;
    int       age, height, weight;
};
```

The argument list is referred to as the signature of a function because it distinguishes between two functions with the same name. The name alone does not necessarily uniquely identify a function. However, the name and its signature *will* uniquely identify a function. For example,

```
class Person
{
 public:    // member functions
    char      getSex();
    void      setSex(char);
    void      setSex(int);
    . . .
 private:    // data members
         char name[40];
         char sex;
         int age, height, weight;
};
```

We can use the setSex() function by using an integer as an argument as well as using char as an argument.[3] This may be necessary because in one application the

---

[3] We will discuss the return type void in chapter 14.

gender may be captured as an integer (e.g., 1 for female, 0 for male), while in another application gender is captured as a character (e.g., f for female, m for male).

Member functions are distinguished from other functions by the following characteristics:

- Member functions have full access privileges to the private, protected, and public members of the class, whereas other functions have access only to the public members of the class.

- Member functions of one class do not have access privileges to members of another class. However, when one class has a relationship with another class, it has access to the other class's public members.

- Member functions are defined only within the scope of the class, whereas ordinary functions are defined at file scope. Member function names are therefore not visible outside the scope of the class. This requires that other classes have access to an instance of the class before they can use the class's services.

- Member functions can overload only other member functions of their class.

Generalization Using Inheritance

IN ADDITION TO CAPTURING THE attributes and the service prototypes, the generalization/specialization relationship must also be captured in the header file. We will look at the code necessary to represent the multiple inheritance for Platypus. Below are the abbreviated class definitions:

```
class Endangered
{// class definition for Endangered}
class OrganicMatter
{// class definition for Organic Matter}
class Animal: public OrganicMatter
{// class definition for Animal}
class Mammal: public Animal
{// class definition for Mammal}
class Platypus: public Animal, public Endangered
{// class definition for Platypus}
```

In this example, "class Animal: public OrganicMatter" tells the compiler that **OrganicMatter** is the superclass of **Animal**. The public keyword means that the public members of **OrganicMatter** will also be public members of **Animal**, the protected members of **OrganicMatter** will also be protected members of **Animal**, and the private members of **OrganicMatter** will also be private members of **Animal**. The line "class Platypus: public Animal, public Endangered" tells the compiler that the platypus has two superclasses as parents, both with public inheritance. In

Chapter 16 we discuss other keywords associated with inheritance. The syntax for implementing generalization/specialization using inheritance follows:

```
class class-tag-name: public parent's class-tag-name
```

Recommended Approach

THE FUNDAMENTAL BUILDING BLOCK OF object-oriented technology is the class. One of the first things we have to do in coding is to translate the classes given in the model into class definitions.

The following guidelines are helpful:

1. Variables (attributes) are declared as *private* members. This is necessary for information hiding.

2. Methods (services) are declared as *public* members. This is necessary for other objects to have access to the public services of an object of this class.

3. Services that are only used by methods within the class are declared as *private* members.

4. Variables (attributes) and methods are declared as *protected* members if they need to be accessible to subclasses (derived classes) and not to the client classes of the derived classes.

5. Data members must be defined in the class declaration.

6. In order to separate the function declaration (interface definition) from the function definition (implementation definition), place the code for the member functions outside the class declaration, either in the same or different file.

7. Do not make a data member public unless (a) you make it read-only or (b) changing the data member has no impact on the behavior of the object.

8. Do not make implementation-related member functions public.

9. Each member function of a class should either modify or provide access to data members of that class (strong cohesion).

10. A class should depend on as few other classes as possible (weak coupling).

11. Classes should not communicate via global variables.

12. Minimize information exchanged between classes. Call by pointer or reference can help.

13. All application generalization relationships are implemented as public inheritance.

14. Use abstract base classes as appropriate.

Example

In C++, the class definition is placed in the header (.h) file. Below is an example of a class definition for the Window class:

```
    // include files are normally first
#include <iostream.h>
#include <string.h>
#include <stdlib.h>
    // we put typedef here for ease of understanding
typedef float Length;
    // forward declarations are placed here for compiler
class Shape;
class LinkScreen;
 // start class definition
class Window
{
public:
    // public services (instance methods)
    void add_box (Length x, Length y, Length width, Length height);
    void add_circle (Length x, Length y, Length radius);
    void move (Length deltax, Length deltay);
    int group_selection ();
    void ungroup_selection ();
private:
    //private attributes (variables)
    Length xmin; Length ymin;
    Length xmax; Length ymax;
    LinkScreen *next;
    //private method(s)
    void add_to_selection (Shape* shape);
};
```

Here we see a typical class definition; the keywords are in bold only for ease of understanding. The include files are given here for tutorial purposes. The iostream.h gives the developer access to cout, cin, and cerr as well as all the standard operators and manipulators associated with stream input/output. The string.h gives the developer access to the standard functions that help manipulate char * like a string. The stdlib.h gives access to the mathematical functions.

Normally, the services in string.h and iostream.h are needed to define operations used in the methods. Thus, they usually only need to be put in the .C files. In general, the only include files that should be in the .h file are the superclass(es) of the class being defined. Normally, all usage of classes in the .h file is by reference or pointer, so only a forward declaration of the other class is needed. However, the exception is when another class is embedded in the class being defined. In this case, the programmer must use an include file, since a forward declaration will not suffice.

■ ■ SUMMARY

The components of a class definition in a header (.h) file are as follows:

1. All the include files
2. All the typedefs
3. All the forward declarations
4. Header (keyword *class* and tag-name) plus inheritance
5. Opening brace: {
6. Keyword *public:*
7. All the public service prototypes
8. Keyword *private:*
9. Attributes (as variables) and private service prototypes
10. Close brace: }
11. Optional instance declarations
12. Semicolon

CHAPTER

14

Implementing Static Behavior

Of things which hold together by nature there are two kinds: those that are unborn, imperishable, and eternal, and those that are subject to generation and decay.

■ Aristotle

One of the major goals in our analysis was to specify the behavior of all the services associated with a class. In the previous chapter, we learned how to declare a service identification using a function prototype. In this chapter, we will see how to turn a service specification into executable code. In the previous chapter, we declared the functions by specifying their prototype in the .h file and within the body of the class definition. Capturing the definitions of the functions (i.e., to capture the behaviors of the services) is discussed in this chapter.

Function Definition

THE FORM OF A FUNCTION definition follows:

```
return-type function-name (list of arguments)
{
  statements
}
```

For example, here is the function definition of a function that returns the greatest common denominator:

```
int greatest_common_denominator(int arg1, int arg2)
{   // return the greatest common denominator
    int temp;
    while (arg2)
    {
      temp = arg2;
      arg2 = arg1 % arg2;
      arg1 = temp;
    }
    return (arg1)
}
```

A function that does not return a value has a return type of *void*. The actions performed when a function is called are specified between the braces. The collection of statements or actions is sometimes called the *body* of the function and is also a block from a programming perspective. A function may cause another function to be executed by calling the other function within its body.

A function call can cause one of the following to occur:

- If the called function has been declared inline, the body of the function is expanded at the point of its call during compilation. This is used to optimize small and frequently called functions and still support the information-hiding principle of object-oriented technology.[1]

- If the function is not declared inline, the function is invoked at run time. A function invocation transfers control to the function being called and suspends execution of the calling function. When the called function has completed, the suspended calling function resumes execution at the point immediately following the call.

---

[1] However, there is a compilation cost to this. Every time a change occurs in the .h file that contains the inline function, all the other files that use the inline function will recompile, even if the change in the .h file has nothing to do with the inline function.

Return Type

The return type plus the argument list defines the public interface of the function. The calling function needs to know only the public interface to call the function. As shown in the previous chapter, the prototype, which includes the public interface, is declared in the .h file of the class.[2]

The return type of a function may be either a native data type, derived type, user-defined type, or void. For example, consider the following lines of code:

```
    //   forward declaration and enum definition
class Dog
enum Gender {male, female};
    //     function declarations
int getAge();
char * getName();
Gender getSex();
void setAge(int newAge);
Dog* getDog();
```

The getAge() function has a native return type, the getName() function has a derived return type, the getSex() function has a user-defined return type, and the setAge() function has a void return type. The getDog() function has a derived, user-defined return type and returns a pointer to an instance of the class **Dog**.

Neither an array nor a function may be specified as a return type. However, a pointer to an array or a function can be specified as a return type. For example,

```
int[100] get100randomNumbers(); // this is not legal
int *   get 100randomNumer();   // this is legal
```

However, when you return a pointer or a reference to an object, there are some pitfalls of which you need to be aware (see "Passing Arguments"). A function without an explicit return value is assumed to have a return type of int; thus a function that does not return a value must declare a return type of void.

Return Statement

The return statement is used to terminate a function that is currently executing and return control to the calling function. There are two forms for the return statement, *return* and *return expression*.

---

[2] Since a function can only be defined once, the function definition is typically specified in its own file with other related functions. Normally, all the function definitions for a single class are contained in one file. This file is called the .C for the class.

The first return statement is used when the return type is void, and the second is used for the nonvoid return types. The expression may be arbitrarily complex and may involve a function. However, for ease of maintenance it is recommended that the expression be only a variable of the return type. An implicit conversion will be applied, if possible, in instances when the variable is not of the return type. A function can return only one value. If the application logic requires that multiple values be returned, the developer might do any of the following:

- Return an aggregate data type that contains multiple values. In this case, the developer will create a class to represent the aggregate and usually will return a pointer or a reference to that class.

- Formal arguments may be defined as either pointer or reference types. This will allow the function to have access to the lvalue of these arguments. Then the lvalue may be used to change the rvalue of these variables.

- A global or static variable may be defined outside the function. Since a global variable is accessible from within any function when properly declared, the function can return a second "return" value via the global variable.

Only the first method is recommended for object-oriented technology when multiple values need to be returned. The second method is used when the function must access the member functions of that variable (object). The third method should rarely be used for the following reasons:

1. The functions that utilize the global variable(s) now depend upon the existence and type of the global variable. This makes reuse more difficult.

2. There is a loss of encapsulation. Global dependencies increase the likelihood of introducing bugs when programs are modified.

3. If a global variable has an incorrect value, the entire program must be searched to find the error; there is no information hiding.

4. Global variables violate the information-hiding and encapsulation principles of object-oriented technology.

5. Recursion is more difficult to manage correctly.

Function Argument List

The argument list of a function may not be omitted. A function that does not take any arguments can be represented either with an empty argument list or the single keyword *void*. For example, the following two declarations of getAge are equivalent:

```
int     getAge()    {return age}
int     getAge(void) {return age}
```

The signature consists of a comma-separated list of argument types. An argument type is any native type, derived type, or user-defined type. An argument name usually follows each type specifier. The argument name is used in the body of the function to access the argument as a variable of the defined type given in the signature.

Since it is used in the body as a variable, each argument name appearing in a signature must be unique and different from the local variable names used in the body. The shorthand, comma-separated type-declaration syntax may not be used in the list of arguments.

If argument names are specified in both the declaration and definition of a function, different names may be used in each. However, the type specifier must be the same. Omitting an argument or using an argument of the wrong type would be caught at compile time, because C++ is a strongly typed language. Both the return type and the argument list of every function call are type-checked during compilation. If there is a mismatch between an actual type and a type declared in the function prototype, an implicit conversion will be applied where possible. However, if an implicit conversion is not possible or if the number of arguments is incorrect, a compile-time error is given.

We suggest that the argument list to any function be small. Some developers limit the number of arguments to seven; thus less than seven. If one wants to adhere to this guideline, what does one do with functions that require a long argument list? There are two ways to handle this:

1. The function may be trying to do too much; you may want to divide the function into two or more smaller specialized functions.
2. Define a class type to do the validity checking. The validity checking can then be performed inside the class member function instead of the using function. This provides better encapsulation and reduces the size of the code of the function.

It is sometimes impossible to list the type and number of all the arguments that might be passed to a function. In this case, you can suspend type-checking by using ellipses (...) within the function signature. Ellipses tell the compiler that zero or more arguments may follow and that the types of the arguments are unknown. The printf() function is an example of the necessary use of ellipses. The printf() function is declared in C++ as follows:

```
printf(const char *,  ... )
```

This requires that every call to printf() be given a first argument of type char*, and after that there can be zero or more arguments. For example,

```
printf("Good Day, you all\n" )
```

uses only one argument, while

```
printf("Good Day %s\n",  userName)
```

uses two arguments. The % indicates the presence of another argument, while the s indicates the type of the argument.

Note that the following two functions are not equivalent:

```
char     func();
char     func( ... );
```

Func() is declared a function that takes no arguments, while func(...) is declared a function that takes zero or more arguments.

Passing Arguments

WHEN A FUNCTION IS CALLED, storage on a structure (referred to as the program's run-time stack) is allocated to the function. Furthermore, each formal argument is provided with storage space within the structure. The storage size is determined by the type specifier for the argument. That storage remains on the stack until the function is terminated. At that point, the storage is freed and is no longer accessible to the program.

The arguments between the parentheses of the function call are referred to as the *actual arguments* of the call. Argument passing is the process of actual arguments initializing the storage of the formal arguments. We will discuss the following argument-passing mechanisms: pass-by-value, reference, or pointer, and passing an array.

Pass-by-Value

The default process of argument passing in C++ is to copy the rvalue of the actual argument into the storage allocated in the structure of the run-time stack for the formal argument. This is called *pass-by-value*.

In the process of pass-by-value, the contents of the actual arguments are not changed because the function access manipulates its local copies, which are on the run-time stack. In general, changes made to these local copies are not reflected in the values of the actual arguments. Once the function terminates, these local values are not accessible to the program. This means that a programmer of the calling function does not need to save and restore argument values when making a function call.

Without a pass-by-value mechanism, each argument would have to be saved before a function call and restored after the function call by the programmer, because they could be altered. The only exception is when arguments corresponding to formal arguments are declared const. Passing-by-value has the least potential for side effects and requires the least work by the programmer of the calling function. Unfortunately, as well-behaved as pass-by-value is, it is not suitable for every function. Examples of these situations include the following:

■ Passing a large object as an argument.[3]
■ When the value(s) of the argument(s) must be modified by the function.

In such situations, either of the following alternatives is available to the programmer:

■ Make the formal argument declaration as a pointer to the type specifier.
■ Make the formal argument declaration as a reference to the type specifier.

Reference or Pointer Argument

The declaration of the formal argument as a reference or pointer overrides the default pass-by-value mechanism. The function receives the lvalue of the actual argument rather than a copy of the argument itself. This now gives the function access to the public data of the object. This is very useful when the function needs to change the values of the actual argument. Remember that the pass-by-value mechanism only allows the function to manipulate local copies of the argument.

Examples

Examples of the three argument-passing mechanisms are shown below.

```
void Collision::calv(Ball ball1, Length deltay)
{
// this is pass-by-value; a copy of Ball is made.
// if we had had Rectangle Ball, a copy of ball as a rectangle
// would be made.
// in addition, a copy of deltay as a Length is given.
}


void Collision::calp (Ball* ball2, Side* top)
{
// this is pass by pointer; pointers to instance of Ball and to
// instance of Side are sent to the routine. We will assume that
// deltay is a data member of Side.
// the routine can call the services of Ball and Side.
}


void Collision::cala(Ball& ball3, Side& lside)
```

---

[3] The time and space required to allocate and copy the class object onto the run-time stack are excessive for a real-world application.

```
{
// this is pass by reference; addresses to Ball and lside are sent
// to the routine. The routine can call the services of Ball and
// Side.
}
```

In C++, the argument-access syntax is different for each mechanism:

```
void Collision::calv(Ball ball, Length deltay)
{
    ball.rect();
    ymin = ymin + deltay;
    // here you use the copies of the values directly.
}


void Collision::calp (Ball* ball, Side* top)
{
    // here we use the operator -> to access the methods of a
    // class in object-oriented C++.
    ball->setYmin (ball->getYmin() + top->getDeltay());
    // assuming there are member functions called setYmin
    // getYmin for class Ball and getDeltay for class Side.
}


void Collision::cala(Ball& ball, Side* lside)
{
    // here we use the operator . to access the methods of a
    // class in object-oriented C++.
    ball.setYmin (ball.getYmin() + top->getDeltay());
    // assuming there are member functions called setYmin
    // getYmin for class Ball and getDeltay for class Side.
}
```

Array Argument

Arrays in C++ do not use the pass-by-value mechanism. Rather, an array is passed as a pointer to its zeroth element. For example, the statement

```
int& getValue(int[10], int);
```

is treated by the compiler as

```
int& getValue(int *, int);
```

The array size of 10 is ignored by the compiler in the declaration of formal arguments. The following declarations are equivalent:

```
// all of the declarations below are equivalent
    int& getValue(int *, int);
    int& getValue(int [],int);
    int& getValue(int [10], int);
    int& getValue(int [40], int);
```

This has the following implications for the programmer:

- The changes to an array argument within the called function (i.e., getValue) are made to the actual array of the call and not to a local copy. In cases where the array being passed as an argument must remain unchanged, programmers need to simulate a pass-by-value mechanism. The most straightforward way to do this is to pass a copy of the array to the function.
- The size of the array is not part of the type specification. Neither the function nor the compiler know the actual size of an array when it is being passed. Array-size checking is not done at compile time.

For example,

```
int& getValue(int [40], int);   // compiler sees it as getValue(int *, int)
main()
{
 int i, *pointer, intArray[20];
 pointer = getValue( &i, 21) // will compile, run-time error
 pointerf = getValue(intArray, 30 ); // will compile, run-time error
}
```

Return Type as Reference or Pointer

THE DEFAULT MECHANISM FOR THE return type is pass-by-value. For object-oriented programming, returning a pointer or reference to an object may be more desirable and more efficient. When a function is returning a pointer or a reference, the programmer should be aware of two pitfalls:

1. Returning a reference to a local object. The local object goes out of scope with the termination of the function. The reference is left aliased to undefined memory. For example,

```
// this code will not work
Person * createPerson(char * name)
 { // the declaration below declares p as a pointer to Person,
   // and the function Person() creates a Person object
     Person *p = Person(name);
            return p;
   // note: p is also undefined when the function is terminated
 }
```

2. The value returned is the actual lvalue of the object. Any modification performed by the calling function will change the object being returned. For example,

```
int& getValue(int * intArray, int j)
  { // this function returns the reference to the j-th element of the intArray
            return intArray[j];
  }
```

```
// let there be an array of digits
int dArray[] = {9, 8, 7, 6, 5, 4, 3, 2, 1}
    // here is a short program that will change the value of dArray
        main()
        {
            getValue(dArray, 0) ++;
            // this will change the value for dArray[0] from 9 to 10.
            // does* the programmer intend to do this?
        }
```

Casting

IN C++, MANY OF THE library functions specify the argument type as a reference. However, in object-oriented programming, programmers deal mostly with pointers. Usually, the function deals with a collection of objects, and collections are easier to handle as an array of pointers. For example, relationships usually return a collection (i.e., array) of pointers to objects. The operator *, used as a unary operator, will cast a pointer to a reference. For example, let us assume we have the following two methods that belong to different objects:

```
        Collision::detect_collision (GO_formation* f, Ball* b)
```

and

```
        Lib_Collider::collide (GO_formation& form)
```

If we need the service of collide in the detect_collision method, we can write the following:

```
        Collision::detect_collision (GO_formation* f, Ball* b)
        {
          Lib_Collider* collider;
          collider->collide(*f)
          // here f is dereferenced into an address
        }
```

Const and Defaults

Const

The proper use of the const keyword will improve the robustness of C++ code. Const controls side effects in the language and is used to replace macro definitions in the language. This is very important if you plan to use a symbolic debugger, because #define is processed by the preprocessor, and its name is not available to the debugger. For example,

```
main()
{
#define Min 1        // this makes Min a constant
                     // Min is not defined for the debugger
const int Max = 10;  // this makes Max a constant
                     // Max is defined for the debugger
};
```

Min is not available to a symbolic debugger because this is translated by the preprocessor to a 1.

Const is also used to guarantee that the function will not alter an argument passed to it by reference or pointer. For example,

```
void function1(Window& win1)
{
// C++ will allow you to modify data members
// of the instance win1.
};

void function2(const Window& win2)
{
// C++ will not allow you to modify data members
// of the instance win2.
};
```

Another use of const is to declare a function that will not alter the data within the object. This is important, because when a function accepts a const pointer to a class as a formal argument, it means that the function may only access a const function of that class.

An example of using const follows:

```
class Point
{
public:
        int X()    {return x_value; }
        void X(int new_x) {x_value = new_x}
```

```
private:
        int x_value;
        int y_value;
};

void function1(const Point& p)
{
   Point local_pt; int local_num;
   local_pt = p;            // Legal
   local_num = p.X();       // Illegal
   p.X(14);                 // Illegal
};
```

However, when the getValue function is declared const (must be done in the function prototype in the .h file),

```
class Point
{
public:
        int X() const {return x_value; }
        void X(int new_x) {x_value = new_x}
private:
        int x_value;
        int y_value;
};

void function1(const Point& p)
{
   Point local_pt; int local_num
   local_pt = p;            // Legal
   local_num = p.X();       // Legal
   p.X(14);                 // Illegal
};
```

The keyword const may be used in two positions in a pointer declaration, as shown below:

```
char* const pointer1 = "Constant Pointer";
const char* pointer2 = "Constant Data";
const char* const pointer3 = "Constant Data and Constant Pointer";
char*  pointer4;
```

In the above examples, const to the left of the * means constant data, while const to the right of the * means a constant pointer.

Default Initializers

A function may provide default argument initalizers for one or more of its arguments by using the initialization syntax within a signature. In object-oriented programming, default initializers are usually used only in constructors.

Identifier Scope

RECALL THAT AN IDENTIFIER IS a name for a data item or object. The identifier must be unique when used, since the program usually uses the identifier to access the data (rvalue). This does not mean, however, that a name can be used only once in a program. A name can be reused if there is some context to distinguish between different instances of the name. A good example of using context is overloading a function name, as in the following:

```
void    setSex(char);
void    setSex(int);
```

This example shows the signature of a function being used as a context. The two functions have the same name (setSex) so the name is overloaded. However, each function has a unique signature.

A second and more general context is *scope*. C++ supports three kinds of scope: *file scope, local scope,* and *class scope.* A name may be reused in a distinct scope; each variable has an associated scope that, together with the name, uniquely identifies that variable. A variable is visible (accessible) only to the code within its scope. For example, a local variable declared within a compound statement is accessible only by the statements within the compound statement.

Local scope is that portion of the program contained within the definition of a function. Each function represents a distinct local scope. Furthermore, within a function, each compound statement (or block) containing one or more declaration statements represents an associated local scope. Local block scopes may be nested. The argument list is treated as being within the local scope of the function.

In class scope, every class maintains its own associated scope. Class scope includes the names of all its class members.[4]

File scope is the outermost scope of a program; it encloses both local and class scope. It is that portion of the program that is not contained within a class or a function definition.

A variable defined at the file scope that is accessible to the entire program is referred to as a *global variable*. Global variables should not be used in object-oriented programming because they violate both the encapsulation and information-hiding principles. In spite of all this, there may be situations where it makes sense to access variables or functions not within the scope of the code. What

---

[4]   Both data members and member functions are within the class scope.

mechanism in C++ supports this? The *scope operator*(::) supports the ability of a line of code to access public functions or variables in another scope. An example of an object-oriented use of the scope operator is provided in Chapter 17 when static members are discussed.

Recommended Approach

IN THE CODE FOR THE class definition in the header file, the data members are defined, but the functions are only declared. We must now define the functions. A function can be defined in either the .h file[5] or the .C file.

Definition in the .h file

The definition of an inline function[6] within the header file may be placed within the class body or defined outside the class body. When the definition of a member function is placed inside the class body, the function is automatically handled as an inline function. For example,

```
class Person
{
 public:   // member functions
      char*    getName();
      char     getSex();
      int      getAge() {return age}
      void     setSex(char s)
      void     setAge(int a) {age = a;}
 private:   // data members
            char name[40];
            char sex;
            int  age, height, weight;
};
```

In this example, the getAge function returns the age of the person as an integer. The setAge function changes the age of the person to the first and only argument passed as part of the signature; it does not return anything. Furthermore, both functions are inline.

If the function definition contains more than two statements, the function should be defined outside of the class body. However, to do this requires using the

---

[5] All functions defined in the .h file are inline functions. For example, code will be generated in line to replace the function call written by the programmer. This will cause the program to run faster, but it will take more storage and execution space.

[6] Inline functions should be only a few lines of code. In fact, inline is only a suggestion to the compiler, which will actually decide if inline will be enforced.

scope operator to identify the function as a member of the correct class. Further-more, if the function is to be inline, it must explicitly declare itself to be inline. For example:

```
inline void
Person::setSex(char s)
{ // sex can only be m or f
    if (s == 'm' || s == 'f')
        {sex = s; return;}
    else
        { // error in input, ignore request
            return;}
}
```

The above code defines setSex as an inline function that is defined outside of the class body. Normally, when this is done, the code follows the class definition.[7]
Note that an inline function has some of the properties of a function:

- It is a class member.
- Type-checking is done at compile time.
- Overloading is permitted on the function by value.

An inline function also has all of the properties of a macro:

- Code is expanded in the calling object.
- Code is linked at compile or link time and not at run time.
- More code space is used.
- Execution time is faster.
- There is no recursion.

The most common functions to inline are the get and set functions because the overhead of a function call far exceeds inlining the couple of instructions for these functions. However, the reader should be aware that inlining violates the encapsulation principle. If you change the .h file of a class, all the other classes may recompile because they are tied to the .h file via the inline function of that class.

Definition in the .C file

In practice, most application functions will be defined in the .C file.[8] Below is an example of placing the definition of setAge in the .C file.[9]

---

[7] The extra code validates the input; nowadays, this is usually done in the user interface. Business applications may assume that what they are getting is a legal value.

[8] .C is an AT&T convention, and .pp is a Turbo C++ convention.

[9] Neither function is inline; inline functions must be defined in the .h file.

```
void Person::setAge(int a)
{
    age = a;
}
```

To help us code the function body, we use the following coding rules for instance member functions:

1. A member function has access to

    ■ All members (data and functions) of the object
    ■ All arguments passed to it via the calling object
    ■ All local variables within its (method) scope
    ■ Global variables within its class scope
    ■ *this*, which is a pseudo–data member of any object (contains the address of the object)

2. When you need to declare local variables, keep variables at the smallest possible scope.
3. When you need to access a function of a superclass, place the superclass name and scope operator before the function name.
4. To increase robustness of code, use the const keyword appropriately. Const should be used to

    ■ Replace macro definitions
    ■ Guarantee that functions will not alter an object passed by reference or pointer
    ■ Declare a function that will not alter the object

To conclude, we will apply the coding rules to our example as follows:

```
class Person
{
 public:   // member functions
      char*    getName() const {return name;}
      char     getSex()   const {return sex;}
      int      getAge() const {return age;}
      void     setSex(const char s) {sex = s;}
      void     setAge(const int a) {age = a;}
 private:   // data members
          char name[40];
          char sex;
          int  age, height, weight;
};
```

■ ■ SUMMARY

To implement the service specification, we can place the code in either the .h file or the .C file.[10] The .h file is appropriate when we have a few lines of code and having this code inlined would be better than a separate subroutine call. However, most application functions should be in the .C file; they are usually more than a few lines of code, and subroutine calls are the most effective way to implement these functions.

Coding the service specification is more restrictive than coding a procedural function. The rules for coding a function are the following:[11]

1.   A member function has access to

- ■ All members (data and functions) of the object
- ■ All arguments passed to it via the calling object
- ■ All local variables within its (method) scope
- ■ Class global (static) variables within its class scope
- ■ *this*, which is a pseudo–data member of any object (contains the address of the object)

2.   When you need to declare local variables, keep variables at the smallest possible scope.

3.   When you need to access a function of a superclass, place the superclass name and scope operator before the function name.

4.   Const should be used to[12]

- ■ Replace macro definitions
- ■ Guarantee that the function will not alter an object passed by reference or pointer
- ■ Declare a function that will not alter the object

---

[10] If the code is going to be part of a library, putting code in the .h file allows a client of that library to change the code; if it is in the .C file, then the client cannot change it.

[11] These are the guidelines for coding an instance member function; not all the rules apply to a static function. The rules for a static function are left to the reader.

[12] To increase robustness of code, use the const keyword appropriately.

Instantiating and Deleting Objects

Had I been present at the Creation, I would have given some useful hints for the better ordering of the universe.

Alfonso the Wise, King of Castile

In the previous implementation chapters, we learned to implement classes and their associated methods. However, actions and tasks that we expect an application/system to perform usually involve specific objects. In fact, we explained the object-oriented communication and control mechanisms as a message-passing paradigm between objects. We should expect that the execution of the program does not operate on classes, but on a specific object(s). For a program to operate on a specific object, it must be able to create and destroy it. In this chapter, we will learn how objects are created and destroyed by the program.

Introduction

AN OBJECT NEEDS MEMORY AND some initial values when it is used by the program and/or function. For most of the native and derived data types that it supplies, the language provides for this through declarations that are also definitions. For example,

```
void Compute::funx()
{
 int n = 300;
 short z[100];
  struct noClass {int i1, int i2} inG2 = {5, 70};
   . . .
}
```

All the objects (i.e., n, z[100] and inG2) are created at function (block) entry when the function funx() is called. Typically, memory space is taken from a run-time system stack. Assuming that we are on a system that defines integers to be 4 bytes and short to be 2 bytes, the int object n would be allocated 4 bytes off the stack, the array of short object z would be allocated 200 bytes off the stack, and the NoClass object inG2 would be allocated 8 bytes off the stack. In each case, the compiler will generate the code for the construction and initialization of these objects. Furthermore, because these are local variables, the compiler will generate the code to deallocate these objects upon exit from the function.

In creating user-defined data types (classes), the user of these data types (classes) can expect similar management of the class-defined objects. A class needs a mechanism to specify object-creation and object-destruction behavior, so that other functions can use objects of this class in a manner similar to the native data types.

Constructors

A CONSTRUCTOR IS A SPECIAL member function with the same name as the class. It allows the client programmer to initialize data values of data members of the object, change values of static variables of a class, and create aggregate objects.[1] It will also involve allocating free store when the keyword *new* is used with the constructor. A constructor is called, or invoked, when its associated type is used in a definition. It is also invoked when pass-by-value is used to pass an argument of this type to a function.

A constructor may be overloaded and can take on arguments; however, it may neither specify a return type nor explicitly return a value. Overloading is commonly used as a vehicle to provide a set of alternative initializations. For

---

[1]   A constructor is called only at instantiation (i.e., when an object is created).

example, let us declare three constructors for the class Person. The first constructor will initialize the private data member "sex," the second constructor will initialize the private data member "age," and the third constructor will initialize the private data member "name." Consider the following example:

```
class Person
  {
    public:
            Person(const char inputSex);
            Person(const int inputAge);
            Person(const char * const input_name);
              . . .
  }
```

This example includes three constructors. The first takes one argument, a single character. The second takes one argument, an integer, and the third takes one argument, a pointer to a character array. The definitions of the three constructors are as follows:

```
Person::Person(const char inputSex)
          { // note: the other data members (name, age)
             // are undefined.
               sex = inputSex;
          }

Person::Person(const int inputAge)
          { // note: the other data members (name, sex)
             // are undefined.
               age = inputAge;
          }

Person::Person( const char * const input_name)
          { // note: the other data members (sex, age)
             // are undefined.
               name = new char[strlen(input_name) + 1];
             strcpy(name, input_name);
          }
```

Note that the constructor has no return type and cannot use a return-expression statement. Because initialization is usually linear code, the return statement is usually not written. Moreover, there is usually nothing complicated about the constructor code.

The constructor's power lies in the mechanism that invokes it implicitly for each object of the class. It is invoked when its class type is used in a definition and when pass-by-value is used for an argument of this type in a function call. When the function is invoked, the mechanism will allocate the storage necessary to contain the nonstatic data members defined in the class. It will allocate storage either from the stack or the heap, depending on whether the keyword new is used.

If no constructor is declared with a class, the compiler provides a default constructor. This constructor requires no arguments and will only allocate space; it will not initialize any data members. One should take care when relying on the default constructor. Data members of built-in types are not guaranteed to be initialized. It is wise to initialize all data members in the constructor. For example, a more practical constructor for the Person class follows:

```
Person(const char * const input_name
                const char inputSex
                const int inputAge
                const int inputWeight
                const int inputHeight)
```

The above constructor will initialize all the data members. However, classes with a large number of data members using a constructor to define an object require programmers to attend to every small detail of the class. It would be nice to be able to provide default values that are, although not universally applicable, appropriate in a majority of the cases. This would free programmers to enter only the values that apply to their function.

A constructor (and any function) may specify a default value for one or more of its arguments using the initialization syntax within the signature. For example, consider the following signature for constructor of Person that initializes only the name, sex and age of a Person object:

```
Person(char* n, char s = 'U',
             int a = -1);
```

This constructor provides default argument initializers that can be invoked with or without a corresponding actual argument. If an argument is provided, it overrides the default value; otherwise, the default value is used. For example,

```
main()
{
    Person Baby1("Undecided");    // This is a baby in infancy
    Person Baby2("Susan",'F'); // This is a baby girl in infancy
    Person Bill("Bill Gates",'M', 35); // This is Bill Gates in middle age
    Person Rich("Rich", , 50); // This is an illegal use of default values
    Person p50(, , 50); // This is an illegal use of default values

};
```

Note that the arguments to the call are resolved positionally. A programmer must then do the following:

- Specify the default initializer for all or only a subset of its arguments.
- Supply the rightmost uninitalized argument with the default initializer before any arguments to its left may be supplied.
- Specify the default initializer(s) in the function declaration contained in the .h file, and not in the function definition in the .C file.
- Arrange the arguments so that those most likely to take user-specified values occur first.[2]

Destructors

A DESTRUCTOR IS A MEMBER function whose name is the class name preceded by the tilde (~). This function is the complement of the constructor and is used to "deinitialize" and "destruct" an object of the class. It performs any necessary cleanup before the object is destroyed. Typically, it is used to destroy complex or aggregate objects, or change values of the static variables of a class. Like a constructor, a destructor may neither specify a return type nor explicitly return a value. Destructors are implicitly invoked when objects of their class must be destroyed. This happens upon block exit and function exit when an object of the class has been declared as a local variable.

A destructor may not take any arguments and, therefore, may not be overloaded. For example,

```
class Person
{
public:
        Person (int AnAge, char SomeSex)
            {Age = AnAge; Sex = SomeSex;}
          Person () {Age = 0; Sex = 'b';}
        ~Person ();    // this is the destructor
    private:
            int Age; char Sex;
        };
```

Note that in the above example there are two constructors (both inline functions) and one destructor.

The destructor has no return type and cannot return a value. For example,

```
class String
  {
    public:
            String (const char * s, int len)   //this is the constructor
```

---

[2]   This is done because once a default is used for an argument, all arguments to the right of it must also be defaulted.

```
                        {length = len;
                          ptrtostr = new char[len + 1]; //this allocates space
                          strcpy(str, s);                //this copies
                        }
                ~String ()     // this is the destructor
                        {delete str;}
        private:
                int length;
                char * ptrtostr;
};
```

A destructor mechanism is automatically invoked whenever an object of its class goes out of scope or the delete operator is applied to the class pointer. First, the mechanism calls the destructor function. After it has executed, the mechanism deallocates the storage associated with that object. However, an object created by using the new operator is always within scope; it needs to be explicitly deleted. Because the "str" memory is allocated via the new operator, the String destructor must explicitly delete it. However, the storage for length does not have to be deleted, since it is a native data type.

The delete operator comes in two forms:

```
delete expression
delete [ ] expression
```

The expression is usually a pointer variable used in the assignment statement from a new operation. The brackets are used when the new operator involves an array of objects. The bracketed delete ensures that the destructor mechanism is invoked on each object in the array. For example, consider the following:

```
String *ptr = new String("new string",10);
```

You must then use the following delete statement—delete [ ] ptr;—before the array created by the String constructor goes out of scope to reclaim storage, or there will be memory leaks.

There are no constraints on what can be done within the destructor. In fact, a common programming technique is to put print statements within both the constructors and destructors. A programmer may cause it to execute any actions and any functions subsequent to the last use of the object.

When either a reference or a pointer to a class goes out of scope, the destructor mechanism is not invoked. In the case of pointers, the programmer must explicitly apply the delete operator to the pointer to delete the object. For example,

```
class Pers
  {
```

```
public:
    Pers (int AnAge, char SomeSex) {Age = AnAge; Sex = SomeSex;}

        // this is inline definition of method

    Pers () {Age = 0; Sex ='b';}
    ~Pers ();
private:
        int Age; char Sex;
};

    //code in a calling method
    f()
    {
        Pers *joe = new Pers(32,'m');
        Pers mary(21,'f');
        Pers *kate = new Pers(50,'f');
        Pers jim;
        jim = Pers(19,'m');
        Pers *baby = new Pers();
        delete joe, kate, baby; //all pointers to objects
        // mary and jim are local variables and
        // will be deleted when the function goes out of scope
    }
```

If the pointer to which a delete is applied does not address a class object (i.e., the pointer has a value of zero), the destructor mechanism is not invoked. It is unnecessary to write the following statement:

```
if (pointer! = 0) delete pointer;
```

If no destructor is declared with a class, the compiler provides a default destructor. One should take care when relying on the default destructor, since it will not free up memory allocated by member functions during the life of the object.

We advise making all destructors of base classes virtual. If this is not done, there may be memory leaks, as illustrated in the following example:

```
Class A
{
public:
        A();
        ~A();
};
Class B: public A
{
```

```
public:
        B();
        ~B();
};
void func()
{
        A* p = (A *) new B();
        delete p;
}
```

In this example, the destructor that will be invoked on p will the ~A(). However, making the destructors of A and B virtual will assure that the destructor for B will be invoked.

Using Constructors and Destructors Properly

NOW LET US LOOK AT how to use the constructor and destructor. There are two ways to create an instance (object) of a class:

1. On the stack as a local variable (instance), as in the following:

```
void    F1()
        {
                Person p; // local to this function
                ...
        };
```

2. On the heap, returning a pointer to the instance, as in the following:

```
void    F2()
        {
                Person* p = new Person; //outlives this function
                ...
        };
```

Similarly, each of the two ways of constructing an instance has a corresponding way of destroying that instance:

1. On the stack as a local variable (instance), as in the following:

```
void    F1()
        {
                Person p; // local to this function
                ...    // p is destroyed when it is out of scope
        };
```

2. On the heap, returning a pointer to the instance, as in the following:

```
void   F2()
       {
           Person* p = new Person; //outlives this function
           ...
           delete p; //p is explicitly destroyed
       };
```

The delete function does not have to be in the same function. However, when you leave it to another function and forget to delete the object, there will be memory leaks (i.e., the object lives for the life of the program).

Generalization and Constructors

LET US GO BACK TO the ancestor tree for Platypus, shown in Figure 15-1. The ancestor tree has been modified to make Platypus inherit from both the Mammal and Endangered classes. Now, let us create an instance of Platypus and see how the constructors for the following classes are involved: Platypus, Mammal, Animal, OrganicMatter, and Endangered. Below are the class constructors:

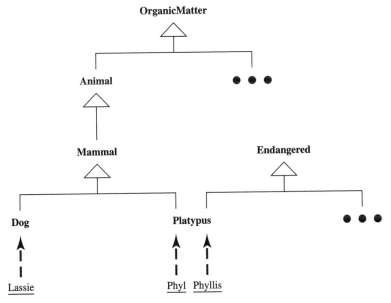

FIGURE 15-1 Inheritance Diagram for a Platypus

```
Endangered::Endangered()
{ //initialization code for Endangered}

   OrganicMatter::OrganicMatter()
      { //initialization code for OrganicMatter}

      Animal::Animal():OrganicMatter()
         {//initialization code for Animal}

         Mammal::Mammal(): Animal()
         { //initialization code for Mammal}

            Platypus::Platypus1(): Mammal(), Endangered()
            { //initialization code for Platypus}
```

The appropriate superclass constructor(s) is specified in the constructor. Generalization/specialization using inheritance for implementation is discussed in depth in a later chapter.

Recommended Approach

Creating an Object

An instance of a class can be created in two ways:

1.   On the stack as a local variable (instance), as in the following:

```
void    F1()
        {
                Person p; // local to this function
                ....
        };
```

2.   On the heap, returning a pointer to the instance, as in the following:

```
void   F2()
        {
                Person* p = new Person; //outlives this function
                ....
        };
```

We can use the array notation (" [ ]") to create more than one instance:

```
void   F1()
```

```
        {
                Person* parray = new Person[10] //10 instances
                parray[0].getAge(); // access first instance
        }
```

This can only be used when you have a constructor that takes no arguments for the class Person.

Destroying an Object

When is an object destroyed?

1. Objects that are allocated on the stack are destroyed (the space on the stack for the object is released) when the object goes out-of-scope. A commonly used idiom to force the destruction of local instances is to wrap them with a scope. This can be useful with transaction-based applications. For example,

```
Create_win::multitran(cal)
{
    {
        Transaction t1;
        /* some database code  */
    } //   t1 destructor is called, which forces the commit of the transaction
    {
        Transaction t2;
        /* some database code */
    } //   t2 destructor is called, which forces the commit of the transaction
}
```

2. Objects that are allocated on the heap must be explicitly destroyed using the delete operator. Examples of the appropriate mechanism for destroying an object are given below:

    a. For a local variable (instance), when it goes out of scope:

```
void   F1()
    {
            Person p; // local to this function
            ...    // p is destroyed when it is out of scope
    };
```

    b. On the heap, using the delete operator:

```
void   F2()
    {
```

```
                     Person* p = new Person; //outlives this function
                     ...
                     delete p; //p is explicitly destroyed
               };
```

    c.   Deleting all instances in an array using [ ]:

```
void    F1()
        {
                Person* parray = new Person[10] //10 instances
                parray[0].getAge(); // access first instance
        };

void    F2()
        {

                ....
                delete [ ] parray; //all 10 instances are deleted
        };
```

The delete operation may be performed from any function that has access to the object. In the last example, the parray of the Person objects were created in the first function, but deleted in the second function. Take care to ensure that other objects having access to this object are not left with an invalid pointer.

Coding Guidelines

This section summarizes coding guidelines for constructors and destructors:

Constructors

- Constructors create instances from a class definition.
- The instance space is allocated before any user-defined constructor is called.
- Constructors can be defined with values intended to initialize data members or to be passed to setup functions.
- Constructors implicitly return an instance of a class (local variable) or a pointer to an instance (when new is used).
- In coding the constructor, do not define a return type or make an explicit return.
- A class can have many constructors, each of which accepts different arguments.
- An array may only be created when there is a constructor with no arguments.

■ Each class should define a default constructor (no args), a copy constructor (arg = a reference to the same class), and an assignment operator (if the class contains pointers).

■ Constructors should be used for data member initialization.

Destructors

■ There is only one destructor per class.

■ If you do not write one, the compiler will provide a standard one, but it may not be what is needed.

■ It deletes instance(s) of a class.

■ The instance space is freed after any user-defined destructors are called. Do not explicitly free the instance space in your code.

■ Destructors do not take any arguments.

■ A destructor method should perform any necessary cleanup before an object is destroyed.

■ Any type of operation can be performed within a destructor. Usually, destructors are used to destroy complex or aggregate objects, or to change the values of the static variables of a class.

■ It is best to declare base class destructors as virtual functions.

■ ■ SUMMARY

We use constructors and destructors to create and delete objects in our application. Below is a review of the earlier sections:

■ To create an instance of a class, use a special constructor operation.

■ Multiple constructors for a single class can be defined, distinguished by the number and types of their arguments.

■ A constructor is executed whenever a new instance of a class is requested.

■ Each class has one destructor.

■ Destructors do not take any arguments.

■ A destructor method should perform any necessary cleanup before an object is destroyed.

■ Any type of operation can be performed within a constructor or destructor.

16

Implementing Generalization/ Specialization

No man is an island.

John Donne

In the previous chapter, we saw how an object is created (instantiated). To create objects properly, however, we also need to establish the proper relationships between objects. Now we will begin to look at implementing relationships. This chapter is devoted to the generalization/specialization relationship.

Inheritance

FROM A MAINTENANCE AND DEVELOPMENT perspective, inheritance is the one mechanism that helps manage code sharing, code reuse, and code extensions. Through inheritance, developers can build new classes on top of an existing hierarchy of classes. This avoids redesigning and recoding every time from scratch. The new classes will inherit both the functions and attributes of existing classes. Inheriting functions enables code sharing and thus reuse, while inheriting attributes enables structure sharing among objects. The combination of these two aspects of inheritance provides a very powerful software modeling and coding mechanism.

In object-oriented analysis and design, generalization/specialization is the mechanism of deriving a new class from an old one. That is, we can add to an existing class and alter the addition to create a specialized class. Since a class becomes a user-defined type in object-oriented programming, generalization/ specialization in C++ is implemented through inheritance via the mechanism of class derivation. In C++, generalization/specialization is implemented as a hierarchy of related types that share code and external interfaces (function prototypes).

In C++, a derived class is used to define a subclass of a *base class* (superclass). A base class is any predefined class definition. A derived class inherits the services (function members) and the attributes (data members) of the *base class* (superclass). It then can be altered by adding both data members and function members, modifying existing member functions, and modifying the access privileges. To modify an existing member function, C++ provides a *virtual* function mechanism. By declaring a function virtual in its base class, a derived class may redefine the function.[1] When a class hierarchy is translated into a set of related derived classes, a base-class pointer may be used to address any object of the derived classes. When a virtual function is accessed via a base-class pointer, C++ will provide the mechanism to execute the appropriate derived or base-class function at run time.

Specifying a Derived Class

A class **Derived** can be derived from another class **Base** using the following form in the header file for **Derived**:

```
#include "Base.h"
    class Derived: public Base
    {
       member declarations
    };
```

---

[1] For example, each derived class may have its own customized method for the virtual function. That customized method is used by objects of the derived class for the virtual function.

The keyword *public* defines the visibility of its inherited members. There is a choice of three keywords: *public, protected,* and *private.* Each keyword specifies different accessibility of the derived class to the base-class members. This will be discussed later in this chapter. Examples of a standard class definition and a derived definition follow:

```
class Person {
   public:
            Person(char* n, char s, int a);
      char*  getName();
      char   getSex();
      int    getAge();
      void   setName(char* n);
      void   setAge(int a);
             ~Person() {}
private:
      char   name[40];
      char   sex;
       int   age, height, weight;
};

class Employee: public Person
{
  public:
   Employee(char* n, char s, int a, int n = 0): Person(n, s, a) {salary = n;}
   int     getSalary() {return salary;}
   void    setSalary(int a) {salary = a; }
           ~Employee() {}
  private:
   int     salary;
};
```

In this example, **Employee** is a derived class, and **Person** is the base class. Using the keyword *public* following the colon in the derived class header means that the protected and public members of the class **Person** are to be inherited as protected and public members of the class **Employee.** Private members of **Person** are not accessible to the class **Employee.** For example, the class **Employee** has no way of accessing the weight data member, but it can access the age via the two functions getAge() and setAge(). "Class Employee" is a subtype of the type "class Person." An instance of **Employee** is also an instance of Person, but an instance of Person is not necessarily an instance of **Employee.**

Frequently a derived class extends the base class by adding new members. In this example, **Employee** has added one new data member (salary) and four new functions (constructor, destructor, getSalary(), setSalary()). The results may be summarized as in Table 16-1.

TABLE 16-1 Relationships Along Lines of Inheritance
for Services and Attributes

Class	Employee Services	Employee Attributes
Person	getName getSex getAge setName setAge	char name[40]; char sex; int age; int height; int weight;
Employee	getSalary setSalary	int salary;

The table shows that every instance of **Employee** has its own data fields for name, sex, age, height, weight and salary, and only the salary attribute is truly an "employee" semantic domain attribute. The other attributes of **Employee** are in the "person" semantic domain. Similar reasoning should be applied to the services. For good cohesion and low coupling, applications dealing with an instance of **Employee** as an "employee" should never need to access the services associated with an employee as a person.[2] However, the services (functions) are shared and available to all the instances. In fact, the common services of **Person** are shared with other instances who are either instances of **Person** or from another derived class of **Person.**

Inheriting from a Derived Class and Implementing Association

A class can be derived from another derived class. For example, let us add **Manager** to the hierarchy of **Person** and **Employee** as follows:

```
const int Max = 20;

class Manager: public Employee
     {
     public:
             Manager(char* n, char s, int a, int n = 0): Employee(n, s, a, n)
                  {for (int i = 0; i< Max; i++)
                        group[i] = 0;}
     Employee   *getEmployee(int n)
                  {return group[n];}
     void       setEmployee(Employee *e, int a)
```

---

[2] The object-oriented paradigm and language allow an application to access only the services of Person when an instance of Employee is viewed as a Person object.

```
                {group[a] = e;}
             ~Manager() {delete [ ] group;}
        private:
        Employee    *group[Max];
   };
```

In this example, **Manager** is the derived class, and **Employee** is the base class. The use of the keyword *public* following the colon in the derived class header means that the protected and public members of the class **Employee** are to be inherited respectively as protected and public members of the class **Manager**. Private members of **Person** and **Employee** are not accessible to the class **Manager**. For example. the class Manager has no way of accessing the weight data member, nor can it access the salary data member directly.

"Class Manager" is a subtype of the type "class Employee," which is a subtype of "class Person." An instance of **Manager** is also an instance of both **Person** and **Employee**, but an instance of **Person** is not necessarily an instance of **Manager** nor an instance of **Employee**.

Manager has added one new data member (*group) and four new services (constructor, destructor, getEmployee(), setEmployee()). The group variable is an array of the pointer to the instances of **Employee**. This is a very common way of capturing an association. Notice that because arrays are not initialized by the language, there is an array-initialization code in the constructor. Also notice the use of the braces in the delete statement of the destructor. The results are summarized in Table 16-2.

Every instance of **Manager** has its own data fields for name, sex, age, height, weight, salary, and group. Once again, the only attribute that is uniquely "managerial" is the group that the manager supervises. The attribute of salary is still tied to the concept of employee, while the rest of the attributes are tied to the concept of person. Conceptually, a manager is an employee and a person. We realize that many developers may not agree with the above statement; however, this is what the model says.

TABLE 16-2 Manager Inheritance

Class	Manager Services	Manager Attributes
Person	getName getSex getAge setName setAge	char name[40]; char sex; int age; int height; int weight;
Employee	getSalary setSalary	int salary;
Manager	getEmployee setEmployee	*group[Max];

Below is a program that uses these three classes:

```
main()
  {//   created as an instance of Employee
      Employee Ed("Edward", m, 21, 20000);
          //   Edward gets a raise!!
      Ed.setSalary(25000);
          //   Time for a boss
      Manager Jane("Jane", f, 25);
          //   Managers get paid a lot!!
       Jane.setSalary(100000);
          //     Put Ed in Jane's group
      Jane.setEmployee( &ed, 0)
          //        Lower Edward's salary
       Ed.setSalary(15000);
   };
```

Adding Polymorphism

A function defined in the base class may be overridden when the keyword *virtual* is specified in the prototype declaration of the function in the base-class header file. A virtual function must be defined in the base class, normally in the .C file. If a derived class wants to override this function, it must declare and define a derived function that matches the original function in name, signature, and return type. The selection of which function definition is invoked is dynamic. For example, it is very common in object-oriented programming to have a collection of pointers to base objects. These pointers normally point to objects of the base class and objects in a derived class (or classes).

Since the virtual function is defined in both classes, there must be a rule by which one of the functions is invoked. The rule is that the function selected depends on the class of the object being pointed to, and not on the pointer type.

If the object being pointed to is an object of the derived class, the function invoked would be a function of the derived class. If a derived class does not have this function declared in its class definition, then the default is to try to find its base class. If the function is not found in its base class, it would search the base class of the base class, and so on until it is found. Remember, the function must be defined in the original base class.

Note that there is a difference between the selection of an appropriate over-ridden virtual function and the selection of an overloaded member function. Overloaded member functions can be determined at compile time because they must have a unique signature. They can also have different return-types, although we have not seen an example of this. An overridden virtual function has an identical signature and return type. It cannot be resolved at compile time. Once a funtion is declared virtual, this property is carried to all redeclarations and redefinitions in its derived classes. It is unnecessary in the derived class to use the function modifier virtual. In the example below, polymorphism is added to setSalary() for **Employee**, so that the company can give bonuses to the managers.

In this example, the **Employee** class code is as follows:

```
class Employee : public Person
  {
   public
     Employee(char* n, char s, int a, int n = 0) : Person(n, s, a) {salary = n;}
    int     getSalary() { return salary; }
virtual void   setSalary(int a) { salary = a; }
          ~Employee() {}
  private:
       int      salary;
  };
```

Note that the only change to **Employee** is to declare setSalary() virtual. This allows the derived class to override this function. Based on the above code for **Employee**, the **Manager** class code is as follows:

```
const int Max = 20;
int bonus () { return 25000; } // big bonuses here

class Manager: public Employee
{
    public:
              Manager(char* n, char s, int a, int n = 0): Employee(n; s, a, n)
                { for (int i = 0; i < Max; i++)
   Employee   *getEmployee(int n)    { return group[n]; }
     void       setEmployee(Employee *e, int a)
                   { group[a] = e; }
     void       setSalary( int s)
                    {Employee::setSalary(s + bonus());}
                 ~Manager() { delete [ ] group; }
    private:
   Employee    *group[Max];
};
```

Note that in class **Manager**, setSalary() is both redeclared and redefined. This means that the implementation of setSalary() is different from that of **Employee**. When all the new salaries are set, all the managers' salaries will increase by an additional bonus of $25,000, while the salaries of the nonmanagement employees will increase only by the set amount. The results are shown in Table 16-3.

TABLE 16-3 Manager Salary Example

Class	Manager Services	Manager Attributes
Person	getName getSex getAge setName setAge	char name[40]; char sex; int age; int height; int weight;
Employee	getSalary ~~setSalary~~	int salary;
Manager	getEmployee setEmployee setSalary	*group[Max];

The strikeout on the setSalary() function in **Employee** means that an object of type **Manager** will not use the function definition given in the class **Employee**. Instead, it will use the setSalary() function definition given in its own class.

The use of polymorphism hides behavior from the user of the services. For example, because of the way we have defined setSalary(), the following program using the latest definition of setSalary() will yield the same results as the earlier main program that used only the employee's setSalary() function.

```
main()
{
    Employee Ed("Edward", m, 21, 20000);
                // Edward gets a raise!!
        Ed.setSalary(25000);
            // Time for a boss
        Manager Jane("Jane", f, 25);
            //Manager gets paid a lot!!; less obvious
        Jane.setSalary(75000);
            // Put Ed in Jane's group
        Jane.setEmployee( &ed, 0)
            // Lower Edward's salary
        Ed.setSalary(5000);
    };
```

In the previous program where the manager inherited without polymorphism, Jane's salary was exactly $100,000, as shown in the main program code where the coder of the main program knows her salary. In this program, however, the coder would have assumed that her salary was $75,000, but in fact it is still $100,000, because when her salary is set, a bonus is added to the base salary. Now, we understand the real reason why managers are so excited about object-oriented technology!

Abstract Class

The base class (also called a root class) of a type hierarchy may contain a number of virtual functions. These are often dummy functions, which have an empty body in the base class and are given a specific meaning in the derived classes. In C++, the pure virtual mechanism is used to handle this situation. In a pure virtual function, the function definition is given in the derived classes. Thus the body of the function is undefined in the base class. Notationally, it is declared in the base class as follows:

```
class BaseClass
{
  public:
      virtual int      foo() = 0;   // This defines foo as a pure virtual function
};
```

A class with at least one pure virtual function is an *abstract class*. For example, consider the following:

```
class Item
{
  public:
      virtual void      cut() = 0;
      virtual void      move(Length dx, Length dy) = 0;
      virtual Boolean   pick(Length px, Length py) = 0;
      virtual void      ungroup() = 0;
};

class Shape: public Item {
  public:
      void              cut() = 0;
      void              draw() { write(Color_Foreground);}
      void              erase() { write(Color_Background);}
      void              move(Length dx, Length dy) = 0;
      virtual Boolean   pick(Length px, Length py) = 0;
      void              ungroup() {}
      virtual void      write(Color color) = 0;
  protected:
            Length x; Length y;
};

class Box: public Shape
{
  public:
```

```
                      Box (Length x0, Length y0, Length w, Length h);
                      ~Box ();
   Boolean            pick(Length px, Length py);
       void           move(Length dx, Length dy);
       void           cut();
  protected:
          Length width; Length height;
};

class Circle: public Shape
{
  public:
                      Circle (Length x0, Length radius);
                      ~Circle ();
   Boolean            pick(Length px, Length py);
       void           move(Length dx, Length dy);
       void           write(Color color);
       void           cut();
  protected:
          Length radius;
};
```

Here, there are two abstract base classes: **Item** and **Shape.** All the functions of Item are pure virtual. **Shape** defines only one of these functions, ungroup(). In addition, it added a new virtual function, write(). **Box** and **Circle** do not have any pure virtual functions, so they are sometimes called *concrete classes*. The reason is that the program can instantiate an instance of a concrete class, but it may not instantiate an instance of an abstract class. From the above discussion this must be so, as an abstract class has undefined methods. However, we can still use a pointer of the abstract class to refer to instances of the derived classes.

Multiple Inheritance

Multiple inheritance allows a derived class to be derived from more than one base class. The syntax of the class declaration for the derived class is extended to allow for a list of base classes. The template for the header file of a derived class with multiple inheritance from base classes **Bc1**, **Bc2**, **Bc3**, **Bc4** is as follows:

```
#include "bc1.h"
#include "bc2.h"
#include "bc3.h"
#include "bc4.h"

class Derived: public Bc1, public Bc2, public Bc3, public Bc4
```

```
{
    member declarations
};
```

For example, consider the following two base classes:

```
class Font
{
public:
                    Font ( Length w, Length h);
                    ~Font ();
        void        write(Color color);
private:
            Length width; Length height;
};


class String
{
public:
            String( char *c);
            ~String ();
    char    *getString(); // return the string
    void    print(); // to stdout
};
```

A class **Text**, in order to be created, needs to inherit the font capabilities from Font and the character capabilities from **String**. Below is the class definition of **Text** that uses multiple inheritance:

```
#include "Font.h"
#include "String.h"

class Text : public Font, public String
{
 public:
        Text ( Length width, Length height, char *pointer) :
            Font( width, height), String ( pointer)
                { other initialization code      }
          ~Text ();
            ...    // new member functions
 private:
            ...    // new data members
};
```

Once again, we see how multiple inheritance works, as shown in Table 16-4. Note that the services and attributes are not indented. This is to show that **String** is

TABLE 16-4 Multiple Inheritance

Class	Text Services	Text Attributes
Font	write()	Length width Length height
String	*getString() print()	
Text		

not a derived class of **Font**. When an instance of **Text** is being created, it will first create an instance of **Font** and then create an instance of **String**, Both of these instances will then become part of the new instance of **Text**. Specifically, the instance of **Text** inherits the print service from **String** and the write service from **Font**.

In deriving from multiple base classes, it is possible to have identically named members from different classes. This may result in ambiguities. For example, consider the following, where class **Font** has added a print function to its definition:

```
class Font
{
 public:
                    Font ( Length w, Length h);
                    ~Font ();
        void        write(Color color);
        void        print(); // to stdeer
 private:
                    Length width; Length height;
};

class String
{
 public:
                    String( char *c);
                    ~String ();
    char            *getString(); // return the string
    void            print(); // to stdout
};
```

Now suppose we want to add a display function to **Text** that prints the string in the correct font. We want to reuse code, and we write the following code:

```
class Text : public Font, public String
{
 public:
```

```
             Text ( Length width, Length height, char *pointer) :
                 Font( width, height), String ( pointer)
                 { other initialization code      }
          ~Text ();
       void display() {print();}
          ...    // new member functions
    private:
          ...    // new data members
    };
```

This will result in a compile-time error, because the compiler does not know which print() function it should use. This ambiguity is shown in Table 16-5.

TABLE 16-5 Ambiguity of print due to inheritance

Class	Text Services	Text Attributes
Font	write() print()	Length width Length height
String	*getString() print()	
Text	display()	

Text has two print functions defined. Determining which one to use is normally solved by using the scope operator. For example, if **Text** intended to use the print() function of **String**, the following code would apply:

```
       void display() {String::print();}
```

Another source of ambiguity arises when a derived class inherits from classes that are derived from a common base class. For example, consider an employee who is also a customer.[3] We want to create a new class **Employee/Customer** that inherits from both **Employee** and **Customer**. However, **Customer** is also a derived class of **Person**. To represent this situation, this instance (Person) would have classes (**Employee** and **Customer**) that are both derived classes of **Person**. Below is the code used to add the two new classes. Table 16-6 shows the results of the inheritances.

```
       class Customer : public Person
       {
          public:
```

---
[3] For example, an instance of Employee that is also an instance of Customer.

TABLE 16-6 Class C/E

Class	C/E Services	C/E Attributes
Person (superclass of Employee)	getName getSex getAge setName setAge	char name[40]; char sex; int age; int height; int weight;
Employee	getSalary setSalary	int salary;
Person (superclass of Customer)		char name[40]; char sex; int age; int height; int weight;
Customer	getSaving setSaving	int saving;
C/E		

```
          Customer(char* n, char s, int a, int n = 0)
                : Person( n, s, a)
                { saving = n; }
    int       getSaving() {return saving;}
virtual void  setSaving(int a) {saving = a;}
              ~Customer() {}
private:
          int  saving;
};

class C/E
      : public Customer, public Employee
{
public:
              ...    // new member functions
private:
              ...    // new data members
};
```

There are two sets of values for the attributes of **Person.** The functions are not duplicated, since they are the same for instances of **Person.** If the functions are all public functions and we want to maintain two sets of data, then we must access the appropriate data by scoping the public functions. For example, to access the age, which is stored as part of **Customer,** we write the following code:

```
int custAge = Customer::getAge();
```

To change the age of **Employee** to 20, use the following code:

```
Employee::setAge(20);
```

This will change only the age data member associated with **Employee;** the age data member associated with **Customer** is unchanged.

How can we use multiple inheritance and still have only one copy of **Person?** C++ includes a mechanism called *virtual inheritance* that allows a derived class to inherit from other classes with the same base class. Only one copy of the base class is inherited. In the following example, we modify the inheritance of **Employee** and **Customer** to use virtual inheritance:

```
class Employee : virtual public Person
{
public:
                Employee(char* n, char s, int a, int n = 0)
                : Person( n, s, a)
                        { salary = n; }
        int     getSalary() { return salary; }
virtual void    setSalary(int a) { salary = a; }
                ~Employee() {}
private:
        int   salary;
};


class Customer : public virtual Person
{
public:
                Customer(char* n, char s int a, int n = 0)
                : Person( n, s, a)
                        { saving = n; }
        int     getSaving() {return saving;}
virtual void    setSaving(int a) {saving = a;}
                ~Customer() {}
private:
        int   saving;
};
```

The keyword *virtual* has been added. The order of public and virtual does not matter (they can be reversed). Now, the **Customer/Employee** class can be defined using the revised **Customer** and **Employee** classes as follows:

```
class C/E : public Customer, public Employee {
 public:
```

```
                C/E(char* n, char s,   int a, int n = 0, int sav = 10000)
                : Person( n, s, a),
                  Employee( n, s, a, n),
                  Customer(n, s, a, sav)
                  {  ...       }
private:         ...   // new data members
};
```

In **Customer/Employee**, the base class **Person** is explicitly initialized. The results of this new code are shown in Table 16-7. Now there is only one set of values for **Person**.

TABLE 16-7 Class C/E

Class	C/E Services	C/E Attributes
Person	getName getSex getAge setName setAge	char name[40]; char sex; int age; int height; int weight;
Employee	getSalary setSalary	int salary;
Customer	getSaving setSaving	int saving;
C/E		

Virtual Destructors

HOW DO THE MODEL AND the language handle a **Person** object for a person who is deceased? Ideally, you would like to delete that person as a **Person** object and delete all of its derived classes. Unfortunately, when you delete a specific person who is also an employee, only the destructor of **Person** is called; you must call the destructor of Employee. This becomes more complex when the person is a manager.

Without another mechanism, one would have to know all the derived classes of the deceased person. However, there is a mechanism that will support the destruction of a **Person** object without knowing all of its derived classes. This mechanism is a *virtual destructor*. Specifying the destructors in a derivation hierarchy as virtual guarantees that the appropriate destructors will be invoked whenever delete is applied to a base-class pointer. The destructor of a class that is derived from a class that declares its destructor virtual is also virtual. In the following example, virtual destructors are added:

```
class Person
{
 public:
                 Person(char* n, char s, int a);
        char*    getName();
        char     getSex();
        int      getAge();
        void     setName(char* n);
        void     setAge(int a);
      virtual    ~Person() {}
 private:
              char name[40];
              char sex;
              int  age;
};
class Employee : public Person{
 public:
                   Employee(char* n, char s, int a, int n = 0)
                         : Person( n, s, a)
                         { salary = n; }
           int     getSalary() { return salary; }
   virtual void    setSalary(int a) { salary = a; }
        virtual    ~Employee() {}
 private:
              int  salary;
};
const int Max = 20;
class Manager: public Employee{
 public:
                   Manager(char* n, char s, int a, int n = 0)
                       : Employee(n, s, a, n)
                         { for (int i = 0; i < Max; i++)
                             group[i] = 0;}
  Employee    *getEmployee(int n)
                       { return group[n]; }
     void             setEmployee(Employee *e, int a)
                         { group[a] = e; }
        virtual    ~Manager() { delete [] group;}
 private:
    Employee    *group[Max];
};
```

Derived Class Visibility

ONE OF THE DIFFICULTIES FOR novices when programming functions of derived classes is knowing what data members they may access. Figure 16-1 is a visual aid

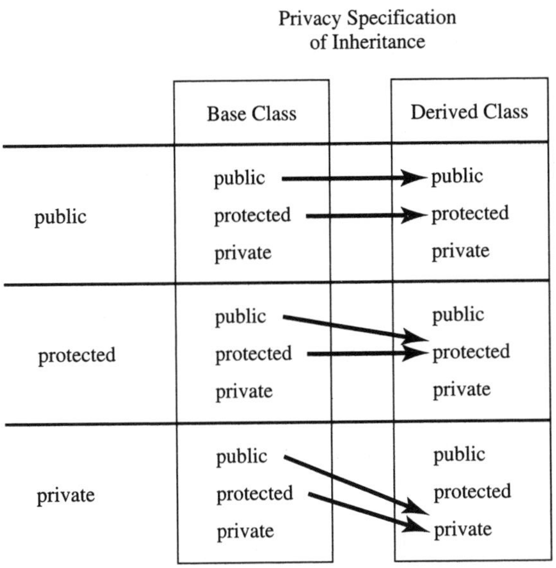

Privacy Specification
of Inheritance

FIGURE 16-1 Derived Class Visibility

to help you while you are programming. Let **X** be the base class, and let **Y** be it's derived class via public inheritance. Let **Z** be the derived class of **Y**, and let **F** be a friend of **X**. Table 16-8 shows how the privacy specification of inheritance affects the accessibility of the derived class to the various data members in the base class.

TABLE 16-8 Derived Class Visibility

Defined in Class X	private	protected	public
Used in Class X	Yes	Yes	Yes
Used in Class Y	NO	Yes	Yes
Used in Class Z	NO	Yes	Yes
Used in Class F	Yes	Yes	Yes
Other code	NO	NO	Yes

■ ■ SUMMARY

In object-oriented programming, the derived class capabilities and its supporting mechanisms, including virtual functions and virtual destructors, are used to implement the generalization/specialization hierarchy of the object-oriented model. Key points to remember follow:

■ Superclasses are base classes in C++.
■ Subclasses are derived classes in C++.

- Polymorphic functions are implemented as virtual functions.
- Virtual destructors are used to support the deletion of instances of derived classes from base-level functions.
- Multiple inheritance may be used to capture behavior and attributes that are part of separate semantic domains.
- Abstract classes are used to capture concepts that help organize the domain.

Here is a summary of inheritance and some C++ coding reminders:

- Variables (attributes) declared in the base class are inherited by its derived classes and need not be repeated in the derived classes.
- However, the derived classes can only directly access variables that are *public* or *protected*.
- Furthermore, if the base class is *privately* inherited, then the inherited public members of the base class become private members of the derived class. Clients of the derived class then have no access to the inherited methods or variables.
- Functions declared in a base class are also inherited in the derived classes.
- Constructors, destructors, and friends are not inherited.
- If a function can be overridden by a derived class, then it must be declared *virtual* in its first appearance in a base class.
- Virtual functions are called using the same syntax as nonvirtual functions.
- Functions that override inherited functions must be declared in the derived class.
- *Virtual* as a keyword prefix to a member function declaration in a class header allows the function to be replaced by any derived class.
- The *virtual* keyword is required only at the first definition of a member function within the hierarchy, that is, at the base class where it is first defined.
- All usage of virtual in subsequent derived classes is optional. However, it is usually considered good documentation practice to include it in the derived classes.
- A virtual function and its overridden versions must have the same name, signature, and return type.
- All member functions except constructors and overloaded *new* can be virtual.
- In a pure virtual function, the function prototype is provided by the base class. In other words, implementation must be provided by a derived class.
- Specifying the destructors in a derivation hierarchy as virtual guarantees that the appropriate destructors will be invoked whenever delete is applied to a base-class pointer.
- When a base class needs constructors or destructors to allocate, initialize, or deallocate base-class objects, the derived class must call the constructor or destructor of the base class.
- In multiple inheritance, construction of a derived class, by default, is done by constructing the base classes in the same order as their declaration.

CHAPTER **17**

Implementing More Relationships

In the previous chapter, we discussed the implementation of generalization/ specialization. However, as we built the analysis model, we used two additional types of relationships, aggregation and association. Although aggregation and association are not explicitly supported in many object-oriented languages, including C++, we believe that they should be implemented in a standard way. In this chapter, we look at some accepted mechanisms for implementing these two relationships.

Introduction

SOME OF THE ISSUES INVOLVED in implementing association and aggregation were presented in the design chapter. They are repeated here for reference, since these issues are usually revisited during implementation.

Implementing Association

There are two approaches to implementing associations: buried pointers and distinct association objects. Since C++ (like most languages) does not support association objects, buried pointers are used.

A binary (one-to-one) association is usually implemented as an attribute in each of the association classes. If you have access to a library that has a Dictionary class, you can also implement a binary association as two Dictionary objects, with each dictionary mapping in one direction across the association.

A many-to-one association requires either a set of objects or an array of objects (if the association is ordered). In this case, a collection class object from a class library is the best implementation.

In implementing associations, the implementor must consider the access pattern and the relative frequencies of the different kind of access. If the number of hits from a query is low because only a fraction of the objects satisfy the criteria, an index should be used to improve the access to objects that are frequently retrieved. However, this is costly; it will use more memory and updates will be slower. Sometimes adding a new association that is derived from the base association will provide for direct access to the appropriate data.

The simplest association to implement is one in which the association is only traversed in one direction. In this case, it can be implemented as an attribute that contains an object reference. If the multiplicity is 1, it is simply a pointer to the other object. If the multiplicity is more than 1, it is a pointer to a collection. If the collection is not ordered, then the pointer is to a set of pointers to objects. If the collection is ordered, a list is used in place of a set. If the collection is qualified, then it can be implemented using a dictionary object.

There are three ways to implement a two-way association:

1. Add an attribute to the class on one side of the association and perform a search when a reverse traversal is required.
2. Add an attribute to both sides of the association. Use the same multiplicity techniques as for an association that is traversed in one direction.
3. Create an associate class, independent of either class. An associate class is a set of pairs of related objects stored in a single-variable-size object. For efficiency, it is common to implement an associative object as two dictionary objects.

If most of the traversal is from the "many" side to the "one" side and new members are added frequently to the links, then number 1 is recommended.

When updates are infrequent and speed of access in both directions is critical to your application, number 2 is recommended. An associative class is recommended when maximum flexibility is needed for future enhancements and performance is not an issue.

Implementing Attributes of an Association

If the association has attributes but no services, then its attributes can be implemented as follows:

1. If the association is one-to-one, the association attributes can be stored as attributes of either class.
2. If the association is many-to-one, the association attributes may be stored in the class on the "many" side.
3. If the association is many-to-many, it is best to create an associative class and assign the association attributes to the associative class.

Implementing Aggregation

Since aggregation is also not supported in most object-oriented languages, including C++, it is implemented using rules similar to those for association. There are two approaches: buried array of pointers and embedded objects.

1. An aggregation can be implemented as an array of pointers to objects. This is done when we want either replaceable components or directly accessible components in the aggregation.
2. An aggregation can also be implemented as a distinct contained object. This is done when we want the components of the aggregation to be changed only through methods of the container object.

Pointers

Since the foundation of implementing association and aggregation is a pointer to an instance of a class and an array of pointers to instances of a class, pointer variables will now be discussed in depth.

In C++, pointers are used to reference variables or machine memory addresses. As we have shown, pointers are intimately tied to array and string processing. Both the string and the array may be thought of as special forms of pointers, where the pointer is associated with a contiguous piece of memory for storing an indexible sequence of values.

Pointers are used in programs to access variables. If x is a variable, then &x is the address (lvalue) in memory of its stored value (rvalue). The variable that contains the address as its stored value (rvalue) is called a pointer variable; pointer variables can be declared in a program and then used to take addresses as values. The form for declaring a pointer is as follows:

```
type * variable;
```

The type may be a native type, a derived type, or a user-defined type, and the variable is an identifier. For example, the declaration

```
Person *p;
```

declares p to be a pointer type that points to an instance of **Person**. The legal range of values for p (or any pointer) includes the special address 0 (zero) and a set of positive integers that are interpreted as addresses on a computer.

Here are some examples of assignment statements using p:

```
Person Jim("Jim", m, 30)
  p = &Jim;                  // the address of Jim is the rvalue
  p = 0;                     // rvalue = 0
  p = (Person *) 1234;       // rvalue = 1234
```

In the first assignment statement, we can think of p as either referring to Jim, pointing to Jim, or containing the address of Jim. All are correct. Note that the compiler decides the actual address to assign to the variable Jim. This can vary from computer to computer, and may be different for different executions on the same computer. The second assignment statement is the special value 0. This value is typically used to indicate an exception condition. For instance, the operator *new* returns a pointer value of 0 when free storage is exhausted. This value is also used to indicate that the object requested was not found in function calls. The third assignment statement assigns an actual memory address. The cast is necessary to avoid a type error. However, assigning a memory address is not recommended for any application.[1]

In using pointers for programming, one of the difficulties is that earlier C++ libraries use pass-by-reference as an argument type to pass objects instead of pass-by-pointer. To use the libraries, the programmer must use the dereferencing or indirection operator *. If p is a pointer to a variable v, then *p is the rvalue of v.[2] The indirect value of p is the rvalue (stored value) of v. In a sense, the dereference operator * is the inverse operator for the address operator &. The following code may clarify this:

```
Person Jim("Jim", m, 20), unknown;   // unknown is uninitialized
Employee *Donna("Donna", f, 21, 40000);
Dog   *d = new Dog()    //create an instance of Dog
Person *p;              // p is uninitialized
p = &jim               // p has an address of Jim
unknown = p;           // illegal assignment
```

---

[1]   This may need to be done in hard real-time systems for the sake of performance.

[2]   In other words, the direct value of p is the lvalue (address) of v.

```
unknown = *p          // legal, assuming the assignment operator has
                      // been defined for Person class
   p = &unknown;      // legal; p now points to unknown
   p = d;             // legal in K&R C; illegal in C++
   p = (Person () d;  // legal, but should not to be done
   p = Donna;         // legal; Employee is a derived class of Person
                      // note: if inheritance was private, then this is illegal
                      // private inheritance is treated as an unrelated class
   Donna = p;         // illegal
```

The following rules will help you deal with pointers:

- Pointers to different classes (types) may not be equated without casting.
- The exception is that a public inherited subclass (derived class) pointer can be assigned to a superclass (base-class) pointer.
- A base-class pointer must always be cast to a legal derived-class pointer.
- An object pointer may always be assigned the void pointer. However, a void pointer must be cast to a legal object pointer.

Arrays

AN ARRAY IS USED TO capture a large number of values of the same data type. The elements (values) of the array are accessible using subscripts. Arrays of all types are possible, including arrays of arrays. An array declaration allocates memory starting from a base address. In C++, an array name is a pointer constant to the base address of the array.

An array can be initialized by a comma-separated list of expressions enclosed in braces, as in the following:

```
int array[5] {23, 11, 107, 706, 1};
```

When the list of initializers is shorter than the size of the array, then the remaining elements are initialized to zero. An array declared with an explicit initializer and no size expression is given the size of the number of initializers. Therefore, the statement

```
char jane[ ] = {'j','a','n','e','\0'};
```

is the same as

```
char jane[5] = {'j','a','n','e','\0'};
```

If external and static arrays are not explicitly initialized, the compiler will automatically create code to initialize all elements of these arrays to zero.

However, this is not true for automatic arrays; their elements will hold undefined values.

To illustrate these ideas, a program to sum the values of an array is shown below:

```
#include <iostream.h>
const int SIZE = 7
main()
{
    // this defines v array as having 7 elements. Their values are
    // v[0] = 7, v[1] = 6, v[2] = 5, v[3] = 4, v[4] = 3, v[5] = 2, v[6] = 1
    int v[SIZE] = {7, 6, 5, 4, 3, 2, 1};
    // initialize the sum to zero
    int sum = 0;
    for(int i = 0; i < SIZE; i++)
    {
        cout << "v[" << i << "] =  " << v[i] << '\t';
        sum += v[i];
    }
    cout << "\nsum = " << sum << end;
}
```

The array v requires memory to store seven integer values. The zeroth element is always the first element of the array. If we assume that a system needs 4 bytes to store a value of type int and that v[0] is stored at location 100, then the remaining array elements are stored at 104, 108, 112, 116, 120, and 124.

We recommend that C++ programmers use symbolic constants for the size of any array, since the code will need to use this value. This makes it possible to change a single value when the array needs to be resized. Notice that the *for* statement is neatly tailored to provide a terse notation for dealing with array computations. Also note that the subscript must lie in the range of 0 to SIZE-1. An array subscript value outside this range will usually cause a run-time error because the subscript cannot be checked at compile-time. An "out-of-bound" subscript can cause system-dependent errors at run time, and thus be very confusing. It is the responsibility of the programmer to ensure that all subscripts stay within bounds.

Pointer arithmetic provides an alternative to array indexing. Below is a program that does the same computation using pointer arithmetic:

```
#include <iostream.h>
const int SIZE = 7
main()
{
    // this defines the v array as having 7 elements. Their values are
    // v[0] = 7, v[1] = 6, v[2] = 5, v[3] = 4, v[4] = 3, v[5] = 2, v[6] = 1
    int v[SIZE] {7, 6, 5, 4, 3, 2, 1};
```

```
   // initialize the sum to zero
   int sum = 0, * p;
   for(p = a; p < &v[SIZE]; p++)
   {
       sum += *p;
   }
   cout << "\nsum = " << sum << end;
}
```

In this example, the pointer variable p is initialized to the base address of the array v. The successive values of p are equivalent to &v[0], &v[1], . . . &v[SIZE-11]. The basic rule for pointer arithmetic is

If j is a variable of type int, then p + j is the jth offset from the address p. The value of p + j is computed as follows:

```
pointer value + sizeof(type of pointer) * j
```

Assume that we have the following program on a system where long double is 8 bytes:

```
#include<iostream.h>
main()
{
    long double v = 0, *p = &v, *newp;
    newp = p + 1;
    cout << "next location is" << newp << endl;
}
```

The output of newp is the address in memory 8 bytes after the address of v.

Friends

IN SOME INSTANCES, WE NEED to give nonmembers of a class access to the non-public members of the class. When this is the case, C++ has a mechanism called *friend* to provide this capability in a controlled manner that preserves some of the information hiding necessary for encapsulation. The friend mechanism has been shown to be needed for overloading the stream input (<<) and output (>>) operators and iterators.

Friends are functions or classes that have direct access to all the members (private, protected, and public) of another class. A friend function can itself be a member function of another class declaration. Friend breaks the encapsulation and information-hiding principles and should rarely be used. However, using a friend is better than making a data member public.

Static Members

SOMETIMES ALL OBJECTS OF A particular class need to access the same variable. For example, there may be some condition flag or counter related to the class that changes dynamically in program execution, as with averages and running totals. Sometimes it is more efficient to provide one variable for all objects in one class than to have each object maintain its own copy. Examples of this are error-handling routines common to the class, and pointers to free storage for the class. For these situations, a static class member is an effective mechanism to use.

A static data member acts as a global variable for its class. For object-oriented programming, there are three advantages to using a static data member over a global variable:

1. Information hiding can still be enforced. A static member can be made nonpublic; a global variable cannot.

2. A static member is not entered into the program's global name space. This reduces the possibility of an accidental conflict of names.

3. Even if the static member is public, a weak form of encapsulation is preserved. Nonmembers require the use of a scope operator (e.g., X::PublicStaticMember) to access the static member, while a member function can access a global variable (e.g., PublicStaticMember) directly.

There is only one instance of a static data member of a class, a single shared variable that is accessible to all objects in the class. Static members obey the public/private/protected access rules in the same manner as nonstatic members. Static data members may also be constant, class objects, or pointers to class objects.

A static member function is used to access static data members of the class. It is not allowed to access any nonstatic data member. A static member function does not contain a *this* pointer; therefore, any explicit or implicit reference to a *this* pointer will result in a compile-time error. Note that an attempt to access a nonstatic class member is an implicit reference to a *this* pointer and will result in a compile-time error.

The definition of a static function is the same as that of a nonstatic member function.; however, a static member function may not be declared *const* or *volatile*. A static member function may be invoked through a class object or a pointer to a class object in the same manner that a nonstatic member function is invoked. However, a static member function can be invoked directly even if no class object is ever declared.[3]

---

[3] This is done by using the class scope operator.

Implementing Association

Binary Association

Since libraries are presently not part of the C++ language, we will not show how to implement association using a **Dictionary** class from a library. Instead, we will show how to implement a binary association as an attribute of each class.[4] Here is an example using buried pointers:

```
class Person
{
  public:
                    Person(char* n, char s, int a);
    Person*   getSpouse()
                    {return spouse;}
        void    setSpouse(Person* p)
                    {spouse = p; return;}
                    ...
                  ~Person() {}
  private:
            char name[40];
            char sex;
            int  age;  . . .
        Person* spouse;
};
```

In the above example, we have added the spousal relationship, which is a "from-Person-to-Person" relationship. By adding an attribute that is a pointer to the Person class, this relationship is captured. The setSpouse() function establishes one side of the relationship, while the getSpouse() function navigates the relationship. The reader should note that it is the programmer's responsibility to establish and update both sides of the relationship.

If there are attributes of the association, each attribute should be added to only one of the classes. The frequency of accessing the attribute within the functions of each class should be used as the criteria for assigning the attribute.

Many-to-One Association

One way to implement a many-to-one association is to have buried pointers to the object as an attribute on the "one" side from the "many" side. Then the program can navigate the relationship directly from the "many" side to the "one" side.

---

4   This allows traversal in both directions.

However, navigating from the "one" side to the "many" side requires a search of all of the objects on the "many" side using the association attribute. The following is an example of how to implement many-to-one association using buried pointers:

```
class Person
{
  public:
                            Person(char* n, char s, int a);
        Person*         getFather()
                                {return father;}
        Person*         getMother()
                                {return mother;}
        Person *c[ ]    getChildren();
                            ...
                    ~Person() {}
  private:
            char name[40];
            char sex;
            int   age;  . . .
        Person* father;
        Person* mother;
        void                setFather(Person* p)
                                {father = p; return;}
        void                setMother(Person* p)
                                {mother = p; return;}
};
```

In the above example, two many-to-one relationships have been implemented: children-to-father and children-to-mother. The data member "Person * father" is the implementation of the buried pointer on the "many" side for the children-to-father relationship. The setFather() function is used to establish the relationship from the child to the father; setFather() is declared as a private function because it should be restricted to creation time. In fact, the best way to implement this is to have a father and a mother as required arguments in the constructor of the **Person** class. Then, a **Person** object may not be created without a father or a mother. If this is done, the two private functions, setFather() and setMother(), would not be needed. The getFather(0 function is used by the child to get to the father. The getChildren() function is the function on the "one" side of the relationship and allows a father or mother to navigate either the children-to-father or the children-to-mother relationship to get all of its children. The code for this is not given. If this is implemented in a relational database, an SQL call that searches the appropriate column for a match is appropriate; in an object-oriented database, however, a link list may need to be traversed. In either case, a collection of pointers to the **Person** objects is returned.

Note that if the relationship is between two classes, this function would be in the class on the "one" side, and all the other functions and attributes would be in the class on the "many" side. It should also be noted that there is no set function on the "one" side because there is no attribute added to the class on the "one" side. The traversal from the "one" side to the "many" side can be very expensive.

Rumbaugh et al. suggest that if fast traversal is critical, then it would be better to add attributes to both sides of the association. In this case, the attribute added to the class on the "one" side is not a buried pointer, but a set of pointers to a class object on the other side. This has the disadvantage of making updates of the relationship fairly complex.

If there are attributes of the association, they should be kept in the class on the "one" side of the relationship.

Many-to-Many Association

A many-to-many association can be implemented in either of the following ways:

1. Add an attribute to both sides as a set of pointers to class objects of the other side. This is good for traversal, but involves update complexity.

2. Implement a distinct association object that is independent of either class in the association. An association object is a set of pairs stored in a single variable-size object. The set would consist of two pointers, one to each of the classes in the association.

To better understand the second technique, let us add the class **Company** and the relationship "works-for" between **Person** and **Company**. Initially, you might decide that this is a many-to-one relationship. However, an individual may work for more than one company, and a company usually has more than one employee. This is a many-to-many relationship. Using the association object, we can create an object that has a set of pairs of pointers. In each pair, the first pointer points to a **Person** object, and the second pointer points to a **Company** object, as shown in Figure 17-1.

The first pair captures that person1 works for company1, and the second pair captures that person1 works for company2. The rest of the pairs should be self-explanatory. A very maintainable way of implementing an association object is to use **Dictionary** objects. From a performance perspective, however, they are not very fast.

Implementing Friends

FRIENDS ARE METHODS OR CLASSES that have direct access to all the members (private, protected, and public) of another class. A friend breaks the encapsulation and information-hiding principles and should rarely be used. However, using a friend is better than making a data member public. A friend method can itself be a member method of another class declaration. A good use of a friend is for iterators for a collection of classes.

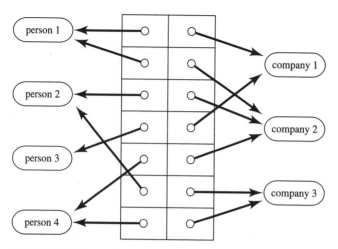

FIGURE 17-1 Association Object: works-for

Class as a Friend

Here is an example that makes a class **GoodGuy** a friend to the class **Text**:

```
class Text: public Font, public String
{
friend class GoodGuy;
public:
Text (Length width, Length height, char *pointer):
        Font(width, height), String (pointer)
        {other initialization code    }
~Text ();
...   // new member functions
private:
...   // new data members
};
```

The friend statement declares that the class **GoodGuy** and all its functions may have direct access to all the members of class **Text**.

Function as a Friend

Here is an example of making a function **GoodMethod** a friend:

```
class Text: public Font, public String
{
friend int Goodguy::GoodMethod(char *);
```

```
public:
Text (Length width, Length height, char *pointer):
        Font(width, height), String (pointer)
        {other initialization code    }
~Text ();
...    // new member functions
private:
...    // new data members
};
```

This is more restrictive than the previous example, since only the function **Good-Method** may access all the members of the class **Text**.

The following example shows a function f1() that can access the members of two classes:

```
class Y; // Forward declaration of Y
class X
{
public:
      friend void     f1(X* x, Y* y);
private:
            int x1; int x2;
};
class Y
{
public:
      friend void     f1(X* x, Y* y);
private:
            int y1, y2;
};
void f1(X* x, Y* y)
{
        y->y1 = x->x1;
        y->y2 = x->x2;
}
```

The function f1() has access to the private members of both class **X** and class **Y**. Both classes are declared with a friend function for f1. Obviously, if every class declares f1 as a friend function, f1 becomes a function that can access any data.

Implementing a One-to-Many Association Using a Friend

The following is an example that uses friend to implement adding and removing an item from a group. The group may be used to capture the many side of an association.

What follows are the two class definitions:

```
class Item
{
friend    Group::addItem(Item*);
friend    Group::removeItem(Item*);
public:
        // some public stuff
      Group*        getGroup () {return group}
private:
      // some private variables, etc.
      Group*        group;
};
class Group: public Item
{
public:
              Group (); //create an empty set
              ~Group (); //destroy a set
    void      addItem (Item*); //add an item
    void      removeItem (Item*); //delete an item
Boolean       includes (Item*); // test for an item
     int      size (); //get number of items in set
private:
    void      add (Item*); //add an item to the set
    void      remove (Item*); //delete an item
                          //from the set
};
```

In the previous example, the friend declarations for services addItem and removeItem allow these services of **Group** to access the private data of **Item**, namely the attribute Group*. This means that **Group** can maintain the integrity of the instances of Item by ensuring that they have a valid pointer as a data item for the attribute Group*. If it is necessary to add a member to the group (add a link), both pointers must be updated. Similarly, removing (or deleting) a member also requires that both pointers be updated. The code for the addItem and removeItem functions follows:

```
void Group::addItem (Item *item);
{
// make referential variable = "this" group
item->group = this;
// add an item to the set of "this" group
this->add (item);
}


void Group::removeItem (Item *item);
{
// make an item member of "null" group
```

```
item->group = 0;
// remove item from "this" set
this->remove (item);
}
```

In the addItem service, the line "item->group = this" directly accesses the group variable of Item. Technically, this violates the encapsulation principle of object-oriented technology. However, remember that a relationship is not truly an attribute,[5] and a relationship implemented as an attribute violates the encapsulation principle. In order to manage the integrity of the relationship, we need to access the relationship attribute that is stored within Item. A friend then becomes a very valuable ally because we want the relationship updated simultaneously on both sides.

Implementing Aggregation

THERE ARE TWO WAYS TO implement an aggregation: buried pointers and embedded objects.

Buried Pointers

Buried pointers are implemented in a way similar to that used to implement an association. To understand this, let us add two more classes to our **Person** example. The two classes are **Hand** and **Body**. Since a person should have a body and two hands, we will use this example to show how to implement composition (aggregation).

The following code is for the buried pointers implementation:

```
class Person
{
 public:
                Person(char* n, char s, int a);
                    ...
                ~Person() {}
 private:
        char   name[40];
            ...
    Person*  spouse; //binary relationship
      Body*  body;   //ptr to body
      Hand*  l_hand; //ptr to left hand
      Hand*  r_hand; //ptr to right hand
};
```

---

[5]   It is implemented as an attribute, so we have lost some information that needs to be managed.

The constructors for initializing the pointers are the same as for an association. Similarly, since each object (body, l_hand, and r_hand) of the composition exists by itself, other functions may access the other objects directly. This is also true with the spouse object in the association.

Embedded Objects

Using the same example, here is the implementation using embedded objects for composition:

```
class Person {
 public:
                   Person(char* n, char s, int a);
                   ~Person() {}
 private:
       char   name[40];
    Person* spouse; //binary relationship
       Body   body;   //object within object
       Hand   l_hand; //object within object
       Hand   r_hand; //object within object
};
```

In this implementation, the objects body, l_hand, and r_hand are not accessible directly by any other class and any nonmember function of this class. The objects are embedded within an instance of **Person.** Only that object has access to these objects. Furthermore, embedded objects must be initialized in a manner similar to inheritance. A sample constructor is shown below:

```
Person::Person(char* n, char s, int a)
        : l_hand(5), r_hand(5)
    // body is implicitly constructed
    // l_hand and r_hand are
    // explicitly constructed
{
            . . .
};
```

The disadvantage of this method is that the arguments of the constructor call for l_hand and r_hand are hard-coded. A more flexible constructor is given below:

```
Person::Person(char* n, char s, int a,
                   int lh_f, int rh_f)
        : l_hand(lh_f), r_hand(rh_f)
{
            . . .
};
```

Implementing Static Members

IT IS THE UNIQUE PROPERTY of a static data member that its variable (a single instance) exists independently of any objects in the class. This allows it to be used in ways that are illegal for nonstatic data members. For example, static members are accessible wherever the class is in scope, and static data members act as global variables for the class. Normally, a static data member holds data that needs to be shared among all instances of the class. It is declared with the keyword *static* and is accessible in the form "className::identifier," when the variable has public visibility. For example,

```
class Person{
 public:
      static int    pubdata;
 private:
      static int   pridata;
};

main()
{
int tmp1 = Person::pubdata; // legal since pubdata is public
int tmp2 = Person::pridata;  // illegal since pridata is not public
};
```

Pridata does not have public visibility, so it is not accessible to any function, including the main() function. However, pubdata has public visibility and is accessible to all functions that use the proper form for accessing it.

The initialization of static data members is different from that of nonstatic data members. Static data members must be initialized once in a single source file. The source file is not within a function, and initialization must be done before main is called. Within the source file, static members are initialized in their sequence in the source file. All static data members (public and private) must be initialized. The syntax for initialization is similar to variable initialization with scoping. An example is

```
int Person::pubdata = 15;  // this initializes pubdata to 15
```

Static member functions are services that are provided by the class, and do not require an instance of the class in order to be accessed. A static member function can be called without an instance prefix, and is accessible by the form "className::functionName" (signature). For example,

```
class Person
{
 public:
      static int getTotal(); // get the number of person instances
```

```
      ...
 private:
      static int no_of_people; // this is incremented by the constructor
                               // and decremented by the destructor
};

main()
{
  int total = 0;
  total = Person::getTotal()
  Person* p;
  int ptotal = 0;
  ptotal = p->getTotal();
};
```

The static function getTotal() is accessed directly by using its class name and the scoping operator in the second statement of main(). In the fifth statement of main(), it is accessed as a function (service) of an object of the class **Person**. Both means of access are legal.

However, a static member function may only use static variables and arguments of its signature in its function definition. The following example illustrates what is legal and illegal in a static member function:

```
class Person
{
 public:
        static int    pubdata;
        static int    clsfcn1();
              int    instdata1;
              int    instfcn1();
 private:
        static int    pridata;
        static int    clsfcn2();
              int    instdata2;
              int    instfcn2();
};

Person::clsfcn1()
{
int tmp1 = Person::pubdata; // legal
int tmp2 = Person::pridata;  // legal
int tmp3 = Person::instdata1; // illegal
int tmp4 = Person::instdata2; // illegal
int tmp5 = Person::instfcn1(); // illegal
int tmp6 = Person::instfcn2(); // illegal
int tmp7 = Person::clsfcn2(); // legal
};
```

Thus, a static function may access any static data members or any other static functions of the class within its function definition. However, it has no access to the nonstatic members.

Recommended Approach

BECAUSE DATABASE-LAYER SOFTWARE FOR object-oriented systems often uses pointers and collections of pointers, we recommend using the buried pointer approach to implement both association and aggregation. Static functions are used as a mechanism to access shared data among objects of the same class.

■ ■ SUMMARY

In this chapter, we learned about pointers, arrays, friends, and static members. We also learned how to use these mechanisms to support the implementation of association and aggregation. Furthermore, we learned how to use static data and static functions to handle the "global data" shared by objects in the same class.

The following are the key points of this chapter:

- ■ Pointers are used to implement association and aggregation.
- ■ Remember the following rules regarding pointers:

    a. Pointers to different classes (types) may not be equated without casting. The exception is that a public inherited subclass (derived class) pointer can be assigned to a superclass (base-class) pointer.

    b. A base-class pointer must always be cast to a legal derived-class pointer.

    c. An object pointer may always be assigned the void pointer. However, a void pointer must be cast to a legal object pointer.

- ■ An array is used to implement the "many" side of a relationship.
- ■ Friends give a nonmember object access to the nonpublic members of the class. Since this violates the encapsulation and information-hiding principles, they should rarely be used.
- ■ Aggregation may be implemented either by buried pointers or by embedded objects.

Case Study: Breakout

When you started to play tennis, one of the most tedious exercises for improving your return was hitting the ball against a backboard or a brick wall. Wouldn't it have been more interesting if you received points for hitting a specific spot or a specific brick? This would help focus your returns on specific spots and thereby increase your accuracy (critical in playing against an opponent). However, if a spot or a brick always had the same value, the tendency would be to focus on the brick with the highest value. This would not help your game, since you would return the ball to one specific spot. To lead you to return to a variety of spots, the point value of each spot or brick would have to vary periodically. This would motivate you to learn to return the ball accurately to a variety of spots by attempting to make the highest score. This would help your game.

Our case studies are based on a game very similar to "solitaire tennis." The game is Breakout. Most readers may already be familiar with this game, since it was one of the first interactive computer video games. The game is very simple and yet requires the use of all the major concepts and mechanisms of object-oriented technology. We have used this game to teach object-oriented technology for many years and have found it extremely effective.

Requirements

BREAKOUT IS AN INTERACTIVE VIDEO game. The playing field consists of three sides and a wall of bricks. The player is given a paddle that can be moved horizontally. It is used to hit a ball against the wall of bricks. The goal of the game is to score points by removing bricks from the wall. A diagram of the game appears in Figure 18-1.

There are two types of bricks in our game: regular and speed bricks.[1] When a ball hits a brick, the following may happen:

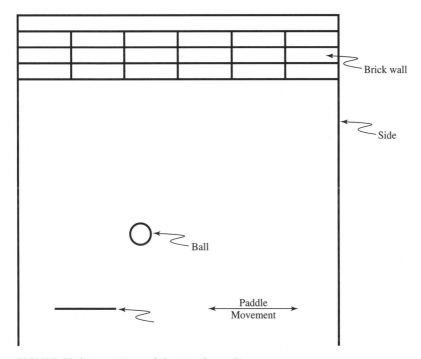

Brick wall

Side

Ball

Paddle
Movement

FIGURE 18-1 User View of the Breakout Game

---

[1]   Though the present requirements is for two type of bricks, we are considering adding other types of bricks to the system later.

■   The ball bounces off.

■   Regular bricks disappear and score 10 points.

■   Speed bricks speed up the ball by a factor of 2 and score 20 points.

When the last brick is removed from the wall, a new wall is displayed (put into play), and the game resumes with the new wall. Whether the new wall is the same as the original wall in design is left to the developers.

Obviously, the ball will also bounce off the paddle and the three sides. However, the "bottom side" (below the paddle) is missing; thus when the ball passes behind the paddle, it is basically lost.

Play begins with the ball taking off from the paddle and moving in a random upward direction. The ball maintains a constant speed and direction until it hits something or is lost. When it hits something, it bounces off and changes direction. It does not change its speed unless it hits a speed brick. The ball continues to move if it is in the field of play. When a ball is lost, the next ball comes into play after a one-second delay. The game is over when the last ball is lost (no balls are left to be put into play). In the design of this game, we will allow each player three balls.

Acquiring Domain Expertise

THE PREVIOUS SECTION IS A typical requirements document. Like most requirements documents, it is incomplete and lacks the specific domain details needed to accurately model the application. One of the most common questions asked is, "How do we get the missing domain information?" The simple answer is to get academic or on-the-job training. Because the world changes so rapidly, we must find other, more immediate, ways to acquire this expertise, like the following:

■   Observe first-hand. That is, go to the field and see what is happening.

■   Listen to a domain expert. This usually means a one-to-one discussion where you ask a lot of questions.

■   Check against previous model(s). This is especially useful in an industry like communications, where many of the standards already use the object-oriented paradigm to describe their needs.

■   Check competitors, since they have probably published their models in some conference proceeding.

■   Read, read, read. There is written literature on everything.

■   For a novice, the *Encyclopedia Britannica* is an excellent source to learn the foundations as well as the terminology of the field. Once you have done your homework, a domain expert is usually more receptive to helping you acquire the additional knowledge necessary to do your job. Try textbooks and professional journals in the field.

■   If you are pioneering a new domain, prototyping may be the best and only means.

In any event, we have chosen the Breakout game as the case study because most of us are at least quasi-domain experts. To further help you in following the case study, we describe additional information that analysts/developers have acquired from experts. This is needed in the third step of our method for specifying the behaviors of the objects in the game.

Expert's Knowledge

Mechanics of Breakout

When a ball hits another object, there are two issues: What happens to the ball, and what happens to the other object? First, we will apply some basic physics. The ball will rebound at the same angle as its entry angle when it hits a flat surface. It is safe to assume that the ball hits a flat surface because in nearly all computer games, objects are modeled as rectangles. We can even assume that the ball is a square and all the other objects are rectangles. For instance, a side is a very narrow rectangle. The ball's reaction is a new direction based on the norm of the flat surface of the obstacle (object) that it hits. This is shown in Figure 18-2.

A ball can hit multiple objects simultaneously. Examples are (1) a side and a brick and (2) two bricks simultaneously. The angle of reflection in those situations is the net effect of the individual reflections of each collision without considering other collisions.

A library subsystem is provided to handle certain details of the game, which we would expect as members of a software company that produces video games.

Time Sequencing in Simulations

In the early 1960s, there were two schools of computer engineers: analog and digital. The analog school felt that the future of the computer was in analog computers because the real world is continuous and not discrete. As we know today, the digital school won. There are two reasons why the digital school won. First, many of the applications that needed automation were already being

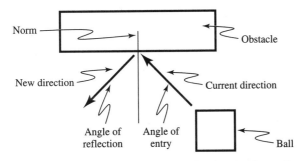

FIGURE 18-2 Collision Mechanics for the Breakout Game

modeled using a discrete model. Second, it was always possible to model any continuous action as a sequence of discrete actions.[2]

The decision to use digital computers also fit very nicely in the information technology world since nearly all the applications/systems that are built fit the digital model. Unfortunately, most engineering (especially process control) applications do not fit nicely into the digital model. In engineering applications, we have always had to find the right granularity of time necessary to make a digital model effective.

There is a similar problem with the Breakout game. The ball and paddle both move continuously in an idealized environment. To simulate continuous movement, we must determine a time slice small enough. In engineering, the control frequency necessary to maintain a stable process is usually the driving factor for the granularity of the time slice. Similarly, the frequency needed to update the display device for Breakout is the driving factor determining the granularity of the time slice.

Video-game developers know that you must refresh the screen every 66.7 milliseconds to give the illusion of continuous motion. To build an optimal game, it is necessary to display a new location for both the ball and the paddle every 66.7 milliseconds. This is implemented as an external event that is generated every 66.7 milliseconds. From a modeling perspective, we can consider the external event as telling the application that another 66.7 milliseconds has elapsed. When this occurs, both the ball and the paddle must provide a "move" service based on elapsed time.

There is a second external event (i.e., start button) that puts the game into play. This event causes the objects to be created and placed in the proper positions so that the game can be played. However, during analysis, we normally do not worry about how to create the objects. Later, usually during design, we will use the "start button" event to sequence the creation of the appropriate objects. For now, we will assume that the wall of bricks is in place, the paddle is displayed in the middle of the screen, and the ball is on the paddle with a velocity in an upward (toward the wall of bricks) direction.

Provided Technology Services

AFTER MODELING A BUSINESS SOLUTION for your problem, you must decide on an approach to implement that solution using available technology. This is usually called the design. We advocate that a design should involve the addition of implementation objects to the domain objects to help realize the domain model on the computer. In this section we describe three provided subsystems and their associated classes to help you implement the Breakout game.

---

[2]   The trick here is to find a granularity small enough so that no key event is lost.

1. Geometric subsystem

The geometric subsystem provides the rectangle class and all the geometric services that we associate with a rectangle. It provides a Cartesian coordinate system for the rectangles to reside in (using Point class) and services to tell whether two rectangles intersect. It also provides services to move the rectangles in the Cartesian coordinate. This is illustrated in Figure 18-3.

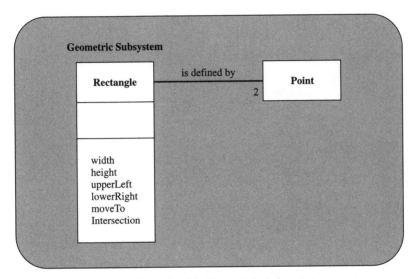

FIGURE 18-3 Class Diagram for the Geometric Subsystem

2. Display subsystem

The display subsystem provides services that superimpose bitmaps onto displayable rectangles so such that the extent of the bitmap is considered a rectangle (**Displayable** class). It provides the following bitmaps: ball, paddle, scoreboard, top, side, slow brick, speed brick, and digits (0–9). The bitmaps are in the **Bitmap** class. The **PicTable** class is used to link the **Bitmap** objects to **Displayable** objects. It also provides support for getting input signals (events) from the "human player" by supporting a **Mouse** class. Finally, it provides window initialization (**GfxEnv** class) to deal with all the details of creating an x-window. Figure 18-4 shows the ball bitmap. The graphics subsystem is shown in Figure 18-5.

FIGURE 18-4 Bitmap of Ball

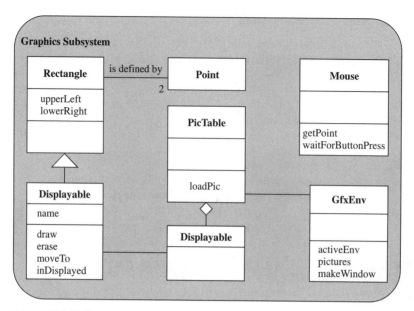

FIGURE 18-5 Class Diagram for the Graphics Subsystem

3. Collision Subsystem

The collision subsystem provides a generic representation of stationary objects (**Gr_obj class**). More important, it provides a mechanism for forming a collection of stationary objects (**GO_formation class**) and handling collisions between a moving rectangle and any stationary object that is in the collection. Given an initial position of a rectangle in motion and a collection of stationary objects (**GO_formation**), it can determine when a collision occurs and compute the rebound position of the rectangle. The collision subsystem is shown in Figure 18-6.

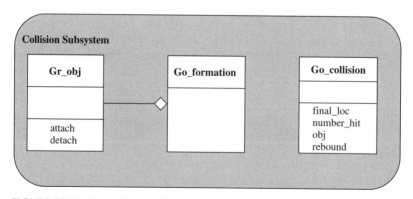

FIGURE 18-6 Class Diagram for the Collision Subsystem

Detailed Class Descriptions

WHAT FOLLOWS ARE DETAILED DESCRIPTIONS of the classes.

Geometric Subsystem Classes

The geometric subsystem contains classes associated with geometry. It is comprised of two classes: **Point** and **Rectangle**, which are described in Figures 18-7 and 18-8.

CLASS NAME	Point
Responsibilities	
This is a 2D Cartesian point.	
It can create a point given *x* and *y* values. It can delete a point.	
Clients can get and change its values. Addition and subtraction of another point are allowed. Division and multiplication by an integer are allowed. Equality using "==" is defined (1 if the same, 0 if different).	
SERVICES	
Point()	// a new point at (0,0)
Point(int a, int b)	// a new point at (a,b)
int X()	//give abscissa value
int Y()	//give ordinate value
void X(int new_x)	//change abscissa value
void Y(int new_y)	//change ordinate value
Operators: / and * may be used with integer and Point.	
Operators: +, −, and == maybe used with Point types.	
Operators: * between two Points is a dot product.	
Variables	
int: abscissa	
int: ordinate	

FIGURE 18-7 CRC Card for Point

CLASS NAME	Rectangle
Superclasses	Point
Subclasses	Displayable, etc.

Responsibilities
This is a 2D Cartesian rectangle. Operators: == and != are defined
It can create a rectangle   given the upper left point and given the lower right point. It can delete a rectangle.
Clients can get values: width, height, upperLeft, lowerRight.
Clients can request it to move by delta x and delta y.
Clients can request it to move defining a new upperLeft.
Clients can ask if a point is contained in the rectangle.
Clients can ask if it intersects with another rectangle.
Clients can obtain the intersection rectangle.
Clients can obtain the smallest rectangle enclosing two rectangles.

Variables
Point: upper left corner
Point: lower right corner

SERVICES
Rectangle()   // a new rectangle at (0,0);

Rectangle(Point& a, Point& b)   // a new rectangle;
             Point: upperLeft
             Point: lowerRight

~Rectangle()   //delete rectangle
Operators: == and != are defined
int width()   //give width of rectangle
int height()   //give height of rectangle
Point upperLeft()   //give upper left point

Point lowerRight()	//give lower right point
void move(int dx, int dy)	//move me by deltas
void moveTo(Point& p)	//move me by changing upperLeft to p
int contains(Point& p)	//return 1, if p is within me; 0 otherwise
Rectangle hull(Rectangle& r)	//return enclosing hull
Rectangle intersection(Rectangle& r)	//return intersection rectangle
int intersectWith(Displayable* d)	//Return 1, if intersection. Return 0 otherwise.

FIGURE 18-8 CRC Card for Rectangle

Display Subsystem Classes

The display subsystem is composed of classes associated with displaying the elements of our model. The drawing constructs available to you in a graphics library are given in Figures 18-9 through 18-16.

You may use the images via an instance of the class **PicTable.** The height and width are given in pixels. The name is the name that you would use with getPic. For example, to get a ball image, which is pictorially a square, you would use the method as follows:

CLASS NAME	**Mouse**
Responsibility	
Keep track of the real mouse.	
SERVICES	
Mouse()	// create a mouse object
~Mouse()	//delete a mouse object
Point getPoint() //retrieve where the mouse is currently pointing	
void waitForButtonPress() //return when user presses a mouse button	

FIGURE 18-9 CRC Card for Mouse

```
PicTable* pre_defined_icons = new PicTable();
char *pointer_ball = "Image_ball";
Picture *pic_ball;
   ...
   pic_ball = pre_defined_icons->getPic(pointer_ball);
   ...
```

CLASS NAME	Displayable
Superclasses	**Rectangle**
Subclasses	**TBD**
Responsibility	
This object places the images (icons) that are available via PicTable on the screen.	
Once an instance of the class is defined, clients can ask it to be drawn, erased, moved on the screen.	
Clients can also ask if the object (instance of Displayable) is visible or not visible to the user.	
Clients can get values: width, height, extent, position.	
Clients can change its image to a new image.	
Clients can ask if another Displayable intersects with it.	
Clients can ask if it intersects with a rectangle or with another Displayable.	
Clients can obtain said intersection as a rectangle.	
Clients can obtain the smallest rectangle that includes the Displayable and another rectangle.	
SERVICES	
Displayable(char* name)	// an icon of "name" at Point (0,0) on the screen
Displayable(char* name, Point& p)	// an icon of "name" at Point p on the screen
Displayable(Displayable& d)	// Create a copy of d
~Displayable()	// Delete displayable

SERVICES	
int draw()	//Draw me at my present position. Return 0, if OK. Else return 1. It is a noop if already displayed.
int erase()	//Stop displaying me; if already so, noop. Return 0, if OK. Otherwise return 1.
void move(int dx, int dy, int disp_flg = 1)	//Move me by deltas. Return 0 if OK. Else return 1. If disp_flg is non-0 and I am currently displayed, redisplay me in new location
void moveTo(Point& p, int disp_flg = 1)	//Move my position to p. Return 0 if OK. Else return 1. If disp_flg is non-0 and I am currently displayed, redisplay me in new location.
int inDisplayed()	//return 0, if not displayed.
Rectangle& rect()	//return my extent.
Point position()	//return my position.
int width()	//return my width.
int height()	//return my height.
int setPic(char* new_pic)	//Set my image to new_pic. Return 0 if OK. Else return 1. If I'm currently displayed, this is an error.
int setPic(Picture* pp)	//Set my image to pp.
int intersectWith(Displayable* d)	//Return 1, if intersection. Return 0 otherwise.

FIGURE 18-10 CRC Card for Displayable

Name	Height	Width
Image_ball	16	16
Image_paddle	5	30
Image_scoreboard	100	200
Image_top	15	500
Image_side	800	15
Image_brick	16	32

Image_slow_brick	16	32
Image_speed_brick	16	32
Image_hello_world	64	64
Image_zero	18	18
Image_one	18	18
Image_two	18	18
Image_three	18	18
Image_four	18	18
Image_five	18	18
Image_six	18	18
Image_seven	18	18
Image_eight	18	18
Image_nine	18	18

FIGURE 18-11 Image Sizes

CLASS NAME	Bitmap (typedef for Picture)
Responsibilities	
This is the figure building block.	
It ties pixel images of objects to a name for showing on the screen.	
Clients can request the height, width, and pixel bitmap of the object.	
Clients can use the = operator to create copies.	
SERVICES	
Bitmap(int width, int height, const Pixmap& stip) // create a picture	
Bitmap(int width, int height, char the_bits[]) // create a picture using Images_*	
int width() // get my width	
int height() // get my height	

Pixmap& pixmap()   // get my pixmap
Bitmap& operator = (const Bitmap&)

FIGURE 18-12 CRC Card for Bitmap

CLASS NAME	PicTable
Responsibilities	
This is a table that ties a name to a bitmap image.	
Clients can request the present and maximum size of the table.	
Clients can ask for the creation and deletion of the table.	
Clients can load the table with a picture (bitmap image) with an associated name.	
Clients can request the picture using the associated name.	
SERVICES	
PicTable() // create a table object.	
int maxSize() // get maximum number of entries table will hold.	
int size() // get current number of entries in table.	
int loadPic(char* name, Picture& pp) // load table with bitmap image pp and tie it to name.	
Picture* getPic(char* name) //return a pointer to bitmap image associated with the name. // If no such name exists, return pointer to bitmap image with name "Default."	
void deletePics() //empty picture table.	

FIGURE 18-13 CRC Card for PicTable

CLASS NAME	PicPak
Responsibilities	
Abstract base class that builds a picture table for PicTable.	
Used to build any game images.	

METHODS	
PicPak( )	// Initialize the PicTable
virtual void load(PicTable&)	// Load the PicTable

FIGURE 18-14 CRC Card for PicPak

CLASS NAME	**GfxEnv**
Responsibilities	
Encapsulates device-dependent graphics environment concerns.	
Initializes and cleans up the environment, and provides scope to any necessary globals.	
SERVICES	
GfxEnv() // initialize the graphics environment Only one GfxEnv may be created at a time. Subsequent attempts will abort the program.	
GfxEnv(PicPak) //initialize graphics environment	
int ok() //return 1 if the graphics environment is OK return 0 if not	
PicTable& pictures() //return the picture table	
int envWidth() //return the width of the graphics environment	
int envHeight() //return the height of the graphics environment	
int wndwWidth() //return the width of the window	
int wndwHeight() //return the height of the window	
int makeWindow(const Rectangle& r) // make a window Only one window may be created	
static GfxEnv* activeEnv() // get active environment	

FIGURE 18-15 CRC Card for GfxEnv

CLASS NAME	Gr_obj
SUPERCLASSES	TBD
SUBCLASSES	TBD

Responsibilities

Gr_obj represents a graphic object for a screen-oriented game. Graphic object is an object as it is (or could be) seen on a screen, is stationary, and can (potentially) be hit by a moving Projectile.

The actual game object must be derived from Gr_obj, and both a virtual function and an unsafe cast must be used to get back the game object. (These need only be performed on Gr_objs that are hit.) (This is necessary because C++ currently lacks mechanisms for genericness; i.e., either templates or checked downcasting.)
A Gr_obj is associated with a GO_formation. (The GO_formation records what Gr_objs are present in the field of play at any one time.)
A Gr_obj may be associated with only one GO_formation at a time. An attempt to violate this will result in a fatal error.
Copying or assigning a Gr_obj will leave the new copy unassociated with any GO_formation. Gr_obj mixes algorithmic details and an oversimplified object interface. (You can have simplicity, efficiency, and generality, but don't count on getting all three at once.)

Attributes:
Rectangular 'location + extent';
Information representing the game object attachment to a GO_Formation.;

Services:
Create/delete a Gr_obj. (Creation is protected, so Gr_obj can only be used as a base (super) class.
Attach/detach from a GO_formation.
Change the Gr_obj's location and rectangular extent.
(The Rectangle's functions will be made available to derived classes.)
(Virtual) Return (as a void*) the address of the object as one of its sub (derived) classes.

SERVICES

Gr_obj(GO_formation*, Rectangle loc) (protected)

int attach() // Returns 0 if already attached to a GO_formation

int detach() // Returns 0 if not attached to some GO_formation

Rectangle rect() // Returns the rectangle at which the GO_obj lies
Point upperLeft() Point lowerRight() int width() int height() void move(Point) void moveTo(Point)

virtual void* real_identity()   // Must be overridden in a common
                                          derived class to return a pointer to
                                this object AS that class WITH type void*
Code that gets the GO_objs back from the collision and expects them to
have a certain type must cast the void* back:
// GO_obj* go = collision.obj(1);
// Real_obj* ro = (Real_obj*) go->real_identity();
   // (if Real_obj overrides real_identity.)

FIGURE 18-16 CRC Card for Gr_obj

Collision Subsystem Classes

The collision subsystem contains the classes associated with the collision of two graphic objects. These classes are shown in Figures 18-17 and 18-18.

CLASS NAME	GO_formation
Responsibilities	
The collections of Gr_objs that are "live" and can be hit at any given time. The number of Gr_objs that can be attached at any one time will be limited to some number not less than 256.	
Attributes: The list of derived Gr_objs.	
Services: Create, Delete—Internal services for use by GO_collision.	
SERVICES	
GO_formation() // Create an instance of GO_formation.	
~GO_formation() // Delete an instance of GO_formation.	

FIGURE 18-17 CRC Card for GO_formation

CLASS NAME	GO_collision

Responsibilities

Perform the game-independent part of moving a rectangular projectile on a straight path for some distance through a "formation" of objects, of which it may strike as many as two at once.
Perform the Breakout-specific parts of a collision, using the class to perform the general elastic collision.
Attributes: Initial and final locations of the projectile; projectile velocity.   The part of its assigned motion that the object completed before striking.   The number and identity of GO_objs struck; the unit normal for the rebound.
Services: Compute those attributes that are not provided (done on initialization).   Return each attribute.   Compute a reflection (rebound) around the unit normal of reflection.
Collaboration: GO_formation

SERVICES

GO_collision (Rectangle init_projectile, Point Motion, GO_formation)
Rectangle initial_loc()
Rectangle final_loc()
Point motion()
int pct_traveled()   // The hundreths of its intended motion the projectile had completed when it first hit something.
int number_hit()   // The number of GO_objs the projectile struck.
GO_obj* obj (int which) // Retrieve the nth GO_obj involved in collision.
Point normal()   // Unit normal vector for the reflection.
Point rebound(Point velocity)   // Compute the rebound after an elastic collision.

FIGURE 18-18 CRC Card for GO_collision

UML Description of the Subsystems

WHAT FOLLOWS ARE DETAILED DESCRIPTIONS of the subsystems using UML notation.

Geometric Subsystem

The geometric subsystem (part of the display subsystem) is shown in Figure 18-19.

Display Subsystem

The display subsystem is shown in Figure 18-19 (detail of the geometric subsystem) and Figure 18-20.

Collision Subsystem

The collision subsystem is shown in Figure 18-21.

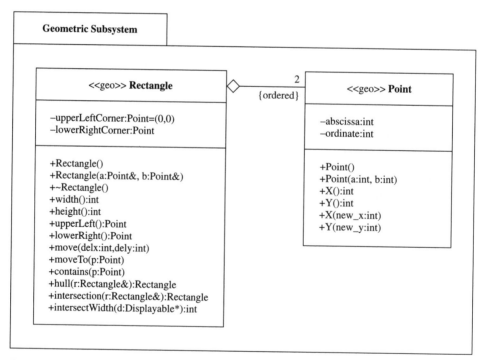

FIGURE 18-19 Geometric Subsystem of the Display Subsystem

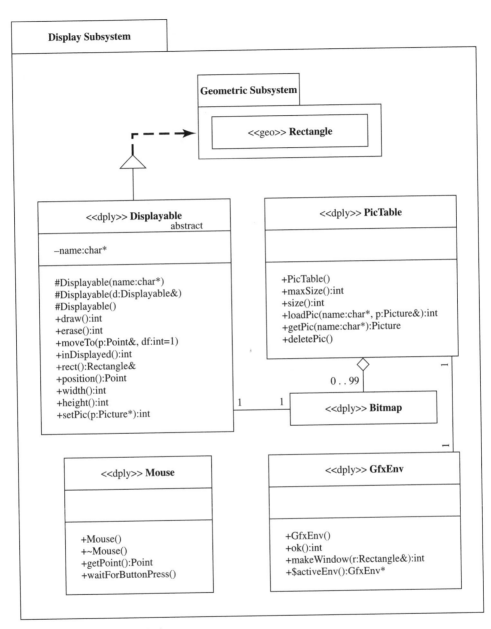

FIGURE 18-20 Display Subsystem

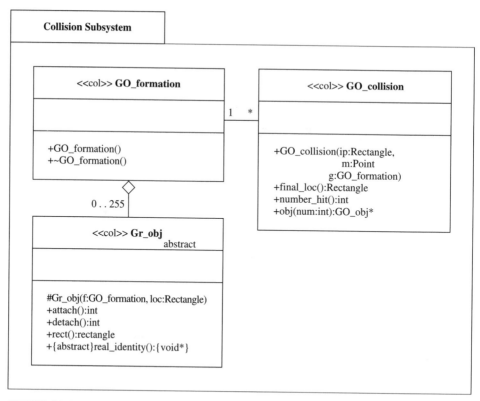

FIGURE 18-21 Collision Subsystem

CHAPTER

19

Case Study:
Team 1

T he first case study follows the efforts of a team that used a minimalist approach to object-oriented analysis. We follow them as they move through the first five steps of our method.

Step 1: Finding the Objects

THE GOAL OF STEP 1 is to find the objects. Team 1 uses the nouns, pronouns, and noun phrases as given by Abbott and Booch to identify the objects in the Breakout game. The results of their work appear in Table 19-1. As you can see, Team 1 identified classes only. They have assumed instances of each of the classes are the same. This premature assumption will cause them to ignore subclasses.[1]

TABLE 19-1 List of Potential Objects

BreakoutGame	Points
Brick	Wall
Ball	Player
Score	Paddle
Playing Field	Side

Step 2: Identifying Responsibilities

THE GOAL OF STEP 2 is to find business attributes and services that are useful to your business problem domain. This step is the beginning of our abstraction process as we start to identify the relevant attributes and services, thus narrowing our problem/application space.

Looking at Adjectives

The suggested process is to look first at the adjectives in the requirements document. From the requirements document, the four potential adjectives/nouns that may be useful are regular brick, speed brick, last ball, and last brick. Here is where the advice of just using adjectives is a little tricky.

In the case of the last brick, the "last" is not a property of any specific brick; a brick becomes the last brick only when all the other bricks are gone. This is different from another attribute of brick, namely, point value. As stated in the requirements, each brick has a point value, and that point value is applicable to all the bricks. Thus, point value is an attribute of brick, while "last" is not an attribute.[2]

---

[1] This is a bad habit that sophomoric object-oriented analysts/developers acquire. It leads to drawing conclusions without all of the relevant data.

[2] For an attribute to be in a class, it must apply to every instance (object) in the class.

For ball, however, "last" ball could be preset and unchangeable. We may also want to make "last" an attribute of the "last ball." As tempting as this is, Team 1 recognized that this is not a very flexible model.[3]

For "speed brick," Team 1 argued that since the requirements said that the speed factor presently is 2, the speed-up factor could be hard-coded into the code for the method. A rejected alternative was to add an additional attribute called "speed" to every speed brick. This was suggested to capture the speed-up factor that the brick possesses. Again, this is possible, but Team 1 has programmers who want to write code. Team 1 has modeled the requirement in a manner that leads to software that is inflexible and hard to maintain. The second alternative of adding a speed attribute is better, because different speeds can be individually assigned to each brick.[4]

Asking Question 1

Team 1 then asked Question 1, "How is this object described in general?" Their results are shown in the CRC cards that follow (Figures 19-1 through 19-9). Figure 19-8 shows a description of a paddle for tennis or ping-pong; we will later discover that these may not be the best choices. Figure 19-9 defines PlayingField as the area within which the game is played. The boundary of this rectangular playing field is defined by its four sides. In Figure 19-17 Team 1 has assumed that the Sides define the boundary of the PlayingField. It can be argued that a Side is like a line with no width. This may be conceptually correct, but in practice all lines have some thickness.

OBJECT NAME	BreakoutGame
ATTRIBUTES	
none	

FIGURE 19-1 CRC Card for Breakout Game

---

[3] Team 2 will find a better vehicle for capturing both the "last ball" and the "last brick" than to make "last" an attribute of the ball object or of the brick object.

[4] Even this alternative is not the correct object-oriented analysis model solution. Team 2, in the next case study, will find the correct analysis model solution.

OBJECT NAME	Points
ATTRIBUTES	
none	

FIGURE 19-2 CRC Card for Points

OBJECT NAME	Brick
ATTRIBUTES	
length, width, depth, color, position, density, weight	

FIGURE 19-3 CRC Card for Brick

OBJECT NAME	Wall
ATTRIBUTES	
length, width, depth, color, position, weight	

FIGURE 19-4 CRC Card for Wall

OBJECT NAME	Ball
ATTRIBUTES	
diameter, color, position, weight	

FIGURE 19-5 CRC Card for Ball

OBJECT NAME	Player
ATTRIBUTES	
name, height, weight, skillLevel, etc.	

FIGURE 19-6 CRC Card for Player

OBJECT NAME	**Score**
ATTRIBUTES	
pointsAccumulated	

FIGURE 19-7 CRC Card for Score

OBJECT NAME	**Paddle**
ATTRIBUTES	
length, width, handleSize, weight, hittingSurfaceMaterial, etc.	

FIGURE 19-8 CRC Card for Paddle

OBJECT NAME	**PlayingField**
ATTRIBUTES	
length, width	

FIGURE 19-9 CRC Card for Playing Field

Asking Question 2

The most difficult question to answer is, "What is our problem domain?" This will have an impact on the reusability of the classes (templates for instantiating an object) that are designed. Question 2 is really the process of abstraction (the object only keeps attributes that are applicable to the problem domain). The attributes that are considered germaine are determined by the scope of the problem domain. Team 1 defines the problem domain as the world of interactive video games.

They now revisit their objects and their attributes within this bounded domain. For the objects in the following figures, the team has changed the attribute list. A deleted attribute is shown with a strikeout, and a new attribute is shown with an underline. Objects with no attributes are eliminated. The results are shown in Figures 19-10 through 19-17.

In present interactive video games, density and weight are not attributes captured in abstraction. Depth can be debated; we are starting to see three-dimensional interactive video games. Color is also an issue, since color screens on PCs are commonplace.

OBJECT NAME	Brick
ATTRIBUTES	
length, width, depth, color, position, ~~density~~, ~~weight~~, <u>pointValue</u>	

FIGURE 19-10 CRC Card for Brick

Since Wall is a collection of Bricks, it is reasonable to assume that the color will be defined for each brick and that the "color" of the wall is determined by the brick. In a sense, the "color" of the Wall is derivable. Again, the weight is not captured in the abstraction for this problem domain. This is shown in Figure 19-11.

Velocity, which is speed * direction, is added (see Figure 19-12) to make the ball move in a direction as well as with speed. This is very vice encapsulation, as the ball has all the data it needs to perform the move itself.

Player represents an abstraction of a person, so that we know who is actually playing the game and can keep the player's point_total. This is shown in Figure 19-13. Team 1 does not have the point_total as an attribute because they assumed that score was a separate object. We will see later that we can capture score as a relationship, embedded attribute, or attribute. We will discuss each of the schema in later chapters.

If we were dealing with system modeling, we would need a separate object (i.e., HumanPlayer) to represent the person who is actually playing the game by moving the keyboard/joystick. However, the HumanPlayer is actually an implementation object.

Skill-level was left as an attribute, because we may want to entice players at different levels to compete with each other, thus increasing our revenue. Name was kept as a way to identify a player who makes the highest score list.

As described in the requirements section, the paddle is abstracted into a rectangle. Many of the attributes of a "real paddle" are not applicable to this abstraction. Team 1 eliminated all attributes except for length and width, and added depth for consistency, as shown in Figure 19-15.

PlayingField is defined as the area within which the game is played. Team 1 has decided that either PlayingField is a derived object, since it can be obtained by knowing all the sides, or that the concept itself is not useful to the problem domain. In order to be consistent with the three-dimensional concept, and the fact that even a conceptual rectangular boundary must have some depth, Team 1 has added the attributes width and depth. This is shown in Figure 19-16.

OBJECT NAME	Wall
ATTRIBUTES	
length, width, depth, ~~color~~, position, ~~weight~~	

FIGURE 19-11 CRC Card for Wall

OBJECT NAME	Ball
ATTRIBUTES	
diameter, color, position, ~~weight~~, <u>velocity</u>	

FIGURE 19-12 CRC Card for Ball

OBJECT NAME	Player
ATTRIBUTES	
name, ~~height~~, ~~weight~~, skill-level, ~~etc.~~	

FIGURE 19-13 CRC Card for Player

OBJECT NAME	Score
ATTRIBUTES	
pointsAccumulated	

FIGURE 19-14 CRC Card for Score

OBJECT NAME	Paddle
ATTRIBUTES	
length, width, ~~handleSize~~, ~~weight~~, ~~hittingSurfaceMaterial~~, ~~etc.~~, <u>depth</u>.	

FIGURE 19-15 CRC Card for Paddle

OBJECT NAME	PlayingField
ATTRIBUTES	
~~length, width~~	

FIGURE 19-16 CRC Card for PlayingField

OBJECT NAME	Side
ATTRIBUTES	
length, ~~width/depth(?)~~, position, <u>width, depth</u>	

FIGURE 19-17 CRC Card for Side

Asking Question 3

Once Team 1 had identified some bounded attributes, they applied the Western school of thinking to object-oriented analysis. They looked at the minimal specification of attributes necessary to satisfy this application.

From the requirements document, it is clear that the writer/buyer is specifying a two-dimensional game. Furthermore, color does not seem to be a requirement. Thus, they assumed the vendor was going after the low-end market of noncolor monitors. However, the buyer may want the game to be portable to color devices without using the color capabilities of more expensive and advanced devices. The actual display device (hardware) to be used is not part of the application domain.

Team 1 then revisited their objects and their attributes within this bounded domain. In the application, the world is two-dimensional. The depth of the brick is not applicable to the abstraction. This logic also applies to Wall, Paddle, and Side. The application is also colorless. The results are shown in Figures 19-18 through 19-25.

Here we represent an abstraction of a person, so that we know who is actually playing the game and keeping a point_total. We do not have the pointTotal as an attribute because we assume that score is a separate object. We will see later that we can capture score as a relationship, embedded attribute, or attribute. We will discuss each of the schema in later chapters.

If we were dealing with system modeling, we would need a separate object (i.e., HumanPlayer) to represent the person who is actually playing the game by moving the keyboard/joystick. However, the HumanPlayer is actually an implementation object.

Skill-level was left as an attribute, because we may want to entice players at different levels to compete with each other, thus increasing our revenue. Name was kept as a way to identify a player who makes the highest score list.

In answering Question 2, depth was added as an attribute. In Question 3, however, it is deleted. Adding an attribute to the list and then deleting the attribute is a symptom of an unclear problem domain/application scope. There is also usually much frustration when each individual has a definition of the domain/application that is inconsistent with those of the rest of the team.

Based on the above analysis for the team, a new list of potential objects has been constructed. This list is summarized in Table 19-2. BreakoutGame had no attributes and hence was removed. Points appeared to be used only as an attribute of another object. PlayingField was defined by the sides.

TABLE 19-2 List of Objects (Revised)

~~BreakoutGame~~	~~Points~~
Brick	Wall
Ball	Player
Score	Paddle
~~PlayingField~~	Side

OBJECT NAME	**Side**
ATTRIBUTES	
length, ~~width/depth(?)~~, position, <u>width, depth</u>	

FIGURE 19-18 CRC Card for Side

OBJECT NAME	**Brick**
ATTRIBUTES	
length, width, ~~depth~~, ~~color~~, position, ~~density~~, ~~weight~~, pointValue	

FIGURE 19-19 CRC Card for Brick

OBJECT NAME	Wall
ATTRIBUTES	
length, width, ~~depth~~, ~~color~~, position, ~~weight~~	

FIGURE 19-20 CRC Card for Wall

OBJECT NAME	Ball
ATTRIBUTES	
diameter, ~~color~~, position, ~~weight~~, velocity	

FIGURE 19-21 CRC Card for Ball

OBJECT NAME	Player
ATTRIBUTES	
name, ~~height, weight~~, skillLevel, ~~etc.~~	

FIGURE 19-22 CRC Card for Player

OBJECT NAME	Score
ATTRIBUTES	
pointsAccumulated	

FIGURE 19-23 CRC Card for Score

OBJECT NAME	Paddle
ATTRIBUTES	
length, width, ~~handle size~~, ~~weight, hittingSurfaceMaterial, etc.~~, ~~depth~~.	

FIGURE 19-24 CRC Card for Paddle

OBJECT NAME	PlayingField
ATTRIBUTES	
~~length, width~~	

FIGURE 19-25 CRC Card for PlayingField

Looking at Services

Services are the only things that another object or system sees. In pure object-oriented analysis, we only need to define services for every object. Unfortunately, there is no easy way to find all the services. This is complicated by the fact that from an implementation perspective you can define any service you want for an object. We must limit our definition of services to those that make sense in the application and/or the problem domain. We recommend using the verbs in the requirements document to find services.

The team rereads the requirements and finds the following verb phrases:

1. "Ball hits a brick." The grammatical object of that sentence is Brick. So Brick needs to provide a hit service.
2. "Points are added to the player's score." This implies that an add service needs to be added either to player, score, or both. The easy way is to add the service to both.
3. "Paddle can be moved horizontally." This implies a move service for Paddle.
4. "Ball bounces off." This implies a bounce service for Ball.
5. "Speed bricks speed up the ball." This implies a speed increase service for Ball.
6. "Ball hits the paddle." This implies a hit service for Paddle.
7. "Ball hits the side." This implies a hit service for Side.
8. "Brick removed from the wall." To Team 1, this was immaterial.

The team used these statements to add services to the objects. The results are shown in the figures of the CRC cards that follow. Score was retained, because the team felt it should be a key object.

When Team 1 redefined the scope from the domain of video games to the specific application as given by the requirements, they reduced the number of attributes. The result is a set of objects with fewer extraneous attributes, but at the price of making the objects less reusable. The results are shown in Figures 19-26 through 19-32.

OBJECT NAME	Ball
ATTRIBUTES	
diameter, ~~color~~, position	
SERVICES	
bounce, speedIncrease	

FIGURE 19-26 CRC Card for Ball with Services Added

OBJECT NAME	Brick
ATTRIBUTES	
length, width, depth, color, position, ~~density, weight~~, pointValue	
SERVICES	
beenHit	

FIGURE 19-27 CRC Card for Brick with Services Added

OBJECT NAME	Wall
ATTRIBUTES	
length, width, ~~depth~~, ~~color~~, position, ~~weight~~	
SERVICES	
none	

FIGURE 19-28 CRC Card for Wall with Services Added

OBJECT NAME	Score
ATTRIBUTES	
pointsAccumulated	
SERVICES	
incrementScore	

FIGURE 19-29 CRC Card for Score with Services Added

OBJECT NAME	Paddle
ATTRIBUTES	
length, width, ~~handleSize, weight, hittingSurfaceMaterial, etc., depth~~	
SERVICES	
beenHit	

FIGURE 19-30 CRC Card for Paddle with Services Added

OBJECT NAME	Side
ATTRIBUTES	
length, ~~width/depth (?)~~, ~~color~~, position, ~~weight~~	
SERVICES	
none	

FIGURE 19-31 CRC Card for Side with Services Added

OBJECT NAME	Player
ATTRIBUTES	
both team: name, ~~height, weight~~, skillLevel, ~~etc.~~	
SERVICES	
addPoints	

FIGURE 19-32 CRC Card for Player with Services Added

Step 3: Specifying Behaviors

THE THIRD STEP IS TO specify the behaviors of the objects. The results of this step are shown in Figures 19-33 through 19-41.

For Team 1, the scenarios for the paddle are as follows:

1. Paddle may be moved because there is no obstruction.
2. Paddle movement requested puts the paddle outside of the playing field.

The scenarios for the ball are as follows:

1. Ball may be moved because there is no obstruction.
2. Ball movement requested will take a ball into a side.
3. Ball hits the paddle.
4. Ball hits a brick.

First, Team 1 observes that paddle movement is not determined by time. Paddle movement is determined by the person in control of the joystick/mouse/keyboard. To change the position of the paddle of a joystick/mouse/keyboard, we need another object, call it Mouse, that provides the service. Below are the adjustments made by Team 1 to handle the paddle scenarios.

Team 1 discussed whether this object should just return delta x, since the y value must be fixed according to our requirements. The proper allocation of requirements to the correct objects affects the reuse issue. Returning delta x makes it easier for the Paddle object to do its work. However, this is less flexible. What will happen when you want to use the Mouse object in another application where you want to get delta y also? This is a very subtle issue involving the question "To which object does a constraint apply?" The mouse is actually allowed to move in any direction that makes sense. In fact, what is being requested is that the Paddle object interpret the deltas from the mouse so that only the x values are changed. This would keep the issue in the proper semantic domain, since the mouse is really a technology object and not part of the problem domain.

Position is added to the attribute list in order to compute the hull. In computer graphics, every displayable object is really a rectangle. This is because nearly all pixel maps are rectangles. Thus, the position of a displayable object is by convention the upper left corner of the rectangle.

In specifying the service for Paddle, Team 1 identified three new services for side: getUL, getLR, and inPath. The getUL service will get the position (x, y) of the upper left corner of the side. The "getLR" will get the position (x, y) of the lower right corner of the side. Since the side has some width, the x value for the upper left corner is different from the x value for the lower right corner. The inPath service is very simple; conceptually, it accepts a geometric object with a position as an argument and determines if the side is occupying any of that space.

In physics, the path or the area that an object will travel in a given period of time is called a hull. One of the things that must be determined is whether the hull of the paddle occupies the same space as one of the sides. If it does, the paddle must not be allowed to move beyond that edge.

Now Team 1 was ready to work on the scenario for ball movement. The first scenario is very simple; the ball moves from current position to current position + velocity *time-elapsed. The velocity is speed * direction; direction is an x value and a y value. Team 1 realized each of the obstacles—paddle, side, and brick—reacts or behaves differently when it is hit by the ball. Figure 19-38 shows Team 1's additions and the changes based on the above scenarios for the ball.

Team 1 has replaced the diameter with a width/length; for a square ball, the length is equal to the width. Having added velocity, Team 1 believes that the ball has all the data to move itself.

The paddle is not in the same situation; it cannot perform its move service without help (collaboration) from another object. The paddle cannot have a fixed or predetermined velocity; both the speed and direction of the paddle are determined by how fast the player is moving the controls. This information is provided by the mouse object.

Here again Team 1 notices that not all the time (66.7 milliseconds) may have been used in traveling from the original position to the point of impact. This is correct; however, in most video games, the model is simplified in that it assumes that the remaining time is used in the impact. This serves two useful purposes: first, it means that the model does not have to deal with computing the actual position based on elastic collision; second, from a display perspective, the user will see the ball hit the obstacle. Note that if an obstacle is hit, it will react to the hit as part of the service inPath. The astute reader will notice a flaw in this assumption.

The reader may notice that the hull is not computed perfectly. For simulation and teaching object-oriented programming, however, this is probably adequate. From Team 1's perspective, bounce, which is probably an event, does not need to be captured as an object, because Ball has nearly all the data it needs to compute the bounce. Based on Team 1's analysis, it only needs the norm from the obstacle that got hit.[5]

Team 1 identified more services for other objects, namely Side, Paddle, and Brick. Team 1 has already done a certain amount of abstracting, in that they have chosen to group together all the bricks into one object (more properly one class) and to group all the sides into one object (more properly one class). Thus for each of these objects two services were identified: inPath and getNorm. For Side, the inPath service has already been defined. The getNorm service has been graphically defined, and its actual implementation is left to design. Figure 19-34 illustrates the results of adding these services.

For Brick, the inPath service is similar to that for Side and Paddle, except that the brick needs to respond to being hit. In response, it needs to ask Score to increment its value, and if the brick is a speed brick it needs to ask Ball to speed up. Two new attributes are added to make this happen. The speed_increase service has already been defined for Ball. The Wall brick_removed service and the Score increment_score (pointValue) service are already identified, and their definitions are given in Figures 19-40 and 19-41.

Team 1 did not discover all the scenarios. They forgot two very important ones: (1) when the last brick is hit and a new wall is created and (2) when the ball is lost and a new ball is put into play (end of game?). They also forgot to look in depth at how scoring is done. If they had done these scenarios, they would have found flaws in both their structural and behavioral models. Team 1 continued to fail to perform analysis with enough depth and completeness to address all relevant domain-modeling issues. This is very common when domain analysis is done by people with no development experience.

OBJECT NAME	Mouse
ATTRIBUTES	
previous location	
SERVICES	
prototype: getDelta()	
{ // structured English definition	
get CURRENT POSITION from mouse hardware	
// the real hardware mouse knows where it is	
compute DELTA	

---

[5] Again, an astute reader may see a flaw in reasoning here. However, the principle is accurate. All is fine if the ball only needs the norm from the obstacle to compute rebound direction.

| as CURRENT POSITION minus PREVIOUS POSITION. |
| return as DELTA |
| } |

FIGURE 19-33 CRC Card for Mouse with Services Added

OBJECT NAME	**Side**
ATTRIBUTES	
length, width, position	
SERVICES	
prototype: getUL() //defined earlier	
prototype: getLR() //defined earlier	
prototype: inPath(hull) //defined earlier	
prototype: ~~been_hit()~~ //eliminated	
prototype: getNorm() //details deferred to design	

FIGURE 19-34 CRC Card for Side

OBJECT NAME	**Paddle**
ATTRIBUTES	
length, width, <u>position</u>	
SERVICES	
prototype: move() // defined earlier	
prototype: inPath(hull) //same as Side	
prototype: ~~been_hit()~~ //same as Side	
prototype: getNorm() //same as Side	

FIGURE 19-35 CRC Card for Paddle

OBJECT NAME	Paddle

ATTRIBUTES

length, width, <u>position</u>

SERVICES

prototype: move()

{ // structured English definition

    get DELTA from mouse object

        via getDelta service of mouse.

      // we assume that we can get to the mouse somehow

    get DELTA-x from DELTA.

    compute hull as

        if DELTA-x is positive

            then:

                set hull's POSITION to POSITION + LENGTH.

            else:

                set hull's POSITION to ball's POSITION

            endif:

      set hull's LENGTH to DELTA-x.

      set hull's WIDTH to WIDTH.

    // note: POSITION and LENGTH belong to paddle.

    // before the paddle can move, it must determine if anything is
in its way.

    // ask the left side if it is in the path (hull)

      if left-side->inPath (hull),

        then:

            get LRC (lower right corner) from left-side

                via getLR service of side

            get LRC-x from LRC.

            set POSITION-x to LRC-x.

      else: // if not left-side, then it may be right-side

        if right-side->inPath (hull),

then:
get ULC (upper left corner) from right-side
via getUL service of side
get ULC-x from ULC.
set POSITION-x to ULC-x.
else:
set POSITION-x to POSITION-x + DELTA-x.
endif:
endif:
// this has conceptually moved the paddle.
// when you get here, x value of POSITION has been changed.
// we need to redisplay the object at its new position,
// but this is actually an implementation issue.
// display self at new position (details left to design).
}

FIGURE 19-36 CRC Card for Paddle with Services Added

OBJECT NAME	**Side**
ATTRIBUTES	
length, width, position	
SERVICES	
prototype: getUL()	
{ // structured English definition	
return POSITION.	
// the position is the upper left corner	
}	
prototype: getLR()	
{ // lower right corner is position-x + width and position-y + length	
// we always assume that width is horizontal and length is vertical	

| LR-x = POSITION-x + width. |
| LR-y = POSITION-y + length. |
| return LR. |
| } |
| |
| prototype: inPath (hull) |
| {   // this is a geometric problem |
| if (the hull and the side occupy any space in common) |
| // the detail on how to determine this is left to design |
| then: // there is an intersection |
| return true. |
| else: |
| return false. |
| endif: |
| } |
| |
| prototype: been_hit() |
| { // this service was found earlier |
| // defining it will be deferred till later |
| } |

FIGURE 19-37 CRC Card for Side with Services Added

OBJECT NAME	**Ball**
ATTRIBUTES	
position, width/length, velocity	
SERVICES	
prototype: move (elapsed_time)	
{ // this is based on ball hitting only one obstacle.	
compute DELTA as VELOCITY*ELAPSED_TIME	
// DELTA is the distance the ball moves when nothing is in its way.	

compute hull as
if DELTA-y is positive,
then:
set hull's start POSITION to ball's POSITION.
else:
set hull's start POSITION to ball's POSITION + WIDTH.
endif.
set hull's end POSITION to hull's start POSITION +DELTA.
// check to see if anything is in its way;   if something is in its way, remember who it is.
For each obstacle that can be in the way:
// ask each obstacle whether it is in the way via inPath service.
if obstacle->inPath (hull),
then:
hit_object is obstacle.
endif:
endFor:
If hit_object is not found,
then: // it can move unobstructed.
set POSITION to POSITION + VELOCITY*ELAPSED_TIME.
else: // it has hit an obstacle.
compute new DIRECTION as angle of reflection.
change POSITION to point of impact.
endif:
}
prototype: ~~bounce()~~
// this has been captured as part of the move service.
prototype: speed_increase(speedFactor)
{
set VELOCITY to VELOCITY*SPEEDFACTOR.
}

FIGURE 19-38 CRC Card for Ball with Services Added

OBJECT NAME	Brick

ATTRIBUTES

position, length, width, pointValue, <u>type</u>

SERVICES

prototype: ~~been_hit()~~   //same as Side

prototype: getNorm()   //same as Side

prototype: inPath(hull)

  {

  {   // this is a geometric problem

    if (the hull and the side occupy any space in common)

    // the detail on how to determine this is left to design

    then: // there is an intersection

      ask Score to increment its value by pointValue

        via increment_score service of Score.

      if type is "speed"

        then:

          ask Ball to increase speed by 2

            via speed_increase service.

        endif:

      tell Wall that this brick has been removed

        via brick_removed service

      disappear.

      return true.

    else:

      return false.

    endif:

  }

FIGURE 19-39 CRC Card for Brick with Services Added

OBJECT NAME	**Score**
ATTRIBUTES	
pointsAccumulated	
SERVICES	
prototype: increment_score(points)	
{	
add POINTS to POINTS_ACCUMULATED.	
}	

FIGURE 19-40 CRC Card for Score with Services Added

OBJECT NAME	**Wall**
ATTRIBUTES	
length, width, position, <u>brickCount</u>	
SERVICES	
prototype: brick_removed()	
{ // Assume that brick count keeps track of the number of bricks.	
subtract 1 from brickCount	
}	

FIGURE 19-41 CRC Card for Wall with Services Added

Step 4: Specifying Relationships

STEP 4 OF OUR APPROACH is to specify relationships among objects. Team 1 reread the requirements document and used the specification of services to help define aggregations and links. Team 1 started by using the *is_a* test to find generalization/specialization. The results are shown in Table 19-3. The results of the table show that no generalization/specializations are found.

The team finds the following potential aggregations and links by rereading the requirements document:

TABLE 19-3 Is_a Test Table

Is A a B?	S	Ba	Br	P	S	W
Score	X	n	n	n	n	n
Ball	n	X	n	n	n	n
Brick	n	n	X	n	n	n
Paddle	n	n	n	X	n	n
Side	n	n	n	n	X	n
Wall	n	n	n	n	n	X

A is the row, and B is the column.
Column 1 is score, column 2 is ball, and so on.
In the cells, a = always, s = sometimes, and n = never.

1. Aggregations:

   Wall of bricks

2. Links:

   Brick and score
   Player and paddle

The following potential aggregations and links were identified by reviewing the methods:

1. Aggregations:

   None

2. Links:

   Mouse and paddle
   Hull and paddle
   Left side and paddle
   Right side and paddle
   Hull and ball
   Ball and each obstacle
   Hit_object and obstacle
   Brick and score

Team 1 then discussed the results of their findings before drawing their model. They know that they have found (as with identifying objects) a list of relationships that are potential aggregations and links. The relationships that need to be modeled by aggregations and links are the relatively permanent ones. The temporary relationships are better modeled by requiring the calling object pass them as part of the message (an argument of the function call).

Team 1 required a criterion to determine which of the vehicles it would use to capture these potential relationships. The criterion is as follows:

> If the relationship's existence extends beyond the present method (i.e., survives beyond at least one method), then the analyst/developer should consider modeling it as a relationship. Though this is not clearly stated in most object-oriented books, aggregations and links (i.e., associations) are used to capture the static relationships between objects. Here, static does not mean that it cannot be altered, but that it is applicable over time.

This guideline must be balanced against the fact that the primary purpose of the model is to capture the domain expert's model of reality. Some judgments must still be made as to which potential relationships should be modeled as an aggregation or link.

With this guideline, Team 1 concluded that (from a domain perspective) the wall is made from bricks, and the wall ceases to exist when there are no more bricks. They decided it was an assembly-parts aggregation, with the understanding that it is also a dynamic aggregation, since the number of bricks could vary over time.

For the brick-to-score link, Team 1 formed a link from every brick to the score. This does not appear bad to Team 1 as they consider a brick an object. However, technically there are n bricks, and there would need to be n links to score, since there must be a separate link for each brick.[6]

Regarding the player-to-paddle link, Team 1 had a heated discussion. The difficulty was that Player is being used to represent two different things. First, Player refers to the real person who is moving the joystick/keyboard. Second (from the game's perspective), there is the concept of a player who owns the paddle and the balls.[7] In this situation, player refers to the real person. From the problem domain's perspective, the mouse moves the paddle. This relationship from person-to-paddle is more accurately captured as the person controls the mouse which controls the paddle. Most analysts will consider the real person to be outside of the application domain. Thus, this link is not captured.

The mouse-to-paddle link is a static link since it does not changed over time. This link definitely needs to be captured in this model.

The hull-to-paddle link is interesting as the hull is really computed at every time slice and is not kept between time slices. This is a temporary link that lasts over the life of a single method or transaction. In this situation, using argument passing is a better vehicle. Since the link is temporary, it is a false link.

---

6   This may seem rather ugly. We will show later how to solve this problem.

7   This kind of misunderstanding is very common. An analyst must often be very careful about which meaning of a word is being used.

The paddle-to-left side link and the paddle-to-right side link are very interesting as team 1's method requires the services of both sides at every time slice. From a model perspective, these links appear to be very static and must be in the model.

The hull-to-ball link is a false link for the same reason that the hull-to-paddle link is a false link.

An obstacle can be any of the sides, any of the bricks that have not been hit, and the paddle. For the ball-to-obstacle links, it appears as though the game needs to know about these links from one time slice to another time slice. Although these links may be conditional, this collection of links is important to the game over time. Therefore these links need to be modeled.

Hit_object-to-obstacle is a false, link since a hit_object is defined only for a time slice or a transaction. It is not applicable across time slices.

The brick-to-score link seems necessary because there is no other way a brick can score points. Similarly, the brick-to-wall link seems necessary because the brick needs to use the wall's brick_removed service. The aggregation is shown in Figure 19-42.

In these links, there are multiple instances of Brick, and each brick has its own link to Score. There are really three instances of Side. Only one instance of Side can be the left side, and only another instance of Side can be the right side. Part of the semantics are lost in the diagram of Figure 19-43.

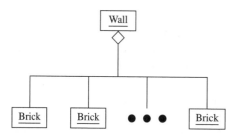

FIGURE 19-42 Team 1's Aggregation Diagram for Breakout Game

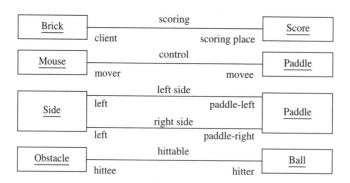

FIGURE 19-43 Team 1's Link Diagram for Breakout Game

Since a new object, Obstacle, was discovered, Team 1 needed to reevaluate their generalization/specialization results. Obstacle was added to the table, and the results are shown in Table 19-4. The generalization/specialization results are shown graphically in Figure 19-44.

TABLE 19-4 Is_a Test Table

Is A a B?	S	O	Ba	Br	P	S	W
Score	X	n	n	n	n	n	n
Obstacle	n	X	n	s	s	s	n
Ball	n	n	X	n	n	n	n
Brick	n	a	n	X	n	n	n
Paddle	n	a	n	n	X	n	n
Side	n	a	n	n	n	X	n
Wall	n	n	n	n	n	n	X

A is the row, and B is the column.
Column 1 is score, column 2 is obstacle, and so on.
In the cells, a = always, s = sometimes, and n = never.

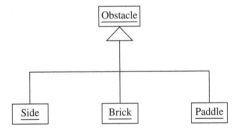

FIGURE 19-44 Generalization/Specialization
Diagram for Team 1's
Obstacle Object

Step 5: Refinement

STEP 5 IS TO REFINE the model. Let us start step 5 by reviewing what we learned from the lawn-mowing example that will help with refinement. First, while very few objects are classes, every class is an object. This is why it is so difficult to differentiate between an object and a class. People have spent a great deal of time trying to develop techniques to help novices deal with this situation. Unfortunately, probably experience is the best technique. Second, there are two forms of polymorphism: (1) the superclass has a default method, and (2) each subclass is required to provide its own method.

FIGURE 19-45 Team 1's Class
              Aggregation Diagram
              for Walled Bricks

For Team 1, the first cut is easy. Their model has only classes as objects. Thus, their classes are **Mouse, Obstacle, Paddle, Side, Ball, Brick, Score,** and **Wall.** The class aggregations are the same as the object aggregations: wall of bricks. All the links are made into associations, since no two are of the same type. **Obstacle** is assumed to be a superclass. Below is a summary of their refinement. The aggregation is shown in Figure 19-45, and the associations are shown in Figure 19-46.

In the second pass, Team 1 recognizes that length, width, and position are attributes for **Brick, Side,** and **Paddle.** In addition, they all have the common services inPath and getNorm. Thus, there is a chance for a superclass. In fact, Team 1 decided that the superclass is **Obstacle,** which they had discovered earlier. All attributes and, more importantly, all services are associated with its being an obstacle to **Ball.**

Now that they had the **Obstacle** class, a member noticed that both **Obstacle** and **Ball** had the same attributes of length, width, and position. These attributes define a rectangle in space. Even though it appeared to be an implementation class, Team 1 added Rectangle to the inheritance tree. The second pass did not cause any change in the aggregation and association diagrams.[8] The results for generalization/specialization of adding rectangle are shown in Table 19-5. The

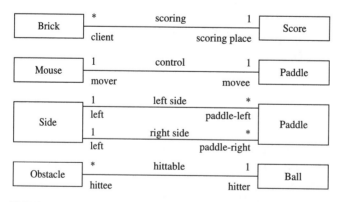

FIGURE 19-46 Team 1's Class Association Diagram

---

[8]   In practice, however, finding new classes may cause these relationships to change in order to capture more accurately the concepts of the problem domain.

IS-A test is shown in Table 19-5. The inheritance diagram in Figure 19-47 shows the results of this iteration. The class descriptions are left as an exercise for the reader.

TABLE 19-5 Second Revised is_a Analysis Table

Is A a B?	R	O	Ba	Br	P	S	W
Rectangle	X	s	s	s	s	s	n
Obstacle	a	X	n	s	s	s	n
Ball	a	n	X	n	n	n	n
Brick	a	a	n	X	n	n	n
Paddle	a	a	n	n	X	n	n
Side	a	a	n	n	n	X	n
Wall	n	n	n	n	n	n	X

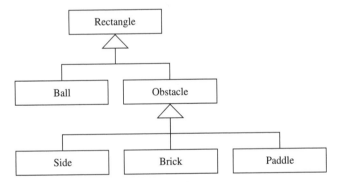

FIGURE 19-47 Inheritance Diagram for Classes Derived from Rectangle

CHAPTER

20

Case Study:
Team 2

Team 2 uses a slightly different strategy than Team 1.

Step 1: Finding The Objects

TEAM 2 ENHANCED THE APPROACH of Team 1 by using categories (as suggested by the leading authors in object-oriented technology) as an aid and their knowledge of the game to identify objects. Their results are shown in Table 20-1.

Team 2 decided to do two things. First, they wisely added the highest score and the list of highest scorers to the requirements. "Real developers" know they are never given all the requirements. Second, Team 2 added a keyboard and a monitor.[1] However, no hardware objects should be included at this time, because they are design objects. Remember that the idea now is to capture the game model of the domain experts.

TABLE 20-1 Team 2's List of Potential Objects

LIST OF POTENTIAL OBJECTS	
BreakoutGame	InteractiveVideoGame
Goal	Score
Points	RemovingBrick
Brick	Wall
Ball	BrickDisappearing
PointsAdded	Player
Paddle	Ball_passes_behind_Paddle
BallxIsLost	Game_over
Ball1	Ball2
Ball3	PlayingField
Side1	Side2
Side3	Brick1,..., n
Paddle	PaddleMove
"BallxMoving"	RegularBrick
SpeedBrick	BallHit_Regular_Brick
BallHitSpeedBrick	BallHit_Paddle
BallHitSide	BallBounce
LastBrick	NewWall
LastBall	GameEnd
Keyboard/joystick	Monitor
HighestScore	ListOfHighestScorers

---

[1] Another team may even want to know the raster size, scan rate, and so on of the monitor.

With the model, we should be able to play the game mentally without any hardware. So we will remove the design objects from Team 2's list. Note that it is common to have both the domain objects and the design objects intertwined in a requirement document. The ability to separate these objects into their proper domain is critical to a quality object-oriented model. Thus, domain expertise is a critical factor in building a high-quality business model.

Step 2: Identifying Responsibilities

REMEMBER THAT THE GOAL OF step 2 is to find *business* attributes and services that will be useful in solving your business problem. This step is the beginning of our abstraction process as we start to identify the relevant attributes and services, thus narrowing our problem/application space.

Looking at Adjectives

The suggested process is to look first at the adjectives in the requirements document. Team 2 follows the same line of thought followed by Team 1. The four potential adjectives/nouns that may be useful are regular brick, speed brick, last ball, and last brick. Here is where the advice of just using adjectives is a little tricky.

Asking Question 1

Now let us ask Question 1, "How is this object described in general?" Team 2's activities in this step were similar to those of Team 1. Their results are shown in Figures 20-1 through 20-33.

OBJECT NAME	BreakoutGame
ATTRIBUTES	
highest score, listOfHighestScorers	

FIGURE 20-1 CRC Card for BreakoutGame

OBJECT NAME	Points
ATTRIBUTES	
none	

FIGURE 20-2 CRC Card for Points

OBJECT NAME	Brick
ATTRIBUTES	
length, width, depth, color, position, density, weight	

FIGURE 20-3 CRC Card for Brick

OBJECT NAME	Wall
ATTRIBUTES	
length, width, depth, color, position, weight	

FIGURE 20-4 CRC Card for Wall

OBJECT NAME	Ball
ATTRIBUTES	
diameter, color, position, weight	

FIGURE 20-5 CRC Card for Ball

OBJECT NAME	Player
ATTRIBUTES	
name, height, weight, skillLevel, etc.	

FIGURE 20-6 CRC Card for Player

OBJECT NAME	PlayingField
ATTRIBUTES	
length, width	

FIGURE 20-7 CRC Card for Playing Field

OBJECT NAME	Paddle
ATTRIBUTES	
length, width, ~~handleSize~~, ~~weight~~, ~~hittingSurfaceMaterial~~, ~~etc.~~, <u>depth</u>.	

FIGURE 20-8 CRC Card for Paddle

OBJECT NAME	Score
ATTRIBUTES	
pointsAccumulated	

FIGURE 20-9 CRC Card for Score

OBJECT NAME	Side
ATTRIBUTES	
length, width/depth(?), position	

FIGURE 20-10 CRC Card for Slide

OBJECT NAME	InteractiveVideoGame
ATTRIBUTES	
none	

FIGURE 20-11 CRC Card for Interactive Video Game

OBJECT NAME	Goal
ATTRIBUTES	
none	

FIGURE 20-12 CRC Card for Goal

OBJECT NAME	RemovingBrick
ATTRIBUTES	
none	

FIGURE 20-13 CRC Card for RemovingBrick

OBJECT NAME	BrickDisappearing
ATTRIBUTES	
none	

FIGURE 20-14 CRC Card for Brick Disappearing

OBJECT NAME	PointsAdded
ATTRIBUTES	
none	

FIGURE 20-15 CRC Card for Points Added

OBJECT NAME	Game_over
ATTRIBUTES	
none	

FIGURE 20-16 CRC Card for Game_Over

OBJECT NAMES	ball1, ball2, ball3
ATTRIBUTES	
same as Ball plus ballNumber	

FIGURE 20-17 CRC Card for Ball1, Ball2, and Ball3

OBJECT NAMES	brick1, brick2, ..., brickn
ATTRIBUTES	
same as Brick	

FIGURE 20-18 CRC Card for Brick1, Brick2, through Brickn

OBJECT NAMES	side1, side2, side3
ATTRIBUTES	
same as Side	

FIGURE 20-19 CRC Card for Side1, Side2, and Side3

OBJECT NAME	Ball_x_is_lost
ATTRIBUTES	
none	

FIGURE 20-20 CRC Card for Ball_x_Is_Lost

OBJECT NAME	Ball_x_moving or Ball_move
ATTRIBUTES	
none	

FIGURE 20-21 CRC Card for Ball_x_Moving

OBJECT NAME	RegularBrick
ATTRIBUTES	
same as Brick plus pointValue	

FIGURE 20-22 CRC Card for RegularBrick

OBJECT NAME	SpeedBrick
ATTRIBUTES	
same as regular brick plus speedFactor	

FIGURE 20-23 CRC Card for SpeedBrick

OBJECT NAME	Ball_passes_behind_Paddle
ATTRIBUTES	
none	

FIGURE 20-24 CRC Card for Ball_Passes_Behind_Paddle

OBJECT NAME	New Wall
ATTRIBUTES	
newPattern, etc.	

FIGURE 20-25 CRC Card for NewWall

OBJECT NAME	Ball_hit_x
ATTRIBUTES	
none	

FIGURE 20-26 CRC Card for Ball_Hit_x

OBJECT NAME	LastBall
ATTRIBUTES	
when there is no other ball	

FIGURE 20-27 CRC Card for LastBall

OBJECT NAME	GameEnd
ATTRIBUTES	
when all balls are lost	

FIGURE 20-28 CRC Card for GameEnd

OBJECT NAME	List_of_highest_scorers
ATTRIBUTES	
array of names and the person's score	

FIGURE 20-29 CRC Card for List_of_Highest_Scorers

OBJECT NAME	LastBrick
ATTRIBUTES	
when brickCount is 1	

FIGURE 20-30 CRC Card for LastBrick

OBJECT NAME	PaddleMove
ATTRIBUTES	
none	

FIGURE 20-31 CRC Card for PaddleMove

OBJECT NAME	HighestScore
ATTRIBUTES	
pointValue	

FIGURE 20-32 CRC Card for HighestScore

OBJECT NAME	BallBounce
ATTRIBUTES	
none	

FIGURE 20-33 CRC Card for BallBounce

Asking Question 2

The most difficult question that we need to answer is, "What is our problem domain?" This will have an impact on the reusability of the classes (templates for instantiating an object) that are designed. Asking question 2 is really the process of abstraction—we let the object keep only the attributes applicable to the problem domain. The relevance of attributes is determined by the scope of the problem domain. Let us define the problem domain as the world of interactive video games.

Team 2 revisited their objects and attributes within this bounded domain. Their results are shown in Figures 20-34 through 20-45. A deleted attribute is shown with a strikeout, and a new attribute is shown with an underline.

OBJECT NAME	BreakoutGame
ATTRIBUTES	
highest_Score, list_Of_Highest_Scorers	

FIGURE 20-34 CRC Card for BreakoutGame

OBJECT NAME	Brick
ATTRIBUTES	
both teams: length, width, depth, color, position, ~~density~~, ~~weight~~	

FIGURE 20-35 CRC Card for Brick

OBJECT NAME	Wall
ATTRIBUTES	
length, width, depth, ~~color~~, position, ~~weight~~	

FIGURE 20-36 CRC Card for Wall

OBJECT NAME	Ball
ATTRIBUTES	
diameter, color, position, ~~weight~~	

FIGURE 20-37 CRC Card for Ball

OBJECT NAME	Player
ATTRIBUTES	
name, ~~height~~, ~~weight~~, skillLevel, ~~etc.~~	

FIGURE 20-38 CRC Card for Player

OBJECT NAME	PlayingField
ATTRIBUTES	
length, width, <u>depth</u>	

FIGURE 20-39 CRC Card for Playing Field

OBJECT NAME	Side
ATTRIBUTES	
length, ~~width/depth(?)~~, position, <u>width, depth</u>	

FIGURE 20-40 CRC Card for Side

OBJECT NAME	"Ball x is Lost"
ATTRIBUTES	
none	

FIGURE 20-41 CRC Card for Ball x is Lost

OBJECT NAMES	Side1, Side2, Side3, <u>Side4</u>
ATTRIBUTES	
same as Side	

FIGURE 20-42 CRC Card for Side1, Side2, Side3, and Side4

OBJECT NAMES	Brick1, Brick2, ..., Brickn
ATTRIBUTES	
same as Brick plus <u>pointValue</u> and sometimes <u>speedFactor</u>	

FIGURE 20-43 CRC Card for Brick1, Brick2, through Brickn

OBJECT NAME	RegularBrick
ATTRIBUTES	
same as Brick plus pointValue	

FIGURE 20-44 CRC Card for RegularBrick

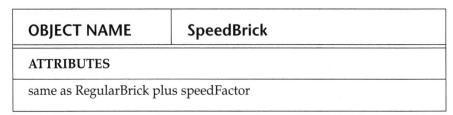

OBJECT NAME	**SpeedBrick**
ATTRIBUTES	
same as RegularBrick plus speedFactor	

FIGURE 20-45 CRC Card for SpeedBrick

In current interactive video games, the density and weight are not attributes that are captured in the abstraction. Depth can be debated, since we are starting to see three-dimensional interactive video games. Color is also an issue, since color screens on PCs are becoming commonplace. This is shown in Figure 20-35.

Since Wall is a collection of Bricks, it is reasonable to assume that the color will be defined for each brick and that the color of the wall is determined by the brick. In a sense, the color of the Wall is derivable. Again, the weight is not captured in the abstraction for this problem domain.

SkillLevel was left as an attribute, because the team wants to entice players at different levels to compete with each other, thus increasing revenue. Name was kept as a way to identify a player who makes the highest score list. This is shown in Figure 20-38.

As you can see in the requirements documentation, the paddle is abstracted into a rectangle. Thus, many of attributes of a "real paddle" are not applicable to this abstraction. Team 2 eliminated all attributes except for length and width, and added depth for consistency, as shown in Figure 20-8.

PlayingField is defined as the area within which the game is played. Team 2 has decided that the concept of a playing area is useful for determining when a ball is still in play.

Remember that the idea here is to capture the objects (concepts) that are meaningful to the domain experts. Does a domain expert in video games use the concept of a playing area that determines if the ball is in play? If it helps, isn't the playing area written into most rule books about games?

Depth is added to the list of attributes to handle three-dimensional video concepts. This is shown in Figure 20-39.

In order to be consistent with the three-dimensional concept and the fact that even a conceptual rectangular boundary must have some depth, we have added the attributes width and depth. Team 2's concept of a side also includes a nonvisible side so that the playing area will be bounded. This is sometimes called an open side of the playing field. This is shown in Figure 20-40 and Figure 20-42.

Figure 20-41 is a consequence of "Ball passes behind Paddle." The original thinking based on the written requirements is that this is due to the fact that the ball passes "behind the Paddle." Observing other video games, however, we realize that the requirements writer assumed that once the ball goes behind the paddle, there is no way for it to stay in the field of play. But the real requirement is that the "ball is lost" when it leaves the playing field.

Thus, knowing or capturing the playing field as a concept is fundamental to the video game. This kind of unintentional misstatement of requirements is very common in documents. One of the most difficult tasks of the analyst/system engineer is to capture the intent, not just the statements, of the user/customer.

From the game definition, we recognize that each of the bricks that will be part of the "wall of bricks" needs to have a point value so that the player can score points when the ball hits a brick. However, some bricks, specifically speed bricks, will also speed up the ball by some speed factor.

Team 2 recognized, however, that not all the bricks in the wall will be speed bricks. This leads to a very interesting discussion: whether the speed factor is an attribute of all the bricks in the wall.

One team member brings up the fact that for the regular brick, we just make the speed factor equal to 1. This would make all the bricks alike. However, another team member argues that this is not proper because one of the rules for determining an attribute is that the value is always needed and is used.

If you do not enforce the rule, everything is formed from an object type in which most of the attributes are not used. Team 2 will take the purist approach that some of the bricks have a speed factor and other bricks do not have a speed factor. Thus, the wall is composed of two different types of objects (speed bricks and regular bricks). This is shown in Figures 20-43 through 20-45.

Asking Question 3

Now that Team 2 has bounded attributes, they apply the Western school of thinking to object-oriented analysis. They look at the minimal specification of attributes necessary to satisfy this application. From the requirements document, it is clear that the writer/buyer is specifying a two-dimensional game.

Team 2 revisited the objects and attributes within this bounded domain. The results are shown in Figures 20-46 to 20-57.

In the application, the world is two-dimensional; thus, the depth of the brick is not applicable to the abstraction. This is also true for the wall and for all objects with depth as an attribute. The result of assuming a two-dimensional world is shown in Figure 20-46 and Figure 20-48.

In answering question 2, both teams added depth as an attribute. In answering question 3, however, they deleted the same attribute. Adding an attribute to the list and then deleting the attribute is a symptom of an unclear problem domain/application scope. There is usually much frustration when each individual has his or her own definition of the domain/application that is inconsistent with those of the rest of the team.

Based on the above analysis, a new list of potential objects has been constructed; see Table 20-2.

Team 2 eliminated Goal and Points because these objects did not have any attributes and were not used as independent objects. All the events (i.e., RemovingBricks, Ball_Hit_Paddle), were eliminated because Team 2 found no attributes. This is very common with events; in the attribute step, the analysis discovers no attribute.

OBJECT NAME	Brick
ATTRIBUTES	
length, width, ~~depth~~, ~~color~~, position, ~~density~~, ~~weight~~	

FIGURE 20-46 CRC Card for Brick

OBJECT NAME	BreakoutGame
ATTRIBUTES	
highest_Score, list_Of_Highest_Scorers	

FIGURE 20-47 CRC Card for Breakout Game

OBJECT NAME	Wall
ATTRIBUTES	
length, width, ~~depth~~, ~~color~~, position, ~~weight~~	

FIGURE 20-48 CRC Card for Wall

OBJECT NAME	Ball
ATTRIBUTES	
diameter, ~~color~~, position, ~~weight~~	

FIGURE 20-49 CRC Card for Ball

OBJECT NAME	Player
ATTRIBUTES	
name, ~~height~~, ~~weight~~, skillLevel, ~~etc.~~	

FIGURE 20-50 CRC Card for Player

OBJECT NAME	Paddle
ATTRIBUTES	
length, width, ~~handleSize~~, ~~weight~~, ~~hittingSurfaceMaterial~~, ~~etc.~~, <u>depth</u>.	

FIGURE 20-51 CRC Card for Paddle

OBJECT NAME	PlayingField
ATTRIBUTES	
length, width, <u>~~depth~~</u>	

FIGURE 20-52 CRC Card for PlayingField

OBJECT NAME	Side
ATTRIBUTES	
length, ~~width/depth(?)~~, position, <u>width, depth</u>	

FIGURE 20-53 CRC Card for Side

OBJECT NAMES	side1, side2, side3, <u>side4</u>
ATTRIBUTES	
same as Side	

FIGURE 20-54 CRC Card for Side1, Side2, Side3, and Side4

OBJECT NAMES	brick1, brick2, ..., brickn
ATTRIBUTES	
same as Brick plus <u>pointValue</u> and sometimes <u>speedFactor</u>	

FIGURE 20-55 CRC Card For Brick1, Brick2, through Brickn

OBJECT NAME	RegularBrick
ATTRIBUTES	
same as Brick plus pointValue	

FIGURE 20-56 CRC Card for RegularBrick

OBJECT NAME	SpeedBrick
ATTRIBUTES	
same as regular brick plus speedFactor	

FIGURE 20-57 CRC Card for SpeedBrick

TABLE 20-2 List of Potential Objects After Step 2

BreakoutGame	~~Interactive Video Game~~
~~Goal~~	~~Score~~
~~Points~~	~~Removing Brick~~
Brick	Wall
Ball	~~Brick Disappearing~~
~~Points Added~~	Player
Paddle	~~Ball passes behind Paddle~~
~~"BallxIsLost"~~	~~"Game over"~~
Ball1	Ball2
Ball3	PlayingField
Side1	Side2
Side3	Brick 1, ...,Brickn
Paddle	~~PaddleMove~~
~~BallxMoving~~	RegularBrick
SpeedBrick	~~BallHitRegularBrick~~
~~BallHitSpeedBrick~~	~~BallHitPaddle~~
~~BallHitSide~~	~~BallBounce~~
~~Last Brick~~	~~NewWall~~
~~Last Ball~~	~~GameEnd~~
~~Keyboard/joystick~~	~~Monitor~~
Highest_Score	List_Of_Highest_Scorers

Looking at Services

Team 2 applies the Abbott/Booch technique of looking at verbs in the requirements document. Then they analyze the method for providing those services. In rereading the requirements, they found the following verb phrases:

1. "Ball hits a brick." The grammatical object of that sentence is Brick. So Brick needs to provide a hit service.
2. "Points are added to the player's score." This implies that an add service needs to be added either to player, score, or both. The easy way is to add the service to both.
3. "Paddle can be moved horizontally." This implies a move service for Paddle.
4. "Ball bounces off." This implies a bounce service for Ball.
5. "Speed bricks speed up the ball." This implies a speed-increase service for Ball.
6. "Ball hits the paddle." This implies a hit service for Paddle.
7. "Ball hits the side." This implies a hit service for Side.
8. "Brick removed from the wall." This implies a removal service for Wall.

Figures 20-58 through 20-64 show the CRC cards created by the team after adding the services to the objects.We do not show CRC cards for objects in which no services were found using verbs.

OBJECT NAME	Brick
ATTRIBUTES	
length, width, depth, color, position, ~~density~~, ~~weight~~	
SERVICES	
beenHit	

FIGURE 20-58 CRC Card for Brick After Adding Services

OBJECT NAME	Ball
ATTRIBUTES	
diameter, ~~color~~, position, ~~weight~~, speed	
SERVICES	
bounce, speedIncrease	

FIGURE 20-59 CRC Card for Ball After Adding Services

OBJECT NAME	Player
ATTRIBUTES	
name, ~~height, weight~~, skillLevel, ~~etc.~~	
SERVICES	
addPoints	

FIGURE 20-60 CRC Card for Player After Adding Services

OBJECT NAME	Score
ATTRIBUTES	
pointsAccumulated	
SERVICES	
incrementScore	

FIGURE 20-61 CRC Card for Score After Adding Services

OBJECT NAME	Side
ATTRIBUTES	
length, ~~width/depth(?)~~, position, <u>width</u>, <u>depth</u>	
SERVICES	
beenHit	

FIGURE 20-62 CRC Card for Side After Adding Services

OBJECT NAME	Wall
ATTRIBUTES	
length, width, ~~depth~~, ~~color~~, position, ~~weight~~	
SERVICES	
brickRemoved	

FIGURE 20-63 CRC Card for Wall After Adding Services

OBJECT NAME	Paddle
ATTRIBUTES	
length, width, ~~handle size~~, ~~weight~~, ~~hittingSurfaceMaterial~~, etc., <u>~~depth~~</u>.	
SERVICES	
beenHit	

FIGURE 20-64 CRC Card for Paddle After Adding Services

Step 3: Specifying Behaviors

THE TEAM WAS NOW READY to analyze the scenarios to identify and specify additional services that each of the objects must provide to make this game work. The results of their work are shown in Figures 20-65 through 20-75.

The paddle scenarios were identified as follows:

1. Paddle may be moved because there is no obstruction.
2. Paddle movement requested puts the paddle outside of the playing field.
3. Paddle strikes the ball in moving.

The ball scenarios were identified as follows:

1. Ball may be moved because there is no obstruction.
2. Ball movement requested will take a ball into a side.
3. Ball hits the paddle.
4. Ball hits a brick.
5. Ball hits a brick and a side.
6. Ball hits two bricks.
7. Ball hits three obstacles (not very likely, but theoretically possible).

For the first scenario, Team 2 came to the same conclusion as Team 1. However, for the second scenario, it decided to add range limits (maximum x value and minimum x value) as attributes of Paddle. For scenario 3, the team first considered having Paddle invoke a service of Ball to change direction, but decided that the move algorithm handled this situation. Team 2's adjustments to the paddle object and the addition of the mouse object are given in Figure 20-65 and Figure 20-66.

Team 2 decided that speed bricks and regular bricks did not behave the same, so they specified the method for each object. Brick and brick1, brick2, and so on are all now either speed bricks or regular bricks. Finally, Team 2 decided that scoring was to be done by informing the player that the score needed to be incremented. In fact, many other teams have decided that score or points accumulated is not an object, but just an attribute of the player. The objects for Team 2 appear in the following figures.

Team 2 has not done a complete analysis. In cases when a ball gets out of play, the creation of a new wall has not been addressed. This is a common practice, since practitioners really perform the first few steps in an interactive manner. So, as for earlier steps, we will not be very concerned about completeness at this time. However, notice that each object assumes that it can access any object it wants. This is not correct. In the next section, the team will address the various ways for objects to access the services of other objects.

OBJECT NAME	Paddle
ATTRIBUTES	
length, width, <u>position, min-x, max-x</u>	
SERVICES	
prototype: move()	
{ // structured English definition	
get DELTA from mouse object	
via getDelta service of mouse.	
// we assume that we can get to the mouse somehow.	
get DELTA-x from DELTA.	
// before the paddle can move, it must determine if it is being asked to move outside of its range.	
//check both left and right limits.	
if POSITION-x + DELTA-x is less than MIN-x,	
then:	
set POSITION-x to MIN-x.	
else:	
if POSITION-x + DELTA-x is greater than MAX-x,	
then:	
set POSITION-x to MAX-x.	
else:	
set POSITION-x to POSITION-x + DELTA-x.	
endif:	
endif:	
// this has conceptually moved the paddle.	
// when you get here, x value of POSITION has been changed.	
// we need to redisplay the object at its new position,	
// but this is actually an implementation issue.	
display self at new position (details left to design).	
}	

FIGURE 20-65 CRC Card for Paddle with Services Defined

OBJECT NAME	Mouse
ATTRIBUTES	
previous location	
SERVICES	
prototype: getDelta() // same as team 1	

FIGURE 20-66 CRC Card for Mouse with Services Defined

OBJECT NAME	Score
ATTRIBUTES	
pointsAccumulated	
SERVICES	
prototype: incrementScore(points)	
{	
add POINTS to POINTS_ACCUMULATED.	
}	

FIGURE 20-67 CRC Card for Score with Services Defined

OBJECT NAME	RegularBrick
ATTRIBUTES	
position, length, width, pointValue	
SERVICES	
prototype: inPath(hull) //same as Side	
prototype: getNorm() //same as Side	
prototype: beenHit()	
{ // this is now simple	
ask Player to increment its value by pointValue	

via add_points service of Player.
tell Wall that this brick has been removed
via brick_removed service
disappear.
}

FIGURE 20-68 CRC Card for RegularBrick with Services Defined

OBJECT NAME	**SpeedBrick**
ATTRIBUTES	
position, length, width, <u>pointValue, speedFactor</u>	
SERVICES	
prototype: inPath(hull)　　//same as Side	
prototype: getNorm()　　　//same as Side	
prototype: beenHit()	
{　// this is now simple	
ask Player to increment its value by pointValue	
via add_points service of Player.	
ask Ball to increase speed by SPEEDFACTOR	
via speed_increase service.	
tell Wall that this brick has been removed	
via brick_removed service	
disappear.	
}	

FIGURE 20-69 CRC Card for SpeedBrick with Services Defined

OBJECT NAMES	Ball, Ball1, Ball2, Ball3
ATTRIBUTES	
position, width/length, velocity	
SERVICES	
prototype: move(elapsed_time)	
{ // this is based on ball hitting only one obstacle.	
compute DELTA as	
VELOCITY*ELAPSED_TIME.	
compute hull as	
if DELTA-y is positive,	
then:	
set hull's start POSITION to ball's POSITION.	
else:	
set hull's start POSITION to ball's POSITION + WIDTH.	
endif.	
set hull's end POSITION to hull's start POSITION + DELTA.	
ask collision to move me	
via the moveBall service.	
return	
}	
prototype: changeDirection (new_direction)	
{	
set DIRECTION to NEW_DIRECTION.	
}	
prototype: changePosition (new_position)	
{	
set POSITION to NEW_POSITION.	
}	

prototype: speedIncrease(speedFactor)
{
set VELOCITY to VELOCITY*SPEEDFACTOR.
}

FIGURE 20-70 CRC Card for Ball with Services Defined

OBJECT NAME	**Collision**
ATTRIBUTES	
????	
SERVICES	
prototype: moveBall(hull)	
{ // this handles simultaneous hits.	
For each obstacle that can be in the way:	
// ask each obstacle whether it is in the way.	
if obstacle->inPath(hull),	
then:	
hit_object is obstacle.	
endif:	
endFor:	
If hit_object(s) is not found,	
then: // it can move unobstructed.	
ask ball to set its POSITION to POSITION + VELOCITY*ELAPSED_TIME via setPosition service.	
else: // it has hit an obstacle(s).	
compute NEW_DIRECTION as net effect of all the angles of reflection. (Details are left to design.)	
ask ball to set its DIRECTION to NEW_DIRECTION via setDirection service.	

For each obstacle that is hit:
ask the object to respond via its been_hit service.
endfor:
endif:
return
}

FIGURE 20-71 CRC Card for Collision with Services Defined

OBJECT NAMES	Side, side1, side2, side3
ATTRIBUTES	
length, width, position	
SERVICES	
prototype: getUL() // same as Team 1	
prototype: getLR() // same as Team 1	
prototype: inPath(hull) // same as Team 1	
prototype: been_hit()	
{ // this service was found earlier;	
// does nothing	
}	

FIGURE 20-72 CRC Card for Side with Services Defined

OBJECT NAME	Player
ATTRIBUTES	
name, skillLevel	
SERVICES	
prototype: addPoints(points)	
{	
ask score to add POINTS via increment_score service.	
}	

FIGURE 20-73 CRC Card for Player with Services Defined

OBJECT NAME	Wall
ATTRIBUTES	
length, width, position, <u>brickCount</u>	
SERVICES	
prototype: brickRemoved()	
{ // Assume that brick count keeps track of the number of bricks	
subtract 1 from brickCount	
}	

FIGURE 20-74 CRC Card for Wall with Services Defined

OBJECT NAME	BreakoutGame
ATTRIBUTES	
ball_array[3], active_ball, lost_flag	
SERVICES	
prototype: start() // this is called at beginning of game	
{ // structured English definition	

set ball_array[1] to ball1.
set ball_array[2] to ball2.
set ball_array[3] to ball3.
set active_ball to 1.
set lost_flag to false.
}
prototype: awake() // this is called by system every 66.7 milliseconds
{ // structured English definition
ask paddle to update its position
via move service of paddle.
ask ball_array[active_ball] to update position, direction, and speed
via move service of ball.
If lost_flag is true,
then:
reset lost_flag to false.
// take active ball out of play
set active_ball to active_ball + 1.
if active_ball > 3,
then: //all three balls are played
end game.
else:
// initialize new ball to starting position.
endif:
endif:
}
prototype: ball_lost()   // this is called by side4
{ // structured English definition
set lost_flag to true.
}

FIGURE 20-75 CRC Card for BreakoutGame

Step 4: Specifying Relationships

TEAM 2 REREAD THE REQUIREMENTS document and used their specification of services to help define aggregations and links for them. Team 2 started by using the *is_a* test to find generalizations/specializations. The results are shown in Table 20-3.

TABLE 20-3 Use of is_a Table

Is A a B?	Ba	ba	S	s	PF	Br	RB	SB	b1	b2
Ball	X	s	n	n	n	n	n	n	n	n
ball?	a	X	n	n	n	n	n	n	n	n
Side	n	n	X	s	n	n	n	n	n	n
side?	n	n	a	X	n	n	n	n	n	n
Playing Field	n	n	n	n	X	n	n	n	n	n
Brick	n	n	n	n	n	X	s	s	s	s
Regular Brick	n	n	n	n	n	a	X	n	s	n
Speed Brick	n	n	n	n	n	a	n	X	n	s
brick1	n	n	n	n	n	a	a	n	X	n
brick2	n	n	n	n	n	a	n	a	n	X

The generalization/specialization found is shown graphically in Figure 20-76. Objects that are underlined are really instances. They will be removed from the model in the refinement step.

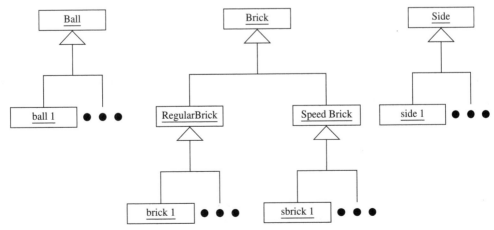

FIGURE 20-76 Team 2's Object Generalization/Specialization Diagram for BreakoutGame

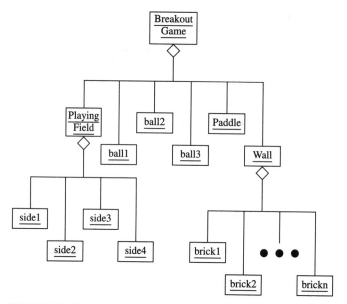

FIGURE 20-77 Team 2's Object Aggregation Diagram for BreakoutGame

For Team 2, the following potential aggregations and links were identified by rereading the requirements document. Their results are shown in Figure 20-77 and Figure 20-78 with the following:

1. Aggregations:

    Wall of bricks
    Playing field consisting of 4 sides

2. Links:

    Brick and score
    Player and paddle

The following potential aggregations and links were identified by reviewing the methods:

1. Aggregations:

    Breakout with everything

2. Links:

    Mouse and paddle
    Ball and collision
    Collision and obstacle

Hit_object and obstacle

Brick and score

Brick and wall

Player and regular brick

Wall and regular brick

Player and speed brick

Ball and speed brick

Wall and speed brick

Player and score

Team 2's discussion went as follows. For the wall and brick aggregation, Team 2 came to the same conclusion as Team 1. However, they added that there are two types of bricks, and they debated whether the wall cared about the type of brick each one was. Team 2 concluded that if the wall is to create itself, then it would need to know the type of brick to be placed in each slot. However, after the bricks have been placed, the wall only needs to remember the number of remaining bricks. Therefore, other than when it is created, the wall does not need to know the type of any given brick. In fact, another member of the team noticed that a wall is an aggregate of brick1, ...,brickn, where brick1 is a tangible tangle object, while Brick and SpeedBrick, though objects, are conceptual. This is a correct analysis of the game.

The playing field is considered the region where the ball is in play. Team 2 has observed that it is bounded or defined by the three sides as well as by a fourth side, which is invisible. In fact, one of the team members pointed out that the requirement for "ball lost" is not stated properly. The ball really disappears when it goes out of the playing area. This is a correct analysis of the problem. Again, a common problem with requirements documents is that they do not say exactly what they mean.

If you think about a paddle as being able to move in any direction, this is a better analysis than the original idea of a ball being lost when it goes behind the paddle. Team 2 came up with the idea that the ball is lost when it hits this fourth, invisible, side, since this fourth side does not behave the same way as the other three sides to the service request been_hit. The original three sides do nothing, while this fourth side will take the present ball out of play.

The brick-to-score link is a false link, because scoring is done via brick-to-player-to-score in Team 2's model. The player-to-paddle link is also a false link (see Team 1's analysis).

Even though many object-oriented authors will argue against it, the aggregation of the Breakout Game as an assembly of parts is very useful. Team 2 chose to use this concept. The game is an aggregate of a wall of bricks, a player, a score, a paddle, a playing field of four sides, and three balls.

The mouse-to-paddle link is necessary (see Team 1's analysis). The ball-to-collision link and the collision-to-obstacles link are more complex, as they capture a richer semantic. Here, the ball is using the collision object to determine its new direction and its final position when it needs to move. It really does not care what obstacles are in the way or what the obstacles do when they are hit. However, for the collision to determine the new direction and final position of the ball, it needs to know about all the obstacles. Moreover, the collision is being used to encapsulate a sequence of function calls that are related to the fact that a collision occurred.

One of the team members, James, suggested that both links should be in the model. This seems very strange to the other team members, since they were concerned about reusability. If Ball has a link to Collision and you want to reuse Ball, you need to also use Collision. Since Collision has links to all the obstacles, you also have to include a list of all the obstacles.

Now we see why a lot of object-oriented authors argue that all relationships (aggregation, link, association, and inheritance) violate the encapsulation principle and should not be allowed. As we have seen with abstraction, any simplification means that some information is ignored.

In order to build the sophisticated systems of tomorrow, developers need a richer set of mechanisms/constructs than the primitive constructs of today's programming languages. With the latter, we are forced to make simplifications that eventually come back to haunt us. We will return to this issue in design.

There are ways in C++ to implement these links without losing the data semantics and still retain reasonable flexibility, maintainability, and decent performance. However, Team 2 felt very uncomfortable with these links, so it decided that the ball should only create the Collision object for the life of the move method of ball. Certainly, this is the only time it is used.

However, with that decision Team 2 created a problem with the obstacle-to-collision link. If the Collision object is dynamic and destroyed at the end of Ball's move method, every time a Collision object is created it must be told what ball and what obstacles are involved in this iteration. Thus, the ball now also needs to know all the obstacles. This, however, does not seem to be information that Ball should be keeping.

So who should keep the list of obstacles that are hittable by the ball? After lengthy discussion, Team 2 concluded that the object that should know what is hittable is the BreakoutGame object. This seems to make sense because Breakout-Game contains all the objects of the game. So Ball_move would require a list of hittable obstacles as an argument.

The reader should note that the two suggestions are not equal. In James's model, the collision was required to have knowledge of obstacles. This is consistent with the actual specification of the methods, because Ball does not directly use any services of the obstacles.

In Team 2's model Ball is passed the list of obstacles as an argument. This implies that ball requires knowledge of the obstacles to perform the move service. Team 2's model gives the flexibility for Ball to change or modify the list of obstacles that Collision uses. This can be both good and bad. In James's model, Ball cannot change or modify the list of obstacles. Again, this can be good or bad.

The key issue Team 2 should have considered in determining whether the consensus model or James's model is better is whether a list of obstacles resides outside or within the control of ball's move method. From the game's description, a strong case can be made that the obstacles are not within the control of Ball_move, and James's model may capture the data semantics better than consensus model.

Unfortunately, such team results are common in object oriented-analysis and design. Any analysis and design based on consensus will have to cater to the lowest common denominator. In our opinion, many applications and systems built using object-oriented technology will not reach their fullest potential. It is not because it cannot be done for technical reasons; it just cannot be done with the people involved. Most developers who have been doing leading-edge development most of their lives will tell you that the most difficult issues were not those of the technology, but the resistance to and lack of in-depth knowledge of the new technology by both fellow workers and management.

The link between hit_object and obstacle was eliminated because one of the team members suggested that the hit_objects are a subset of all the obstacles. Moreover, this subset does not exist for more than the life of the method. The method itself has the criteria for forming the subset (list) of obstacles that are hit_objects and that subset is not used by any other object.

The four links (player-to-regular brick, wall-to-regular brick, player-to-speed brick, and wall-to-speed brick) are needed to score points or to decrement the brick_count.

The ball-to-speed brick link appears to be needed to speed up the ball. However, there are some data semantics at issue here. This link is attempting to capture the speeding up of the ball that is actually in play. Capturing this by using a link requires that every time a new ball is put into play, all the links would have to change to the new ball. This suggests that a link may not be a very good way of capturing this situation.

Team 2, remembering that there is a second way of getting a handle to another object, decides that the calling object should pass the handle to Ball as an argument. This now means that the caller determines when the ball gets speeded up. This frees the speed brick from having a link to any ball. Thus, speed brick-to-ball is a false link.

The player-to-score link was kept for scoring. One of the members brought up the idea of making points_accumulated an attribute of Player and getting rid of Score, so that the link does not have to be maintained. Team 2 rejected the idea. The link and aggregation diagrams for Team 2 follow. The aggregation diagram does not include obstacles because Team 2 did not know what to do with them. These issues will be revisited in the next step.

In this step, Team 2 also made discoveries that caused them to modify the list of objects they created and the behaviors they specified in earlier steps. This is common in practice in most methodologies. Team 2 made the changes shown in the following figures. This will work if there is only one paddle and one ball. However, as we know, this is not true. There are three balls; for the above service to work, BreakoutGame must know which ball is in play. Since balls are part of the game, it is not unreasonable for the game to keep track of which ball is in play.

Team 2 recognized that there were a couple of problems with side4 taking the ball out of play. First, it is not natural for a side to have a relationship (link, aggregation, or inheritance) with the active ball or all the balls. Second, a side really should not have the responsibility of taking the ball out of play, nor should it be the object that causes a new ball to be put into play.

If these are not responsibilities of side4, what object should have these responsibilities? After a lengthy discussion, Team 2 concluded that taking the current ball out of play and determining the next ball to be in play, if any, is the responsibility of BreakoutGame. However, Team 2 recognized that the event of the ball hitting side4 is the trigger for the above actions.

There are two ways to connect an event with its resulting actions. In situations where the actions can be completed immediately, the event can cause the actions to occur as part of its method. For example, in our case the been_hit method could either ask the active ball to become inactive or deleted, or ask the game to put the next ball in play. If we did this, however, the active ball would immediately disappear. This would cause a technical problem. If you remember, this method is being called as part of the ball move for the active ball (i.e., Ball_move called collision's moveBall that called side4's been_hit service). So if we remove the ball now, Collision's moveBall return path would be broken.

This means that we cannot perform all the actions associated with the response to the event immediately. Thus, we must use the second way of connecting events to actions. The second way is for the event recognizor (side4's been_hit service) to signal the object with the responsibilities that the event has occurred. Then it is the notified object's responsibility to ensure that the actions are taken at the appropriate time. This technique was used by Team 2. We have avoided the discussion of creating the new wall; this is discussed in the next chapter.

OBJECT NAME	BreakoutGame
ATTRIBUTES	
To be defined	
SERVICES	
prototype: awake() // this is called by the system every 66.7 milliseconds	
{ // structured English definition	
ask paddle to update its position	
via move service of paddle.	
ask ball to update its position, direction, and speed	
via move service of ball.	
}	

FIGURE 20-78 CRC Card for BreakoutGame

OBJECT NAMES	side4
ATTRIBUTES	
length, width, position, not visible	
SERVICES	
prototype: getUL() // same as Side	
prototype: getLR() // same as Side	
prototype: inPath(hull) //same as Side	
prototype: beenHit()	
{ // this service should take the ball out of play;	
//however, you have to be careful when you delete an object	
}	

FIGURE 20-79 CRC Card for Side4

OBJECT NAMES	side4 (revised)
ATTRIBUTES	
length, width, position, not visible	
SERVICES	
prototype: getUL() // same as Side	
prototype: getLR() // same as Side	
prototype: inPath(hull) //same as Side	
prototype: beenHit()	
{ // this service requires that we add // a link between breakout game and side4	
tell breakout that ball is now lost	
via ball_lost service.	
}	

FIGURE 20-80 CRC Card for Side4 (revised)

Step 5: Refinement

TEAM 2 IDENTIFIED THE FOLLOWING classes after the first pass:

- BreakoutGame
- PlayingField
- Paddle
- Ball
- VisibleSide
- InvisibleSide
- Wall
- SpeedBrick
- RegularBrick
- Player
- Score
- Mouse

The class aggregations are as follows:

- Breakout Game with every Class
- Wall of Speed and Regular Bricks
- Playing Field of Visible and Invisible Sides

In this step, all the object generalizations are converted to class generalizations, and instances of a class are dropped. The results are shown in Figures 20-81 to 20-83. Instances are created via the constructors and are not part of the generalization structure. All the links are directly converted to associations. The generalization, aggregation, and association diagrams after the first pass are shown in Figures 20-84 through 20-86.

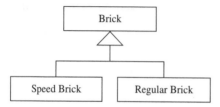

**FIGURE 20-81 Team 2's Class Generalization
Diagram for Classes
Derived from Brick**

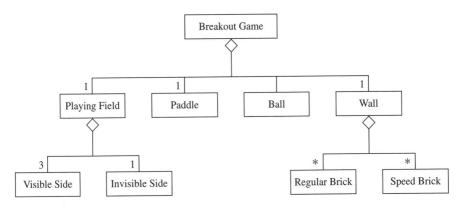

FIGURE 20-82 Class Aggregation Diagram for BreakoutGame

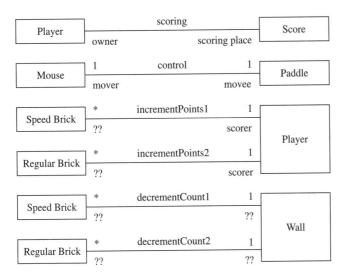

FIGURE 20-83 Team 2's Object Link Diagram for BreakoutGame

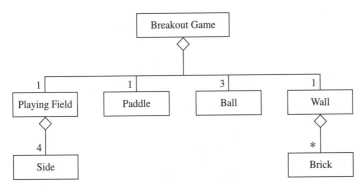

FIGURE 20-84 Revised Class Aggregation Diagram for BreakoutGame

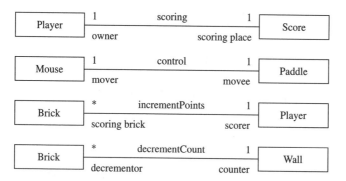

FIGURE 20-85 Revised Class Association Diagram

FIGURE 20-86 Revised Class Inheritance Diagram

In the second pass, Team 2 noticed that it could eliminate the funny relationship of Player and Wall to both SpeedBrick and RegularBrick by using the superclass Brick to capture the relationship.

There was also a long discussion on whether the wall is a collection of bricks. This is confusing. Before being formed, the wall needs to know about the two types of bricks. When formed, however, the wall considers all of them bricks.[2] The new diagrams after the second pass are shown in Figures 20-87 through 20-89.

The team continues to iterate. The discussion during each iteration and the changes to the model are described below. The complete class specifications are shown in Figures 20-90 through 20-108.

Team 2 made a major addition to BreakoutGame's methods. In its "start" method, it now creates and maintains the list of obstacles that are hittable. This list is needed by BreakoutGame to use as one of the arguments to the move service of Ball.

Collision is not shown in any of the diagrams since it is a dynamic object/class. It is never kept over a time slice. The diagram shows relatively static relationships between relatively static classes. Side is where the Playing Field-to-Side

---

2   Wall does not use the fact that there are two types of bricks that make up the wall. Technically, the model should only reflect the steady state or static state of the model; as such, the better model is to make Wall a collection of bricks. Changing relationships as new superclasses are discovered is very common.

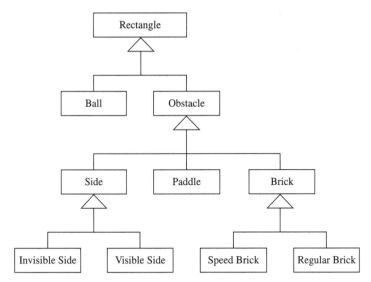

FIGURE 20-87 Final Class Generalization Diagram

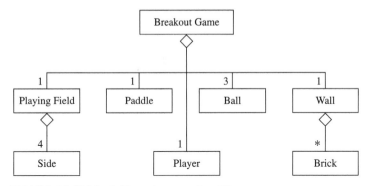

FIGURE 20-88 Final Class Aggregation Diagram

aggregation is established, so even though it has no additional attributes or methods, this class should be kept, at least in analysis. It should be quite clear that Side is a useful concept in the application domain; that alone should be adequate reason to keep this class during analysis.

A case could be made to move the method for the been_hit service of RegularBrick to this superclass. Team 2 felt that the method should stay with the class.

Now the team was ready for the two other aggregate classes, Playing Field and Wall. It is usually very difficult to determine aggregate type, because many aggregates have all characteristics of the various types. However, when this aggregate is used in a specific application domain, it should always clarify the aggregate type.

Team 2 addressed this issue as follows. First, one member suggested that PlayingField is defined when all four sides are defined. It has no attributes and

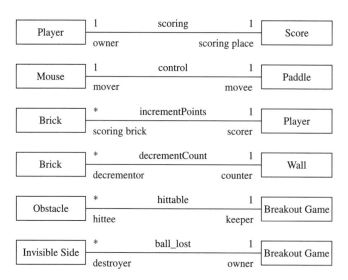

FIGURE 20-89 Final Class Association Diagram

provides no services directly, so this concept is not needed. This certainly is what the person had read in object-oriented books. It also would make the model have fewer classes and objects; thus, it must be good. This would be right, if the goal of object-oriented analysis/design were to make things as simple as possible.[3]

A second member of the team argued that PlayingField is a basic concept of the game. It led the team to come up with the fourth side. Another team member argued that it organizes the game. If you do not have PlayingField, the four sides would all be part of BreakoutGame, and the concept that the sides form a boundary would be lost.

Now we have a very concrete example of how difficult it is to determine whether a concept is used or not used in an application domain. In any event, Team 2 decided that PlayingField was a useful concept.

The wall seems easier, since all the team members considered it an assembly-parts type. In fact, the brickCount attribute is tied to its being made from bricks. Even though they recognized that the wall could be thought of as a rectangular region with position, length, and width, this fact was not being used. Therefore, the attributes were dropped by the team. Then, the team added the final three classes—Player, Score, and Mouse—for completeness. Now, the team still had one more issue to resolve—creating a new wall. This can be done very simply. When

---

[3]   However, we think that is the wrong goal. It is our opinion that many of our problems come from trying to solve complex problems with constructs that are too simple to capture all the rich data semantics, procedural semantics, structural semantics, and declarative semantics of the application domain. We do not believe that developers intentionally write spaghetti code and forget to capture important information; instead, for years developers/programmers have been trying to build skyscrapers with a hammer and saw (simple to use), instead of the sophisticated tools that professional builders use. It is no wonder why so many software projects are failures.

brickCount, which Wall decrements, is zero, it is time to create a new wall. Thus, they could just add a few lines to the method brick_removed for Wall.

However, careful analysis by Team 2 revealed two flaws. First, as for Ball_lost, there is a technical problem with creating a new wall within the method brick_removed; the last brick has not been removed. Second, even without the technical problem, there is a business problem. The chances are that when the last brick is hit, the ball will be within the area that will be used for the new set of bricks. If the application just places the wall back onto the playing surface, the ball would be trapped within the wall. This would make it very easy for the player to score points.

As usual, the requirements are not quite accurate. What the customer wants is for the ball to clear the area where the new set of bricks will be placed before the new wall is created. The team decides that the best way to do this is for Breakout-Game to handle testing for when a new wall will be created.

Wall will provide three new services: (1) isBrickCountZero, which returns True when the brickCount is zero; (2) create_new_wall, which creates a new wall; and (3) isInSpace, which returns True if the object being passed as an argument is in the space of the wall. To be able to do this, the team needed to revive the attributes of position, length and width for Wall.[4] The changes to Wall and Breakout-Game to handle creating a new wall are given in Figures 20-90 through 20-108.

CLASS NAME	PlayingField
ATTRIBUTES	
none // organizes the four sides	
SERVICES	
none	

FIGURE 20-90 CRC Card for PlayingField

---

[4] The team wanted to use the fact that the wall is both a rectangular region and an assembly of bricks. In object-oriented technology, this is done very easily. Consider how you would do this with conventional paradigms.

CLASS NAME	Ball
SUPERCLASS	Rectangle

ATTRIBUTES
velocity   // plus all attributes of Rectangle

SERVICES
prototype: move(elapsedTime, listOfObstacles)
{
compute DELTA as
VELOCITY*ELAPSED_TIME.
compute hull as
if DELTA-y is positive,
then:
set hull's start POSITION to ball's POSITION.
else:
set hull's start POSITION to ball's POSITION + WIDTH.
endif.
set hull's end POSITION to   hull's start POSITION +DELTA.
ask collision to move me
via the moveBall service.
return
}
prototype: changeDirection (new_direction)
{
set DIRECTION to NEW_DIRECTION.
}
prototype: changePosition (new_position)
{

set POSITION to NEW_POSITION.
}
prototype: speedIncrease(speedFactor)
{
set VELOCITY to VELOCITY*SPEEDFACTOR
}

FIGURE 20-91 CRC Card for Ball

CLASS NAME	**Collision**
ATTRIBUTES	
none // this is a method that has been made into an object	
SERVICES	
prototype: moveBall(ball, hull, List_of_Obstacles)	
{ // this handles simultaneous hits.	
For each obstacle in the List_of_Obstacles:	
// ask each obstacle whether it is in the way.	
if obstacle->inPath(hull),	
then:	
hit_object is obstacle.	
endif:	
endfor:	
If hit_object(s) is not found,	
then: // it can move unobstructed.	
ask ball to set its POSITION to POSITION + VELOCITY*ELAPSED_TIME via setPosition service.	
else: // it has hit obstacle(s).	

compute NEW_DIRECTION as   net effect of all the angles of reflection. (Details are left to design.)
ask ball to set its DIRECTION to NEW_DIRECTION   via setDirection service.
For each obstacle that is hit:
ask the object to respond
via its been_hit service.
endfor:
endif:
return
}

FIGURE 20-92 CRC Card for Collision

CLASS NAME	Obstacle
SUPERCLASS	**Rectangle**

ATTRIBUTES
none   // inherit attributes of rectangle

SERVICES
prototype: inPath(hull)
{ // this is a geometric problem
if (the hull and the side occupy any space in common)
// the details of how to determine this are left to design
then: // there is an intersection
return true.
else:
return false.
endif:

}	
prototype: getNorm() //details deferred to design	

FIGURE 20-93 CRC Card for Obstacle

CLASS NAME	Side
SUPERCLASS	**Obstacle**

ATTRIBUTES
none   // inherit attributes of rectangle and obstacle

SERVICES
none   // inherit services from rectangle and obstacle

FIGURE 20-94 CRC Card for Side

CLASS NAME	BreakoutGame

ATTRIBUTES
ball_array[3], active_ball, lost_flag

SERVICES
prototype: start() // this is called at beginning of game
{ // structured English definition
set ball_array[1] to ball1.
set ball_array[2] to ball2.
set ball_array[3] to ball3.
set active_ball to 1.
set lost_flag to false.
establish the members of the "hittable" association.
}
prototype: awake() // this is called by system every 66.7 milliseconds
{ // structured English definition

| ask paddle to update its position |
| via move service of paddle. |
| ask ball_array[active_ball] to update its position, direction, and speed |
| via move service of ball. |
| if lost_flag is true, |
| then: |
| reset lost_flag to false. |
| // take active ball out of play |
| set active_ball to active_ball + 1. |
| if active_ball > 3, |
| then: //all three balls are played |
| end game. |
| else: |
| // initialize new ball to starting position |
| endif: |
| endif: |
| } |
| prototype: ballLost()
// this is called at beginning of game |
| { // structured English definition |
| set lost_flag to true. |
| } |

FIGURE 20-95 CRC Card for BreakoutGame

CLASS NAME	**Rectangle**
ATTRIBUTES	
length, width, position	
SERVICES	
prototype: getUL()	
{ // structured English definition	

return POSITION.
// the position is the upper left corner
}
prototype: getLR()
{   // lower right corner is position-x + width and position-y + length
// we always assume that width is horizontal and length is vertical
LR-x = POSITION-x + width.
LR-y = POSITION-y + length.
return LR.
}

FIGURE 20-96 CRC Card for Rectangle

CLASS NAME	InvisibleSide
SUPERCLASS	Side

ATTRIBUTES
none   // inherit attributes of rectangle, obstacle, and side

SERVICES
none   // inherit services from rectangle, obstacle, and side
prototype: beenHit()   // this overrides obstacle's method
{ // this service requires that we add   // a link between breakout game and side4
tell breakout that ball is now lost
via ball_lost service.
}

FIGURE 20-97 CRC Card for InvisibleSide

CLASS NAME	Paddle
SUPERCLASS	Obstacle

ATTRIBUTES
min-x, max-x   //inherit attributes of rectangle and obstacle

SERVICES
// inherit services from rectangle and obstacle
prototype: move()
{ // structured English definition
get DELTA from mouse object
via getDelta service of mouse.
// we assume that we can get to the mouse somehow
get DELTA-x from DELTA.
// before the paddle can move, it must determine if it is being asked to move outside of its range
//check both left and right limits
if POSITION-x + DELTA-x is less than MIN-x,
then:
set POSITION-x to MIN-x.
else:
if POSITION-x + DELTA-x is greater than MAX-x,
then:
set POSITION-x to MAX-x.
else:
set POSITION-x to POSITION-x + DELTA-x.
endif:
endif:
// this has conceptually moved the paddle
// when you get here, x value of POSITION has been changed
// we need to redisplay the object at its new position,
// but this is actually an implementation issue

	// display self at new position (details left to design)
}	

FIGURE 20-98 CRC Card for Paddle

CLASS NAME	Brick
SUPERCLASS	Obstacle
ATTRIBUTES	
pointValue // inherit attributes of rectangle and obstacle	
SERVICES	
none // inherit services from rectangle and obstacle	

FIGURE 20-99 CRC Card for Brick

CLASS NAME	RegularBrick
SUPERCLASS	Brick
ATTRIBUTES	
none // inherits attributes of rectangle, obstacle, and brick	
SERVICES	
// inherit services from rectangle, obstacle, and brick	
prototype: beenHit()	
{ // this is now simple	
ask Player to increment its value by pointValue	
via add_points service of Player.	
tell Wall that this brick has been removed	
via brick_removed service	
disappear.	
}	

FIGURE 20-100 CRC Card for RegularBrick

CLASS NAME	VisibleSide
SUPERCLASS	Side

ATTRIBUTES

none   // inherit attributes of rectangle, obstacle, and side

SERVICES

none   // inherit services from rectangle, obstacle, and side

FIGURE 20-101 CRC Card for VisibleSide

CLASS NAME	SpeedBrick
SUPERCLASS	Brick

ATTRIBUTES

speedFactor   // inherits attributes of rectangle, obstacle, and brick

SERVICES

// inherits services from rectangle, obstacle, and brick

prototype: beenHit()

{   // this is now simple

   ask Player to increment its value by pointValue

     via add_points service of Player.

   ask Ball to increase speed by SPEEDFACTOR

     via speed_increase service.

   tell Wall that this brick has been removed

     via brick_removed service

   disappear.

}

FIGURE 20-102 CRC Card for SpeedBrick

CLASS NAME	Wall
ATTRIBUTES	
~~position~~, ~~length~~, ~~width~~, brickCount	
SERVICES	
prototype: brickRemoved()	
{ // Assume that brick count keeps track of the number of bricks	
subtract 1 from brickCount	
}	

FIGURE 20-103 CRC Card for Wall

CLASS NAME	Player
ATTRIBUTES	
name, skillLevel	
SERVICES	
prototype: add_points(points)	
{	
ask score to add POINTS via increment_score service.	
}	

FIGURE 20-104 CRC Card for Player

CLASS NAME	Score
ATTRIBUTES	
pointsAccumulated	
SERVICES	
prototype: incrementScore(points)	
{	

add POINTS to POINTS_ACCUMULATED.

}

FIGURE 20-105 CRC Card for Score

CLASS NAME	Mouse
ATTRIBUTES	
previous location	
SERVICES	
prototype: getDelta()	
{ // structured English definition	
get CURRENT POSITION from mouse hardware.	
// the real hardware mouse knows where it is.	
compute DELTA	
as CURRENT POSITION minus PREVIOUS POSITION.	
return DELTA.	
// note: there was a discussion whether this object should just return delta x, since the y value needs to be fixed according to our requirements.	
// This is a very subtle issue regarding to which object a constraint applies. The mouse is actually allowed to move in any direction that makes sense. In fact, what is being requested is that the Paddle object interpret the deltas from the mouse so that only the x values are changed.	
// The proper allocation of requirements to the correct object also affects the reuse issue. If it returns delta y, then it is easier for the Paddle object to do its work. However, this is less flexible. What will happen when you want to use the Mouse object in another application where you also want to get delta x?	
}	

FIGURE 20-106 CRC Card for Mouse

CLASS NAME	Wall
ATTRIBUTES	
position, length, width, brickCount	
SERVICES	
prototype: brickRemoved()	
{ // assume that brickCount keeps track of the number of bricks	
subtract 1 from brickCount	
}	
prototype: is_brickCount_zero( )	
{	
if brickCount is zero,	
then:	
return true.	
else:	
return false.	
endif:	
}	
prototype: createNewWall( ) //left to design	
prototype; isInSpace( ) //left to design	
// we will discover that this and inPath are	
// the same function	

FIGURE 20-107 CRC Card for Wall

CLASS NAME	BreakoutGame
ATTRIBUTES	
ball_array[3], active_ball, lost_flag	
SERVICES	
prototype: start()	// this is called at beginning of game

{ // structured English definition
set ball_array[1] to ball1.
set ball_array[2] to ball2.
set ball_array[3] to ball3.
set active_ball to 1.
set lost_flag to false.
establish the members of the "hittable" association.
}
prototype: awake()
{ // structured English definition
ask paddle to update its position
via move service of paddle.
ask ball_array[active_ball] to update its position, direction, and speed
via move service of ball.
if lost_flag is true,
then:
reset lost_flag to false.
// take active ball out of play
set active_ball to active_ball + 1.
if active_ball > 3,
then: //all three balls are played
end game.
else:
// initialize new ball to starting position
endif:
endif:
ask Wall if brickCount now zero
via is_brickCount_zero service.
if brickCount is zero,
then:
ask Wall if the ball is in its space
via is_in_space service.

if ball is not in Wall's space,
then:
ask Wall to create new wall
via create_new_wall service.
endif;
endif:
}
prototype: ballLost()
{ // structured English definition
set lost_flag to true.
}

FIGURE 20-108 CRC Card for BreakoutGame

CHAPTER

21

Case Study: Design & Implementation

For design and implementation, we will continue the case study with Team 2's domain model.

Design

IN THE FORMATION OF SUBSYSTEMS, a starting point is to try to use existing subsystems. In the case study, three subsystems are made available to the team during design. Armed with these three subsystems of classes that they might be able to use, the team started to design its application.

The discussion went as follows. The mouse is very useful, and one team member suggested that the "main program" (i.e., the awake method of the breakout game) should use the mouse getPoint service to get the new values and then pass them to Paddle as arguments. This is certainly the way most procedural programmers would have done it, so it must be so in the object-oriented approach. However, another team member pointed out that knowledge of the mouse is not part of the game; it is an implementation object that is needed only by Paddle.

By having the breakout game get data from Mouse, the suggestion has broken the encapsulation principle. A third team member asked, "How can this be done without breaking the encapsulation principle?" After some thought, the second team member recognized that Mouse is actually a collaborator of Paddle in Paddle's performing its move service, and relationships with collaborators are usually captured by using associations. The second team member suggested that there should be an association between Paddle and Mouse that was already captured in the actual model.

This scenario is very common in projects. Even though the team has properly identified key concepts such as an association between Paddle and Mouse, they revert to a procedural way of implementing the application. This negates the benefits of having performed the object-oriented analysis, and the application will not benefit from object-oriented technology.[1]

After recognizing that giving Paddle an association to access the mouse service is better object-oriented programming, the first team member decided that he could still use his prior experience to save the day. He noticed that Displayable inherits from Rectangle and that Ball and Obstacle also need to inherit from Rectangle. Furthermore, both Ball and Obstacle are displayable. So he recommended that the team take advantage of the fact that Displayable inherits from Rectangle by simply replacing Rectangle in its inheritance diagram with Displayable.

However, another team member had a problem with this. She raised the issue that Rectangle in a graphic subsystem must be in raster units of the display device, while the rectangle in the original model is in engineering units. They are not the same semantic rectangle, so the team should not be using the same rectangle to capture two semantically different concepts. Of course, the first team member argued that performance would be faster if the team just mentally converted everything to raster units, since it will have to be done anyway.

---

[1] In our experience, implementation constraints, especially when developers have to meet interfaces of legacy systems that are defined for procedural programming as well as having to meet performance constraints and language limitations, may compromise the main benefits (flexibility and maintainability) of moving to object-oriented technology. Unfortunately, it is not that the object-oriented approach does not live up to its promises; it is more that developers/organizations have not made the changes necessary for it to happen.

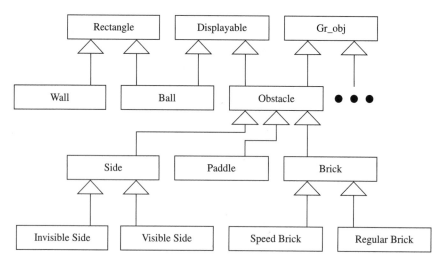

FIGURE 21-1 Revised Inheritance Diagram

Wisely, the team recognized that if they accepted the first team member's argument, it would not be free. In fact, there were many maintainability and portability issues in this case. As a result, the team decided that it would sacrifice performance to preserve the semantic definitions.[2] Figure 21-1 shows the revised inheritance diagram for Team 2.

Something very powerful happened here. The team is now able to reuse the Rectangle class in two different semantic domains. Both Wall and Ball inherit directly from Rectangle, and Obstacle inherits from Gr_obj, which has embedded in it a rectangle.

These objects use Rectangle with application domain (engineering) units, which could be miles, feet, meters, and so on. However, all the displayable objects also inherit from Displayable, which also inherits from Rectangle. However, the rectangle in Displayable is in raster units or the units of the display device. Here the team has used multiple inheritances very effectively to handle different semantic domains. This is a very powerful way to model objects/classes that operate in multiple semantic domains, when it seems natural for all the attributes and services of the superclass to be part of the subclass.

However, in the case of the mouse and the paddle, it is not natural for a paddle to be a subclass of a mouse. In this instance, the team links the two classes together via a relationship. The team felt that this was a very weak relationship and represented it by an association.[3] Now the team was ready to look for oppor-

---

[2] This is not a trivial issue. In real projects with performance constraints, whenever independent classes are collapsed into one class for performance, the system is less flexible and harder to maintain. We recommend that you upgrade your hardware instead of collapsing the classes, because hardware is getting cheaper faster than the cost of software maintenance and development.

[3] Although it is rare that aggregation is used to integrate implementation classes/objects into the model, it should be considered when you are in the design stage.

tunities to use polymorphism for handling services and began to look at the services of all the objects. The first service that the team found in common was the move service. Both Ball and Paddle have move services, and from the perspective of the caller, BreakoutGame, they have the same semantic meaning.

However, the signatures are quite different. The ball's move service has two arguments, while the paddle's move service has no arguments. Furthermore, both services are used only once in the application. Thus, with what they thought was good implementation judgment, the team decided to ignore the semantic commonality.[4]

The team had a very long discussion on the been_hit service of InvisibleSide, RegularBrick, and SpeedBrick. A team member said that from the caller's perspective, all three classes are providing the same service. In fact, the Collision object that uses this service does not even know whether it has hit a brick, side, or paddle. However, another member said that they were not the same service because their methods (behaviors) are different. Furthermore, VisibleSide and Paddle do not even have such a service. However, the first team member remembered very well how to solve these issues; she suggested that they define the service in the superclass and declare it as a no-op method for the superclass. Furthermore, any argument differences could be handled by adding the missing argument to the signature and ignoring them in the method. Her suggestion was taken by the team. The revised class specifications are shown in Figures 21-2 through 21-8.

Now the team was ready to address the associations. The team accepted the player-to-score, mouse-to-paddle, and brick-to-wall associations. In fact, the brick-to-wall association would be implemented using the aggregation relationship, since the semantic meaning is consistent and compatible. However, the team had issues with the remaining three relationships. First, the team did not believe it was natural for Brick to have a relationship with Player solely for the purpose of scoring.

A team member recognized that scoring is really not part of a service of Brick, but is really a result of a collision. That person suggested that a point value be returned to Collision by Brick instead of having Brick do the scoring. This means that Brick does not have to have an association with Player. However, Collision must now know how to score. To create an association between Collision and Player is still not natural, since we would not expect collision to know about a player. However, if they created a new object called Scoreboard, scoring could be done by telling the scoreboard to update the score. This seems reasonable. In fact, now it seems plausible for either Brick or Collision to have this relationship.[5] Note

---

4   This is actually bad judgment. What happens when there are a multitude of moving objects?

5   This is again another very common problem; the relationship is captured by the wrong object or at the wrong abstract class. So it is correct to have the relationship at Brick or at Collision. The answer is that it all depends on the application. If scoring is the result of a collision, then the relationship belongs to the Collision object. However, if scoring is really a property of the brick, then the relationship should be established for Brick. For example, if we decide that you can score the brick value by not hitting the brick for 50 seconds, then scoring is more a property of Brick then it is of Collision.

that object-oriented technology does not force you to choose exclusively. You can implement both relationships. It is semantically very rich. In this case, the team decided that scoring was a property of Collision.

Even with that decision, it still seems very awkward for Collision to have access to a specific instance of a scoreboard. The problem is that scoring is not in the same semantic domain as a collision. In fact, scoring, with its associated objects, Player, Score, and Scoreboard, really forms another subsystem of its own. However, using an association to get to these subsystem services is a bit awkward. It would be nice to be able to access the services of another subsystem without establishing an association, and obviously, there is a way.

By definition, a class is also an object; as such it has attributes and services. How does one access class services? Every object has access to class services by knowing the class name, its service name, and its signature. This is the closest thing to a global service (or function). The Collision or Brick objects can use a class service of Scoreboard to access the scoring service of the scoring subsystem. This very nicely separates the issue of who should have points added to the score from the issue of when scoring should occur.

A similar issue arises with the association between Obstacle and Breakout-Game. Again, this problem is solved differently. Here the library of classes from the collision subsystem removed our concerns. This should seem correct to the reader, because this relationship is really part of the collision subsystem. The team recognized that the GO_formation object is, in fact, the list.

The discussion about the association between InvisibleSide and Breakout-Game was very complex. A well-encapsulated resolution to this issue is to have InvisibleSide notify Collision that the ball is lost. Then, Collision would notify Ball that it is lost, and finally, when the game can delete the ball, it would ask Ball for permission. However, the team decided that this was very complex and difficult to follow. So they took advantage once again of the class services and made Ball_lost a class service of BreakoutGame.

CLASS NAME	Obstacle
SUPERCLASS	Rectangle

ATTRIBUTES
none   // inherit attributes of rectangle

SERVICES
prototype: inPath(hull)
{   // this is a geometric problem
if (the hull and the side occupy any space in common)

| // the detail on how to determine this is left to design |
| then: // there is an intersection |
| return true. |
| else: |
| return false. |
| endif: |
| } |
| prototype: getNorm()   //details deferred to design |
| prototype: been_hit( ) |
| { |
| // do nothing |
| } |

FIGURE 21-2 CRC Card for Obstacle

CLASS NAME	**InvisibleSide**
SUPERCLASS	**Side**

ATTRIBUTES
none   // inherit attributes of Rectangle, Obstacle, and Side

SERVICES
none   // inherit services from Rectangle, Obstacle, and Side
prototype: been_hit()   // this overrides Obstacle's method
{ // this service requires that we add   // a link between BreakoutGame and side4.
tell breakout that ball is now lost
via ball_lost service.
}

FIGURE 21-3 CRC Card for InvisibleSide

CLASS NAME	RegularBrick
SUPERCLASS	Brick

ATTRIBUTES
none   // inherit attributes of Rectangle, Obstacle, and Brick

SERVICES
// inherit services from Rectangle, Obstacle, and Brick
prototype: been_hit()   // this overrides Obstacle's method
{   // this is now simple
ask Player to increment its value by pointValue
via add_points service of Player.
tell Wall that this brick has been removed.
via brick_removed service
disappear.
}

FIGURE 21-4 CRC Card for RegularBrick

CLASS NAME	SpeedBrick
SUPERCLASS	Brick

ATTRIBUTES
speedFactor   // inherit attributes of Rectangle, Obstacle, and Brick

SERVICES
// inherit services from Rectangle, Obstacle, and Brick
prototype: been_hit()   // this overrides Obstacle's method
{   // This is now simple
ask Player to increment its value by pointValue
via add_points service of Player.
ask Ball to increase speed by SPEEDFACTOR

| via speed_increase service. |
| tell Wall that this brick has been removed |
| via brick_removed service |
| disappear. |
| } |

FIGURE 21-5 CRC Card for SpeedBrick

CLASS NAME	**MouseX //library use Mouse**
ATTRIBUTES	
previous location	
SERVICES	
prototype: getDelta()	
{ // structured English definition	
get CURRENT POSITION from mouse hardware.	
// the real hardware mouse knows where it is	
compute DELTA	
as CURRENT POSITION minus PREVIOUS POSITION.	
return DELTA.	
}	

FIGURE 21-6 CRC Card for Mouse

CLASS NAME	**BreakoutGame**
ATTRIBUTES	
ball_array[3], active_ball, lost_flag	
SERVICES	
prototype: start() // this is called at beginning of game	
{ // structured English definition	

set ball_array[1] to ball1.
set ball_array[2] to ball2.
set ball_array[3] to ball3.
set active_ball to 1.
set lost_flag to false.
establish the members of the "hittable" list.
initialize the display (graphic) environment.
}
prototype: awake()
{ // structured English definition
ask paddle to update its position
via move service of paddle.
ask ball_array[active_ball] to update its position, direction, and speed
via move service of ball.
if lost_flag is true,
then:
reset lost_flag to false.
// take active ball out of play
set active_ball to active_ball + 1.
if active_ball > 3,
then: //all three balls are played
end game.
else:
// initialize new ball to starting position.
endif:
endif:
ask wall if brick count now zero
via is_brickCount_zero service.
if brickCount is zero,
then:
ask wall if the ball is in its space
via is_in_space service.

| if ball is not in wall's space, |
| then: |
| ask wall to create new wall |
| via create_new_wall service. |
| endif; |
| endif: |
| } |
| prototype: ball_lost() |
| { // structured English definition |
| set lost_flag to true. |
| } |

FIGURE 21-7 CRC Card for BreakoutGame

CLASS NAME	**Wall**
SUPERCLASS	**Rectangle**

ATTRIBUTES
brickCount
SERVICES
prototype: brick_removed()
{ // Assume that brick count keeps track of the number of bricks
subtract 1 from brickCount
}
prototype: is_brickCount_zero( )
{
if brickCount is zero,
then:
return true.
else:
return false.

endif:
}
prototype: create_new_wall( )   // left to design
prototype: is_in_space( )   // left to design
// we will discover that this and inPath are
// the same function.

FIGURE 21-8 CRC Card for Wall

Implementing Class

THE MOST EFFECTIVE WAY TO learn how to translate classes into C++ is to start with a simpler version of the Breakout game. This version, as shown in Figure 21-9, will have just four walls, the paddle, and one ball.

In the process of doing detailed design, a team member decided that both the paddle and the wall were part of the field because the paddle and the wall use it as a boundary.

FIGURE 21-9 Simplified Version of BreakoutGame

The revised diagrams of aggregation, inheritance, and association are shown, along with any revisions, in Figure 21-10, Figure 21-11, and Figure 21-12. The revised CRC cards for the necessary classes are shown in Figures 21-13 through 21-20.

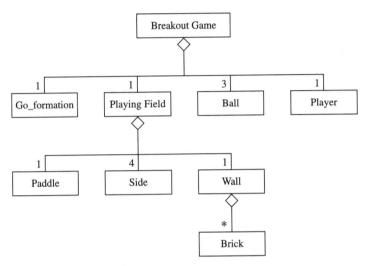

FIGURE 21-10 Class Aggregation for Simplified Version of Breakout Game

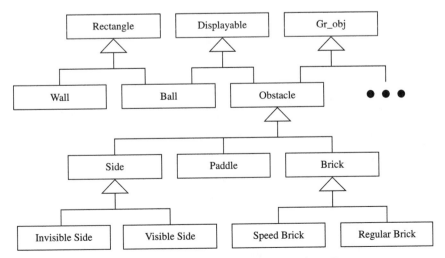

FIGURE 21-11 Inheritance Diagram for Simplified BreakoutGame

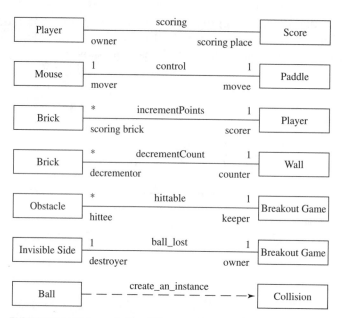

FIGURE 21-12 Association Diagram for BreakoutGame

CLASS NAME		BreakoutGame	
Responsibility		**Collaboration**	
Provide "play the game" service to Main		GO_formation	
Manage its aggregation		Scoreboard	
		Field	
		Players	
METHODS			**Variables**
Game( ) // create a game object			form
~Game( ) // destroy the game object			sb
void play_game( ) // play the game, see awake			fld
static Point convertGtoD(Point x) // conversion			plys
static Point convertDtoG(Point x) // conversion			

FIGURE 21-13 CRC Card for Game

CLASS NAME	Obstacle	
SUPERclasses	Gr_obj, Displayable	
SUBclasses	Side, Paddle, Brick	
Responsibility	Inheritance	
Provide foundation object for hittable.	Gr_obj	
Provide display capabilities.	Displayable	
Provide link to GR_obj		
METHODS		Variables
Obstacle(GO_formation *f, Rectangle loc, char *name, Point p		
~Obstacle()		
virtual SpeedFactor respondToBeingHit (Collision *c) // this is been_hit, // except that this returns a speed factor. // this team has decided that speedup // is caused by the collision. // this has the advantage that if you hit two // speed bricks simultaneously, // the program can decide to speed up by, // say, 3 or anything you want.		
void *real_identity() //need by GO_collision		

FIGURE 21-14 CRC Card for Obstacle

CLASS NAME	Paddle
SUPERclass	Obstacle
Responsibility	Inheritance/Collaboration
Move itself as a movable.	Obstacle
Uses mouse to determine how it moves.	Mouse

Inherits its hit properties.	
METHODS	**Variables**
Paddle(GO_formation *f, Rectangle loc, Point P, int xmax, int xmin	mouse_prev _pos
~Paddle	mouse
void move()	Xmax
	Xmin

FIGURE 21-15 CRC Card for Paddle

CLASS NAME	**Side**
SUPERclass	**Obstacle**
SUBclasses	**ClosedSide, OpenSide**
Responsibility	**Inheritance**
Provide side abstraction.	Obstacle
METHODS	**Variables**
// constructor	
// destructor	

FIGURE 21-16 CRC Card for Side

CLASS NAME	**ClosedSide**
SUPERclass	**Side**
Responsibility	**Inheritance**
Provide closed side abstraction.	Side
METHODS	**Variables**

// constructor	
// destructor	

FIGURE 21-17 CRC Card for ClosedSide

CLASS NAME	Ball
SUPERclasses	**Rectangle, Displayable**

Responsibility	Inheritance	
Provide ball abstraction	Rectangle	
Provide "move" service given time-elapsed and the hittable formation	Displayable	
Provide service to change velocity		
Provide service to change position		
Provide service to get velocity		
Provide service to get rectangle of ball		
METHODS		**Variables**
Ball(Point v, Point a, Point b);		
// destructor		
void move (int time_elapsed, GO_formation *form);		
void changeVelocity(Point v);		
void changePosition(Point new_position);		
Point get_velocity(); // { return velocity; }		
// Rectangle rect() const; // { return rectangle of ball }		

FIGURE 21-18 CRC Card for Ball

CLASS NAME	Collision
SUPERclass	**GO_collision**

Responsibility	Inheritance
Provide collision-detection service	Private inheritance of
Provide scoring service to Hit_objects	GO_collision

METHODS	Variables
Collision(Rectangle init_projectile, Point motion, GO_formation *form)	
~Collision()	
void moveBall(Ball *ball)	
void incr_score(int score)	

FIGURE 21-19 CRC Data for Collision

CLASS NAME	Field	
Responsibility	**Collaboration**	
Manage its aggregation	Wall	
	ClosedSide	
	OpenSide	
	Paddle	

METHODS	Variables
// constructor to create object of type field	w
// destructor to destroy object of this type	top, left, right
getPaddle() // return a pointer to a paddle	bottom
getWall() // return pointer to a wall	pd

FIGURE 21-20 CRC Card for Field

The header files (.h files) for the classes follow:

class.h File

```
#ifndef _CLASS_H
#define _CLASS_H

// all forward declarations for classes
class Game;
class Field;
class Wall;
class Brick;
class Reg_brick;
class Speed_brick;
class Paddle;
class ClosedSide;
class OpenSide;
class Side;
class Obstacle;
class Ball;
class Collision;
class Scoreboard;
class Player;
class Players;
// library classes

class Point;
class Rectangle;
class GO_formation;
class Gr_obj;
class GO_collision;
class Displayable;
class Mouse;


#endif
```

Notice that the class.h file is use to capture all the forward references. This has the advantage of making it easier for the programmer, so the programmer does not have to worry about forward declaration. All the programmer has to do is include the superclasses and any embedded classes. This comes at a price, however, as each new forward declaration you add to the class.h file will cause everything to recompile. For a large system, you may not want this to happen.

Ball.h File

```
#ifndef _BALL_H
#define _BALL_H

#include      "Displayable.h"
#include      "Rectangle.h"
 #include       "class.h"

typedef int    SpeedFactor;

class Ball : public Displayable, public Rectangle
{
   private:
       Point   velocity;
   public:
       Ball(Point v, Point a, Point b);
       virtual ~Ball();
       void   move (int time_elapsed, GO_formation *form);
       void   change_velocity(Point v);
       void   change_position(Point new_position);
       Point  get_velocity();         // { return velocity; }
//     Rectangle rect() const;        //
  { return rectangle of ball }
   };

#endif
```

There are two new public functions: Ball(...) and ~Ball(). The first function is called a **constructor** in C++ and the second function is called a **destructor**.

Paddle.h File

```
#ifndef _PADDLE_H
#define _PADDLE_H

#include      "class.h"
#include      "Obstacle.h"

class Paddle: public Obstacle {

private:
  Mouse *mouse;
```

```
    Point mouse_prev_pos;
    int Xmax;
    int Xmin;
public:
    Paddle(GO_formation *f, Rectangle loc, Point P, int xmax, int xmin);
    virtual ~Paddle();
    void move();
};
#endif
```

Field.h File

```
    #ifndef _FIELD_H
    #define _FIELD_H

    #include "class.h"

    class Field
    {
      private:
          Side      *top, *left, *right, *bottom;
          Paddle    *pd
      public:
          Field(GO_formation *form);
          virtual ~Field();
          Paddle *getPaddle();
     };
    #endif
```

Side.h File

```
    #ifndef _SIDE_H
    #define _SIDE_H

    #include       "class.h"
    #include       "Obstacle.h"

    class Side : public Obstacle
    {
      public:
          Side(GO_formation *f, Rectangle loc, char *name, Point p);
          virtual ~Side();
    };
    #endif
```

Visible.h File

```
#ifndef _CLOSEDSIDE_H
#define _CLOSEDSIDE_H

#include      "class.h"
#include      "Side.h"

class VisibleSide : public Side
{
   public:

        VisibleSide(GO_formation *f, Rectangle loc, char *name, Point P);
        virtual ~VisibleSide();

};
#endif
```

Collision.h File

```
#include      "class.h"
#include "GO_collision.h"

class Collision : private GO_collision {

private:

public:

   Collision(Rectangle init_projectile, Point motion,
                      GO_formation *form);
   virtual ~Collision();

   void moveMe(Ball *ball);

};
```

Game.h File

```
#ifndef _GAME_H
#define _GAME_H

#include       "class.h"

class Game {
```

```
        private:
           GO_formation *form;
           Field *fld;

        public:

           static bool ball_lost_flag;

        public:

           Game();
           virtual ~Game();
            static void ball_lost();
           static Point convertGtoD(Point x);
           static Point convertDtoG(Point x);

        };
        #endif
```

Main.C

```
#include <iostream.h>
#include <new.h>
#include <assert.h>
#include <stdlib.h>
#include <string.h>
#include "GfxEnv.h"
#include "Game.h"

#include "IO.h"
#include "Breakout_Pak.h"

void free_store_empty()
{
  static int i = 0;
  if(i++ == 0)                   // guard against cerr allocating memory
    cerr << "Out of memory\n";   // tell user
  abort();                       // give up
}

static void init( const The& );
static void cleanup();
static Breakout_Pak bk_pak;

main ()
{
```

```cpp
  // handle running out of memory
  set_new_handler(free_store_empty);

  cout << "Here we go" << endl;

  // create the graphics environment
  GfxEnv ge( bk_pak );
  cout << "created ... " << flush ;
  // make the window for our game
  ge.makeWindow(Rectangle(5, 5, 805, 805));
  cout << "windowed ... " << flush ;

  // make sure everything is ok
  assert(ge.ok());
  cout << "OK'd ... " << flush ;

  // do some initialization
  init( ge.the() );
  cout << "init'd ... " << flush ;
  // Construct the breakout object here
  // and start things off
  //void test();
  //test();
  //cout << "Hey, this worked" << endl;
      /* Create game object */
      Game* game = new Game();
      /* Play game */
      game->play_game();
      /* Delete game object */
      delete game;
  cleanup();
  cout << "Play over" << endl;
  return(0);
}

#    include "images/ScoreBoard"
#    include "images/Paddle"
#    include "images/Brick"
#    include "images/SpeedBrick"
#    include "images/SlowBrick"
#    include "images/Ball"
#    include "images/Side"
#    include "images/Top"
#    include "images/d0"
#    include "images/d1"
#    include "images/d2"
```

```
#    include "images/d3"
#    include "images/d4"
#    include "images/d5"
#    include "images/d6"
#    include "images/d7"
#    include "images/d8"
#    include "images/d9"

void
init( const The& )
{
#if 1
  // build Bitmaps from the data
  Pic_init bscoreboard(ScoreBoard_width, ScoreBoard_height, ScoreBoard_bits );
  Pic_init bbrick(Brick_width, Brick_height, Brick_bits );
  Pic_init bspbrick(SpeedBrick_width, SpeedBrick_height, SpeedBrick_bits );
  Pic_init bslbrick(SlowBrick_width, SlowBrick_height, SlowBrick_bits );
  Pic_init bball(Ball_width, Ball_height, Ball_bits );
  Pic_init bside(Side_width, Side_height, Side_bits );
  Pic_init btop(Top_width, Top_height, Top_bits );
  Pic_init bpaddle(Paddle_width, Paddle_height, Paddle_bits );
  Pic_init bboard(ScoreBoard_width, ScoreBoard_height,
                                    ScoreBoard_bits );
  Pic_init bd0(D0_R_18_width, D0_R_18_height, D0_R_18_bits );
  Pic_init bd1(D1_R_18_width, D1_R_18_height, D1_R_18_bits );
  Pic_init bd2(D2_R_18_width, D2_R_18_height, D2_R_18_bits );
  Pic_init bd3(D3_R_18_width, D3_R_18_height, D3_R_18_bits );
  Pic_init bd4(D4_R_18_width, D4_R_18_height, D4_R_18_bits );
  Pic_init bd5(D5_R_18_width, D5_R_18_height, D5_R_18_bits );
  Pic_init bd6(D6_R_18_width, D6_R_18_height, D6_R_18_bits );
  Pic_init bd7(D7_R_18_width, D7_R_18_height, D7_R_18_bits );
  Pic_init bd8(D8_R_18_width, D8_R_18_height, D8_R_18_bits );
  Pic_init bd9(D9_R_18_width, D9_R_18_height, D9_R_18_bits );

  // load pictures of objects
  PicTable& pt = GfxEnv::activeEnv()->pictures();
  pt.loadPic("Image_scoreboard", bscoreboard);
  pt.loadPic("Image_brick", bbrick);
  pt.loadPic("Image_speed_brick", bspbrick);
  pt.loadPic("Image_slow_brick", bslbrick);
  pt.loadPic("Image_ball", bball);
  pt.loadPic("Image_side", bside);
  pt.loadPic("Image_top", btop);
  pt.loadPic("Image_paddle", bpaddle);
  pt.loadPic("Image_zero", bd0);
  pt.loadPic("Image_one", bd1);
```

```
  pt.loadPic("Image_two", bd2);
  pt.loadPic("Image_three", bd3);
  pt.loadPic("Image_four", bd4);
  pt.loadPic("Image_five", bd5);
  pt.loadPic("Image_six", bd6);
  pt.loadPic("Image_seven", bd7);
  pt.loadPic("Image_eight", bd8);
  pt.loadPic("Image_nine", bd9);
#endif
}

void
cleanup()
{
  // nothing to do yet!
}
```

Implementing Static Behavior

BELOW IS THE .C FILE for the classes for the simplified game.

Ball.C file:

```
#include "Ball.h"
#include "Collision.h"
#include "Game.h"


void
Ball::move(int time_elapsed, GO_formation *form)
{
        Point a = Rectangle::upperLeft();
        Point b = Rectangle::lowerRight();
        Rectangle ball_rect(a,b);
        Collision c(ball_rect, time_elapsed*velocity,
                                form);
        c.did_collision_occur(this);
        // c ceases to exist when function exits
}

void
Ball::change_velocity(Point v)
{
        velocity = v;
}
```

```
void
Ball::change_position(Point new_position)
{
        Rectangle::moveTo(new_position);
        Point p1 = Game::convertGtoD(new_position);
        Displayable::moveTo(p1,1);
}

Point
Ball::get_velocity()
{
        return velocity;
}
```

The .h file for the class is included so that the compiler can use the data member definitions. The .h files for the other classes, Collision and Game, are included because the function calls functions that belong to these classes (i.e., the convert function of Game). The .h file of rectangle was not included in the .C file because the include of it is in the .h file.

Collision.C file:

```
#include "Collision.h"
#include "Ball.h"
#include "Hit_object.h"

void
Collision::moveBall(Ball *ball)
{
        ball->change_position(final_loc().upperLeft());
        int sf = 1;              // speed factor
        for(int i = 0; i<number_hit(); i++)
        {
                Obstacle *hitptr =
                        (Obstacle *) obj(i)->real_identity();
                sf *= hitptr->respond_to_being_hit(this);
        }
        Point v = rebound(ball->get_velocity());
        if(v.X() == 0 )
                v.X(1);
        if(v.Y() == 0 )
                v.Y(-1);
        ball->change_velocity(sf*v);
}
```

Field.C file:

```
#include "Field.h"
#include "ClosedSide.h"
#include "Paddle.h"

Paddle *
Field::getPaddle()
{
        return (pd);
}
```

Obstacle.C file:

```
#include "Obstacle.h"

SpeedFactor
Obstacle::respond_to_being_hit(Collision *c)
{
        return(1);      // default SpeedFactor is 1
}
```

Paddle.C file:

```
#include "Paddle.h"
#include "Game.h"
#include "Mouse.h"

void
Paddle::move()
{
        Point newpoint = mouse->getPoint();
        Point delta = newpoint - mouse_prev_pos;
        // convert to game coordinates
        Point game_delta = Game::convertDtoG(delta);
        if( (Gr_obj::upperLeft().X() + game_delta.X()) < Xmin)
               Gr_obj::moveto(Point(Xmin,Gr_obj::upperLeft().Y()));
        else if( (Gr_obj::lowerRight().X() + game_delta.X()) > Xmax)
               Gr_obj::moveto(Point(Xmax - Gr_obj::width(),
                       Gr_obj::upperLeft().Y()));
        else
               Gr_obj::move(Point(game_delta.X(), 0));

        Displayable::moveTo(Gr_obj::upperLeft(),1);

        mouse_prev_pos = newpoint;
}
```

In this implementation, the developer moves the mouse's previous position into the paddle. This is done for performance reasons, because it is very expensive to call a representation of a mouse and the access the mouse library object. However, it is not for free; this change makes the paddle less reusable, because it is now more tightly tied to the library Mouse class.

Instantiating Objects

BELOW IS THE .C FILE with constructors and destructors added for the classes in the simplified game.

Ball.C file:

```
#include "Ball.h"
#include "Collision.h"
#include "Game.h"

Ball::Ball(Point v, Point a, Point b)
      :Rectangle(a,b), Displayable("Image_ball",Point(0,0))
{
        draw();
        Point p1 = Game::convertGtoD(a);
        Displayable::moveTo(p1,1);
        velocity = v;
}

Ball::~Ball()
{
}

void
Ball::move(int time_elapsed, GO_formation *form)
{
        Point a = Rectangle::upperLeft();
        Point b = Rectangle::lowerRight();
        Rectangle ball_rect(a,b);
        Collision c(ball_rect, time_elapsed*velocity,
                           form);
        c.did_collision_occur(this);
        // c ceases to exist when function exits
}

void
Ball::change_velocity(Point v)
```

```
{
      velocity = v;
}

void
Ball::change_position(Point new_position)
{
      Rectangle::moveTo(new_position);
      Point p1 = Game::convertGtoD(new_position);
      Displayable::moveTo(p1,1);
}

Point
Ball::get_velocity()
{
      return velocity;
}
```

Collision.C file:

```
#include "Collision.h"
#include "Ball.h"
#include "Obstacle.h"

 Collision::Collision(Rectangle init_projectile, Point motion,
            GO_formation *form)
         :GO_collision(init_projectile, motion, *form)
{
}

Collision::~Collision()
{
}

void
Collision::did_collision_occur(Ball *ball)
{
      ball->change_position(final_loc().upperLeft());

      int sf = 1;                 // speed factor
      for(int i = 0; i<number_hit(); i++)
      {
            Obstacle *hitptr =
                  (Obstacle *) obj(i)->real_identity();
            sf *= hitptr->respond_to_being_hit(this);
      }
```

```
                Point v = rebound(ball->get_velocity());
                if(v.X() == 0 )
                        v.X(1);
                if(v.Y() == 0 )
                        v.Y(-1);
                ball->change_velocity(sf*v);
        }
```

Obstacle.C file:

```
        #include "Obstacle.h"

        Obstacle::Obstacle(GO_formation *f, Rectangle loc,
                char *name, Point p) : Gr_obj(*f,loc),
                Displayable(name, Point(0,0))
        {
                Point p1;

                draw();
                p1 = Game::convertGtoD(p);      // convert to display coord.s
                Gr_obj::moveto(p);      // move Gr_obj to correct location
                Displayable::moveTo(p1,1);      // move to display coord.s
                                                        //
         and display
                attach();       // add to GO_formation list
        }

        Obstacle::~Obstacle()
        {
        }

        SpeedFactor
        Obstacle::respond_to_being_hit(Collision *c)
        {
                return(1);      // default SpeedFactor is 1
        }
```

Paddle.C file:

```
        #include "Paddle.h"
        #include "Game.h"
        #include "Mouse.h"

         Paddle::Paddle(GO_formation *f, Rectangle loc, Point p,
                    int xmax, int xmin)
```

```
        :Hit_object(f, loc, "Image_paddle", p)
        {
            mouse = new Mouse();
            mouse_prev_pos = mouse->getPoint();
            Xmax = xmax;
            Xmin = xmin;
        }

Paddle::~Paddle()
{
}

void
Paddle::move()
{
    Point newpoint = mouse->getPoint();
    Point delta = newpoint - mouse_prev_pos;
    // convert to game coordinates
    Point game_delta = Game::convertDtoG(delta);
    if( (Gr_obj::upperLeft().X() + game_delta.X()) < Xmin)
        Gr_obj::moveto(Point(Xmin,Gr_obj::upperLeft().Y()));
    else if( (Gr_obj::lowerRight().X() + game_delta.X()) > Xmax)
        Gr_obj::moveto(Point(Xmax - Gr_obj::width(),
                Gr_obj::upperLeft().Y()));
    else
        Gr_obj::move(Point(game_delta.X(), 0));
    Displayable::moveTo(Gr_obj::upperLeft(),1);
    mouse_prev_pos = newpoint;
}
```

Side.C file:

```
#include "Side.h"

Side::Side(GO_formation *f, Rectangle loc, char *name, Point p)
    :Obstacle(f, loc, name, p)
{
}

Side::~Side()
{
}
```

Field.C file:

```
#include "Field.h"
#include "ClosedSide.h"
#include "Paddle.h"

 Field::Field(GO_formation *form)
{
            top = new ClosedSide(form, Rectangle(Point(0,0), Poin
t(500,15)),
                    "Image_top", Point(15,15));
            left = new ClosedSide(form, Rectangle(Point(0,0), Poi
nt(15,800)),
                    "Image_side", Point(15,15));
            right = new ClosedSide(form, Rectangle(Point(0,0), Po
int(15,800)),
                    "Image_side", Point(500,15));
            bottom = new ClosedSide(form, Rectangle(Point(0,0), P
oint(500,15)),
                    "Image_top", Point(15,790));
            pd = new Paddle(form, Rectangle(Point(0,0), Point(30,
5)),
                    Point(250,775), 500, 30);
}

Field::~Field()
{
     delete top;
     delete left;
     delete right;
     delete bottom;
     delete pd;
}

Paddle *
Field::getPaddle()
{
     return (pd);
}
```

Implementing Inheritance

IN THE NEXT STAGE, THE team simplifies the model, so that we can effectively implement a version consistent with what we have discussed so far. Specifically, we will replace the Player class with a Scoreboard class, so that the points can be

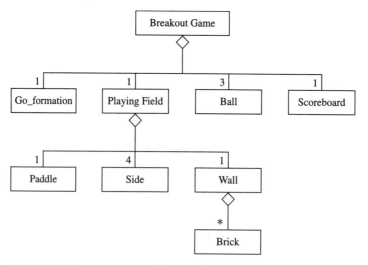

FIGURE 21-21 Aggregation Diagram for BreakoutGame

displayed. The scoring of points also moved from Brick to Collision, since Collision now provides an incr_score service for Brick. This says that scoring is a result of a collision and Brick has some point value that Collision may use for scoring. Note that in the original model, the team concluded that scoring was a responsibility of brick. Figures 21-21 through 21-23 show the revised diagrams, and Figures 21-24 through 21-30 show the new CRC cards.

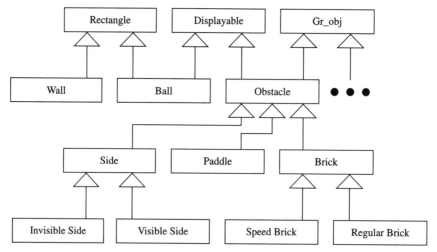

FIGURE 21-22 Inheritence Diagram for BreakoutGame

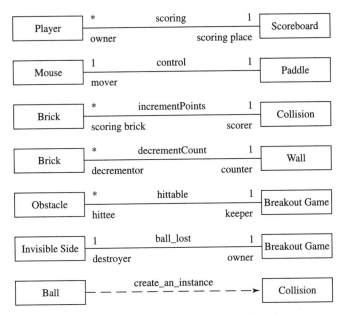

FIGURE 21-23 Association Diagram for BreakoutGame

CLASS NAME	Brick
SUPERclass	**Obstacle**
SUBclasses	**Reg_brick, Speed_brick**
Responsibility	**Inheritance/Collaboration**
Provide brick abstraction	Obstacle
Hold point value of brick	Is = part of Wall
METHODS	**Variables**
// constructor	visibility
// destructor	point_value
respond_to_being_hit(Collision *collision)	
regenerate_brick(GO_formation *f)	

FIGURE 21-24 CRC Card for Brick

CLASS NAME	InvisibleSide
SUPERclass	**Side**
Responsibility	Inheritance
Provide open side abstraction	Side
Provide polymorphic service for respond_to_being_hit	
METHODS	**Variables**
// constructor: how do we make it not visible?	
// destructor	
respond_to_being_hit (Collision *c)	
{ tell game ball is lost; return 1 as SpeedFactor }	

FIGURE 21-25 CRC Card for InvisibleSide

CLASS NAME	Reg_brick
SUPERclass	**Brick**
Responsibility	Inheritance
Provide regular brick abstraction	Brick
METHODS	**Variables**
// constructor	
// destructor	

FIGURE 21-26 CRC Card for Regular Brick

CLASS NAME	Speed_brick
SUPERclass	**Brick**
Responsibility	**Inheritance**
Provide speed brick abstraction	Brick
Provide for SpeedFactor	
METHODS	**Variables**
// constructor	SpeedFactor
// destructor	
respond_to_being_hit(Collision *collision	
{	
do standard brick response	
return a SpeedFactor via data member	
}	

FIGURE 21-27 CRC Card for Speed_Brick

CLASS NAME	Wall
Responsibility	**Collaboration**
Provide wall abstraction	Rectangle
Provide number of bricks left	
Keep track of where bricks are	
METHODS	**Variables**
// constructor	num_left
// destructor	form
brick_off_wall( )	rectangle
	brick-array
void regenerate( )	

bool time_to_regenerate( )	
int intercept(Rectangle rect)	

FIGURE 21-28 CRC Card for Wall

CLASS NAME	Scoreboard
SUPERclass	**Displayable**
Responsibility	**Inheritance/Collaboration**
Provide scoreboard abstraction	Displayable
Provide for display of points	Digits
(version 2: keep score)	
METHODS	**Variables**
// constructor	score
// destructor	num_of_digits
display_score(int)	
incr_score(int n)	

FIGURE 21-29 CRC Card for Scoreboard

CLASS NAME	Brick
METHODS:	
did_collision_occur(Ball *ball)	
{	
Detach this object from hittable list (GO_formation)	
Erase itself off screen	
Set visibility data member to FALSE	
Use collision's incr_score service	
Tell wall brick is no longer part of wall	
Return 1 as value	

}
regenerate_brick(GO_formation *f)
{
Draw self
Set visibility data member to TRUE
Attach this object from hittable list (GO_formation)
}

FIGURE 21-30 CRC Card for Brick

Below are the .h file and the .C file for these classes and the modified classes.

Brick.h file:

```
#ifndef _BRICK_H
#define _BRICK_H

#include     "class.h"
#include     "Hit_object.h"

typedef int   SpeedFactor;

 class Brick : public Hit_object
{
   private:
       bool visibility;
       int    score;
       Wall *wall;
   public:
       Brick(GO_formation *f, Rectangle loc, Point p, bool vis,
             int pv, char *name, Wall *w);
       ~Brick();
       SpeedFactor respond_to_being_hit(Collision *collision);
       void regenerate_brick(GO_formation *f);
};
#endif
```

Collision.h file:

```
#include     "class.h"
#include "GO_collision.h"
```

```
class Collision : private GO_collision {
private:
public:

  Collision(Rectangle init_projectile, Point motion, GO_formation *form);
  virtual ~Collision();
  void did_collision_occur(Ball *ball);
  void incr_score(int score);
};
```

Field.h file:

```
#ifndef _FIELD_H
#define _FIELD_H

#include     "class.h"

class Field
{
   private:
       Wall          *w;
       ClosedSide    *top, *left, *right;
       OpenSide      *bottom;
       Paddle        *pd;
   public:
       Field(GO_formation *form);
       virtual ~Field();
       Paddle *getPaddle();
       Wall   *getWall();
};
#endif
```

Game.h file:

```
#ifndef _GAME_H
#define _GAME_H

#include     "class.h"

class Game {
private:
   GO_formation *form;
   Scoreboard *sb;
   Field *fld;
   int  ballno;
   Ball * BALLS[5];
```

```
      Ball * give_me_a_ball();
   public:
      static bool ball_lost_flag;
   public:
      Game();
      virtual ~Game();
      void play_game();
      static void ball_lost();
      static Point convertGtoD(Point x);
      static Point convertDtoG(Point x);
   };
   #endif
```

InvisibleSide.h file:

```
   #ifndef _OPENSIDE_H
   #define _OPENSIDE_H

   #include        "class.h"
   #include        "Side.h"

   typedef int SpeedFactor;
   class InvisibleSide : public Side
   {
      public:
          InvisibleSide(GO_formation *f, Rectangle loc, char *name, Po
   int P);
          virtual ~InvisibleSide();
          SpeedFactor respond_to_being_hit (Collision *c);
   };
   #endif
```

RegBrick.h file:

```
   #ifndef _REG_BRICK_H
   #define _REG_BRICK_H

   #include        "class.h"
   #include        "Brick.h"

   class Reg_brick : public Brick
   {
      private:
      public:
          Reg_brick(GO_formation *f, Rectangle loc, Point p, bool vis,
                   int pv, Wall *w);
```

```
            virtual ~Reg_brick();
    };
    #endif
```

Scoreboard.h file:

```
    #ifndef _SCOREBOARD_H_
    #define _SCOREBOARD_H_

    #include "Displayable.h"
    #include "class.h"

    class Scoreboard : public Displayable
    {
        private:
            static int      point_scored;
        public:
            static Displayable    *score[10];
            static int            numdigits;
            static char    *digits[10];
            static void    drawscore(int);
        public:
            Scoreboard();
            virtual ~Scoreboard();
            static void    display_score(int);
            static void    incr_score(int);
    };
    #endif
```

Notice that in Scoreboard, the incr_score function used by Collision is defined as a static function. This means that any function may access this service by prefixing the function with the class name and the scope operator. This is used in the Collision function definition, which is in Collision.C

SpeedBrick.h file:

```
    #ifndef _SPEED_BRICK_H
    #define _SPEED_BRICK_H

    #include      "class.h"
    #include      "Brick.h"

    typedef int    SpeedFactor;

    class Speed_brick : public Brick
```

```
{
  private:
      SpeedFactor speed_factor;
  public:
      Speed_brick(GO_formation *f, Rectangle loc, Point p,
              bool vis, int pv, SpeedFactor sf, Wall *w);
      virtual ~Speed_brick();
      int respond_to_being_hit(Collision *collision);
};
#endif
```

Wall.h file:

```
#ifndef _WALL_H
#define _WALL_H

#include      "class.h"
#include      "Rectangle.h"

const int MAX_BRICKS = 90;

class Wall
{
  private:
      Brick *bricks[MAX_BRICKS];
      int num_left;
      GO_formation *form;
      Rectangle bounds;
  public:
      Wall(GO_formation *f, Rectangle loc);
      virtual ~Wall();
      void regenerate();
      void brick_off_wall();
      bool time_to_regenerate();
      int intercept(Rectangle rect);
};
#endif
```

Brick.C file:

```
#include      "Brick.h"
#include      "Wall.h"
#include      "Collision.h"

Brick::Brick(GO_formation *f, Rectangle loc, Point p,
        bool vis, int pv, char *name, Wall *w)
```

```
            :Hit_object(f, loc, name, p), visibility(vis), score(pv),
                wall(w)
    {

        if(visibility == FALSE)
                erase();          // if visibility false, created brick
                                         //
      is hittable, but not displayed
    }

    Brick::~Brick()
    {
    }
    SpeedFactor
    Brick::respond_to_being_hit(Collision *collision)
    {
        Gr_obj::detach();
        erase();
        visibility = FALSE;
        collision->incr_score(score);
        wall->brick_off_wall();
        return(1);
    }
    void
    Brick::regenerate_brick(GO_formation *f)
    {
        draw();
        visibility = TRUE;
        Gr_obj::attach();
    }
```

Collision.C file:

```
    #include "Collision.h"
    #include "Ball.h"
    #include "Hit_object.h"
    #include "Scoreboard.h"

    Collision::Collision(Rectangle init_projectile, Point motion,
                GO_formation *form)
            :GO_collision(init_projectile, motion, *form)
    {
    }

    Collision::~Collision()
    {
    }
```

```
void
Collision::did_collision_occur(Ball *ball)
{
        ball->change_position(final_loc().upperLeft());

        int sf = 1;              // speed factor
        for(int i = 0; i < number_hit(); i++)
        {
                Hit_object *hitptr =
                        (Hit_object *) obj(i)->real_identity();
                sf *= hitptr->respond_to_being_hit(this);
        }
        Point v = rebound(ball->get_velocity());
        if(v.X() == 0 )
                v.X(1);
        if(v.Y() == 0 )
                v.Y(-1);
        ball->change_velocity(sf*v);
}

void
Collision::incr_score( int score )
{       // this is how you call a static function
        Scoreboard::incr_score ( score );
}
```

Notice that the function incr_score() of Collision calls the static function incr_score() of Scoreboard. Here the scope operator is used for a class not in its hierarchy; thus, a static function is almost like a global function in that the program does not need a pointer to an instance of the class to use the function. However, unlike a global function, which is not tied to any class, a static function can be used only if the program knows the class to which it belongs.

Field.C file:

```
#include "Field.h"
#include "ClosedSide.h"
#include "OpenSide.h"
#include "Wall.h"
#include "Paddle.h"

Field::Field(GO_formation *form)
{
            top = new ClosedSide(form, Rectangle(Point(0,0), Point(500,15)),
                "Image_top", Point(15,15));
```

```
        left = new ClosedSide(form, Rectangle(Point(0,0), Point(15,800)),
                "Image_side", Point(15,15));
        right = new ClosedSide(form, Rectangle(Point(0,0), Point(15,800)),
                "Image_side", Point(500,15));
        bottom = new OpenSide(form, Rectangle(Point(0,0), Point(500,15)),
                "Image_top", Point(15,790));

        w = new Wall(form, Rectangle(Point(33, 65), Point(481,113)));
        pd = new Paddle(form, Rectangle(Point(0,0), Point(30,5)),
                Point(250,775), 500, 30);
}


Field::~Field()
{
        delete top;
        delete left;
        delete right;
        delete bottom;
        delete w;
        delete pd;
}


Paddle *
Field::getPaddle()
{
        return (pd);
}


Wall *
Field::getWall()
{
        return(w);
}
```

Game.C file:

```
#include <stdio.h>
#include "Game.h"
#include "Scoreboard.h"
#include "Field.h"
#include "GO_formation.h"
#include "Ball.h"
#include "Paddle.h"
#include "Wall.h"
```

```
bool Game::ball_lost_flag = TRUE;

Game::Game()
{
      ball_lost_flag = TRUE;
      sb = new Scoreboard();
      form = new GO_formation();
      fld = new Field(form);

}

Game::~Game()
{
   delete fld;   // field
   delete form;  // GO_formation
   delete sb;    // scoreBoard

}

void
Game::play_game()
{
      Ball *ball;
      Paddle *paddle;
      Wall *wall;
      paddle = fld->getPaddle();
      wall = fld->getWall();
      ballno = 0;
      for( int i = 0; i < 5; i++)
      {
            BALLS[i] = new Ball(Point(1,1), Point(0,0), Point(16,16));
      }
      while( (ball =  give_me_a_ball()) != NULL)
      {
            // give ball initial velocity and position
            ball->change_velocity(Point(1,1));
            ball->change_position(Point(300,300));
            ball_lost_flag = FALSE;
            while(TRUE)
            {
                  paddle->move();
                  ball->move(1,form);
                  if(wall->time_to_regenerate())
                  {
                        if (wall->intercept((Rectangle) *ball))
                        ;  // do nothing
```

```
                              else
                                 wall->regenerate();
                        }
                        if(ball_lost_flag == TRUE)
                        {
                                 ball->erase();
                                 delete ball;
                                 break;
                        }
               }          //end while(TRUE)
        }  // end while ( (ball= . . .) != NULL)
}


void
Game::ball_lost()
{
        ball_lost_flag = TRUE;
}


Point
Game::convertGtoD(Point x)
{
        // convert from game coordinates to display coordinates
        return(x);
}


Point
Game::convertDtoG(Point x)
{
        // convert from display coordinates to game coordinates
        return(x);
}


Ball *
Game::give_me_a_ball()
{
        if (ballno >= 5) return 0;
        else
        {
        Ball * rb = BALLS[ ballno++ ];
        return rb;
        }
}
```

InvisibleSide.C file:

```
#include "OpenSide.h"
#include "Game.h"

InvisibleSide::InvisibleSide(GO_formation *f, Rectangle loc, char
*name, Point p)
        :Side(f, loc, name, p)
{
        erase();
}

InvisibleSide::~InvisibleSide()
{
}

SpeedFactor
InvisibleSide::respond_to_being_hit(Collision *c)
{
        Game::ball_lost();
        return(1);      // default SpeedFactor is 1
}
```

RegBrick.C file:

```
#include       "Reg_brick.h"

Reg_brick::Reg_brick(GO_formation *f, Rectangle loc, Point p,
        bool vis, int pv, Wall *w)
        :Brick(f, loc, p, vis, pv, "Image_slow_brick", w)
{
}

Reg_brick::~Reg_brick()
```

Scoreboard.C file:

```
#include <stdlib.h>
#include <unistd.h>
#include "Scoreboard.h"

unsigned sleep(unsigned);

char *Scoreboard::digits[] = {
        "Image_zero",
        "Image_one",
```

```
        "Image_two",
        "Image_three",
        "Image_four",
        "Image_five",
        "Image_six",
        "Image_seven",
        "Image_eight",
        "Image_nine"
                    };

int Scoreboard::numdigits = 10;
int Scoreboard::point_scored = 0;

Displayable* Scoreboard::score [ ]= {
                            0,
                            0,
                            0,
                            0,
                            0,
                            0,
                            0,
                            0,
                            0,
                            0
                };

Scoreboard::Scoreboard() :
        Displayable("Image_scoreboard", Point(530, 15))
{
        draw();          // Displayable::draw();
        for (int n = 0; n < 10; n++)
        {
                score[n] = new Displayable("Image_zero");
                score[n]->move(Point((700 - n * 18), 40));
        }

        sleep(1);
        drawscore(0);
}

Scoreboard::~Scoreboard()
{
        for(int n = 0; n < 10; n++)
                delete score[n];
}
```

```
void
Scoreboard::display_score(int n)
{
      drawscore(n);
}

const int XBUF = 15;
const int YBUF = 30;

void
Scoreboard::drawscore(int n)
{

      while(numdigits-- > 0) {
            score[numdigits]->erase();
      }
      // build new score in loop, each time update position
      numdigits = 0;
      // if score is 0, just display "0"
      if (n == 0) {
            delete score[numdigits];
            score[numdigits] = new Displayable(digits[0]);
            score[numdigits]->move(Point((700 - numdigits * 18), 40));
            score[numdigits]->draw();
            numdigits++;
      }
       while (n) {
            int rem = n % 10;
            delete score[numdigits];
            score[numdigits] = new Displayable(digits[rem]);
            score[numdigits]->move(Point((700 - numdigits * 18), 40));
            score[numdigits]->draw();
            n /= 10;
            numdigits++;
      }
}
void
Scoreboard::incr_score( int n )
{
      point_scored += n;
      drawscore( point_scored );
}
```

SpeedBrick.C file:

```
#include       "Speed_brick.h"

Speed_brick::Speed_brick(GO_formation *f, Rectangle loc,
    Point p, bool vis, int pv, SpeedFactor sf, Wall *w)
    :Brick(f, loc, p, vis, pv, "Image_speed_brick", w), speed_factor(sf)
{
}

Speed_brick::~Speed_brick()
{
}


SpeedFactor
Speed_brick::respond_to_being_hit(Collision *collision)
{
      Brick::respond_to_being_hit(collision);
      return(speed_factor);
}
```

Wall.C file:

```
#include "Wall.h"
#include "Rectangle.h"
#include "Speed_brick.h"
#include "Reg_brick.h"


Wall::Wall(GO_formation *f, Rectangle loc)
 :bounds(loc), form(f)
{
      int max_row = bounds.height()/16;
      int max_col = bounds.width()/32;
      for(int row = 0; row < max_row; row++)
      {
            for(int col = 0; col < max_col; col++)
            {
                  Point new_pos;
                  new_pos = bounds.upperLeft() + Point(col*32, row*16);
                  if (col == row) {  // make a speed brick
                        bricks[(row*max_col) + col] =
                              new Speed_brick(f,
                                    Rectangle(Point(0,0), Point(32,16)),
                                    new_pos, TRUE, 20, 2, this);
                  }
```

```
                    else    {   // make a regular brick
                        bricks[(row*max_col) + col] =
                            new Reg_brick(f,
                                Rectangle(Point(0,0), Point(32,16)),
                                new_pos, TRUE, 10, this);
                    }
            }
        }
        num_left = max_row * max_col;
}


Wall::~Wall()
{
        int max_row = bounds.height()/16;
        int max_col = bounds.width()/32;

        for(int row = 0; row < max_row; row++)
        {
                for(int col = 0; col < max_col; col++)
                {
                        delete bricks[(row*max_col) + col];
                }
        }
}


void
Wall::regenerate()
{
        // redraw each brick
        // reattach each brick to form
        int max_row = bounds.height()/16;
        int max_col = bounds.width()/32;
         for(int row = 0; row < max_row; row++)
        {
                for(int col = 0; col < max_col; col++)
                {
                        bricks[(row*max_col) + col]->regenerate_brick(form);
                }
        }
        num_left = max_row * max_col;
}


void
Wall::brick_off_wall()
{
        num_left -= 1;
}
```

```
bool
Wall::time_to_regenerate()
{
        if( num_left == 0)
                return(TRUE);
        else
                return(FALSE);
}


int
Wall::intercept(Rectangle rect)
{
        return(bounds.intersectsWith(rect));
}
```

Implementing Relationships

TO HELP US UNDERSTAND STATIC functions and associations better, we now change
the game to allow multiple players. First, we will add two new classes: Players
and Player. Then, we will modify incr_score() function to handle multiple players.

Figure 21-31 and Figure 21-32 are the modified aggregation and association
diagrams. Figure 21-33 and Figure 21-34 show the class descriptions for the new
classes.

Below are the .h and .C files for Players and Player, and the .C file for Collision with the modified code for incr_score() function, and the modified code for
Game::play_game() function.

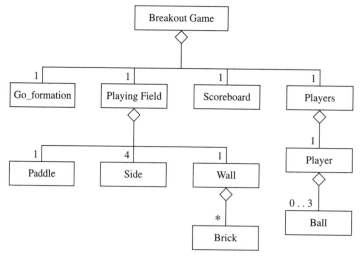

FIGURE 21-31 Aggregation Diagram for BreakoutGame

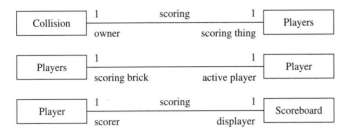

FIGURE 21-32 Association Diagram for BreakoutGame

CLASS NAME	Players
Responsibility	**Collaboration**
Provide players abstraction	Player
Provide list of players	
Keep track of number of players and next player	
METHODS	**Variables**
// constructor	list of players
// destructor	next_player
static void increment_score(int points)	max_num
void respond_to_ball_lost( )	active-player
Ball *give_me_a_ball( )	

FIGURE 21-33 CRC Card for Players

CLASS NAME	Player
Responsibility	**Collaboration**
Provide individual player abstraction	Players
Keep track of player's balls	Ball
Keep track of player's score	

METHODS	Variables
// constructor	score
// destructor	list of balls
void update_score(int)	max_num
Ball *give_me_a_ball()	current_ball
int get_score() cons	
bool any_balls_left() const	

FIGURE 21-34 CRC Card for Player

Players.h file:

```
#ifndef _PLAYERS_H
#define _PLAYERS_H

#include        "class.h"

class Players {
private:
        Player* List_of_p[5];   // list of players
        int nextplayer;
        int maxnum;
public:
        static char *p_names[];
        static Player *active_player;
public:
        Players(int n);
        virtual ~Players();
        static void increment_score(int points);
        void respond_to_ball_lost();
        Ball *give_me_a_ball();
  };
#endif
```

Players.C file:

```
#include <stdio.h>
#include <stdlib.h>
#include "Players.h"
#include "Player.h"
#include "Ball.h"
#include "Scoreboard.h"
```

```
Player * Players::active_player=NULL;

char *Players::p_names[] = { "Player A",
                                              "Player B",
                                              "Player C",
                                              "Player D",
                                              "Player E"
                                            };


Players::Players(int n)
{

      if(n > 5)
            maxnum = 5;
      else
            maxnum = n;
      for(int i = 0; i < maxnum; i++)
      {
            List_of_p[i]  =
                  new Player(p_names[i], 6, 0, Point(530, 300 + i*20
      ));
            // put new player on list
      }
      // active_player to first one
      active_player = List_of_p[0];
      // set next player pointer
      nextplayer = 1;
}

Players::~Players()
{
      // delete all players in list
      for(int i = 0; i < maxnum; i++)
      {
            delete List_of_p[i];
      }
}

void
Players::increment_score(int points)
{
      active_player->update_score(points);
      int score = active_player->get_score();
      Scoreboard::display_score(score);
}
```

```
void
Players::respond_to_ball_lost()
{
}


Ball *
Players::give_me_a_ball()
{
      Ball *newBall;
      if(active_player->any_balls_left())
            newBall = active_player->give_me_a_ball();
      else
      {
            if(nextplayer == maxnum)
                  newBall = NULL;
            else
            {
                  active_player = List_of_p[nextplayer++];
                  newBall = active_player->give_me_a_ball();
                  sleep(5);
            }
      }
      return(newBall);
}
```

Player.h file:

```
#ifndef _PLAYER_H_
#define _PLAYER_H_

#include "class.h"
#include "Ball.h"

class Player
{
   private:
      char*   p_name;
      int     score;
      int curball;
      int maxball;
      Ball* BallPtrList[50];
   public:
      Player(char*, int, int, Point);
      virtual ~Player();
      void    update_score(int);
      Ball    *give_me_a_ball();
```

```
              char*   get_name() const;
              int          get_score() const;
              bool any_balls_left() const;
        };

        #endif
```

Player.C file:

```
#include <stdio.h>
#include "Player.h"
#include "Ball.h"
#include "Point.h"

Player::Player(char* nm, int init_num_balls, int init_score, Point ball_disp)
      : p_name(nm), score(init_score), curball(0)
{
      if (init_num_balls > 50 ) init_num_balls = 50;
      maxball = init_num_balls;
      for(int i = 0; i < init_num_balls; i++)
      {
            Ball *pb;
            Point pos = ball_disp + Point(i*20,0);
            pb = new Ball(Point(0,0), Point(0,0), Point(16,16));
            pb->change_position(pos);
            BallPtrList[i] = pb;   // save ball pointer
      }
}

Player::~Player()
{
      Ball *b;
      while(curball < maxball - 1)
      {
            b = BallPtrList[curball];
            delete b;
            curball++;
      }
}

void
Player::update_score(int n)
{
      score += n;
}
```

```
char*
Player::get_name() const
{
      return p_name;
}

int
Player::get_score() const
{
      return score;
}

bool
Player::any_balls_left() const
{
      return (( curball < maxball ) ? TRUE : FALSE);
}

Ball *
Player::give_me_a_ball()
{
      Ball *b;
      if(curball == maxball)
      {
            b = NULL;
      }
      else
      {
            b = BallPtrList[curball];
            curball++;
      }
       return b;
}
```

Collision.C file:

```
      #include "Collision.h"
      #include "Ball.h"
      #include "Hit_object.h"
      #include "Players.h"

      Collision::Collision(Rectangle init_projectile, Point motion,
                GO_formation *form)
              :GO_collision(init_projectile, motion, *form)
          {
          }
```

```
Collision::~Collision()
{
}

void
Collision::did_collision_occur(Ball *ball)
{
        ball->change_position(final_loc().upperLeft());
        int sf = 1;                // speed factor
        for(int i = 0; i < number_hit(); i++)
        {
        for(int i = 0; i < number_hit(); i++)
        {
                Hit_object *hitptr = (Hit_object *) obj(i)-
>real_identity();
                    sf *= hitptr->respond_to_being_hit(this);
        }
        Point v = rebound(ball->get_velocity());
        if(v.X() == 0 )  v.X(1);
        if(v.Y() == 0 ) v.Y(-1);
        ball->change_velocity(sf*v);
}

void
Collision::incr_score(int score)
{
        Players::increment_score(score);
}
```

The reader should note the use of a static function to separate the scoring from the actual playing of the game. Also by using the Players abstraction, you can add rules for scoring that are independent of Collision. This is a very powerful concept.

Game.C file:

```
#include <stdio.h>
#include "Game.h"
#include "Scoreboard.h"
#include "Field.h"
#include "Players.h"
#include "GO_formation.h"
#include "Ball.h"
#include "Paddle.h"
#include "Wall.h"
```

```cpp
bool Game::ball_lost_flag = TRUE;

Game::Game()
{

      ball_lost_flag = TRUE;
      sb = new Scoreboard();
      form = new GO_formation();
      fld = new Field(form);
      plys = new Players(2);
}

Game::~Game()
{
   delete plys;  // players
   delete fld;   // field
   delete form;  // GO_formation
   delete sb;    // scoreBoard
 }

void
Game::play_game()
{
      Ball *ball;
      Paddle *paddle;
      Wall *wall;
       paddle = fld->getPaddle();
      wall = fld->getWall();
      while( (ball = plys->give_me_a_ball()) != NULL)
      {
            // give ball initial velocity and position
            ball->change_velocity(Point(1,1));
            ball->change_position(Point(300,300));
            ball_lost_flag = FALSE;
             while(TRUE)
            {
                  paddle->move();
                  ball->move(1,form);
                  if(wall->time_to_regenerate())
                  {
                        //if (wall->intercept((Rectangle) *ball))
                        if (wall->intercept( *ball ) )
                        ;  // do nothing
                        else
                        wall->regenerate();
                  }
```

```
                              if(ball_lost_flag == TRUE)
                              {
                                      plys->respond_to_ball_lost();
                                      ball->erase();
                                      delete ball;
                                      break;
                              }
                      }       //end while(TRUE)
              }  // end while ( (ball = . . .) != NULL)
      }


      void
      Game::ball_lost()
      {
              ball_lost_flag = TRUE;
      }


      Point
      Game::convertGtoD(Point x)
      {
              // convert from game coordinates to display coordinates
              return(x);
      }


      Point
      Game::convertDtoG(Point x)
      {
              // convert from display coordinates to game coordinates
              return(x);
      }
```

SELECTED BIBLIOGRAPHY

The following are some of the references used in writing this text. This is a rapidly evolving field, and no single book will give you in-depth coverage of all the topics introduced here. The references are given in alphabetical order by authors.

Booch, Grady. *Object-Oriented Design with Applications.* Benjamin/Cummings, 1991.

Booch, Grady, James Rumbaugh, and Ivar Jacobson. *The Unified Modeling Language for Object-Oriented Development, Version 0.9a Addendum.* Rational Software Corporation, 1996.

Budd, Timothy. *An Introduction to Object-Oriented Programming.* Addison-Wesley, 1991.

Coad, Peter, and Edward Yourdon. *Object-Oriented Analysis.* Yourdon Press, 1991a.

Coad, Peter, and Edward Yourdon. *Object-Oriented Design.* Yourdon Press, 1991b.

Embley, David, W., Barry D. Kurtz, and Scott N. Woodfield. *Object-Oriented System Analysis: A Model-Driven Approach.* Yourdon Press, 1992.

Entsminger, Gary. *The Tao of Objects: A Beginner's Guide to Object-Oriented Programming.* Yourdon Press, 1992.

Graham, Ian. *Object-Oriented Methods.* Addison-Wesley, 1991.

Khoshafian, Setrig, and Razmik Abnous. *Object Orientation: Concepts, Languages, Databases, User Interfaces.* John Wiley, 1990.

Lippman, Stanley B. *C++ Primer.* Addison-Wesley, 1991.

Martin, James, and James Odell. *Object-Oriented Analysis and Design.* Prentice Hall, 1992.

Rumbaugh, James, et al. *Object-Oriented Modeling and Design*. Prentice Hall, 1991.

Shlaer, Sally, and Stephen Mellor. *Object-oriented Systems Analysis: Modeling the World in Data*. Yourdon Press, 1988.

Shlaer, Sally, and Stephen Mellor. *Object Lifecycles: Modeling the World in States*. Yourdon Press, 1992.

Stroustrup, Bjarne. *The C++ Programming Language*. Addison-Wesley, 1991.

Wirfs-Brock, Rebecca. *Designing Object-Oriented Software*. Prentice-Hall, 1990.

INDEX

ACKNOWLEDGMENTS

Preface

Keats, John, "Letter To J.H. Reynolds," May 3, 1818.

Chapter 1

Bloor Research Group, *CASE & Methods Based Development Tools: An Evaluation and Comparison*, United Kingdom, 1994.

Chen, Peter, "The entity-relationship model—Toward a unified view of data," *ACM Trans. on Database Systems*, 1(1), March 1976.

Codd, E., "Extending the database relational model to capture more meaning," *ACM Trans. on Database Systems*, 4(4), December 1979.

Hughes DoD Composite Software Error History

Yourdon, E.N. and L.L. Constatine, *Structured Design: Fundamentals of a Discipline of Computer Program and Systems Design*, Prentice-Hall, Englewood Cliffs, New Jersey, 1979.

Chapter 2

Goldstein, N. and J. Alger, *Developing Object-Oriented Software for the Macintosh Analysis, Design, and Programming*, Addison-Wesley, 1992.

Brooks, F.P., *The Mythical Man-month; Essay on Software Engineering*, Addison-Wesley, 1982.

Chapter 3

Brooks, F.P., "The Silver Bullet, Essence and Accidents of Software Engineering," *Information Processing '86*, (ed.) H.J. Kugler, Elsevier Science Publishers B.B. (North-Holland), 1986.

Kuhn, T., *The Structure of Scientific Revolution (2nd edition),* University of Chicago Press, 1970.

Chapter 4

King, R., "My Cat is Object-Oriented," *Object-Oriented Concepts, Databases, and Applications,* (eds.) Won Kim and Fredrick H. Lochosky, ACM Press and Addison Wesley, 1989.

Booch, G., *Software Engineering with Ada,* Benjamin/Cummings Publishing Co., Menlo Park, California, 1983.

Booch, G., "Object-Oriented Development," *IEEE Trans. on Software Engineering,* vol. SE-12, no. 2, pp. 211–21, February 1986.

Meyer, B., *Object-Oriented Software Construction,* Prentice-Hall International (UK) Ltd., Cambridge, UK, 1988.

Wirfs-Brock, R., *Designing Object-Oriented Software,* Prentice-Hall, 1990.

Coad, P. and E. Yourdon, *Object-Oriented Analysis,* Yourdon Press, 1991.

Schlaer, S. and S. Mellor, *Object-Oriented Systems Analysis: Modeling the World in Data,* Yourdon Press, 1988.

Ross, D., "Applications and extensions of SADT," *IEEE Computer,* April 1985.

Chapter 5

Wordsworth, *The Prelude,* 1850.

Coad, P. and E. Yourdon, *Object-Oriented Analysis,* Yourdon Press, 1991.

Schlaer, S. and S. Mellor, *Object-Oriented Systems Analysis: Modeling the World in Data,* Yourdon Press, 1988.

Chapter 6

McMennin, S.M. and J.F. Palmer, *Essential System Analysis,* Yourdon Press, 1984.

Chapter 7

Jacobson, I., M. Christerson, P. Jonsson, and F. Overgaard, *Object-Oriented Software Engineering—A Use Case Approach,* Addison-Wesley, Wokingham, England, 1992.

McMennin, S.M. and J.F. Palmer, *Essential System Analysis,* Yourdon Press, 1984.

Schlaer, S. and S. Mellor, *Object Lifecycles: Modeling the World in States,* Yourdon Press, 1992.

Chapter 8

Lamb, C., *Last Essays of Elia* (1833).

Winston, M.E., R. Chaffer, and D. Herrmann, "A taxonomy of part-whole relations," *Cognitive Science*, 11:417–44, 1987.

Chapter 9

Kant, E., Logic, (Trans.) Robert S. Hartman and Wolfgang Schwarz, Dover, 1988.

Martin, O. and J. Odell, *Object-Oriented Analysis and Design*, Prentice-Hall, 1992.

Chapter 10

Paine, T., *The Age of Reason*, Pt. ii, par 56, 1795.

Schlaer, S. and S. Mellor, *Object-Oriented Systems Analysis: Modeling the World in Data*, Yourdon Press, 1988.

Rumbaugh, J., M. Blaha, W. Premerlani, F. Eddy, and W. Lorensen, *Object-Oriented Modeling and Design*, Prentice-Hall, 1992.

Chapter 11

Stein, L.A., H. Lieberman, and D. Ungar, "A shared view of sharing: The Treaty of Orlando," *Object-Oriented Concepts, Databases, and Applications*, (eds.) W. Kim and F.H. Lechosky, ACM Press, New York, 1989.

Chapter 12

Stroustrup, B., *The C++ Programming Language*, Addison-Wesley, 1991.

Kernighan, B.W. and D.M. Ritchie, *The C Programming Language*, Prentice-Hall, Englewood Cliffs, New Jersey, 1978.

Chapter 13

Peirce, C.S., "How to Make Our Ideas Clear," *Charles S. Peirce: Selected Writings (Values in a Universe of Chance)*, (ed.) Philip P. Wiener, Dover, 1966.

Chapter 14

Aristotle, "Zoology," *Aristotle*, (Trans.) Philip Wheelwright, The Odyssey Press, 1951.

Chapter 15

Alfonso The Wise (Attributed)

Chapter 16

Donne, J., *Devotions Upon Emergent Occasions*, 1624.

Chapter 17

Solemnization of Matrimony, The Book of Common Prayers